Ronald L. Johnstone

CENTRAL MICHIGAN UNIVERSITY

RELIGION IN SOCIETY
A Sociology of Religion
SECOND EDITION

PRENTICE-HALL, INC. Englewood Cliffs, New Jersey 07632

Library of Congress Cataloging in Publication Data

Johnstone, Ronald L.
   Religion in society.

   Includes bibliographical references and index.
   1. Religion and sociology. 2. United States—
Religion. I. Title.
BL60.J63 1983   306'.6   82-7592
ISBN 0-13-773077-2   AACR2

To Arline

Editorial/production supervision: Richard Kilmartin
Cover design: Miriam Recio
Manufacturing buyer: John Hall

Previous edition published under the title *Religion and Society in Interaction: The Sociology of Religion.*

©1983, 1975 by Prentice-Hall, Inc., Englewood Cliffs, N.J. 07632

Printed in the United States of America
10 9 8 7 6 5 4 3 2

ISBN 0-13-773077-2

Prentice-Hall International, Inc., *London*
Prentice-Hall of Australia Pty. Limited, *Sydney*
Prentice-Hall Canada Inc., *Toronto*
Prentice-Hall of India Private Limited, *New Delhi*
Prentice-Hall of Japan, Inc., *Tokyo*
Prentice-Hall of Southeast Asia Pte. Ltd., *Singapore*
Whitehall Books Limited, *Wellington, New Zealand*

Contents

Preface

This introduction to the sociology of religion in second edition follows an outline that with continuing modifications has worked successfully in two decades of teaching courses variously titled Religion and Society, Sociology of Religion, and Religion in Contemporary Society. The book is intended primarily for a first college-level course in the sociology of religion, taken preferably by students who have had at least an introductory course in sociology.

Yet in writing the text, I also have kept in mind those persons who from time to time have asked me what the sociology of religion is all about. They seem to come primarily from the ranks of organized religion and include seminary professors and denominational administrators as well as clergy and laypeople in local congregations. This book will be an aid to them as they seek information and insight not only about an academic subject but also about the relationship of religion to the society in which they live.

The book consists of four parts. Part I is an introduction to the sociological perspective on religion. It grapples with the problem of defining religion, considers the fascinating but ultimately frustrating question of the origins of religion, and investigates the process by which a person becomes religious, that is, undergoes religious socialization. Part II focuses on the distinctive perspective that sociology has on religion as a social phenomenon. That is, how do general laws and principles of social and group life impinge on religion as it organizes itself into groups and carries on its activities? Also we look closely at the classic church-sect continuum of religious organization and evolution. In Part III we look at the relationship of religion to major social institutions and structural features of society: religion and politics, religion and the economy, religion and social class, and finally religion and the role and perception of women in society. In Part IV we look specifically at some of the major features of religion in the United States—the social environment and experience of a majority of the readers of this text. After exploring several highly important socio-historical developments within American religion, particular attention is paid to American socio-religious developments, namely the black church and the phenomenon of denominationalism. The section concludes by focusing on primary sociological factors that will significantly affect the future of religion.

In this progression the reader will experience firsthand some of the problems inherent in the enterprise we call the sociology of religion and will become involved and somewhat expert in the process of applying the sociological perspective. The reader also will develop insight into the place of religion in society that will supplement one's prior understanding, whether gained from the inside as a believer or from the outside as a serious, or even casual, observer of the religious scene.

While the fundamental thrust and outline of this second edition follows that of the first, the reader will note at least three major changes: (1) the deletion of several chapters and sections of chapters, (2) informational updating throughout, and (3) the addition of substantial bodies of new material. The relationship of women to religion, the development of the New Religious Right, and the process of socialization into religious cults such as Jim Jones's Peoples Temple are major examples of such new material.

In any publication of one's work, debts to others are both many and significant. I wish to mention two sets of people in particular. First are four fellow sociologists who provided extremely helpful suggestions at crucial stages of writing and revision. They are Philip L. Berg (University of Wisconsin—La Crosse), Harold S. Himmelfarb (Ohio State University), Harold W. Melvin (Fitchburg State College), and Anson D. Shupe, Jr. (University of Texas at Arlington). Second, Annette Davis, Kirsten Johnstone, and Donna Johnstone provided typing services not only in good form but with good humor as well.

R.L.J.

I

INTRODUCTION TO THE SOCIOLOGY OF RELIGION

1

The Sociological Perspective

Religion is a social phenomenon and is in an interactive relationship with the other social units that constitute a society. This seemingly obvious assertion, which lies at the very foundation of the sociology of religion, is actually not nearly so simple as it may seem. Nor is it so readily accepted as one might expect.

Many people, particularly the religiously committed, think of religion in an entirely different way. Some prefer to see religion as the context of people's communion with the supernatural, and religious experience as something outside ordinary experience, while others see religion as an expression of an instinctual reaction to cosmic forces. Still others see religion as an explicit set of messages from a deity. These viewpoints certainly de-emphasize, or ignore, or even reject the sociological dimensions of religion. Nevertheless, whether we are talking about religion in general, or a particular religious family such as Christianity or Buddhism, or a specific religious group such as the Four Square Gospel Tabernacle, religion will be seen to interact with other social institutions and forces in society and will follow and illustrate sociological principles and laws.

In other words, whatever else it is (or is not), religion is a social phenomenon and as such is in a continual reciprocal, interactive relationship with other social phenomena. That, in brief, is what the sociology of religion is all about; and this book is basically concerned with the specification and elaboration of this point in a variety of dimensions and on a number of levels.

CHARACTERISTICS OF THE
SOCIOLOGY OF RELIGION

Asserting that religion is a social phenomenon suggests several things. In the first place the statement has a *nonevaluative intent.* Thus we are not going to be able to, or even want to, speak about the truth or falsity of religion. Speaking of religion in terms of the good, the true, and the beautiful may be worthwhile and even stimulating for philosophers and theologians—or anyone, for that matter (even sociologists); but such considerations have nothing to do with sociology. Sociology that claims to describe reality accurately demands that its practitioners approach their subjects—religion no less than any other (and perhaps more than most)—with all the neutrality and objectivity they can muster.

Of course, no sociologist can always (if ever) be perfectly neutral and objective with regard to his or her subject, let alone one so value laden and emotionally charged as religion. Recent studies in the sociology of knowledge, as well as honest discussions that have punctured the myth of a "value-free" sociology, have been sufficient to discourage any such pretentions. Nonetheless, a conscious, deliberate striving for neutrality and objectivity must be present—indeed, it should be evident—in any sociological investigation.

The sociology of religion is also *empirical*—it can only study and reach conclusions about phenomena that are observable. In order to confirm or refute any particular theory, the sociologist must test that theory with relevant empirical observations, or *data.* And since data are by their nature limited to the observable, the measurable, the quantifiable, whatever elements of religion are spiritual or supernatural, in the sense that they cannot be seen with the eye or otherwise measured or recorded, are by definition beyond the purview of sociology.

Our characterization of the sociology of religion so far, as objective and empirical, can be summed up by stating that the sociology of religion is conducted according to the *scientific method.* By the scientific method we mean (1) the systematic search for verifiable data ("facts") firmly rooted in prior knowledge and theoretical formulations, (2) the production of evidence as opposed to hearsay, opinion, intuition, or common sense, and (3) the following of procedures that others can verify and replicate (reproduce under essentially identical conditions).

It is at this point that the sociologist of religion encounters probably the most strenuous objection from the religiously committed, which usually runs something like this: Since religion relates primarily to the supernatural—that is, to forces that are usually unseen—and involves matters of the heart as well, anything the sociologist can say about religion, limited as he or she is to describing the observable, will be at best superficial and unimportant, at worst false and misleading. J. Milton Yinger has supplied some useful imagery in speaking to this issue. He frames the objection to the empirical study of religion with the question, "How is it possible to see a stained-glass window from the outside?"[1] That is, the beauty and the message or picture of a church's stained-glass window is visible only when one is *inside* and can see the sunlight shining through. Professor Yinger goes on to note, however, that the view from the inside constitutes only part of what can be learned about the window. Only from the outside, for example, can the viewer appreciate the exterior framework or context within which that window exists. Furthermore, there are, as Yinger suggests, pieces of information potentially important to understanding the significance of the window that have nothing to do with viewing it from the inside (or from the outside, for that matter): who built it, who installed it, who provides for its repair, who goes in to view it from the inside. We can also consider the reason it was installed, what "outsiders" think of it, how it resembles or differs from other windows, whether the style of newer windows is the same or is changing, and so on.

Rather than belabor the obvious parallel that we are suggesting between this situation and the study of religion, it is enough to note that questions like these can be answered empirically, that they are important questions, and that the answers to them amplify our understanding. Granted, empirical data do not constitute the only information of any importance about religion. Nor can we claim that empirical or observable measures of religion reveal its "essence." Studying religion empirically places a certain restriction on our enterprise—but no more severe a restriction than is placed on the position of those who claim religion to be strictly concerned with spiritual matters and therefore off-limits to empirical investigation. Each "side" of this issue can contribute to an understanding of the total phenomenon.

CENTRAL SOCIOLOGICAL ASSUMPTIONS

Having established that the scientific study of religion is a legitimate endeavor, it remains for us to indicate why, for the sociologist, it is an important one—that is, how it furthers sociology's task of attempting to understand the dynamics of people living in groups. For this purpose it will be helpful to identify some of the central assumptions of sociology, whether applied to the study of religion, the family, the class system, the division of labor, or any other social phenomenon.

The Sociological Perspective

In the first place, what exactly *is* sociology? Very briefly stated, sociology is the study of the interaction of people in groups and of the influence of those groups on human behavior generally and on society's other institutions

[1] J. Milton Yinger, *The Scientific Study of Religion* (New York: Macmillan, 1970), p. 2.

and groups. Thus sociology has a twofold goal: (1) understanding the dynamics of group life—what groups are, how they function, how they change, how they differ from one another; and (2) understanding the influence of groups on individual and collective behavior. One fundamental assumption of sociology implied by this is that all human activity is influenced by groups. Throughout a person's lifetime groups impinge on his or her biological "raw material," shaping it, modifying it, influencing it—*socializing* it, to use the sociologists' term. This process begins with the family and proceeds through the hundreds of educational, associational, peer, and work groups that a person participates in and has contact with throughout his or her lifetime.

In both fundamental senses of the sociological enterprise—explaining group dynamics and explaining group influence—religion qualifies perfectly as a field of sociological study and analysis. Leaving aside for now the question of whether religion is also (or even primarily) an individual phenomenon, it is obviously at least a group phenomenon. Thus to the extent that religions organize themselves into groups—congregations, denominations, dioceses, cells, fellowships, and so on—an important task for sociology is the study of the structure and functioning of these groups simply *as groups.* In other words, we want to determine how and to what extent religious groups follow sociological laws governing group life in general. In what ways does a congregation, for example, operate like any other voluntary association—like, say, the League of Women Voters? Or how and to what degree do major religious denominations function like other large bureaucracies—like, say, General Motors, or the United States Army?

Insofar as religion is organized into groups, it exerts influences not only on its members, but also on nonmembers and on other groups and institutions. The second dimension of our preliminary definition of sociology—as a study of group influence—thus suggests that religious groups have at least the potential for influencing people just as do groups that center around one's family, peers, or workplace. The question is not so much *whether* such influence exits but *to what degree, in what ways,* and *how it can be measured.*

Human Nature

A number of assumptions in sociology center around the definition of human nature. Here we shall emphasize three of these assumptions.

First, and perhaps most obviously, a human being is a *biological organism*—a creature with physiological drives, needs, potentials, and limitations. The socializing influence of groups is thus both directed at and limited by biological factors. Religion is of course among those socializing agents that attempt to influence or modify biological nature. For example, different religious groups have different approaches to, and provide or allow different outlets for, sexual drives. And insofar as people in fact internalize these different emphases—whether they be permissive, compensatory, restrictive, or whatever—to that extent people will have different personalities and evidence different values and attitudes. In short, although the sociological perspective rejects notions of bio-logical determinism, it recognizes as openly as possible that the human being has potentialities and limitations that are biologically provided.

Another sociological assumption regarding human nature that is worth mentioning is the apparently unique *ability of people to symbol.* By this we mean the ability arbitrarily to attach specific meanings to things, sounds, words, acts—meanings which are not intrinsic to the items themselves but which people have created. By establishing consensus on these meanings, groups are able to communicate and to accumulate knowledge. Using lan-guage as the prime symbolic mechanism, people can deal with abstract con-cepts and emotions, such as love, justice, and equality as easily as they can ask someone to pass the potatoes at the dinner table.

The ability to express meanings symbolically is primarily responsible for the variety of groups, cultures, ideologies, and technologies throughout histo-ry. There is no activity in which people are engaged that does not involve acts of symbolizing—whether lecturing, voting, making love, or "being religious." Religion in fact consists entirely of symbols and of activities that are interpreted and mediated by symbols. This is true whether the symbols have empirical referents or not. God, hell, salvation, Star of David, nirvana, guru, mana—all have meaning to those initiated into a particular symbolic system. The meaning of each of these is not inherent in the word itself, or in the com-bination of sounds, but is supplied by the believer. Even if divine truths have been revealed to people by a supernatural being, those truths have been expressed in human language, or are immediately translated into human lan-guage—otherwise the message would have no meaning for people.

Yet another primary sociological assumption about human nature is that *people become human only in groups*—admittedly, a dramatic way of stating that the influence of groups on the human organism through socialization is crucial and far-reaching. We do not propose to debate the academic question of whether the newborn babe is in fact human. The point is simply that the newborn infant is not yet very much of what it is going to become, and that what it does become will be largely attributable to socializing influences. One of those socializing influences is religion, which in fact affects everyone, wheth-er or not they are born into a "religious" family, or attend Sunday school, or are married by a member of the clergy, and so on. For religion also exerts an indirect influence on people, if only in an inverse way as a negative reference group or through its influence on secular institutions.

Human Action Is Directed toward
Problem Solving

A fundamental assumption of sociology is that *every human action is in some form and to some degree a problem-solving act or mechanism.* Whether working at a job, getting married, planning a party, or genuflecting, the human being is engaged in the process of solving or resolving some existing (present) or anticipated (future) problem. The problem may be how to satisfy a biological need for nourishment, how to achieve victory on the athletic field, or how to get God to help you pass an exam this afternoon. In any case, the person perceives a problem that he or she must solve, either now or, if he or she fails to take appropriate action, in the future.

Religious behavior is problem-solving like any other social activity. Praying, attending church services, observing religious laws, and having and talking about "mountaintop experiences," for example, are all religious activities that contribute in some way (at least from the perspective of the religious participant) toward solving a problem, either existing or anticipated. Note that we are not suggesting (or denying) that religion in fact either solves problems or creates them. Rather, our point is that people often engage in religious activities *in the belief* that such behavior can solve problems. Lest there be any misunderstanding, once again we shall emphasize that throughout this book no attempt is made to determine or question the truth or falsity, the efficacy or inefficacy, of religion in general, of any specific religion in particular, or of anyone's personal religious beliefs. Engaged as we are in sociological investigation, we are concerned solely with what can be observed, including what people *believe* exists and happens.

All Social Phenomena Are Interrelated

The final sociological assumption that we need to clarify before delving in detail into the sociology of religion is that *all social phenomena within a given group or society are interrelated*. That is, all social phenomena are continually interacting, and every part becomes linked with every other in at least an indirect way. More specifically, part A may not be influenced directly by part F, but F may be having some indirect influence through a chain of other factors or social phenomena called B, C, D, and E. Most important for our purposes, religion interacts with—is in a dynamic reciprocal relationship with— every other social phenomenon and process. Religion both influences them and is influenced by them; religion both acts and reacts, is both an independent variable and dependent variable, both cause and effect. This principle of the continual dialectic involving religion and other social phenomena is a central theme of this book, for determining the nature and extent of these mutual influences are key tasks in the sociology of religion.

We have now identified in at least an introductory way what sociology is. Now, what is *religion*—the second term in our subject, the Sociology of Religion?

A SOCIOLOGICAL DEFINITION
OF RELIGION

Everyone of course "knows" what religion is. For our purposes, however, such knowledge needs to be systematized. We need to achieve some consensus on the boundaries of our subject matter, which we all recognize as having great diversity, before we can proceed to analyze it. Without denying the validity of any individual's private definition, we need to establish some ground rules that we can follow throughout this text. Clearly there is nothing absolute about a definition—no definition, of any phenomenon, religion included, is inherent in the phenomenon itself. What we require, then, is a *working definition* of religion—specifically, a definition that we can be fairly sure includes the major ideas of this concept, a definition that is moreover flexible and responsive to changing conditions and new evidence—so that we can communicate fairly sensibly not only among ourselves but with others as well. Although we shall not include everything that anyone has ever thought religion might be, we shall try to isolate the core or essential elements.

THE CHARACTERISTICS OF
RELIGION

The English word *religion* has a Latin root; that much is certain. But there is disagreement over whether the Latin root word is *religare*, meaning "to bind together" (suggesting possibly the concept of a group or fellowship), or *relegere*, meaning "to rehearse, to execute painstakingly," referring probably to the repetitious nature of liturgy. Either word makes sense as a root, and each taps a dimension of religion that we will include in our definition. Yet it is clear that etymology by itself will not provide us with an ultimate answer to our problem of definition.

Religion Is a Group Phenomenon

Let us start with the concept suggested by the Latin word *religare*—the concept of the group or fellowship. The assertion that religion is a group phenomenon is significant both for what it says and for what it fails to say, for what it excludes. What it excludes is of course the individual aspect. Certainly religion is an individual matter in any number of ways: in that it involves personal emotions and thoughts; or insofar as one's religion is a matter of personal beliefs; or insofar as individuals are free to commit themselves to whichever religious system they prefer. Still, it would not make sense to expect that one could somehow systematically study every individual's personal religious beliefs. Sociology, being committed to systematic study of group behavior, has no such problem in that it concentrates on the group dimension of religion.[2]

Throughout history and in every corner of the world, people have engaged in religious behavior. Congregations, ceremonial gatherings, denominations, prayer meetings, family pilgrimages, ecumenical councils—all are examples of religious activity. Even when a lone figure is acknowledged to have experienced visions or received supernatural dispensations, he or she frequently attracts others—that is, he or she becomes a leader (perhaps even a prophet) with a following, often whether the person seeks it or not. True, we also see occasional isolated mystics and religious hermits in mountaintop seclusion. Even most of these, however, belong to some subgroup of a major religion (such as Catholicism or Buddhism) which may encourage or even structure and coordinate such activity.

Elaborating our admittedly arbitrary division of religion into its personal and group dimensions, J. Paul Williams suggests that there are at least four types or levels of religiousness: (1) the *secret* level, which a person keeps to himself or herself and does not divulge or discuss; (2) the *private*, which he or she divulges or discusses with only a few carefully chosen intimates; (3) the *denominational*, which the individual shares with many others in a large group; and (4) the *societal*, which the person shares with the members of society at large.[3] Williams's first two categories will occupy very little of our time— not because they fail to involve religion (they obviously do), but simply because of the reasons already mentioned for narrowing our range of coverage, and also, to some extent, because solid sociological research into individual aspects of religion has only recently begun. For example, Chapter 3, while it does not deal with precisely what Williams means by "secret" religiousness, focuses on what we might call the social-psychological dimension of religion— the process of individual internalization of religion. Our primary attention, however, will be on what Williams identifies as denominational and societal religion, with particular emphasis on the former, again reflecting the fact that most research in the sociology of religion has been in this area.

So much for what is excluded by our characterization of religion as a group phenomenon. Now we may ask, What is *included* in this aspect of our definition? Answering this question requires that we specify exactly what a group is; in this regard, fortunately, sociologists are very explicit.

---

[2] This is not to ignore the fact that sociologists, particularly social psychologists, also study the behavior of individuals. For example, the current considerable sociological interest in the nature of religious commitment and in the process of religious socialization and internalization of religious concepts and values obviously necessitates careful attention to individual behavior. Nevertheless, the purpose of such research with individuals is primarily to be able to generalize to larger groups and categories of people.

[3] J. Paul Williams, "The Nature of Religion," *Journal for the Scientific Study of Religion* 2, no. 1 (1962), 8.

According to one definition that most sociologists would accept, a group has six major features. The first and most basic is that *a group is composed of two or more people (members) who have established certain patterns of interaction* (including communication) with one another. Such interaction does not necessarily take place continually, or even daily. Nor does every member of a group interact with every other member. Nor is this interaction necessarily face to face. The point is simply that the people who constitute a group—group members—are aware of one another (perhaps even know one another) and have established patterns of interaction characteristic of their group.

The second major feature of a group, according to our definition, is that *group members share certain common goals*—in fact, this is the reason they came together in the first place (although they may not have known it then). The process of forming a group thus involves the fundamental sociological concept, introduced earlier in this chapter, that all human behavior consists of some sort of problem-solving activity. Saying that a group has common goals implies that individuals who are confronted with common problems have made contact and have agreed to work together toward the goal of solving those problems. Imagine, for example, five individuals, each deeply concerned about industrial-waste pollution in a certain trout stream, who through casual conversation (perhaps while trying to fish the stream) "discover" one another and subsequently form a group called STEP (Save Trout from Environmental Pollution), whose primary goal is reducing pollution in this and other trout streams. Thus what was originally the separate concern of five individuals has become a group concern, which in turn implies a certain common goal or set of goals that they share with one another.

Third, as a result of the above, *a group is guided by shared norms*. For once a group defines its goals, it then determines how to reach them; that is, the group specifies that such and such is what its members will do, as well as when, where, and how. All such specifications are norms—more or less formal expectations concerning appropriate behavior by one or all members of the group.

Fourth, *every group member has a role*, or set of functions, to fulfill. As such, a role consists of a set of specific norms the group wants carried out. The development of different roles within the group gives rise to what is known as *the division of labor*. Thus, whenever a member leaves the group or adopts a new role, the group may need to keep the division of labor in balance by recruiting someone else—either another member or an outsider—for that particular role.

Fifth, *a group functions collectively in accordance with a status system*, a hierarchy in which different amounts of power, authority, and prestige are accorded to different roles and to the individuals in those roles. Different groups, of course, have different criteria for establishing status rankings. Roles involving group coordination, decision making, and interpretation, for example, which inherently carry the greatest authority and prestige, are very often assigned to those individuals who are believed to perform these tasks most ably, although such other factors as seniority, wealth, and kinship can also be influential.

Sixth, *group members feel and express a sense of identification with the group*: "I belong," "This is my group," "Yes, I'm an active member of STEP." The degree of group commitment, dedication, and identification varies from member to member, and most groups are able to tolerate some such variability. But without a certain minimum amount of identification and commitment on the part of its members, a group will soon disintegrate.

These six characteristic features of a group obviously apply to religious groups no less than to any other kind. Thus in studying religion as a group phenomenon, we already know many things to expect and even some questions to ask: How does a given religious group differ from all others in terms of these six aspects? What, for example, are the religious group's goals? its norms? its roles? its status criteria?

Religion Is Concerned with the Sacred and Supernatural

A second characteristic that we wish to include in our definition of *religion* is its involvement with what Durkheim identified as the "sacred," with what Rudolf Otto termed the "holy" or the "wholly other,"[4] and essentially what Mircea Eliade refers to as "sacred space" that is qualitatively different from all other "homogenous" space in which regular, everyday occurrences and activities take place.[5] There is a universal tendency for religion to express awe, reverence, and fear with regard to certain things, beings, or situations and to distinguish them from the ordinary, the mundane—or, as Durkheim defines it, the "profane." Old Testament Jews removed their sandals upon entering the temple, many Christians make the sign of the cross when praying to God, Hindus give cows the right of way, Muslims undertake pilgrimages to Mecca, American Indians avoided disturbing holy plots of ground. All such behavior expresses the recognition of a sacred place or situation. In each instance people acknowledge being in the presence of something special—something above and beyond them that demands adopting special attitudes, performing certain actions, and perhaps articulating special words as well.

For many people—for whole religious systems, for that matter—that "something special," the *sacred*, in fact involves the *supernatural*, a power or being not subject to the laws of the observable universe. Such a power may be

---

[4] Emile Durkheim, *The Elementary Forms of the Religious Life*, trans. Joseph Ward Swain (New York: Collier, 1961), p. 52; Rudolf Otto, *The Idea of the Holy*, trans. John W. Harvey (London: Oxford University Press, 1936), pp. 8–41.

[5] Mircea Eliade, *The Sacred and the Profane*, trans. Willard R. Trask (New York: Harcourt Brace Jovanovich, 1959), p. 20.

personified by Jesus, by Vishnu, by Allah, or by any number of gods, devils, goblins, or spirits. Or perhaps it is simply a vague and diffuse power, such as that identified by the Polynesian term *mana* (which we shall discuss shortly).

In these beliefs a dichotomy of reality is being expressed. On the one hand there are the "profane" (ordinary) events and the visible environment of the routine workaday world. On the other hand there is the invisible, largely uncontrollable, out of the ordinary realm. To a greater or lesser degree, people can control and predict familiar everyday situations—the choice of daily tasks, conversations with others, the acts of eating and copulating, the seeking of nightly rest, and so on. But most people seem to believe that there is more to life than such ordinary situations and events. What about the big bang in the sky last week and the twisting dagger of light that preceded it? What about my friend who dropped dead while running beside me? What about that place in the swamp where a whole hunting party was swallowed up in the mud? Such things are out of the ordinary; they cannot be taken for granted; they elicit fear, awe, respect. We are here in the presence of Otto's "wholly other"—an entirely different order of existence.

It should be emphasized that the experiences that people define as sacred vary considerably and the objects of their awe and reverence are infinitely diverse. Yet every society has its list of such awesome and mysterious things and events. Religion deals with them. Religion provides explanations and answers; religion prescribes methods of placation and of expressing appropriate reverence. The sacred, the holy, the supernatural, together with people's relationship to them, thus constitute the prime subject matter of religion.

Although the term *sacred* may occasionally connote little more than "deserving or demanding respect," with no necessary thought of a supernatural power being involved, it is usual for the two concepts to go together. That which is considered sacred is so precisely because some supernatural force or activity arouses the feeling of awe that surrounds the sacred object, person, place, or situation. While they are not strictly synonymous concepts, the sacred and the supernatural are in most societies so intimately related that most of the time we shall regard them as almost inseparable for the purposes of our definition of religion.

However, in the interests of precision and clarity of the concepts *sacred* and *supernatural,* we shall regard only the sacred as essential to religion. This allows us to include several thought systems that most people would almost intuitively think of as religious systems, yet upon close examination are found to express no concept of the supernatural at all. We would mention as examples Jainism, Ethical Culture, early Buddhism, and early Confucianism.

Religion Involves a Body of Beliefs

A third characteristic of religion, one that is much more straightforward and easy to describe, is that it invariably includes or implies a body of beliefs. This characteristic proceeds directly from the foregoing considerations of the sacred and the supernatural. For in the act of endeavoring to deal with or justify these phenomena and experiences, religious groups develop explanations, work out rationales, and discover "facts" that are eventually systematized into a body of beliefs.

Every major religion has its sacred book or books that spell out or at least provide the basis for determining the beliefs the group holds. Some examples are the Bible, the Koran, the Book of Mormon, and the Bhagavad-Gita. Furthermore, every major religion has beliefs *in addition* to those contained in such "official" or basic writings—the interpretations and extensions of lesser prophets and of other successors to the founder(s) of the religion, for example. Then, too, there is in every religion (and not just in those of preliterate societies) the oral tradition—unwritten explanations, in the form of myths, sagas, and proverbs, handed down to each new generation by word of mouth.

Borhek and Curtis describe seven features of most belief systems. First, there are *values*—definitions of what is good or valuable. Second, *criteria of validity* by which to judge new observations and messages. Third, a "*logic*" that relates one substantive element in the belief system to others. Fourth, a *perspective* that identifies how the group stands in relation to other groups and world views. Fifth, *substantive beliefs* such as "Jesus will come again to reign a thousand years" or "Vishnu is an avatar of the Buddha." Sixth, there are *prescriptions and proscriptions* so far as behavior is concerned. Seventh, there will be a *technology* that consists of means and techniques for obtaining valued goals.[6]

It should be pointed out that we are dealing here with a characteristic that is not unique to religious groups, for groups of all kinds have belief systems. Although we can view beliefs as attitudes or opinions so far as the individual is concerned, group beliefs properly fall under the heading of the norms established or accepted by the group. Norms, in other words, specify not only how a group's members are expected to behave but also what they are expected to believe, how they are to interpret and relate to things and events. The distinctiveness of religious groups so far as beliefs and norms are concerned rests simply with the subject matter of those beliefs. The beliefs of religious groups specifically concern the sacred and very likely also the supernatural.

Religion Involves a Set of Practices

A fourth characteristic of religion is that it universally involves specific practices—which consist of acting out certain normative expectations. One of the most obvious features of any religion—obvious because it consists of behavior rather than beliefs or attitudes or perspectives—is the performance of ritual and the host of other activities generated by its beliefs. The gathering to

[6] James Borhek and Richard F. Curtis, *A Sociology of Belief* (New York: John Wiley, 1975), pp. 9–15.

worship, the rain dance, the sacrifice of animal or person, the ceremonial foot washing, the immersing in water at baptism, the vigil—all these are examples of what we are referring to.

It is important to understand that there is nothing intrinsically religious in a given act—an act or practice becomes religious only when the group defines it as such. Thus the act of eating a meal may be no more than a means of gaining sustenance; or it may be an *agape* ("love feast") of the first-century Christians, or a ceremonial enactment of the Last Supper. One may wear a robe solely to fend off the cold, or (in medieval Europe) to indicate one's academic rank; or one may wear it to indicate that he or she is a holy person or messenger of God. Journeying to a distant town may be for the purpose of conducting business or taking in the sights; or it may be for fulfilling the religious obligation of making a pilgrimage to a holy city at least once during one's lifetime.

Religion Involves Moral Prescriptions

Another feature of religion that, although certainly not unique to religious groups, is emphasized in all of them. That is the moral dimension. This refers to the judgment a religious group or system makes that certain thoughts, certain ideas are good and worthwhile and to be encouraged and positively reinforced, while other actions, thoughts, and ideas are bad, harmful, and to be rejected by the faithful. Another way of saying this is that a religion advocates certain behaviors with the intention of encouraging its adherents to choose such behaviors in everyday situations. Of particular significance here is that religion is unique in claiming a "higher" source or basis for its morality: You should do such and so or refrain from such and so because God wills it or because it is in tune with cosmic forces, not simply because our group says so or because I your leader say so. In other words, religion ultimately invokes the sacred or the supernatural in order to influence the behavior of individuals not only in extraordinary situations or situations defined as "religious," but in all the ordinary, routine ones as well.

A FORMAL DEFINITION OF RELIGION

In attempting to define religion formally we shall go no further than to gather together the ingredients we have discussed. Our definition is thus perhaps less elegant than some, yet more inclusive than many. Sociologically viewed, then, and in terms of what will come under review in this book, *religion* can be defined as *a system of beliefs and practices by which a group of people interprets and responds to what they feel is sacred, and usually, supernatural as well.*

Let it be clearly understood that by employing this definition we are, for purposes of sociological investigation at least, adopting the position of the hard-nosed relativist and agnostic. That is, we are neither affirming nor deny-ing the existence of the supernatural; nor are we stating whether what a group defines as sacred is or is not in fact sacred. We *are* asserting, however, that people in groups often do in fact believe in the supernatural and identify cer-tain beings, events, and so on as sacred. These beliefs and the attitudes and behavior stemming from them thus become the subject matter of the sociology of religion.

It should also be clear by now that the above definition is to be under-stood as neither the final nor the best definition of religion; rather, it is a pragmatic one—one, moreover, that is reasonably in tune with what the ma-jority of people consider religion to be. This latter point is particularly impor-tant, for it is unnecessary, and would even be unwise, deliberately to define religion in a manner too different from the way most people understand it.[7]

APPLICATION OF THE
DEFINITION

Before ending our formal treatment of the definition of *religion* (in a real sense, the remainder of this book represents an elaboration and explication of our definition), two serious questions require discussion. One concerns the ap-plication of our definition, particularly with regard to whether we should in-clude or exclude certain ways of life and thought when speaking of religion. The other involves the issue of whether there is a distinction to be made be-tween religion and magic (not stage magic, of course, but magic in the original sense of using charms and spells to control supernatural forces)—and if there is, where to draw the line—or whether the two are really a single concept.

Should the Various "Isms" Be Called
Religions?

With respect to the former question, there has been much discussion about whether the various "isms," such as communism, fascism, scientism, and humanism, should be included under the heading of religion.

Proponents of this viewpoint are particularly fond of citing the charac-teristics of communism to support their argument, pointing out its "religious" elements—its prophets, its emphasis on orthodox beliefs, its rituals, its sacred shrines, the missionary zeal and unquestioning commitment of its adherents.

---

[7] It might be noted that the above definition is an example of what most sociologists would call a "functional" definition in contrast with a "substantive" one. A functional definition emphasizes more what the phenomenon *does*, whereas a substantive definition places its emphasis on what a phenomenon *is*. Cf. Peter Berger, "Second Thoughts on Defining Religion," *Journal for the Scientific Study of Religion* 13, no. 2 (1974), 125–33; Richard Machalek, "Definitional Strate-gies in the Study of Religion," *Journal for the Scientific Study of Religion* 16, no. 4 (1977), 395–401.

And those who argue that scientism qualifies as a religion find similar patterns: a system of beliefs about the utility of scientific endeavors, a set of practices (the scientific method), prophets of old (the founding fathers of modern science), sacred places (the laboratory, the computer room), supreme loyalty and commitment of its adherents, the missionary zeal, if you will, with which proponents try to win others to share their faith in science.

Although we do not take such analogies with total seriousness, no one can deny the existence of certain striking parallels between such ideologies and thought systems, on the one hand, and religion as we have defined it, on the other. If we want to be precise, however, our characterization of religion as involving the sacred and the supernatural quite clearly places these ideologies and thought systems outside the realm of religion. Before leaving the subject, however, it is only fair to make the observation—and the point can hardly be overstressed—that certain pronounced elements in ideologies like communism are unlike anything else *outside* religion. Certainly the tenets of communism or socialism, for example, are held "religiously," and its adherents frequently exhibit "religious" zeal in pursuing group goals. The importance of this observation is that it helps us understand the behavior of such systems' organizations and adherents. We see commitment and zeal in such systems of thought and practice even if we don't happen to agree with what they espouse or do. Nevertheless, sticking by our definition, we shall not include such thought systems in our discussion of religions in the following chapters.

It should be emphasized that more than a technicality is involved here. If we made our definition of religion progressively broader and our criteria more inclusive, we would soon reach the point where *everything* could be defined as religion. Then *nothing* would be religion, inasmuch as there would be no alternative categories. Subsuming all (or even nearly all) human behavior in a definition of religion would be much like saying that all human behavior is sexual or that all human behavior is economic. In a certain sense, such assertions say something important—they draw attention to the profound fact that sexuality, economics, and religion are pervasive phenomena which touch almost every form of human activity to at least some degree. However, to reduce all human activity to any one of the categories requires stretching that category to absurd dimensions and is ultimately counterproductive. A more reasonable solution (at least this is the consensus within sociology) is to draw somewhat narrower boundaries around one's subject matter by identifying specific characteristics such as we have done above, thereby facilicating more intensive study and analysis of a more manageable body of data.

The Relationship of Religion and Magic

Resolving the issue of the relationship between religion and magic is in some ways more difficult. By way of introduction, let us consider the concept of *mana* (a Polynesian term), which is common in "primitive" religions, and vestiges of which appear in the religious systems of industrial societies as well. Purnell Benson notes, for example, that mana appears in numerous religions under various names—in Hinduism it is *darshan*; in Christianity it is *divine grace*; among American Indians it was called *manito* by the Algonquins, *wakanda* by the Sioux, *orenda* by the Iroquois, and *maxpe* by the Crow.[8]

Mana is a prime ingredient in magic. To those who believe in it there exists in the world, everywhere, and in everything, an elemental force, a primary energy—mana. Mana even exists—it floats, so to speak—in the very air we breathe. Often it is just *there*, not directly attached to anything, simply waiting to be grasped, harnessed, used. Though mana is in people, in things, in animals, in plants, and in the atmosphere, it is impotent until someone or something, or a spirit perhaps, activates it by discovering the secret key that unlocks its energies.

Enter magic, which attempts to exercise power over people and things by controlling the ubiquitous mana. The practice of magic is thus not an expression of ignorance, as is commonly supposed, but a conscious, deliberate attempt to circumvent what might normally be expected to occur. That is, magic is typically used to undercut the predictable by marshaling sufficient mana—elemental force—to change what otherwise would be inevitable.

In those societies where magic is most likely to be practiced and condoned (the more "primitive" societies), people make little if any distinction between magic and religion—or for that matter among scientific knowledge, religious knowledge, common-sense knowledge, and magic. Knowledge is knowledge, be it scientific, religious, or whatever. This lack of categories of course makes the task of distinguishing between magic and religion a bit more difficult.

We may begin, however, by noting the similarities and the differences or contrasts that have been suggested in the long debate over the relationship of religion and magic. First some similarities: (1) both are serious attempts to deal with and solve the basic problems people face; (2) both are based on faith in the existence and efficacy of powers that cannot be seen and can only be inferred by results; (3) both involve ritual activity, traditionally prescribed patterns of behavior; and (4) both are bona fide elements of the group's larger culture.

Some differences or contrasts follow: (1) religion more often centers on such overarching issues as salvation and the meaning of life and death, whereas magic is more likely to be employed in grappling with current, concrete problems (counteracting a viper's bite, bringing rain, defeating the enemy, for example); (2) religion is more often future oriented, while magic is primarily concerned with the here-and-now (or at least the very near future); (3) religion's orientation toward supernatural powers tends to be one of obeisance

---

[8] Purnell H. Benson, *Religion in Contemporary Culture* (New York: Harper & Brothers, 1960), p. 136.

and supplication, involving sacrifice and prayer (such as asking the appropriate deity or spirit to act on one's behalf), whereas magic is more manipulative, more often suggestive of pride than of humility (the magician seeks direct control over things and events, even at times seeking to trick the deity or defeat the deity in a contest if he or she can control enough mana); and (4) religion is characteristically a group activity, with groups of people collectively engaged in rituals and worship, while magic is typically an individual affair—the magician against the world, so to speak. Of course it is important to recognize that the magician conducts his or her work within a group (the society), and that in a real sense it is the group that *allows* the magician to work. Thus even though the magician works alone, his or her work is group sanctioned.

Are religion and magic, then, different phenomena, or two aspects of the same phenomenon? Or is one a subpart of the other? The last alternative is probably the most helpful way to see their relationship. Recalling our definition of religion, we find that magic fulfills each of our criteria—magic consists of beliefs and practices; it very clearly is concerned with the sacred and the supernatural; and it is practiced within a group (in a sense it is "possessed" by a group, although practiced by an individual). In fact, the relationship of magic to religion is virtually a classic example of specialization, for magic is typically practiced where the religious system considers it a legitimate and useful activity and encourages or at least allows its use. Thus magic is probably best seen neither as a competitor with religion nor as an alternative to it, but as a specialized subunit of religion. In fact, rarely is religion without at least some magical elements, just as magic is seldom practiced entirely apart from a larger religious system that legitimates it.

FINAL REFLECTION ON THE DEFINITION OF RELIGION

As the reader reflects a moment on our attention in this chapter to the task of defining religion, he or she might sense some ambivalence. If so, we have achieved one of our purposes in this chapter. Frankly, as we write this text, we face a dilemma which cannot be resolved to the satisfaction of all. The dilemma resides in the recognition that (1) our definition of religion (the five characteristics) is not inclusive of all phenomena that may in some sense be "religious," and it tends to be "conservative" in the sense that the focus is inevitably upon what has been traditionally recognized as religious—the religious institution in society, and (2) that such traditional institutional forms of religion do happen to be a prominent feature of societies and as such merit analysis and understanding.

Thus we have opted in this introductory text to concentrate on what is commonly regarded as religion and seems to fall fairly cleanly within our definition (a fantastically broad array of data and developments as it is). But we recognize and draw attention to the fact that there is likely more than can legitimately be called religion than this. Thus, in one sense we conclude this chapter deliberately leaving the issue of defining religion somewhat open-ended. Yet we also proceed from a close-ended approach as we pragmatically attempt to cover a manageable subject. That is, we shall spend most of our time in this text discussing religion as included in our definition. But we strongly assert that when the discussion is ended, we shall only have begun to talk about what could have been included from other perspectives or definitions.

A CONCLUDING HISTORICAL NOTE: THE DEVELOPMENT OF THE SOCIOLOGY OF RELIGION

A clearly identifiable interest in a formalized sociological study of religion goes back barely a hundred years, roughly coincident with the beginning of formalized sociology in general near the midpoint of the last century. The stimulus for sociological interest in religion seems to have been the reports of anthropologists during the early and middle nineteenth century who encountered and studied "primitive" societies in Africa and Oceania. Two significant observations made by these social scientists were (1) the existence everywhere of some form of religion, and (2) the fascinatingly wide variety of religious forms and behaviors.[9] In other words, religion was observed to be as diverse as it was widespread.

Such had always been true, of course. But as long as societies remained relatively isolated, the diversity and universality of religion was not fully appreciated. The advent of European colonialism and the consequent increase in world trade and commercial interaction after the Middle Ages raised the frequency and intensity of intersocietal contacts and eventually led to ethnographical investigations by social scientists. As a result more and more people began taking an interest in understanding and explaining the worldwide diversity of religion.

The reaction within Western society to revelations of such religious diversity was varied. Many from within the ranks of the Christian Church concluded rather quickly that all these other religious systems are wrong, misguided, benighted—that Christianity is the only correct, the only God-given, religion. Therefore, they tried to convert to Christianity the people who believed differently, and to prevent the spread of the other, what they believed to be, erroneous religious systems. Extensive missionary efforts that had begun in the 1700s were intensified in the nineteenth century. These far exceeded anything since the last of the Crusades in the thirteenth century.

---

[9] This pair of observations and the four responses that follow are suggested by J. Milton Yinger in *Sociology Looks at Religion* (New York: Macmillan, 1961), pp. 11–12.

Others responded to the newly discovered religions by maintaining that all religions are to be understood as sincere efforts to struggle with perplexing human problems, and that therefore each should be considered as good as any other so long as its adherents are satisfied. That is, despite such variation, the essence of religion is common to all of them.

A third reaction, essentially the opposite of the previous one, was that the various claims to religious truth are mutually exclusive and contradictory. Therefore, all are erroneous and should be dispensed with if possible. A variant on this theme was the prediction that as science progressed and eliminated superstition, religion would be increasingly rejected and finally relegated to the status of a relic from prescientific days.

A fourth response was that while each of the various religions has valuable aspects, no one of them is perfect. Therefore, we need to pick and choose the best elements from each for the particular society and age in which we live. Christian Science, Bahai, and various modern Buddhist cults still hold this view. In fact, each of the above points of view has its contemporary advocates. But as we have tried to make clear in the first part of this chapter, none of these positions is appropriate for the social scientist, since each involves value judgments of one sort or another.

Following the initial flurry of social scientists' interest in religion (initiated by early anthropologists), sociological interest in and research on religion, with a few notable exceptions, lay somewhat dormant until fairly recently. David Moberg has suggested several reasons for this: (1) some sociologists, discouraged by the close historical association of religion with philosophy and metaphysics, decided that religion could not be fruitfully studied empirically; (2) other sincerely interested sociologists yielded to the opposition against sociological research on religion that came from many religious groups; (3) those teaching in state universities were fearful of jeopardizing their positions if they should somehow overstep the boundary separating church and state; (4) others, convinced that religion was definitely on its way to extinction anyway, preferred not to waste their time; (5) still others who had personally rejected religion were reluctant to maintain any contact with it—even if only of a research nature.[10]

The notable exceptions included some of the early sociological giants, such as Emile Durkheim, Georg Simmel, and Max Weber, who devoted a significant portion of their scholarly energies to analyzing the role of religion in society. After Weber's publication of his *Sociology of Religion* in 1921, however, little research or theoretical development occurred in the sociology of religion until after World War II, when there was a dramatic upsurge in religious activity, particularly in the United States. Significant increases in church membership and attendance at religious services, extensive building programs, and

[10] David O. Moberg, *The Church as a Social Institution* (Englewood Cliffs, N.J.: Prentice-Hall, 1962), p. 13.

the establishment of hundreds of new congregations each year engendered serious talk of a religious revival.

Sociologists became interested. Here was a social phenomenon to be explored and explained, a development that was particularly intriguing in that many social scientists had long been predicting the eventual and even precipitous demise of religion, particuarly in its institutional form. The sociologists' new research interest in religion, which began in the late 1940s and early 1950s, has continued essentially unabated to the present. One reason for this is that these new developments in religion, which clamor for investigation and explanation, have continued at a rapid pace. Furthermore, the persistence of religion in its various forms has finally forced sociologists to renew the effort, initiated by early fathers of sociology like Durkheim and Weber, of attempting to understand the nature and function of religion. For both these reasons this book concentrates on systematizing sociological research and theoretical efforts that have appeared during the past twenty years or so—not because the newest efforts are necessarily the best ones, but simply because most of the empirical work in the field is of relatively recent vintage. Indeed, it appears that social scientists are beginning to fulfill in part the prophecy of the anthropologist James Frazer, who predicted a half-century ago that the time would come when the religions of the world would no longer be regarded in terms of their truth or falsehood, but simply as phenomena to be studied like any other expression of humanity.[11]

[11] James Frazer, *The Gorgon's Head* (London: Macmillan, 1927), pp. 281–82.

2

The Sources of Religion

We now approach what is admittedly a highly speculative, but at the same time a highly fascinating, issue in the sociology of religion—the question of the origins and sources of religion. When we realize that the question is phrased, not so often "Where does religion come from?" but instead "Why are people religious?" we see that the question of origins and sources is a relatively common one—one that has intrigued philosophers throughout the centuries, and scientists more recently. When people observe what we have come to think as religious behavior and become curious why people are doing or saying what they are, they are raising a question that by implication goes far beyond the immediate event and the persons involved in it. Ultimately the question is: from where did these ideas and practices come? Or, to be more ultimate yet, how did the idea of a God, or supernatural and sacred forces and entities originate in the first place? The answers to such questions, whether immediate or ultimate, have been many and varied, although we will soon discover that they can fairly conveniently be organized into relatively few categories.

The question of religion's origin per se is no longer pursued by social science, for any evidence of an origin or origins has been lost in prehistory. Attempts to reconstruct origins by examining contemporary preliterate societies have in fact served only to delay slightly the admission that such evidence, if it ever existed, is lost in antiquity. It is important to recognize that the scientific method is limited in this regard; in fact, it is incapable of establishing absolutely verifiable conclusions about past events on the basis of present or even past realities. Thus even when substantial evidence appears to support an attractive theory, any hypothesis regarding religion's origins is doomed to remaining forever tentative. More on this problem later in the chapter.

Yet despite such limitations in the pursuit of religion's origins, we propose to explore the question briefly. We do this because of the historical value and intellectual stimulation such a look at the past provides; but more important, such an exploration will serve to introduce us to several relevant contemporary issues in the sociology of religion that we will discuss more fully later. These are such issues as the functional view of religion, the nature and extent of social influences upon religion, and to some extent the conflict between theology and sociology regarding an analysis of religion.

With regard to prehistoric people, it seems reasonable to assume on the basis of available evidence that they seldom had questions about the sources of their religious beliefs and practices. Their religious elements were such integral parts of their culture and normative system that they most likely saw them simply as "in the nature of things." Things were that way and always had been. Therefore, there was little likelihood that questions of religious origins as such would occur to these people. There were often myths and tales of the origins of human beings or of one's society in particular, but seeing religion as something distinct from the rest of one's beliefs and practices in society was not likely.

REVELATION AS ORIGIN

With the beginning of both Christianity and, before that, Judaism, part of the answer was extremely simple—God was the originator of religions. God created the world and the people in it; he already in the Garden of Eden established some general principles and laws; he later spoke through selected prophets, and they recorded God's words and their own God-inspired commentary. God himself was directly at work instructing his people, and in the process was creating religion through the process of revelation.

This hypothesis or explanation of a divine origin of religion is not unique to Judaism and Christianity. Even Gautama Buddha, the founder of Buddhism, reports having experienced heavenly inspiration of a sort as he sat under the bo tree, practically at the end of his rope in his quest for truth. The insight around which he developed his religious system hit him out of the blue, so to speak; he had a "revelation." The revelation that inspired Mormonism was in the form of golden plates buried in the hill called Cumorah in New York State. Muhammad reported receiving visions (revelation) from the angel Gabriel in a cave near Mecca.

All such cases report the belief that either God himself or some other cosmic, supernatural force intervened in history, altered the normal course of events, and deliberately added to what had been previously known. Whether by personal contact with the divine power, an experience with an intermediary, sudden inspired insight, discovery of secret written messages, or whatever, it is the direct intrusion of a supernatural power with new knowledge and insight for humanity.

In turn, of course, such religious leaders, as they speak and write for the followers that gather around them, are themselves sources of revelation for the religious system that has begun to develop. As they become defined as gods or, at the very least, spokespersons for divinity, what they utter is revelation.

It is important to realize, of course, that such revelational explanations for the origins of religion concern what believers consider to be the only "true" religion—that is, their own. Proponents of the revelation hypothesis usually refer only to their religion as the one revealed by God. Other religions may exist, but their source is something else, an inferior source, although it is likely that other religions are hard at work trying to find the very truth that God has given only to "us."

THE "NATURAL-KNOWLEDGE-OF-GOD" EXPLANATION

Christian theologians, claiming direct revelation from God for their gift of "true" religion, have always been intrigued by the existence of other religions. If God revealed himself directly only to the Chosen People of Israel, they asked themselves, how did the religions of other peoples arise? The answer they finally settled on, based on scattered verses from the Bible, was the "natural-knowledge-of-God" concept: All human beings are born with a fundamental awareness of the divine, a rudimentary knowledge that God or some power is ultimately responsible for what they see around them. All other religions, then, are the result of peoples' striving to build on this fundamental awareness and make some sense out of it. The great diversity of religious systems is then relatively easy to explain. Because the initial awareness of God is so vague and diffuse, people are forced to call upon their imagination and experience in developing these systems. And since the imagination and experience of people are so diverse, the religious systems they evolve consequently differ.

Associated with the natural-knowledge-of-God idea is the "witness-of-nature" concept: The wonder and complexity of nature reinforces people's innate knowledge of the divine and motivates them to seek explanations. What I see around me—the cycle of seasons, the wonder of the flora and fauna, the majesty of the mountains, the splendor of the sun by day and the moon and stars at night—must have been brought into existence by someone or some power, some god or gods. And perhaps that god has helpers and supervisors of specific spheres and activities, such as the oceans, farming, lovemaking, and war. Eventually a complex system evolves from an original "seed of divine awareness."

Sociologists can obviously neither confirm nor refute such a hypothesis. Note, however, that except for the idea of inherent initial awareness, this attempt to explain the origins of religion is basically in harmony with modern sociological concepts. That is, there is a recognition that people themselves create their norms and beliefs and thought systems in response to their experiences and surroundings, and that a fundamental factor in such experiences is their contact with the physical environment. But more on such sociological views later in this chapter.

ANTHROPOLOGICAL EXPLANATIONS

We now turn from explanations of theologians to those of social scientists, who have attempted to explain the sources or origins of religion on the basis of empirical observations. We first focus on the anthropologists, particularly those of the nineteenth century who were so instrumental in stimulating investigation of religion from the perspective of social science.

The views of the early anthropologists on this subject are too diverse to even summarize here. It is worth noting, however, that all believed that religion somehow arose in response to the experiences of people in the world in which they lived. As preliterate people encountered awesome, mysterious, even terrifying events—thunder and lightning, earthquakes, tidal waves and floods, illness, birth and death—they felt the need to understand their causes. Religious systems thus gradually evolved out of people's need to assign causes for so-called natural phenomena and other recurrent experiences.

Some differences in emphasis and focus among early anthropologists are also worth noting. Max Müller, for example, is a representative of the "naturistic" school, which emphasized the role of physical acts of nature—natural events like storms, sunrises, tides.[1] Prehistoric people were fearful and almost completely defenseless and at the mercy of these events: Why do they happen and why to me in particular? Müller suggests that since prehistoric people saw other people cause events—push rocks, throw stones, shoot arrows, fell trees, and so on—they reasoned that *everything* that happens must be caused either by other human beings or humanlike agents. What evolved then was the belief in spirits—invisible beings much like people in the sense that they possessed wills and abilities to bring about effects by their actions. It is these spirits who *cause* natural events. Thus prehistoric people might suggest that a spirit crashes giant cymbals and produces thunder; that a fire-

---

[1] See F. Max Müller, *Anthropological Religion* (London: Longmans Green, 1892); idem, *Lectures on the Origin and Growth of Religion* (London: Longmans, 1878).

breathing spirit spits out lightning; that a spirit heaves itself out of the bowels of the earth and causes an earthquake; that a spirit takes the sun out of its basket and puts it on a shelf in the sky each morning; and so on.

Early anthropologists discovered among the "primitive" peoples they studied an apparently universal belief in such spirits, a phenomenon termed *animism*—the belief that all sorts of inanimate objects as well as living, growing things and moving creatures possess a life principle or soul of some kind. Rocks, trees, animals, and people have spirits in them, whereas some spirits are freewheeling and unattached to things. All spirits, however, are conceived of in a thoroughgoing anthropomorphic fashion—that is, they have shape, mind, feelings, and will, though they are invisible beings. They are much like people in that they can be amenable to sound arguments or placating gifts, particularly when they are in a good mood. They can also be quarrelsome, nasty, and dangerous when upset or angry. They like flattery, loyalty, and deference. So one must be continually vigilant to stay on their right side.

Thus when a coconut fell nearby, the prehistoric person is less likely to have said, "The coconuts are ripe; it's coconut season again," and more likely to have asked, "Who threw it? What did I do now to make a spirit angry?" Or tripping over a root in the path, they were less likely to curse their clumsiness and more likely to ask why the root's spirit reached out and grabbed them: Was it only a playful jest, or a warning that worse may happen if I don't shape up in some way?

Whereas Müller emphasized the external events of nature, Edward Tylor, who represents the "animistic" school, focused on such personal experiences as dreams, and seeing one's reflection in the water.[2] When I dream of sexual conquest, or felling the enemy on the field of battle, or running from a tiger, what is happening is that the spirit that resides in me (my soul) is out for the night—having a ball, displaying his or her valor, or running into a bit of trouble. My image in the stream? Why it is none other than my spirit looking up at me. See, when I smile, it smiles; when I frown, it frowns.

Another representative anthropologist, Robert Lowie, focused on those experiences that generated a sense of "mystery and weirdness" in people. For Lowie, religion is not simply a matter of identifying spirits or distinguishing body and soul. Rather, religion only arose when one's emotions became involved and a sense of mystery pervaded one's observations of the activities that spirits engage in.[3]

Many more hypotheses developed by anthropologists could be cited, but the above examples are enough to make the point that what we are calling anthropological explanations for the origin of religion focus primarily on people's belief in spirits and in what these spirits do. Such beliefs arise essentially from needs of prehistoric people to explain natural events in the physical environment as well as their own experiences. In a real sense this is a need for ra-

[2] See Edward B. Tylor, *Primitive Culture* (London: Murray, 1871).
[3] Robert Lowie, *Primitive Religion* (New York: Boni & Liveright, 1924), p. xvi.

tionality of a sort, for a means of making coherent the many things one has no control over.

This is what social scientists call the "cognitive need" explanation for religion. That is, people want to know and understand the "what" and the "why" of the goings on around them. Explanations evolve that place the source of mysterious events at the hands of supernatural beings and forces.

PSYCHOLOGICAL
EXPLANATIONS

Another broad area of explanation, the psychological perspective, in general treats the origins of religion in terms of people's emotional needs—in other words, not so much like Müller and Tylor, who emphasized people's cognitive needs to explain the mysterious, but more in terms of their need to resolve and adjust emotionally to the mysterious and the disastrous, more like Lowie's emphasis. In this view, people seek to maintain emotional stability in the face of danger, insecurity, and disruption, particularly as they encounter illness, accident, and death: How can I keep going as my world (health, personal relationships, and so on) crumbles about me? Why do disasters happen to me and to those I love? Can I make any sense out of it all? How can I find strength to go on?

E. Goodenough expresses this perspective clearly when he describes religion as the response of human beings to constant threats to their safety, security, and future existence. In particular, people face great insecurity and anxiety related to the knowledge not only that they shall ultimately perish but that it could happen at any moment. He calls this the "tremendum"—a Latin word referring to "that which must be feared" or the "source of terror."[4]

As an extension of this, a common psychological explanation suggests that people seek solutions and answers for such frustration, anxiety, and fear by trying to fit their experience into the larger framework of a divine plan with a long-range perspective: All things work out for those who love God; things will be better in the by and by; he died because God needed him more than we did; God is testing me to see if I am worthy; my sins have caught up with me and I am being punished.

Psychologist Walter Huston Clark has borrowed W. I. Thomas's idea that people basically have four "wishes" or drives—for security, response, recognition, and new experience—and contends that these are reasonably comprehensive for understanding the psychological need and appeal of religion.[5]

---

[4] Erwin R. Goodenough, *The Psychology of Religious Experiences* (New York: Basic Books, 1965), p. 6.

[5] Walter Huston Clark, *The Psychology of Religion* (New York: Macmillan, 1958), p. 67; William I. Thomas, *The Unadjusted Girl* (Boston: Little, Brown, 1923), pp. 4ff.

This leads us beyond the idea of emotional adjustment just expressed, although we are still dealing quite specifically with emotional needs that the individual strives to fulfill—specifically, according to Clark's approach, through religion.

Another psychologist, George S. Spinks, agrees with Clark by speaking of religion as actively fulfilling fundamental human needs, but takes this idea a step further by emphasizing the uncertainties and terrors that continually threaten to overwhelm the individual.[6] As such, he and Goodenough say the same thing.

Sigmund Freud, the "father of psychoanalysis," sees religion stemming primarily from a sense of guilt derived at least partly from the Oedipus complex and the attempts by the male to reconstruct a father image after his "love affair" with his mother and his ritual "killing" of his father. Thus for Freud, religion is a mechanism that allows people to sublimate many primitive instincts that society represses.[7]

Another perception that Freud uses extensively is the concept of projection. In projection, the god characters are really representations (projections) of wishes and conflicts within the person. God the Father, Christ, the stories of the original Paradise and the Fall into Sin, the ideas of the devil and immortality—these are all projections from the unconscious mind. Freud believed that gradually psychology would fathom the relationships.

Freud adds that a basic desire of people is to control some of the terrifying forces that surround them. A model for such control appears early in the lives of many persons—that model is the child's father. Thus, the family setting and role functions within the family (the patriarchal father role in particular) become the basis for projection of "fatherly" qualities both of authority and of problem solving and answer giving to the gods and supernatural powers that make up religious systems. We might add here, although getting ahead of the story just a little, that Freud is really quite sociological in his perspective at this point. The group setting and the role structure of that group play significant parts in Freud's analysis.

In general, then, from the psychological point of view, religion serves an adjustment function. That is, it helps people survive frustration in trying to fulfill or serve drives and needs, and in trying to adapt to the frightening experiences that threaten their emotional integrity.

While we earlier credited, so to speak, anthropologists, with the cognitive need explanation as an important component in understanding reasons for the development of religion, particularly its supernatural elements, this is an emphasis within psychology as well. A prominent contemporary psychologist, Abraham Maslow, says that a person has a "cognitive need to understand." Life needs to have a meaningful framework for the person to survive. Thus, a

---

[6] George S. Spinks, *Psychology and Religion* (Boston: Beacon Press, 1963), pp. 46–47.

[7] Sigmund Freud, *The Future of an Illusion* (New York: Liveright, 1928).

person "needs a religion or religious surrogate to live by, in about the same sense that he needs sunlight, calcium, or love."[8]

SOCIOLOGICAL VIEWS

We now turn to the sociological treatment of the issue of religion's sources or origins. Actually, to continue using the term *origins* would be misleading. Certainly contemporary sociologists no longer use the term; nor did the early representatives of sociology that we shall soon cite. A more appropriate term is *social correlates* (or simply *correlates*) of religion—that is, associations between various events and features on the one hand and religious forms and expressions on the other. As shall be evident throughout this text, one of the central concerns of contemporary sociology of religion is tracing the interaction of social factors and religion, not pretending or even hoping to discover "origins," but only influences on and modifiers of religion. In an important sense it makes little difference to the social scientist whence religion came originally anyway. The fact that it exists is more than sufficient to merit our attention and analysis.

As we might expect, sociologists who seek to discover the "influences" on and "correlations" of religion focus on the various processes involved in social interaction and group life. Theirs is not so much the anthropologists' emphasis on personal experiences with the physical environment, or the psychologists' emphasis on personal emotional adjustment, but theirs is an emphasis on models of what transpires in group interaction processes. These models are in a sense copied and reiterated in the religious system.

In elaborating the sociological position we shall first consider the contribution of the pioneering social theorist Georg Simmel. Patterns of social interaction that are themselves nonreligious, Simmel asserted, exert a prime influence on religion. Many feelings and patterns of expressions commonly termed "religious" are also found in other areas of life and in fact are basic ingredients of social interaction in general—exaltation, commitment, fervor, love, and so on are common to all forms of human experience and relationships. Faith, for example, is a common ingredient in relationships between individuals. Most of our interactions with people are founded on faith—faith that an approaching stranger will not shoot me as I reach out to shake his hand; faith that the pilot of the plane knows how to fly, is not on a suicide mission, and is sober; faith that the cook at the drive-in has not laced the hamburger relish with arsenic; and so on. *Religious* faith, then (to continue the example), is a supreme form of a prime factor in everyday interaction. "In faith in a deity," Simmel writes, "the highest development of faith has become

---

[8] Abraham Maslow, *Toward a Psychology of Being* (Princeton, N.J.: D. Van Nostrand, 1963), pp. 57–64.

incorporate, so to speak; has been relieved of its connection with its social counterpart."[9]

Implicit in what Simmel says here is a crucial sociological assumption concerning religious "origins"—namely, that the models for many if not all religious sentiments, expressions, and beliefs reside orignially in society at large, in its patterns of interaction. In other words, society precedes religion. Before religion can develop, there must first exist general patterns of social interaction—that is, a society—that can serve as a model.

Another pioneer, and Simmel's contemporary, Emile Durkheim, devoted much of his theoretical and research energies to studying religion and was particularly intrigued by the question of religion's origins and social correlates. Durkheim emphasized religion's role in influencing and reinforcing societal integration—in legitimating society's values and norms by providing divine sanctions for behavior that society defines as normative and by periodically bringing people together for ritual activities that strengthen their feeling of unity. Like Simmel, Durkheim believed that general patterns of social interaction provide models and precursors for religion. But Durkheim goes further in asserting (quite dramatically) that society's norms, roles, and social relationships are so closely reflected by religion that the latter is nothing more than these characteristics expressed in somewhat different form. The extreme of this position is Durkheim's contention that the real object of veneration in any religion is society itself—that which is venerated may be *called* "God," but it is really society.

In talking about god and the society, Durkheim makes much use of the concepts of "totem" and "totemic principle." A totem is an object or a living thing, such as a bird or animal or plant, that a group regards with special awe, reverence, and respect. It is what has often been mistaken by outside observers of so-called primitive people as an object of worship—a false god or idol—in Christian terms. Durkheim says the object is not worshipped per se. What is important is what the totem *represents*; it is that which is worshipped, if you will. But the totem is only a symbol of something more fundamental. Durkheim himself says

> Thus the totem is before all a symbol, a material expression of something else. But of what?
>   From the analysis to which we have been giving our attention, it is evident that it expresses and symbolizes two different sorts of things. In the first place, it is the outward and visible form of what we have called the totemic principle or god. But it is also the symbol of the determined society called the clan. It is its flag; it is the sign by which each clan distinguishes itself from the others, the visible mark of its personality, a mark borne by everything which is a part of the clan under any title whatsoever, men, beasts or things. So if it is at once the symbol of the god and of the society, is that not because the god and the society

[9] Georg Simmel, "A Contribution to the Sociology of Religion," *American Journal of Sociology* 11, no. 3 (1905), 336–67.

are only one? . . . The god of the clan, the totemic principle, can therefore be nothing else than the clan itself, personified and represented to the imagination under the visible form of the animal or vegetable which serves as totem.[10]

Undergirding Durkheim's view that society personifies itself in the form of totems or gods to revere and worship (that is, society itself is the real object of worship), is his perception of the need of society to reaffirm itself, that is, affirm its legitimacy and worth. This involves for Durkheim the creation of an "ideal" society. That ideal society is very literally the *idea* it has of itself— what it is like, what it stands for, where it has been, where it is going, and so on. This is more than the strictly *material* side of society that would include the people themselves, the ground and pavement on which they stand, the things they use, and the gestures they make. Integral to this process of maintaining the ideal aspect of society (its essence, so to speak) is religion that personifies the societal ideal and is the primary mechanism for its maintenance.

As a further extension of this idea of the essential identity of god and society is Durkheim's view of the idea of a person's soul. John Wilson points out that Durkheim saw in the belief in the soul "a symbolic representation of the relation between the individual and society."[11] The moral authority of the society is the reality that stands behind the concept of the soul. So, when people refer to their souls, they are referring (without of course being aware of it) to a social element within them. This social element will of course live long after the people themselves. One would have to think at this point of the Hindu and Buddhist concept of samsara and the traditional Greek and Christian concept of the immortality of the soul.

At this point, we can not avoid reintroducing Durkheim's concept of the sacred that was discussed briefly earlier and described as an integral part of our definition of religion. The sacred refers to those things and situations and places that are *set apart,* very special, emitting an aura of the holy, and so on. But Durkheim also says that the sacred consists of "all sorts of collective states, common traditions and emotions, (and) feelings which have a relationship to objects of general interest."[12] He contrasts profane things as those that each of us constructs from our own sense data and experiences. As purely individual impressions they do not have the same prestige and influence as the more societal and collective elements that constitute the sacred.

Another way to help understand how Durkheim views religion and how intimately it is associated with the society itself is to see religion as a *function-*

---

[10] Emile Durkheim, *The Elementary Forms of the Religious Life,* trans. Joseph Ward Swain (New York: Collier, 1961), p. 236.

[11] John Wilson, *Religion in American Society* (Englewood Cliffs, N.J.: Prentice-Hall, 1978), p. 19.

[12] Emile Durkheim, "Concerning the Definition of Religious Phenomena," in W. S. F. Pickering, *Durkheim on Religion* (London: Routledge & Kegan Paul, 1975), p. 95.

al element in society. That is, religion performs a beneficial function within society, for all religious acts (in Durkheim's view) tend to reaffirm society's legitimacy and bind its members more closely together. Durkheim's views of the functional (integrative) role of religion are well illustrated in his discussion of the social functions of religious and ceremonial ritual, as summarized by Alpert.[13] Durkheim sees four primary social functions of such ritual: (1) It serves a disciplinary and preparatory function—that is, ritual imposes a self-discipline that is necessary for social life. Members of society need to accommodate constraints, controls, boundaries. Learning to follow religious rituals facilitates development of this ability. (2) Ceremonial ritual provides a cohesive function—that is, it brings people together, reaffirms their common bonds, and reinforces social solidarity. By doing things jointly and repetitively, the members of the group strengthen their bonds of relatedness. "The essential thing is that men are assembled, that sentiments are felt in common, and that they are expressed in common acts."[14] (3) It serves a revitalizing function—that is, it makes members of the society aware of their common social heritage. It links them to the past: What we do has a history; we ourselves have a history. Such awareness can provide motivation and inspiration to carry on. (4) It serves a euphoric function. It aids in establishing a pleasant feeling of social well-being. This function takes on special significance when a group is faced with calamities, disappointments, losses of treasured members, and other threats to its stability. It helps straighten out the sharp curves and adds some rays of light in the dark tunnels of disappointment and despair.

It is appropriate at this point to mention a more contemporary application and suggestion of functional theory by Robert Merton. He speaks about the possibility of "functional alternatives." That is, although a given action or role of a particular subunit in a social system may be seen as functional, it should not be concluded that such is the only action or performance that may be functional in that particular place and time.[15] This is of particular relevance to the identification of religious functions. The fact that religion performs certain functions and satisfies certain needs of society and its individual members does not mean that religion is either inevitable or nonexpendable. Other systems or mechanisms could conceivably satisfy these needs as well or better. Actually, this may help explain why some persons are "religious" while others are not at all religious, at least not in ways traditionally defined as such by that society. That is, while some people practice major religions, others avail themselves of nonreligious functional alternatives or of religious alternatives outside the mainstream of formalized religion.

[13] Harry Alpert, *Emile Durkheim and His Sociology* (New York: Russell & Russell, 1961), pp. 198–203.

[14] Durkheim, *Elementary Forms,* pp. 431–32.

[15] Robert K. Merton, *Social Theory and Social Structure* (Glencoe, Ill.: Free Press, 1956), pp. 33–34.

More recently Guy E. Swanson has adopted Durkheim's basic position but modified it somewhat in conducting a monumental piece of research. Starting with the basic sociological assumption that all human ideas arise from the experience of people with their environment,[16] both physical and social, Swanson attempted to discover examples of specific human experiences giving rise to certain forms of religious belief. In this 1960 study *The Birth of the Gods* Swanson focused on religion's preoccupation with the supernatural in an attempt to determine the origin of this concept. Like the early anthropologists, Swanson noted the predominance of spirits and of the concept of mana in "primitive" religious systems. What are the sources of the belief in such phenomena? Swanson suggests that spirits, which he defines as "organized clusters of purposes" having a personal identity and access to mana, grow out of, and consequently stand for, social patterns already present in the society.[17] That is, as Durkheim and Simmel both maintained earlier, society serves as the model for religion.

Swanson then asks, What social relationships do the experiences with spirits correspond to? He suggests four conditions or types of social patterns or groups: (1) social relationships in which there is an evident connection between cause and effect, associated with the belief that spirits have a purpose and a will; (2) relationships regarded as persisting over the generations, which relates to the belief that spirits are immortal; (3) particular groups that are the source of particular spirits, which means that every spirit has a specific identity; and (4) groups that have distinctive purposes, associated with the fact that spirits differ in purpose and role.[18]

Using this general orientation to the source or basis of belief in spirits, Swanson analyzed data drawn from preliterate and early historical societies in order to trace the relationship between certain kinds of belief (such as monotheism, polytheism, and the beliefs in ancestral spirits, in reincarnation, in the immanence of the soul, and in the efficacy of witchcraft) and various social conditions and relationships. That is, he sought correlations between religious beliefs and practices, on the one hand, and, on the other, such social factors as the society's source of food, its amount of food production, the degree of danger of attack from alien societies, size of the population, the degree of private-property ownership, the emphasis on communal vs. noncommunal specialties within the society, social stratification, the nature and frequency of unlegitimated contacts with members of other societies, the variety and kinds of social organizations, and so on. In some cases Swanson found a surprisingly high correlation between a set of social factors and a particular religious belief or practice—that is, a particular belief was always (or almost always) present *only if* certain social factors were also present, and always (or nearly always)

---

[16] Guy E. Swanson, *The Birth of the Gods* (Ann Arbor: University of Michigan Press, 1960), p. 1

[17] Ibid, p. 18.

[18] This typology is summarized from ibid., pp. 19–20.

absent *only when* the same factors were absent. In all cases, he found fascinating and highly suggestive correlations, whether of high magnitude or not. For example, the belief and practice of witchcraft, Swanson discovered, tend to occur in societies where people must interact with one another on important matters with no clear norms, controls, and structures to guide them.[19] Thus people resort to witchcraft apparently as a substitute, as a compensatory device for attempting to explain and above all to control what happens to them. Or to take another example: The belief in reincarnation is more likely to appear in societies where the pattern of settlement is dominated by "small hamlets, compounds of extended families, small nomadic bands, scattered rural neighborhoods, or other units smaller than a village."[20] The apparent logic underlying this is that there is a greater probability that a person will be regarded as living on through reincarnation where there are intimate, highly interdependent, long-lasting relationships within a relatively small but fairly independent social unit—where, in other words, the social unit is thought to survive the members who constitute it at any given time. The individual and his or her idiosyncrasies within such groups are of considerable interest and importance. As Swanson points out, "The particular potentialities of each member are appreciated as limiting or facilitating the lives of all the others, and those effects persist after a member dies."[21] These effects are such things as "his technological inventiveness, his habits of shirking work, his fecundity, or the qualities of his voice in the ceremonial songs [that] have shaped adaptations of his fellows . . . [and that] continue after his death."[22] In other words, "the memory lingers on." Moreover, the social relationships and structure of the group provide a "model" for the development of a belief in personal reincarnation.

While Swanson himself admits that even strong positive correlations do not conclusively establish cause-and-effect relationships between social factors and religious beliefs, his achievement lies in having shown that certain beliefs are extremely unlikely to occur and be accepted unless certain social factors, conditions, or relationships are present. For example, it is extremely unlikely that a society lacking a certain degree and type of organizational complexity will accept belief in a monotheistic "high god" (one considered responsible for creating the world), even if the belief is suggested by a member of the group, revealed by a deity, or diffused from another society. Specifically, societies that accept such a belief have a hierarchical arrangement of three or more "sovereign groups" (groups having ultimate decision-making authority over specified areas of life).[23] Although Swanson stops short of asserting any causal relation-

[19] Ibid., chapter 8.
[20] Ibid., p. 113.
[21] Ibid., p. 112.
[22] Ibid.
[23] Ibid., pp. 62–65.

ship here and would simply affirm that this social structure is likely the model for the emergence of monotheism much of the time, the relationship is strong enough to at least tempt the reader to begin thinking of talking about necessary and sufficient conditions for the development of that particular belief.

CONCLUSION

Although the origins and ultimate sources of religion can never be known with certainty, research and speculation on these subjects has not been fruitless. The hypotheses we have summarized—the anthropological theories that emphasize people's interaction with nature; the psychological theories that stress people's fears, frustrations, and emotional needs; and the sociological theories that focus on the social context in which religion exists—at the very least contribute to our understanding of what religion is, why it has come about, and perhaps also why it persists.

In summary, then, it seems reasonable to advance the following propositions concerning the forces that sustain religion, if not give rise to it: (1) People are continually and universally threatened with failure, frustration, and injustice. (2) Religion becomes the attempt of people in groups to "relativize" such threats to their wholeness by placing them within a context of a larger system or plan and by "explaining" much that happens in terms of supernatural intervention into and control over earthly events. (3) At the same time, threats similar to those experienced by individuals also affect social relationships—and, in fact, society itself. (4) Religion arises as an attempt by society to cushion such threats (both to itself and to its members) by bringing people into a ritual fellowship of common belief. Religion is thus a response to both individual and group needs. (5) The characteristic form of religious belief and interpretation in a given society is significantly conditioned by the type and complexity of existing social patterns and relationships.

3

Becoming Religious

As we look at the impact of religion on society and the people that constitute society we shall begin at the beginning, so to speak. That is, we shall look at the process by which people become religious in the first place. We assume that newborn infants have no "religious instincts." While they may have certain needs for which religion might, among other institutions as well, provide some satisfactions—such needs as security, protection, explanation, reinforcement (cf. Chapter 2)—they are not born with a ready-made religious system inside them just waiting to bloom. That they must learn, just as they learn language, table manners, the rules and techniques of playing baseball, and how to drive a car. All of this, including the learning of the contents of a particular religious system, is included within the fundamental social process called socialization. Thus we continue to work with the simple but basic observation that religion is a group phenomenon and that a member of a religious group is either born into it or joins it at some later stage in the life cycle; in either case he or she is taught the norms of the group and integrated into the life of the group. In this process the group socializes (it teaches and trains), and the individual internalizes the norms (he or she learns). Throughout this chapter we shall move back and forth between these two foci of the socialization or learning process.

ELEMENTS IN RELIGIOUS SOCIALIZATION

We begin with the group and the desire to socialize new members. The group desires to bring a person (a member) into a committed, functional relationship with other members of the group so that the new member knows what the group stands for, can fill a role within the group, and can further the aims of the group and help it reach its goals. Some of this process is nonstructured and occurs through informal contacts and interactions with other members; much of it is structured and formal, channeled through educational agencies and processes.

In "primitive" societies (that is, preliterate and/or prehistoric societies usually with a hunting and gathering economy), religious socialization, as with nearly all socialization, is primarily informal. The child gradually learns the beliefs and understandings of the group through conversation and by hearing his or her elders recount the sagas and tales passed down through the generations. In a similar manner, the child learns practices associated with and growing out of religious beliefs. As indicated in Chapter 2, religious socialization is seldom distinguishable from general socialization in primitive societies, inasmuch as their members seldom distinguish the religious from other spheres of thought or knowledge.

There is nevertheless some degree of organization and planning in the socialization of primitive religion. For example, Wallace distinguishes two forms, in addition to individual expression, in which primitive religion is manifested: the shamanic and the communal. A shaman (such as a witch doctor or medicine man) is one who is believed to possess greater access to and control over mana and who performs service rituals for people. Obviously, viewing shamanic activity is a learning experience for the neophyte. Similarly with the communal form of religious expression, conducted both by natural subcommunities (such as nuclear families, larger kinship groups, and affinity groups such as those determined by age or sex) and by the total community acting in concert, there are rites of passage from one stage in the life cycle to another (such as puberty rites), for example, or tribal totem celebrations in which everyone gathers around the symbol or symbols of their common origin and loyalty in order to reaffirm their unity as well as their common past.[1] Certainly a great deal of socialization and learning take place at all these levels of primitive religion. Nor do these forms of socialization disappear as societies evolve. A child observes the family religious activities so common in orthodox Buddhist and Confucian religious systems, and the congregational worship activities in the Judeo-Christian heritage. And the child learns.

[1] Anthony F. C. Wallace, *Religion: An Anthropological View* (New York: Random House, 1966), pp. 86–91.

However, although informal socialization still exists and remains influential in both agrarian and industrial societies, with the greater specialization of roles and differentiation of activities in these societies, religious socialization becomes more formalized. Religious teachers deliberately teach neophytes specifically religious norms, and formalized religious ceremonies are conducted during which neophytes learn about religious activities and gradually begin to participate in them.

The socializing or educative intent of religious groups is summarized in a classic manner by Jesus: "Go therefore and make disciples of all nations, . . . *teaching* them to observe all things whatsoever I have commanded you."[2] This refers to socialization pure and simple—transmitting knowledge as well as training in appropriate activities. Most religious groups view this process as a lifelong one. Worship services in the Western tradition are in significant ways of a socializing nature, extending or expanding on what is already known. A sermon, for example, expounds and explains, not simply exhorts and directs. The various communal ceremonies of most religious groups, in fact, are fundamentally socializing experiences. In addition to recognizing the deity through giving praise and thanksgiving and performing rituals believed to please the god or gods, joint activities perform a reinforcement function, reminding participants of their beliefs and of how they are to conduct themselves before the deity.

Worship services and ceremonial gatherings may also bring about the conversion or full commitment of newcomers, another aspect of socialization. When people hear something or learn something that moves them to attach themselves to the group, socialization has begun; now formal educational processes take over. The person's commitment is also reinforced through new informal socialization contacts.

Thus several things are involved in religious socialization. First the group convinces the newcomer to make a commitment to the group and what it stands for, often on the basis of very little knowledge or contact. (By newcomer we mean either a potential convert or the child of a group member.) Second, there is the core process of building on that commitment through teaching the newcomer the norms of the group—its beliefs and appropriate behaviors and rituals. (Note that these stages are interchangeable—that is, people may be involved in the process of learning norms for some time before being converted or committing themselves.) Third, the group tries to extend its influence over the person to those situations where he or she is not in direct contact with the group or its members. That is, the group tries to influence *all* the individual's values; this is essentially the morality dimension that many suggest is an integral feature of religion. Finally, there is the reinforce-

---

[2] Matthew 28:19–20 (Revised Standard Version). Emphasis added.

ment and encouragement aspect of continuing socialization. One reason religious groups encourage their members to continue participating in ceremonies, attending education classes, and listening to sermons after having learned the "basics" of the religion is to "strengthen" and reinforce the members' commitment.

METHODS OF RELIGIOUS SOCIALIZATION

Formal Methods

We have already touched on the socialization methods of religious groups. At this point we need merely to systematize them. There is first the formal mechanism that most religious groups establish—in a strict sense of the term, the educational system. All groups establish explicit teaching activities, which may take the form of a guru gathering a few persons around him, an evangelist on a tree stump or a soapbox, a Bar Mitzvah preparatory class, or a Sunday sermon. The teaching function has been an integral and important part of religion from the beginning of the major religious systems that exist worldwide today. Certainly the founder of any religion or religious group teaches as he or she tries to get across his or her message and vision. Once established, the religious group uses diverse methods, both formal and informal, to get across its ideas and the body of its knowledge, beliefs, and practices to the neophyte member. The effectiveness of such socialization is a major topic of this chapter and is discussed at several points in the chapters that follow.

Informal Methods

Another way in which socialization takes place is informally—through interaction with the members of a religious group. Such socialization or learning from others occurs in all kinds of groups, of course. The general socialization of children into the society that occurs through interaction with peers, for example, is of primary importance and well documented. And it is popular knowledge that what you learn from associates in a work group through casual conversation is at least as important—if not more so—than the socialization that occurs through participating in formal orientation programs or by studying job descriptions.

Those who have been introduced elsewhere to major sociological concepts and theories will recognize this as an application of "symbolic interactionism." That is a widely held theory of socialization and learning which holds that the primary and certainly most effective and long-lasting method of teaching what the group stands for and wants done is through imitation and emulation, through mimicking and role taking. That is, we observe, then we do. Children mimic the behavior of adults and other children around them. This theory objects in particular to another widely held theory called the "behavioral learning theory" in which people learn what the group wants by being rewarded for "appropriate" behavior and punished for "inappropriate" behavior—positive and negative reinforcement.

Interestingly, many religious groups recognize the importance of informal socialization and consequently often deliberately encourage it. A term frequently used by religious groups in this connection is *fellowship;* members of religious groups are encouraged "to fellowship" with fellow members. Such formal mechanisms as religious youth groups, men's clubs, ladies' auxiliaries, and senior citizens' groups are organized in great part with the hope and expectation that members of the larger organization—for example, the congregation—will develop friendships and maintain ties outside formal religious contexts. What is involved here is recognition of the importance of reinforcement —through continued and frequent contact with others of your religious group, the formal norms and beliefs you have been taught and have accepted will be reinforced and, as it is often expressed, "your faith will be strengthened."

Considerable empirical evidence has been gathered that tends to support this strategy, though it is difficult to determine which is cause and which effect—whether such contact strengthens one's faith, or whether those of strong faith seek out fellowship in the first place. Thus studies have shown that the person whose close personal friends are mainly members of his or her religious group tends to be more orthodox in his or her beliefs, a more regular participant in religious organization. Glock and Stark, for example, constructed an index of "religious experience," based on whether respondents were certain of having "a feeling [of being] somehow in the presence of God," "a sense of being saved in Christ," and "a feeling of being punished by God for something you had done." Almost invariably, regardless of Christian denomination, respondents with a greater number of best friends who were also members of their congregation scored higher on this index.[3]

An intensive extension of the fellowship mechanism for religious socialization occurs through marriage. Religious groups urge endogamy—that is, marriage within the group—assuming (rightly) that a marriage between two persons from the same religious group will encourage both persons to participate and remain with the group. Intermarriage with a person of another religious group introduces the risk of losing your member to the other group, and may reduce the level of participation and commitment of your member even if he or she does not defect. There is of course the possibility of gaining a new member through intermarriage of one or your members with an outsider. Some groups in fact appear to be net gainers through this process. Yet few groups wish to advocate such an approach because of the risks involved. Thus,

---

[3] Charles Y. Glock and Rodney Stark, *Religion and Society in Tension* (Chicago: Rand McNally, 1965), p. 164.

religious groups have traditionally forbidden (or all but forbidden) interfaith marriage. Until very recently Roman Catholics, for example, could not be married by a priest in church if the non-Catholic partner refused to join the Catholic Church or would not sign a statement agreeing that any children born of the marriage would be reared as Catholics. Many Orthodox Jewish families ostracize children who marry Gentiles. In the face of high rates of interfaith marriage, most groups have been relenting on this issue, although the official stance of discouraging interfaith marriage remains.

THE EFFECTIVENESS OF RELIGIOUS SOCIALIZATION

The Impact of Attendance at Worship Services

We now turn to the question of the impact or effectiveness of mechanisms, primarily the formal ones, that religious groups use to socialize their members. One major subject of sociological investigation has been the impact within Western industrial societies of the formal instruction and inspiration that takes place in the regular religious ceremony—the classic example being the weekly (Sunday or Saturday morning) worship service. Many studies have focused on differences among the regular attenders at such services, on the one hand, and less regular attenders, infrequent attenders, and nonattenders on the other. We have occasion to refer to such studies in the Appendix as we look at attempts by sociologists to define and measure religiosity. Here we are interested in the same or similar data from another perspective. That is, if effective socialization in fact takes place in formal religious services, then we should find differences along a continuum of attendance at (or at least, exposure to) such services. Specifically, we would expect to find evidence of greater knowledge, firmer belief, stauncher commitment, and a greater sense of morality among those more often exposed.

Before attempting to validate this hypothesis it should be pointed out that in the United States there is considerable religious illiteracy even among members of religious groups. Schroeder and Obenhaus, for example, reach pessimistic conclusions about the level of biblical knowledge and of cognitive understanding of the Christian faith in Corn City (the fictitious name of a real town in Iowa). They note that of the town's church members who are of above average intellectual ability and who are reasonably strongly committed to and involved in church life ("nuclear" and "modal" members), less than half were able to relate a reasonably accurate version of the story of the good Samaritan.[4]

---

[4] W. W. Schroeder and Victor Obenhaus, *Religion in American Culture* (New York: Free Press, 1964), p. 147.

In my own study of Lutheran young people, only 8.7 percent of those sampled who attended church services regularly and also attended a parochial school could correctly identify Nathanael as one of Jesus' disciples, and only 25 percent correctly identified Enoch as the Old Testament character who is described as never experiencing physical death.[5]

In a nationwide survey of adults in the United States conducted in 1970, only 15 percent correctly identified five prominent biblical figures (Moses, Daniel, Jonah, Peter, Paul). In fact, a greater number of respondents (17.5 percent) were unable to identify even a single figure, and less than half (46.4 percent) were able to identify three.[6]

These and similar studies indicate that such a high rate of religious illiteracy exists among even regular church members that we should not expect the impact of regular participation in formal religious activities on behavior to be particularly dramatic. If concepts and knowledge do not "sink in," then we can hardly expect them to exert much measurable influence.

With this caution in mind, we can proceed to examine how exposure to the religious group and its teachings influences beliefs and behavior. The data in Table 3-1 indicate some fairly clear and consistent correlations between frequency of church attendance and likelihood of (1) accepting certain traditional conservative Christian beliefs, and (2) exhibiting superior biblical biographical knowledge. Keep in mind, of course, that these are correlations and not necessarily cause-and-effect relationships. Many other factors besides church attendance affect religious beliefs and knowledge. Also, it is even possible that holding certain traditional beliefs is part of what makes people attend church regularly. Further, there is no control in these data for respondent's relative liberalism or for their denominational affiliation—religious liberals are combined here with conservatives, Protestants with Catholics. Nonetheless, the evident correlation between frequency of church attendance and conservative beliefs connotes at least some influence of the former on the latter.

If we single out for study two generally conservative denominations (Baptists and Lutherans), the relationships observed in Table 3-1 become more dramatic and lend greater support to our hypothesis—that is, the data (see Table 3-2) show higher correlations between church attendance (in this case, at relatively conservative churches) and conservative doctrinal views. Table 3-2's data clearly show that the more frequent a respondent's church attendance (at a conservative church), the more likely he or she is to give conservative doctrinal responses and the greater is likely to be his or her biblical knowledge. Three additional observations can be made by comparing or combining data in the two tables: (1) The conservative subsample of Baptists plus Lutherans (cf. Table 3-2) is both more doctrinally conservative and more biblically knowledgeable than the total sample (cf. Table 3-1). (2) Respon-

[5] Ronald L. Johnstone, *The Effectiveness of Lutheran Elementary and Secondary Schools as Agencies of Christian Education* (St. Louis: Concordia Seminary Research Center, 1966), p. 100.

[6] Ronald L. Johnstone (project director), national survey data gathered by the National Opinion Research Center for the Lutheran Council in the U.S.A., 1970.

TABLE 3–1 *Percentage of Church Members Agreeing with Selected Biblical Doctrines and Evidencing Knowledge of Biblical Biography, by Frequency of Church Attendance*

	FREQUENCY OF CHURCH ATTENDANCE			
	WEEKLY OR NEARLY SO	ABOUT ONCE A MONTH	SELDOM	NEVER
"The Devil actually exists and is an active and evil influence in the world."				
Definitely agree§	65%†	48%	39%	38%
Definitely disagree	12	16	28	27
"Jesus will actually return to the earth someday and the world will be destroyed after he has separated the believers from the nonbelievers."				
Definitely agree§	58	48	39	39
Definitely disagree	11	15	22	31
"A child is already sinful when it is born."				
Definitely agree§	37	19	12	18
Definitely disagree	44	60	72	72
"The real purpose of religion should be to help people with their problems and needs rather than help them to get to heaven."				
Definitely agree	26	44	40	45
Definitely disagree§	27	17	17	14
"He was in a lion's den."				
Correctly identifies Daniel	66	57	54	53
"A voice spoke to him from a burning bush."				
Correctly identifies Moses	48	36	33	26
"He was swallowed by a great fish or whale."				
Correctly identifies Jonah	73	62	65	57

TABLE 3–1 *Percentage of Church Members Agreeing with Selected Biblical Doctrines and Evidencing Knowledge of Biblical Biography, by Frequency of Church Attendance*

	FREQUENCY OF CHURCH ATTENDANCE			
	WEEKLY OR NEARLY SO	ABOUT ONCE A MONTH	SELDOM	NEVER
"He is the disciple who denied Jesus three times."				
Correctly identifies Peter	41	34	25	19
"He wrote many letters or epistles that are in the New Testament."				
Correctly identifies Paul	46	21	18	18
Total N*	652	273	394	74

*Excluded from the total sample of 1490 persons are the 96 (6.4 percent) who reported no religious membership or preference.

† Note that only the "definitely agree" and "definitely disagree" responses are reported. This explains the fact that percentages listed do not total 100 percent and differ in totals from one question to another.

§ The responses marked with this symbol are those generally considered the more orthodox or traditional responses to the question. It should be noted, however, that there is definite disagreement among various traditions within Christianity on the third and fourth questions, and between Christians and Jews on all four questions.

Source: Ronald L. Johnstone (project director), national survey data gathered by the National Opinion Research Center for the Lutheran Council in the U.S.A., 1970.

dents, regardless of theological orientation or frequency of church attendence, are more familiar with the Old Testament characters than with the New Testament characters. (3) The differences between those who seldom and those who never attend church are small (and in fact the "nevers" are even more likely than the "seldoms" to expect the return of Jesus and to believe that a child is born sinful). Probably one should not expect large differences between two categories of church members both of whom evidence low involvement. Further, the number of those making up the category of members who never attend conservative churches (Table 3–2) is quite small, and therefore conclusions based on percentages in that category tend to be less reliable than otherwise.

The Impact of Parochial Schools

One primary socializing agent for several religious groups which has attracted considerable research and journalistic attention in recent years is the

TABLE 3–2 *Baptists and Lutherans Agreeing with Selected Orthodox Christian Doctrines and Evidencing Knowledge of Biblical Biography, by Frequency of Church Attendance*

	FREQUENCY OF CHURCH ATTENDANCE			
	WEEKLY OR NEARLY SO	ABOUT ONCE A MONTH	SELDOM	NEVER
Definitely agree that the Devil exists and is active in the world	82%	62%	52%	48%
Definitely agree that Jesus will return to earth someday	80	60	50	57
Definitely agree that a child is already sinful at birth	53	26	11	24
Definitely disagree that the purpose of religion is to help people with problems, not to help them get to heaven	16	35	39	43
Correctly identifies Daniel	76	64	53	52
Correctly identifies Moses	54	35	31	29
Correctly identifies Jonah	77	62	65	62
Correctly identifies Peter	59	39	24	14
Correctly identifies Paul	52	21	16	14
Total N	189	117	124	21

Source: Ronald L. Johnstone (project director), national survey data gathered by the National Opinion Research Center for the Lutheran Council in the U.S.A., 1970.

parochial school—elementary, secondary, and college. Historically these schools illustrate the full-blown socializing intent of religious groups more fully than any other agency or mechanism. Not only is there usually daily formal instruction in religious beliefs and ritual (especially in elementary parochial schools), but there are over thirty hours a week (that is, school time) of "fellowship" with members of one's religious group. Also, the system increases the likelihood of marrying within the religious group, particularly if it is a parochial high school or college under discussion. Religious groups have established such schools with very specific intentions of preserving pure doctrine, encouraging maximum participation in religious activities, improving religious character, developing a rich devotional life, and particularly for Jewish schools, preserving a traditional lifestyle.

The question is then, How effective are parochial schools? That they aid in the religious socialization process is clear, though the success is not unequivocal. Several relatively recent studies bear on the subject: one on Catholic eduction, one on Lutheran parochial school education, one on fundamentalistic schools, one on Mennonite education, and one on Seventh-Day Adventist schools. Each study is replete with data and observations, but we shall make only a few comments based on their findings as they relate to our concern in this chapter with religious socialization.

The Catholic study by Greeley and Rossi found that education in Catholic schools had a measurable impact on those who experienced it. In general, the greater the number of years a person attended a Catholic school (including elementary, secondary, and college levels), the higher his or her religious performance and knowledge of doctrine. However, it was also noted that the most significant positive correlation between religious education and religious behavior was among those who had devout parents and later married a devout Catholic mate. The authors' comment on these findings emphasizes such reinforcement:

> Something of a pattern begins to emerge: Religious education does indeed have an impact on the adult lives of its students, but only when the social context of childhood or adulthood supports and emphasizes the values learned in the school. Religious education apparently works when there is constant reinforcement from outside the school.[7]

In my study of Lutheran adolescents, the data concerning proportion of total education in Lutheran parochial schools lead one to conclude that parochial school education has a significant impact on doctrinal knowledge, biblical knowledge, and religious activities. However, many (though not all) differences apparently related to parochial schooling wash out if we apply a control variable for type of family background the student had experienced— that is, if we take into account how much family and home reinforcement there is for religious values and practices. If the family was what we termed an "ideal" or "nuclear" Lutheran family or even (in most cases) an "average" or "model" Lutheran family, the parochial school training did not seem to add significantly to what a student brought with him or her from home so far as measures of religiosity are concerned. The parochial school education of those from "marginal" Lutheran families, on the other hand, produced marked results, in the sense of significantly increased levels of religious knowledge and participation in religious activities.[8]

---

[7] Andrew M. Greeley and Peter H. Rossi, *The Education of Catholic Americans* (Chicago: Aldine, 1966), p. 104.

[8] Johnstone, *Effectiveness of Lutheran Schools,* ch. 5 and 10.

Larry Lewis's study of a sample of 574 Seventh-Day Adventist adults, some of whom had attended Seventh-Day Adventist parochial schools and some of whom had not, yielded similar results in terms of minimal impact of the parochial school except for those from less religious families. He observes: "Apparently highly religious parents can make up for a lack of parochial education while parochial education can make up for a lack of highly religious parents."[9] Again, the family religious background and environment was crucial.

Erickson's study of 212 elementary-school-age students from fundamentalist churches in the Midwest and Southwest resulted in findings that "lend no support to the view that sectarian [parochial school] education is more conducive to religious development than is public education"[10] Erickson reaches this conclusion, it should be noted, after controlling for the religiousness of parents, congeniality in the home (communicative relationships with parents), and level of student church involvement.

In summarizing several studies of the impact of Mennonite religious schools, Donald Kraybill concludes that there is very little evidence to suggest an accumulative effect of such ethnic schools on orthodox beliefs and behavior.[11] Nor does such education appear to increase "avoidant behavior," that is, avoidance of certain activities permitted in the surrounding culture but tabood as "worldly" behavior by the religious group (drinking alcoholic beverages, smoking, premarital sexual intercourse, social dancing, and gambling).[12]

Attempting to integrate these studies represents a challenge inasmuch as the samples consist in some cases of adults, in others of adolescents, and in others of children. Further, different research instruments and analytic tools were used, and different foci were intended. All of which helps explain why their conclusions do not totally agree. Yet one observation or tentative conclusion seems to come through all of them fairly clearly. That is that parochial school socialization does little but reinforce what the religious group teaches so far as children of both "nuclear" and "modal" members are concerned. On the other hand, for those children with relatively little religious influence in the home, the parochial school can raise the levels of doctrinal knowledge, ritual participation, ethnic preference, and avoidance behavior. However, many of the studies note that children in this latter category are less likely to attend parochial schools than children of the nuclear and modal religious families. That is, one of the elements in being a member in good standing in a religious

[9] Larry M. Lewis, *Religious Effects of Seventh-Day Adventist Parochial Education* (Ph. D. dissertation, Boston University, 1974), p. 133.

[10] Donald A. Erickson, "Religious Consequence of Public and Sectarian Schooling," *School Review* 72, no. 1 (1964), 29.

[11] Donald B. Kraybill, *Ethnic Education: The Impact of Mennonite Schooling* (San Francisco: R & E Research Associates, 1977), p. 99.

[12] Kraybill, *Ethnic Education, pp. 101–2.*

group that sponsors a religious school is commitment to the value of parochial education and a willingness to send one's children there, should such a school be available in the community.

INTERNALIZATION OF RELIGION

We have been focusing on the agents and processes of religious socialization, and in assessing the effectiveness of such socialization we have focused on the group. We now turn in our discussion of socialization to the obverse of socialization—namely, internalization. What are some of the processes involved, stages of development, and differences in outcome for individuals who are being socialized?

In considering the process of the internalization of religion we are immediately required to distinguish between those who internalize the religious concepts and practices of a group from birth and those who undergo a conversion experience at some later point in life. We first look at the most common pattern—that of "growing up religious" within a particular religious context.

"Growing Up Religious"

A fundamental observation is that individuals internalize the religion of their group essentially the same way they learn the language of their culture, or their sex role, or the lifestyle of their social class. The process is intimately tied up with the development of one's personality and the evolution of one's concept of self. A person internalizes—makes a part of himself or herself—what he or she hears, sees, and both consciously and subconsciously considers applicable to himself or herself. The person hears words, is introduced to concepts, and is confronted with various phenomena at the intellectual, or cognitive, level. But he or she also—especially initially—emulates or imitates what he or she sees. In a sense the person absorbs many patterns, norms, and values through the experience of seeing them exemplified by parents, peers, and others long before he or she confronts them intellectually.

Just as a child learns to talk before he or she is exposed to the rules of grammar and spelling, so he or she attains an orientation toward the supernatural (and, if he or she is a Christian, perhaps a concept of self as a sinner) long before he or she confronts such issues in the form of religious doctrines and propositions.

This orientation fits into the broad framework of the development of the self—a process in which religion plays a part. Early in the process of this development the child becomes aware of himself or herself not simply as an "I" or subject—the center of the universe, so to speak—but also as a "me," an object with certain characteristics that others react to and interact with. He or she begins to learn how others expect him or her to behave if he or she is to interact successfully as well as satisfy his or her personal needs. The child begins to see himself or herself from various perspectives and in his or her various roles—male or female, son or daughter, friend or stranger, American or foreigner, and so on. As he or she is exposed to religious influences in the family and in the family's religious group, he or she also acquires the rudiments of a religious self. He or she begins to regard himself or herself as related not only to the so-called natural and social worlds of things and people that he or she sees and interacts with, but also as related to an unseen world of the supernatural. This person begins to have an orientation toward the sacred, however, that is defined by the group. He or she begins to see himself or herself in relation to that other world and expands his or her image of self accordingly.

At this point, depending on the specific religious group context, great diversity may appear. One child begins to see himself or herself as a worthless sinner utterly helpless in the face of the supernatural, while another sees himself or herself as a special object of creation with great worth and potential. For most, a combination of both perspectives applies. In any case, the individual becomes aware of unseen powers in the universe. To some extent this may be comforting knowledge, a convenient way of explaining much that is incomprehensible. To some extent it may be frightening, particularly as one considers or learns the ways in which he or she can incur the wrath of those supernatural powers and even be punished by them.

In short, then, what a child is learning about himself or herself from religious group sources supplements what he or she is learning about himself or herself from interaction with playmates, television, siblings, and so on. Initially this learning is almost exclusively through informal observing and intuiting, only later to be supplemented by more formal cognitive learning. Most children in any society in fact derive some of their self-concept from religious sources, even if they are born into families which espouse no formal religious group affiliation. For everyone is at least indirectly influenced by religion through contact with other people and institutions.

It will be obvious to some readers that the foregoing description of the process of internalizing religion leans heavily on the symbolic interaction perspective in sociology, a basic premise of which is that people relate to things, events, and other people on the basis of the meanings they assign to them. These meanings in turn develop within the person during the process of social interaction. The religious expressions of other people and the religious institutions themselves contribute to the construct of meanings people develop. Obviously the particular set of observations and interactions that a given individual makes and experiences have a crucial influence on whatever religious meanings develop within him or her.

Gaining Religious Identity

Although religious socialization primarily aims at providing a person with an appropriate stance in relation to the supernatural and instructs him or her in the nature and function of the supernatural, another important socialization process involves teaching the child his or her religious identity. David Elkind has conducted research which indicates that even this process is complex. Children, Elkind contends, proceed through certain stages in learning who they are religiously. Thus a child of five who says, "I am a Catholic" understands that identification differently from a child of nine or a child of twelve. Elkind found that from the age of five or six most children know their religious identity and will freely admit they are, say, Protestant, or Catholic, or Jewish. But such an identity for them is not at all what it is for older children or adults. The young child tends to confuse religious identity with nationality and racial designations. Their religious identification is a name with no clear referent. By eight or nine years of age, however, children have a more concrete conception of their religious identity. They can distinguish religious from nonreligious designations and can attach behavioral description to various religious groups. However, it is not till the age of ten to twelve that an abstract dimension of religious identification is added—only then do youngsters begin to speak of cognitive elements such as beliefs and try to explain why particular religious groups engage in certain activities.[13]

The Role of the Family

As mentioned earlier in this chapter, much religious socialization occurs outside the formal structure of the organization, with a significant portion taking place in family interaction. Religious groups recognize this. Some have programs which focus on trying to help parents perform this task, while others at least point out the importance of the family. However, John L. Thomas, a Jesuit sociologist, found through research that the kind of religious socialization that the Catholic Church hopes parents will conduct for their children is not in fact occurring on the scale expected. Thomas states that although persons professionally involved in promoting organized religion agree that an important function of the family is the inculcation of religious beliefs and practices in their children, he finds that the religious training of the Catholic preschool child at home falls far short of traditional expectations.[14] Family influences are nevertheless significant in the sense of reinforcing and filtering religious influences from elsewhere, particularly from formal agencies such as parochial schools, as noted earlier.

[13] David Elkind, "Age Changes in the Meaning of Religious Identity," *Review of Religious Research* 6, no. 1 (1964), 36–40.

[14] John L. Thomas, "Religious Training in the Roman Catholic Family," *American Journal of Sociology* 62, no. 2 (1951), 178–83.

In a study of male college students, Gordon Allport and his associates found that family influence was extremely important regarding their present "need" for some form of religious orientation or belief system. They found that a firmly declared need continued for 82 percent of those who had what they termed an "outstanding" religious education during their childhood. Religious need was expressed by decreasing proportions of students as the quality of their childhood religious socialization declined. Thus 78 percent of those who received an "ordinary" religious education, 52 percent of those who described their religious socialization as "superficial," and only 32 percent of those who received no religious education described themselves as having a present clear need for religion.[15] Although the measure of religious socialization or "upbringing" used by Allport does not distinguish family socialization from the socialization stemming from the religious institution itself, it seems reasonable to assume, with the authors, that the prime referent is the influence and training of the family.

The family's religious influence can be important in negative ways as well. For example, John Kotre interviewed a number of graduate students who had attended Catholic schools for sixteen years, some of whom at the time of his study defined themselves as still "in" the Catholic church and others of whom considered themselves "out," and found a strong correlation between being "out" and the existence of religious conflict in the home—conflict operationally defined as either an interfaith marriage or one parent a nonpracticing Catholic.[16]

RELIGIOUS CONVERSION

As stated at the outset of the preceding section, the process of internalizing religion and developing the religious self is, so far as can be determined, essentially similar to the process of internalizing other knowledge, beliefs, and skills, and merely adds another dimension to one's initial concept of self. A more dramatic form of religious internalization is that of conversion.

We shall not delve deeply into the conversion phenomenon itself, which is of course strongly psychological in nature and for the most part nonempirical. We cannot, for example, determine whether a particular individual's conversion is in fact a personal experience with God Himself in which the Holy Spirit enters the person and leads him or her to certain convictions. We can, however, provide some sociological insight into the context within which conversions occur, point out that conversion is not wholly a psychological

[15] Gordon W. Allport, J. M. Gillespie, and J. Young, "The Religion of the Post-War College Student," *Journal of Psychology* 25, no. 1 (1948), 3–33.

[16] John Kotre, *The View from the Border* (Chicago: Aldine, 1971), p. 143.

phenomenon, and note that it does not occur in a wholly religious context as distinct from a social one.

The Group Context

First we must note the somewhat obvious yet important fact that conversion as a form of behavior or process is affected by the group within which it occurs. That is, what constitutes conversion, what one can expect to experience, and even whether one should expect a conversion experience at all are matters defined by the religious group one belongs to or happens to be under the influence of at the moment (during an evangelistic service, for example).

In a study of young people in the fundamentalist Swedish Mission Covenant Church, Hans Zetterberg found a number of group influences on the conversion phenomenon, which he defined as itself a stage in the social role of membership. For one thing, every member had a clear background of being religiously influenced before entering the group and undergoing the conversion experience; in fact, eight of every ten converts came from families in which at least one parent was already a member of the group. Secondly, conversion does not necessarily imply a change in one's way of life—the convert already has "pious habits and right belief." Conversion is simply a signal of a more conscious acceptance of this life. Third, a clear majority of conversions occur under conditions that are created and manipulated by the group (revival meetings, church camps, and the like). Fourth, although a sudden change in lifestyle may be the stereotype of conversion, such conversions are relatively unlikely. Zetterberg found that only 16 percent of his sample had conversions of this type. Much more likely are two other, more modest, types of conversion. Most likely is "sudden role identification," in which a person who has been undergoing socialization by the group suddenly feels certain of his or her salvation (although behavior does not change noticeably because he or she had been living the role of the converted for some time). The other type of conversion is "role assimilation," in which the person gradually becomes sure of his or her saved condition over an extended period of membership.[17]

Borhek and Curtis are even less impressed with the common stereotype of conversion as a sudden reversal or change of direction and commitment on the part of an individual. They suggest that the actual conversion (such as might occur in a revivalist service) is a *rite de passage* "differing from other such rituals only in the fact that the participant may be largely unconscious of its ritual, conventional character."[18] They suggest further that conversion expe-

[17] Hans Zetterberg, "The Religious Conversion as a Change of Social Roles," *Sociology and Social Research* 36, no. 1 (1952), 159–66.

[18] James T. Borhek and Richard F. Curtis, *A Sociology of Belief* (New York: John Wiley, 1975), p. 98.

riences are often "so highly conventionalized that it requires real effort not to view them as rituals *learned for the occasion.* " [19]

The Age Factor

A second major point about conversion is that—in its dramatic form, at least—it is primarily an adolescent phenomenon. It is understandably no accident that the Jewish boy has his Bar Mitzvah and the Jewish girl her confirmation in early adolsecence. Similarly in most liturgical Christian churches, confirmation is in early adolescence, and in nonliturgical churches baptism and/or profession of faith occur at this time. Walter H. Clark cites two early studies in the psychology of religion by E. D. Starbuck and E. T. Clark (1899 and 1929 respectively) that found the most common age for conversion of males to be about sixteen and for females about fourteen or fifteen.[20]

David Elkind makes the point that until adolescence the child "knows much more than he understands about his religious identity."[21] Gordon Allport describes adolescence as the time when the person must transform his religious attitudes from secondhand to firsthand fittings of his personality.[22]

There is some indication that sexual guilt feelings and sexual anxieties among people who have only recently begun to struggle with their sexual development, desires, and propensities are strongly influential here. The traditional stereotyped conversion in a tent meeting or evangelistic service almost invariably includes a discourse and series of prayers and altar calls that have touched on "sexual sins" more than any others and have been designed to produce admission of guilt for what are essentially universal feelings and urges. Thouless states: "The typical adolescent conversion may be regarded psychologically as the sudden emergence into consciousness of a previously repressed system of feelings belonging to the sex instinct, which is now admitted into consciousness because it is sublimated, purified and directed to a religious end. "[23]

That conversion should frequently occur during adolescence is probably not surprising considering the hormonal changes, opportunities for new experiences, and intellectual awakening that occur at this stage in the life cycle. Religion may be one among many other new ideas and systems to embrace. Or, religion that began to be internalized many years earlier may have developed to a peaking point at this time. Although we shall not discuss them at this point (see Chapter 13), it is no mere coincidence that most "Jesus freaks" and most American devotees of Eastern religions are adolescents, with most of the

---

[19] Borhek and Curtis, *A Sociology of Belief,* p. 98. Emphasis added.

[20] Walter H. Clark, *The Psychology of Religion* (New York: Macmillan, 1958), p. 207.

[21] Elkind, "Age Changes," p. 40.

[22] Gordon W. Allport, *The Individual and His Religion* (New York: Macmillan, 1957), p. 32.

[23] Robert H. Thouless, "The Psychology of Conversion," in *Conversion,* ed. Walter E. Conn (New York: Alba House, 1978), p. 143.

others just barely out of adolescence. Further, converts to many cults (to be discussed in Chapter 5) are young people.

Not all conversions occur during adolescence, of course. But something akin to the psychological and emotional dislocations that occur during adolescence happen at other times in people's lives as well. Catherine Robins, in analyzing conversion of women into the East African Revival—a large scale Protestant revival movement in Central Africa—notes that among Kiga women from Southwest Uganda it is common for a "life crisis" to have precipitated conversion.[24] She notes that among Hima women from the same region a common precondition for conversion appears to be a marital crisis, whether that means being forced into an unwanted "arranged" marriage or finding oneself in a marriage that is dominated by a conflict of Christian values with traditional values that allow, for example, a husband's male kin sexual access to his wife.[25]

Stages in Conversion

Our third sociological observation about conversion focuses on its socialization aspect. In describing the process of conversion into a small cult called the Divine Precepts, John Lofland distinguishes between (a) predisposing conditions—attributes of persons prior to contact with the group—and, (b) situational contingencies—social factors and influences in operation after contact with the group is made.

The first of three predisposing conditions is tension and emotional dislocation, which those who later became converts perceived themselves to have been enduring at fairly high levels for some time. Such tension could have resulted from failing grades in college, a broken love affair, career uncertainties, and the like. Second, the potential converts for various reasons did not avail themselves of more conventional mechanisms for solving problems and reducing tension. Such tension-relieving mechanisms could have been psychological counseling, immersion in political or public service activities, or pure avoidance-escape techniques, such as drug or alcohol use, as a means of temporarily blotting out or dulling the impact of unpleasant reality.[26] Third, having found no psychological or socio-political avenue for releasing their tension, they

---

[24] Catherine Robins, "Conversion, Life Crises, and Stability Among Women in the East African Revival," in *The New Religions of Africa,* ed. Bennetta Jules-Rosette (Norwood, N.J.: Ablex Publishing Corporation, 1979), p. 197.

[25] Catherine Robins, "Conversion, Life Crises, and Stability Among Women in the East African Revival," p. 199.

[26] To this list Richardson, Stewart, and Simmonds would add particularly what they call the "conventional" responses of "muddling through," or doing other more or less conventional things, such as moving, changing jobs, taking a holiday, getting married, and getting divorced, before taking the more dramatic route of affiliating with an offbeat religious cult. Cf. James T. Richardson, Mary White Stewart, Robert B. Simmonds, *Organized Miracles* (New Brunswick, N.J.: Transaction Books), pp. 238–39.

sought a religious solution in conventional religious organizations and/or in reading self-help and other religious literature—all without significant resolution of the tension and emotional discomfort with which the individuals began.

Four situational factors now developed. These are what Lofland and sociologists everywhere would stress as factors that are for all practical purposes "outside" the individual, highly *sociological* in nature, if you will. The first Lofland calls the "turning point"—that is, when the preconverts first encountered the Divine Precepts cult, they had reached or were about to reach a crisis in their lives, for whatever they had done before either had been disrupted, was completed, or had failed. In other words, some serious change in their social environment had occurred. Second, there developed or already existed an "affective bond" between the potential recruit and one or more group members. That is, a social relationship of some meaning and significance had developed for the potential recruit (convert). In this case the relationship was with a member and committed affiliate of a particular group. Third, the preconvert's affective relationships outside the cult were either weak or ineffectual. Again, something of significance had happened to the potential convert's social relationships that had preceded. In this case they did not amount to much; they did not constitute much by way of competition. Fourth, total conversion required a period of intensive interaction, often abetted by residence in the group's communal dwelling.[27] Here, of course, we are talking about social interaction pure and simple—interaction that can be intensive and thorough and probing, and can as a result be very effective in producing changes in people (conversion).

What has just been described, then, is not some sudden, instantaneous experience, but a process—what Richardson and Stewart call a conversion "career."[28] In describing conversion as "career" we would observe that conversion is progressive (that is, it involves stages and a progression from one level to another), and it has a background of predispositions within a person that are based on prior socialization experiences. Thus, when conversion occurs we can observe a blending of situational and social-environmental prerequisites, psychological needs, receptivity on the part of the individual, and, above all, active socialization efforts by members of the group to which the person is converting.

CONCLUSION

Religious socialization, the process of becoming religious, is not some unique or unusual process. It is simply socialization by a group into a body of norms that provide a set of meanings and interpretations that individuals internalize

[27] John Lofland, *Doomsday Cult* (Englewood Cliffs, N.J.: Prentice-Hall, 1966), pp. 31–62.

[28] James T. Richardson and Mary Stewart, "Conversion Process Models and the Jesus Movement," in *Conversion Careers: In and Out of the New Religions,* ed. James T. Richardson (Beverly Hills: Sage Publications, 1978).

and relate to the large body of other meanings they possess. Although the ultimate authentication of particular meanings may be different (revering a supernatural being or a sacred book, for example), the process and ultimate outcome is not unlike learning the role and meaning construct of Italian citizen, Venezuelan mother, or offensive center for a professional football team. Certain elements common to all in a social category are learned. Yet a unique pattern emerges, for each individual has a unique combination of interactions and observations that eventuate in his or her meaning construct. Thus, although we continue to search for significant commonalities, differences, and consequent generalizations so far as religious behavior is concerned (the basic assignment for the remaining chapters in this text), we recognize that religion is at some ultimate point unique to the individual; for socialization, religious and otherwise, is a unique experience for each individual. What we are saying is that the powerful social influences and factors ultimately impinge on the individual and must be internalized. Thus, psychological processes are involved. But our major point is that what we observe is not something internal to the individual "coming out," so to speak, but something being created and induced "from without" through socialization processes.

II

RELIGION AS SOCIAL
ORGANIZATION

4

Religion as a Group Phenomenon

In Chapter 1 we made the point that as a social phenomenon religion exhibits patterns of interaction and process that duplicate at many, if not all, points the patterns that all other social groups exhibit, and we suggested quite explicitly that religion is a group phenomenon. We now pick up on these fundamental sociological observations and expand them as we look more specifically at the social organization of religion. That is, we want to see how religious ideas, regardless of their real or supposed source, become embodied in groups, and how in turn these groups proceed to function, evidence similarities among themselves and with other groups, and distinguish themselves both from one another and from other kinds of groups in society.

RELIGION AND THE
CHARACTERISTICS OF A
GROUP

In Chapter 1 we briefly defined *group* as two or more interacting people who (1) share common goals or aims that stem from common problems and a desire to resolve them; (2) agree upon a set of norms they hope will help them achieve their common goals; (3) combine certain norms into roles that they expect persons within the group to fill and carry out in the interests of the group; (4) agree (often only implicitly) on certain status dimensions and distinctions on the basis of which they rate one another; and (5) identify with the group and express or exhibit some degree of commitment to the group, what it proposes to do, and how it proposes to do it.

Clearly, religious organizations meet all of these criteria. Religious groups are concerned with problems and with expressing aspiration, hopes, and goals. They want to know why certain things happen (cognitive understanding of accident, death, thunder, or whatever); or they want to express their dependency relationship with a deity (proper worship and ritual activity); or they want to devise methods of gaining rewards from the deities (techniques of prayer or magic); or they want to achieve a proper existence after this present life (salvation). In each case we are observing goals and the process of establishing goals.

Intimately associated with goal establishment, of course, is agreement on norms. To agree that it is an appropriate goal to appease a jealous god is to establish a norm—namely, that there is such a god, that so and so is his or her name, and so on. Any belief or assertion about the supernatural, any explanation of what it does, any established practice or ritual directed toward it is a norm. Christianity, with its elaborate doctrines, dogmas, and theological tomes, clearly possesses an extensive normative system. Its historic emphasis on "right belief" becomes partially understandable in this context. Yet "primitive" religions that appear more to emphasize behavior—the ritual that involves proper steps and stages in the rain dance, the puberty rite, or the battle preparation—equally emphasize norms—norms of right behavior perhaps more than norms of right belief.

As immediately as norms follow goals, so do roles follow both. The group agrees on a leader (priest, shaman, rabbi, guru, prophet, pastor) and defines his or her duties. It specializes ritual functions into dancers, cantors, sorcerers, choirs, treasurers, acolytes, deacons, temple prostitutes, theological professors, executive secretaries of evangelism, directors of research and survey, public relations directors, news release writers, members of the commission on church literature, ushers, chairpersons of the annual spaghetti supper, and so on.

Partly, but not solely, as a result of such specialization of roles, status differences appear in religious groups. Quite naturally the leader, the coordinator, the spokesperson, and the teacher of religious truths early acquire greater status—greater prestige and respect, if nothing else—than the rank-and-file participant. The status of such persons also involves greater authority and, perhaps as a spinoff, greater power as well. Possibly greater wealth and more leisure may accrue. But there are other status distinctions, too. There are those members who appear to follow the norms of the group more closely than others. Such behavior will likely be recognized by many members, who will characterize those who are most assiduously normative as "very religious," "most sincere," "Zoroastrian of the Decade," "Methodist of the Year," and the like.

Related to such ideas of status differentiation is the factor of group identification. Identification and commitment are variables that range from low (if not zero) to high. Groups tend to tolerate variability here, though most strive for high commitment from all members. Of course, as we will point out shortly, the larger the group, the more likely that the range of commitment and identification will increase.

The major point we are making is that although the subject matter of religion may be unique and although it may claim a unique (namely, supernatural) source for its norms and roles, yet as the religious group organizes itself and sets about doing what it feels it should be doing, it exhibits all the features of any and all other groups. At the level of organization and structure it is no different from other groups. The focus of the goals may be different, the specific set of norms may be different, the combination of norms into particular roles may be unique, the criteria for status assessment may vary. But the religious group, as any other group, will have all of these ingredients and must constantly work at resolving differences of interpretation and application of its goals, norms, and roles. It must adjust them, expand them, and so on, just as any group must. Just as nations or social clubs or political parties or nuclear families differ among themselves yet also evidence similarities in the problems they need to adjust to and the ultimate resolutions and patterns they exhibit, so too religious groups, though unique in certain ways, evidence similarities among themselves and in fact with all other social groups.

This all suggests by way of practical application that the problems and challenges that any group must deal with on a day-to-day basis will be there for a religious group to deal with also. Just as a family needs certain tasks to be performed—cooking meals, washing clothes, mowing the lawn, bringing home spendable income in the form of wages or salary—so a religious group needs someone to lead the group in worship, someone to clean up afterwards, someone to provide leadership in music, and someone to keep tabs on revenues and expenditures. Just as political parties meet in convention periodically to define and refine their platforms and address new issues facing the nation, so churches gather in convention to refine their theological positions on various issues and address new issues that are brought before them. Just as a society devises a court and penal system to provide a fair hearing for those accused of deviation from society's norms and in turn to punish and attempt to rehabilitate those who are found guilty, so religious groups establish procedures to provide a fair hearing but then punish if the person is found guilty, perhaps to the point of excommunication if the individual persists unrepentant in his or her deviance—be it called heresy, immorality, heterodoxy, or whatever.

In short, a group is a group is a group.

RELIGION AND THE FIVE
FUNCTIONAL PREREQUISITES
OF GROUP LIFE

Recruitment and Reproduction

By way of a more systematic and thorough treatment of what we have suggested above we can point out that religious groups, no less than other groups, are involved with meeting the challenges of the five functional prerequisites of group life.[1] First, any group must pay attention to the prerequisite of recruitment or reproduction to replace its members who die, defect or become incapacitated. Societies accomplish this through natural reproduction (births), acceptance of immigrants, or annexation of neighboring territories and populations. Other groups rely primarily on natural reproduction and recruitment of new members through voluntary affiliation with the group. Religious groups have historically not been unmindful of meeting this prerequisite for group continuity. In fact, many religious groups have explicitly urged maximum natural reproduction. Prohibitions against birth control, emphasis on conception as the only valid motive for sexual relations, and social ridicule or pity for the barren woman all enter in here. Although the Old Testament injunction to be fruitful and multiply has more recently been interpreted simply as a predictive statement of what would naturally happen as men and women mated, it was historically interpreted as a divine command to reproduce as prolifically as possible. Some groups have explicitly urged their members to bear as many children as possible so as to increase the numbers of God's people. Many religious groups have also worked hard at adding to their numbers through recruitment of members from outside the group—by conversion or proselytizing. Jesus' injunction quoted in Matthew, "Go ye therefore, and teach all nations," has been followed to greater and lesser degrees throughout history. Ever since (and even before) Charlemagne "converted" the barbarians through mass baptisms in 722, Christian missionaries have been attempting to expedite conversion of nonbelievers and pagans. Actually, however, it was not until the eighteenth and nineteenth centuries, when the new worlds of the Americas, Asia, Africa, and the Pacific experienced extensive exploration and colonization, that Christian groups began subsidizing significant missionary activity.

All Christian groups continue today to support missionary work throughout the world, though somewhat curtailed because of political unrest in various nations, the development of political nationalism that is often accompanied by religious nationalism (for example, in Iran note the intimate relationship of Islamic religion with the political revolution that deposed the shah), and a slightly declining financial support from parent denominations.

---

[1] David Aberle, "The Functional Prerequisites of a Society," *Ethics* 60, no. 2 (1950), 100–111.

Much of the current missionary activity is highly traditional in the sense of going out into the jungles and villages to meet the indigenous peoples where they are and establish congregations. However, increasing emphasis is being placed on work within the expanding urban centers as one after another of the underdeveloped nations begins to industrialize. Along with this ministry to the urban centers often goes increasing attention to a radio and television ministry designed to reach out to the masses.

With respect to contemporary mission work a familiar sight to almost everyone is the pairs of young Mormon men in suits, white shirts, and ties plying the streets and neighborhoods of towns and cities in many countries trying to find receptive ears for the story and message they have to tell. They are required to devote two years before marriage to full-time mission work, some in the home country, others in a foreign one.

Or look at the cult members such as those in the Unification Church ("Moonies") who divide their time between fund raising from those they are unlikely to recruit, and charming the rootless, uncommitted young person into social contact with the group and convincing him or her to stick around and find out more. It was few people indeed who in the 1970s did not run into or at least observe such young people at work in airports and busy city streets.

Other major religions, such as Islam and Buddhism, have also actively courted nonmembers, not infrequently using force and political means when ordinary persuasion was insufficient. In fact, in Islam the political-military and religious motivations are so mixed as to be impossible to separate (true throughout the history of Christianity also, of course). Early in the history of Islam the conquering of both surrounding and distant territories for both booty and land became an absorbing goal and activity. Subjugated peoples were of course also pledged to the religion of Islam. Buddhism used religious missionaries, monks, and teachers to spread their message. In fact, as early as two centuries after Gautama Buddha's death, the Indian emperor Asoka, who came to the throne in 273 B.C., conceived of Buddhism as a world religion and sent missionaries as far as Egypt and Greece.[2] These missions left no trace, however, and these attempts to spread Buddhism were apparently quite ineffective. In Sri Lanka (Ceylon) it was a different story. Buddhist missionaries sent by Asoka's son, Mahinda, in 240 B.C. were so successful that Buddhism quickly became the state religion of Sri Lanka and remains so until this day.[3]

A classic example of a group's failure to meet the requirement of reproduction and recruitment of new members is that of the American religious group called the Shakers, founded in 1787. One of their primary tenets was strict separation of the sexes and complete sexual continence. Therefore, a

[2] John B. Noss, *Man's Religions* (New York: Macmillan, 1949), pp. 175–76.
[3] Edward Conze, *A Short History of Buddhism* (London: George Allen & Unwin, 1980), p. 42.

prime source of new members (natural reproduction) was deliberately eliminated. Sole reliance was placed on adult conversion to the faith. Perhaps in great part because of the limited number of persons willing to observe sexual continence, the group had trouble gaining enough new members to maintain itself. Not surprisingly, the group consists today of but a very few elderly people.

Socialization

A second prerequisite any group must be concerned with is developing a process of training and educating new members—what we have been calling socialization. The norms and practices of the group must be taught to the new member, whether he or she is a child of current members, a convert, or a conquered subject. Religious groups of course face this challenge continually. The doctrines and the practices of the group must be inculcated in the new member. He or she must know and believe certain bits and bodies of doctrine and ritual first of all for his or her own good and also if he or she is to become and remain a member in good standing. Further, the person must know and believe certain things if he or she is to help in preserving the group's beliefs and practices and in handing them down to succeeding generations of followers.

Accordingly, the teaching or educative function of religion becomes a major task for religious groups. It is not by chance, for example, that the full-time religious leader in Judaism, both ancient and contemporary, has the title *rabbi*, meaning "teacher." In "primitive" religions, of course, the socialization process was largely informal and accomplished through emulation as the young watched the old and began to participate in the ritual activities and as they listened to the sagas and tales that elaborated the group's beliefs. However, religious systems that also emphasize various systematic cognitive elements of understanding and belief develop formal mechanisms for conveying such knowledge and for training in ritual performance: confirmation classes, Sunday or other church and sabbath schools, and study groups of all kinds. Religious groups that tend to rely on generalists called ministers or priests may at some point add specialists to their staff called ministers of education. An early development among American Christian denominations, for example, was to establish a publishing house to produce aids to ritual activities (for example, hymnbooks) and educational material designed to aid the religious growth and maturation (socialization) of members.

Producing Satisfactory Levels of Goods and Services

A third prerequisite for the continued existence of all groups is the production and distribution of a level of goods and services that will satisfy at least the minimal requirements or demands of their members. In the case of a total society, this task involves satisfying at least the minimal survival needs of its citizens for such items as food, shelter, and clothing. For voluntary associations such as contemporary religious groups it means giving members what they have come to the group to find, or else running the risk of members losing interest and leaving. Presumably, members of religious groups receive certain expected benefits from their affiliation, or they will not stay or would not have joined in the first place. Perhaps they are seeking eternal salvation, or comfort and reassurance, or good fellowship, or a vehicle through which they can help those in need. A religious group therefore must either "deliver the goods," so to speak—or at least convince its members that the goods are being delivered or will be in the hereafter—or see its constituency evaporate. Although this may sound almost crass, perhaps even sacrilegious, when talking about religious groups, these very religions must "deliver" something that people want, or the people will go elsewhere.

Religious groups that we will be defining as "cults" in the next chapter, which tend to be centered around a charismatic leader, are notoriously unstable and likely to disband as quickly as they formed when the leader becomes discredited or dies or the competition promises more. Followers may decide they are not receiving what they were seeking, or believe that they will more fully or more quickly receive what they seek from the competition that has appeared on the scene.

The relationship of most members to their religious group is of course not so tenuous or easily shifted as what we just described in cults. Certainly lifelong adherents to a group must overcome apathy and inertia, if nothing else, if they wish to defect—yet defect they will (and do) if evidence accumulates and the conviction mounts that what was sought has not been found or is no longer being offered fully enough by the group.

Researchers have recently been observing declining memberships in several major denominations in the United States (and increasing membership in others). Interestingly, those with declining memberships tend to be more theologically and socially liberal; those with increasing memberships tend to be conservative on both counts. We shall not at the moment evaluate the hypothesis that people are increasingly becoming disenchanted with liberal theology and the intrusion of liberal social and political views into the major Christian denominations and as a consequence are leaving such groups to join more traditional groups that emphasize personal comfort and the reassurance of absolute rather than relative truths. But we can certainly agree that most people who leave a religious group, whether or not they affiliate with another one, are expressing a dissatisfaction with the "goods and services" delivered by that group—it no longer provides them what they want, or at least not enough of what they want to maintain their allegiance.

Preserving Order

The fourth primary task that groups must perform is that of preserving order. Essentially this task involves coordinative and supervisory roles, but above all it means motivating members to pursue group goals while employing and abiding by group norms. Within total societies this centers in the political process and the exercising of governmental controls and sanctions—the range of rewards and punishments meted out for adherence to or deviation from the norms, as the case may be. On the positive side, it involves encouraging members to cooperate with one another and to supplement, rather than interfere with, the performance of others' roles. It involves providing a context for freedom of movement and action of individuals within limits agreed upon by the group. On the negative side, it may involve incarceration, the death penalty, or ostracism.

So far as religious groups are concerned we think here of the three major types of church government established to reach the organization's goals. First, there is the episcopal type (for example, Episcopal and Roman Catholic churches), in which authority rests with the congregation's clergyman and with higher-ranking clergy such as popes and bishops. Second, the presbyterian type, in which authority rests with representative committees of clergy and church members. Third, the congregational type, in which ultimate organizational authority resides in local church members and with their representatives meeting periodically in regional or national convention or assembly.

We also think of heresy trials and inquisitions, in which those accused of deviating from official doctrine or practice are sought out, tried, and punished. Fundamental here is the conviction that if such controls are not employed, radical changes may be introduced that would result in the alienation and loss of members to the point of ultimate dissolution and destruction of the group.

Maintaining a Sense of Purpose

The fifth primary prerequisite that groups must fulfill if they hope to survive is the maintenance of a sense of purpose among its members. This task is concerned with the sixth feature of groups mentioned in Chapter 1—namely, the identification factor. Groups must develop and maintain among members a feeling of commitment to and identification with the group. Groups that fail continually to reinforce members' commitment run the risk of takeover or collapse in the face of internal opposition or outside threat. A society, for example, needs citizens sufficiently committed to pick up arms and risk death on the battlefield in the face of enemy invasion. A religious group wants to be able to count on sufficient loyalty and commitment among its members so that they are not swayed (or possibly even converted) by every fragrant new wind of doctrine that blows by. They want members who take pride in their affiliation and who will resist the wiles of other groups or philosophies that may try to win them away. Most religious groups (except most Jews and Hindus) in addition want members who will in fact try to bring others into their fold. "We've got a great group here and would like you to share its benefits with us!" Failing to maintain a sense of purpose can bring a group to the brink of destruction just as can failure in any of the other four primary tasks already discussed.

THE EFFECTS OF INCREASING
GROUP SIZE

Having examined one aspect of religion as a group phenomenon—in terms of the tasks that face all groups, not just religious ones—we now turn to a discussion of the pressures for change that religious groups (no less than other groups) experience. Of particular interest and significance is the effect on groups of increasing size. Important changes occur, and new challenges develop as groups grow. Although a group may in one sense be successful by increasing its membership, serious problems may arise as a consequence. Paul Mott has summarized well the various developments associated with a group's increasing size.[4] We include only some of them—those with particular salience to religious groups.

As groups increase in size, the degree of consensus among members concerning goals and especially norms declines. In great part a basic problem of communication and interaction is involved here. As groups grow, a point is reached when not everyone can interact with everyone else; nor can any one person interact with all others. Levels of understanding and commitment to goals and norms cannot be maintained. Not only can people not share as fully with one another and reach truly common understandings by involving everyone in decision and policy making, but also problems of increasing diversity arise as more members come in. In fact, each new person is a potential disrupter, if not a potential revolutionary, inasmuch as the ideas he or she brings or those that he or she may develop may challenge fundamental beliefs of the group. Obviously the tightknit, integrated, primary-group-like relationship that may have existed at a group's inception and during its early development begins to submit to increasing diversity and more specialized interests as different elements enter.

An almost inevitable outcome of increased diversity and reduced consensus resulting from an increase in size is increasing deviance from group norms. Since norms influence behavior, the introduction of diverse or conflicting norms results in diverse behavior. Some members may assent to many of the group's norms (they probably would not be members otherwise), yet not share others. They are likely to act consonant with their norms, thereby deviating from the group's expectations. For example, a religious group may have explicit norms defining alcoholic beverages as the Devil's tools of destruction. The member who would still like a nip or two is more likely to depart from the group norm as the group grows larger. Perhaps the norm and its importance to the group has not been explained fully to him or her or is no longer reinforced through discussion and conversation; perhaps this person does not feel as closely united with the other members as he or she did when the group

---

[4] Paul E. Mott, *The Organization of Society* (Englewood Cliffs, N.J.: Prentice-Hall, 1965), pp. 48–69.

was small, and thus does not feel so bad about disappointing them should they find out about his or her deviance. Actually, as the group grows larger it becomes physically and emotionally impossible to feel or express as much concern about other individual members as was possible when the group was smaller and members more intimate.

As groups increase in size the ratio of formal norms to informal ones increases. That is, when a group is small and when the members can interact almost at will with one another and with the leader, norms and ideas can be shared with everyone in an informal way. But when the group grows to the point that not everyone can talk readily with everyone else and perhaps does not even know everyone else, the group will find it necessary to formalize its norms and principles and beliefs by writing them down. It is not coincidental that almost without exception holy books and bibles are written *after* the religion has been established awhile, has gained converts, and has moved beyond small group status. For one thing, the leader can no longer speak to everyone. So someone copies down some of his or her sayings and pronouncements and passes copies around to the membership.

A fourth development as groups grow larger is that roles tend to become more specialized, and part-time roles tend to become full-time ones. Such specialization removes the nonspecialist from intimate contact with the tasks of various roles. Greater autonomy for roles develops. Members who originally were involved to some degree in almost everything the group did and decided now know less and less about what others are doing.

As groups increase in size there is greater need for coordination. As the number of roles increases there is greater need for coordinators to interrelate those roles and insure that they are performed in proper sequence. Nothing wrong with that, of course. But in the process, the coordinators gain greater knowledge about the operation of the total organization than ordinary members possess; having by definition greater authority, they become increasingly isolated from the rank and file. Obviously the original intimacy and democracy of the group fade fast in the face of this tendency. There are also, of course, increased opportunities for abusing one's power and perpetuating oneself in office, for example.

And so on. Mott lists thirteen developments within groups related to increasing group size. The five discussed here, however, are sufficient to make the point that one measure of success that groups often use—namely, membership growth—sets them on an irreversible course involving change along a variety of dimensions. In the next chapter we shall refer back to these dimensions in our discussion of the church-sect typology. First, however, we want to look more closely at one of the developments in groups related to increasing size—the bureaucratization trend that we identified earlier as an increase in the coordinative element in groups.

THE BUREAUCRATIZATION OF
RELIGION

In the preceding section we talked about the need for increased coordination as groups grow larger. This introduced us to the concept of bureaucracy which has as its essential feature the coordinating idea. That is, as specialized roles appear and as decisions need to be made certain persons assume or are given coordinating roles. These tend to be ranked in a hierarchy of authority. The whole idea is that greater efficiency should be achieved because someone is organizing the activities of others so that the whole group does not need to meet and take a lot of time reaching a democratic decision. Further, these co-ordinators have a broader picture of what is being done and can determine the most efficient sequence of activities.

But we also need to point out that although bureaucratization appears to be an inevitable trend in groups as they grow large and develop an increasingly complex division of labor requiring careful coordination, it may also create problems and have unintended and unwanted consequences. As Hammond and Johnson point out, a key issue in the Protestant Reformation of the fifteenth century concerned how authority was to be exercised within the church. Implicitly this was a question of what to do about the church bureaucracy.[5] Certainly the Roman Catholic Church had long been organized along rather classic brueaucratic lines. An elaborate hierarchy of authority passed down through pope, archbishops, bishops, and priests, with other levels in between. Specialized training and experience were required of those who filled various specialized roles. Explicit rules were in effect for nearly every situation and role. An air of impartiality and impersonality pervaded relationships among leaders and between them and members.

But the leaders of the Protestant Reformation wanted greater involvement and a stronger voice for the laity. A key theological tenet stressed within early Protestantism was that every person can have direct contact with and access to God. No intermediary such as church, pope, or priest was required. Some groups were convinced that no church authority should exist or exercise control beyond the democratic assembly of each local congregation—no level of authority above the congregation (except God himself) should require the member or the congregation to do anything. Congregationalists, Lutherans, and Baptists are among Protestant denominations that still espouse this principle, though in modified form in each case.

How successful have such religious groups been in implementing this philosophy, in avoiding the bureaucratization that sociologists have document-

[5] Philip E. Hammond and Benton Johnson, *American Mosaic* (New York: Random House, 1970), p. 149.

ed in other types of groups? We gain some insight into the issue when we observe what happens when an individual or a local body of believers strives to maintain its autonomy but also finds it expedient to cooperate with other individuals or congregations in various joint ventures. Perhaps several congregations discover that training future clergy members is a difficult task to accomplish alone and so they join together in establishing a theological seminary. Or they may want to send missionaries to foreign lands. A single congregation usually can not afford to support a missionary, but several congregations can. So they establish a missionary society or board or commission to handle the details, such as collecting mission contributions from the several congregations. Or they may want to produce lessons and literature for their Sunday schools, but local ministers don't have the time or perhaps lack the specialized skill. Therefore several congregations organize a Sunday School Board and organize a Commission on Church Literature to handle the planning, writing, editing, and publishing tasks.

The outcome of such developments is that, although no one particularly intends it, the local congregations lose some of their autonomy. The boards or agencies or commissions assume some measure of authority and independence and in turn gain influence over the congregations. It is a reciprocal relationship—while local congregations may have established the goals and even some of the policies for such administrative groups, once in existence the latter influence the congregations. They train the ministers, organize and supervise the missionary endeavors, and write the Sunday school material. Thus they become innovators and not simply implementers of policy.

The relationship between such boards and the local congregation and its members can therefore become somewhat uncertain. Such a situation is highlighted when one or more congregations discover they do not like the theological inclinations of their seminary's ministerial graduates, or feel that heretical ideas are slipping into their Sunday school material. The congregation of course has the option of severing the relationship, but then it faces the problem of carrying on all these tasks by itself or linking up with yet another organization. The common reaction is to go along with the established pattern, even though the congregation loses some of its cherished autonomy in the process.

A method observed by Paul Harrison in the American Baptist church that bridges the gap between national boards and local independent congregations is the action of the executive who heads a board or agency. If the executive secretary or other administrator of a national board or commission has charismatic qualities, he or she can gain broad-based support among local clergy and laypeople that grants him or her greater flexibility and autonomy and ultimately substantial authority and influence over local decisions.[6] Of course, even without charisma the denominational executive will have some

---

[6] Paul M. Harrison, *Authority and Power in a Free Church Tradition: A Social Case Study of the American Baptist Convention* (Princeton, N.J.: Princeton University Press, 1959), pp. 74–77.

measure of autonomous power because much of his or her day-to-day work goes on unseen and unknown by most of the constituency. As Harrison points out, most lay members have no knowledge of the internal operation of the larger church body, never attend national, state, or even local associational meetings, and most likely do not even know the names of their officials, let alone the policies they set.[7]

In other words, a bureaucracy, once formed, tends to take on a life of its own, initiates and implements policy partly of its own making, and may begin to direct the larger organization of which it is a specialized part in new directions.

Robert Michels's classic "iron law of oligarchy" can be seen operating in many religious groups. This refers to the tendency, as responsibilities and authority are transferred to leaders (a process seemingly inherent and inevitable in group life), for a number of developments in combination to lead to oligarchy. Delegating responsibility and power to leaders, for example, concentrates both skills and informal prerogatives in their hands. Leaders become more skilled than rank-and-file members in administration, coordination, manipulation, diplomacy, and so on, and they have access to information not available to others. Along with such skills and knowledge goes power. The gratitude and allegiance of members to their leaders for doing jobs they would not care to do also strengthens the leaders' position of power and influence. Further, leaders tend to be self-perpetuating in their positions. They like their power and privilege, and they want to keep it. As a result, incumbents are hard to remove.[8]

Religious organizations are not immune to such organizational tendencies. In fact, they join on an equal footing with all other democratic organizations in this tendency. This is true regardless of how jealously a group may strive to remain a pure democracy. Even those religious groups which make a strong theological point that local and individual religious autonomy is sacred are faced with the tendency to oligarchy. Of course, other religious groups, such as the Roman Catholic church, stress a hierarchical authority pattern in the first place and have little problem living with the oligarchic tendency. Although there has been some change recently, with laypeople demanding more input into decision and policy making, the issue in such a group has traditionally been less one of laypeople wanting to curtail the power of bureaucratic church executives than of church officials trying to keep the laypeople from becoming too independent and freethinking. It is a struggle for power either way. It is a struggle based on the two characteristics of groups, religious or otherwise: (1) diversity in a number of dimensions within the group, and (2) the oligarchic tendency for leaders to accumulate power. Internal diversity

---

[7] Ibid., p. 92.

[8] Robert Michels, *Political Parties,* trans. Eden and Cedar Paul (Glencoe, Ill.: Free Press, 1949). First published in England in 1915.

within a group makes effective total control next to impossible, yet oligarchic tendencies serve to override diversity in the interests of bureaucratic efficiency.

THE "OPEN SYSTEMS" THEORY OF RELIGION

As a culmination of the foregoing discussion of various purely sociological features of religion we shall look at an approach to the analysis and understanding of religious organizations that makes use of all of the ideas already presented, and some others as well. It is purely *sociological* theory in the sense that the subject is the group or organization itself and not the individuals who make up that group. By way of a shorthand designation it is commonly called the "open systems" theory of religious organization.

The term "open systems" is intended to suggest that religious groups, like any other group, are "open" in the sense that the surrounding social environment that consists of other groups, social institutions, social movements, political and economic structures, and any other social feature can and likely will have an influence on that group. The group is not closed in the sense that it has an impervious shell that allows nothing from outside to influence it. On the contrary, the group finds itself interacting with first one part or aspect of the surrounding social environment, then another. This theory holds that religious groups not only are highly complex structures but also, just like any other group, to quote Ross Scherer,

> continuously confront competing choices which produce conflict, strain, imbalance, or less than full satisfaction at any one point in time. In other words, because modern society is complex and changing, denominations too become complex and must continually face "dilemmas" which require adjustments in goals and strategies for mission. Like a logger riding on a turning log, they must continually act to maintain "balance." At times, denominations can be assertive and aggressive over against society, and at other times retreating and withdrawing. For each choice and solution, there is a gain and there is a price.[9]

Scherer points out that the focus of this theory is on how a group relates to the social environment within which it exists. He indentifies several ideas or assumptions that amplify this central idea.[10] Keep in mind that while we are talking about groups in general, we are particularly interested in making specific applications to religious groups.

1. A group is basically a transformation system. That is, its members take resources, do something with and to them, and exchange the product with other groups and persons in their social environment. For example, a re-

[9] Ross P. Scherer, *American Denominational Organization* (Pasadena, Calif.: William Carey Library, 1980), p. 2.

[10] Ibid., pp. 9–10.

ligious group can take some people with skills in persuasion and some money and can create a political lobby in a nation's capital and persuade legislators to pay more attention to protecting the civil rights of citizens. By the same token, those same people and that same amount of money could have been used to create a paramilitary organization engaged in sniper attacks on Blacks and Jews emerging from their places of business. In either case, a group is performing as a transformation system.

2. It is crucial for the group to come to terms with the social environment in which it exists because in an ultimate sense its survival depends on that environment. The group would experience entropy (that is, it would run down, gradually lose its energy) if it did not replenish its resources from the environment. The Shakers that we mentioned earier experienced entropy in the extreme as they were unable to procure sufficient resources (converts) from outside in the social environment of the society and produced no new member resources by natural reproduction so as to maintain a viable membership. By way of further extension of this idea, if a group's ideology and behavior are so far out of line with acceptable belief and practice in the society that the society determines that extermination of the group is its only recourse, then the group will almost surely face a problem of entropy down the road. The Mormons escaped this eventuality only by finding the wide open spaces and isolation of frontier Utah Territory to establish themselves in, and then later by modifying their position on issues such as polygamy when their contact with the rest of American society increased.

3. The group filters and interprets the reality that is external to it. It "maps" and "codes" that external reality for its members and stores away those readings and interpretations. This idea recognizes that the group is not totally "at the mercy" of the surrounding social environment. The Flat Earth Society, for example, screens out all the everyday evidence available in the surrounding world that speaks to the spherical nature of the planet earth. Thus, accounts of jet planes flying around the earth or science textbooks describing the earth rotating on its axis are tricks and lies intended to confound the faithful members who *know* that the earth is indeed flat.

4. Such selectivity and group-dictated interpretations produce an at least temporary or partial "steady state" in which the members of the group feel reasonably secure about their group's reading and description of the reality around them. This would suggest that groups might hold a fairly "far-out" idea that is judged as relatively harmless by the surrounding society so long as most of what the group says and does is fairly conventional. Members of the Flat Earth Society, for example, continue to hold jobs and perform as citizens without persecution either by our government or their neighbors.

5. The group not only exists within the broader history that surrounds it, but it also in itself has a history. That is, a group is not static and in some kind of state of suspended animation, but is at least to some degree dynamic and changing. This all but presupposes that there will be some degree of inno-

vation and deviance from within the system that will produce at least a minimum level of change and adaptation. Groups do not have total control over their members, particularly as the groups increase in size. New ideas both from within and from without will begin to surface. Again, in very simple terms, the group does not exist in isolation from the social environment around it.

6. Although the group lives by the stabilizing influence of its structure of roles, rules, and mutual understandings, there turns out to be really no single "best way" but rather a variety of alternatives by which a group might reach its objectives. Thus our attention is drawn to the continuous importance of the group members as decision makers and creators of principle and policy.

And so, by way of the briefest of summaries, a religious group, just as any group, is an "open system" that has both internal dynamics and external environmental influences that encourage and produce change and adaptation. While this does not suggest that a religious group is really nothing more than what its surrounding social environment wants it to be and has shaped it to be, such a group is not autonomous and self-determining either. There is continuous interaction of one with the other. Whatever else it is or may be, religion is a group phenomenon and evidences the principles and laws of group life and adaptation.

5

The Church-Sect Continuum of Religious Organization

In the previous chapter we explored ways in which religious groups are both similar among themselves but also similar to other groups and social organizations. We now turn to some important distinctions among religious groups — distinctions that are fundamentally matters of organization — that is, sociological, not theological, differences. We begin with the *church-sect typology* — a way of identifying differences among religious groups that was given its fullest early conceptualization by the theologian Ernst Troeltsch, but was introduced into sociology by his teacher Max Weber and has been used and expanded by numerous sociologists since their time.

As we shall soon see, the dichotomy of church and sect actually only identifies two polar types of religious organization. That is, the church and the sect occupy the ends of a social continuum that has several gradation points (other types of organization) in between. We first shall contrast the polar types and then discuss three other types of religious organization that investigations following those of Troeltsch and Weber have shown to be important additions to the typology.

THE SECT

Demerath and Hammond suggest that differences between churches and sects can be observed from either of two perspectives, one concerning the internal characteristics of the organization, the other the external relationships of the group with the features of its social environment.[1] Focusing on internal differences, we can observe the following about sects: (1) A sect sees itself as a fellowship of the elect—that is, an embodiment of true believers. (2) Sects encourage spontaneity of religious expression involving extensive group participation. (3) Sects de-emphasize organization and strive to maintain maximum democratic participation of members within an explicitly nonbureaucratic structure. (4) A sect is usually small, and deliberately so. (5) Sects utilize laypeople as leaders. Frequently part-time, such leaders likely have little if any formal theological training. Commitment to the principles avowed by the group is seen as more important than "book learning." The element of charisma is a common feature of leaders. (6) A sect emphasizes purity of doctrine and usually demands a return to original religious teaching. This involves a renunciation of the doctrinal perversions and aberrations that it accuses the established denominational religious groups of having allowed to intrude into true religion. (7) A sect emphasizes traditional ethical principles and strives to influence its members along a broad spectrum of behavior. (8) Sects tend to concentrate on otherworldly issues (salvation, deliverance, heaven and hell) and discount or deprecate this world's concerns. Even their emphasis on ethics (point 7) is focused more on its relevance to ultimate otherworldly concerns, less on the relationship of person to person. (9) A sect gains new members primarily through conversion. It is initially a fellowship of adults, although eventually they must turn their attention to the religious socialization of children. (10) A sect draws disproportionately from the lower social classes in the society.

Implicit in many of the characteristics just outlined is the prime characteristic of a sect, namely, protest. Usually it is protest against both (1) established traditional religious forms and groups that sect members feel have strayed too far from pristine religion, and (2) the surrounding secular society, which is viewed as embodying all kinds of evil. A sect thus reflects schism—a breaking away from and a rejection of established patterns, both religious and secular. It is at this point that we encounter most directly the external relationships of a sect to its surrounding social environment that we mentioned earlier. The sect in its protest against the evils of the surrounding society engages in some kind of rejection of that social structure. The form may be withdrawal in both a figurative and literal sense from most of the typical activities people engage in. Communal groups such as the Amish and Hutterites would fit here and would be the most extreme form of withdrawal and rejection. They refuse to participate in the surrounding community's politics (they do not vote); they send their children to school only to learn to write, read, and do basic math, and try to keep them from going beyond the eighth grade; they subscribe to no newspapers or magazines; they own and listen to no radi-

---

[1] N. J. Demerath III and Philip E. Hammond, *Religion in Social Context* (New York: Random House, 1969), pp. 70–71.

os or TV sets; and they engage in only occasional commerce with the surrounding community, being nearly self-sufficient on their communal farms.

We might mention here in passing that there are of course many other types of sects. Although we shall not get into a description of the various types here, two typologies the reader may wish to explore are those of Elmer T. Clark and Bryan Wilson. Clark distinguishes the pessimistic-adventist sects, the perfectionist-subjectivist sects, the charismatic-pentecostal sects, the legalistic-objectivist sects, and the communistic sects.[2] Wilson distinguishes the revolutionist, introversionist, manipulationist, thaumaturgical, reformist, and utopian sects.[3]

THE CHURCH

Before presenting the corresponding characteristics of the church type we need to make clear that the church (the sect also) is clearly what in sociology we call an ideal type. That is, the concept of church or sect or any of the other types of religious organization that we shall describe later in the chapter represents a summary or distillation of social characteristics and phenomena that frequently appear together, and that in combination help to distinguish one set of organizations from another. It is a kind of model that expresses in pure, complete form the central characteristics of a pattern of organization or behavior. Although we do not expect to find all the characteristics of an ideal type in pure form in a particular organization at a given moment in time, we will expect most of them. In a sense an ideal type is used for dramatic purposes to heighten one's awareness of salient characteristics of a social phenomenon. For example, we listed ten characteristics of the sect. Yet a religious group may accurately be identified as a sect and yet lack one or two of the characteristics on the list, or not reproduce all ten characteristics in "pure" form. Similarly the church type represents one "extreme" form of religious organization that may have appeared at some time in history in essentially all its characteristics, but probably never in pure form on all dimensions. That is, an ideal type is more a concept and less an empirical reality, though based on substantial empirical observations. Its value lies in providing a clear-cut base of comparison for what we observe empirically at a given point in time. Although we may be unable to observe an empirical example of a "church" at this point in history, we can understand more clearly what we do observe because of either its similarities to or differences from the ideal type we have as a base of contrast.

But now to the major characteristics of the *church* type of religious organization. The church (1) claims universality and includes all members of the

[2] Elmer T. Clark, *The Small Sects in America* (Nashville: Abingdon, 1949).
[3] Bryan Wilson, *Religious Sects* (New York: McGraw-Hill, 1970).

society within its ranks; there is a strong tendency for "citizen" to be equated with "member;" (2) exercises religious monopoly and tries to eliminate religious competition; (3) is very closely allied with the state and secular powers; frequently there is overlapping of responsibilities and much mutual reinforcement; (4) is extensively organized as a hierarchical bureaucratic institution with a complex division of labor; (5) employs a professional, full-time clergy who possess the appropriate credentials of education and formal ordination; (6) almost by definition gains new members through natural reproduction and the socialization of children into its ranks.

A prime example of a church is the medieval Roman Catholic Church. Another close approximation was the Russian Orthodox Church of the nineteenth century. For that matter, contemporary European state churches approximate this model, though they all now at least formally tolerate religious diversity and competition—something the pure church type does not do. Although there is no really good example of a church type of religious organization to be observed today, the concept retains considerable value as a point of reference for understanding the other types of religious organization that are in clear evidence today.

Although we shall not elaborate them here, the reader should be aware that refinements and further specification of the church type have been made. For example, J. Milton Yinger has distinguished the "universal church" from the "ecclesia" (Greek word for church) and has further divided both into institutionalized and diffused forms.[4]

THE DENOMINATION

The *denomination* is in a mediating position between the church and the sect, and as such is the most important addition to the original dichotomous church-sect typology. When the church loses its position of religious dominance and monopoly, denominationalism is the result. In fact, the moment the protesting, struggling sects that have been striving to attain autonomy are tolerated, however reluctantly, by the established church, the church is by definition dead and is immediately transformed into a denomination—that is, one religion among several. As some of the protesting sects evolve (we will discuss this evolutionary process later in the chapter), they too become denominations, and this type of religious organization—denominationalism—becomes a distinct, identifiable type.

A denomination can be defined as follows: (1) It is similar to the church, but unlike the sect, in being on relatively good terms with the state and secular powers. The denomination's most extreme stance in this respect would be

---

[4] J. Milton Yinger, *The Scientific Study of Religion* (New York: Macmillan, 1970), pp. 256–64.

"loyal opposition." It is at home in the halls of government and occasionally tries to exert some influence in that direction—something few sects try to do. (2) A denomination maintains at least tolerant and usually fairly friendly relationships with other denominations in a context of religious pluralism. (3) It relies primarily on birth for membership increase, though it will also accept converts; some groups even actively pursue evangelistic programs, though directed primarily to the unconverted, unchurched citizens, not persons presently members of other denominations. (4) A denomination accepts the principle of at least modestly changing doctrine and practice, and tolerates some theological diversity and dispute—something a true sect will not do. (5) It follows a fairly routinized ritual and worship service that explicitly discourages spontaneous emotional expression. (6) It trains and employs a professional clergy who must meet certain formal normative requirements before certification. (7) It recognizes competing demands from other affiliations upon its members' commitment and involvement; thus it accepts less extensive involvement from members than a sect does, but often expects more than the church (where by virtue of the citizen–church member equation it is recognized that many persons will be minimally or noninvolved members). (8) A denomination draws disproportionately from the middle and upper classes of the society.

Before proceeding to look at two other important types of religious organizations within the framework of the church-sect typology—namely, the cult and the institutionalized sect—we need to analyze a bit further the relationship between sect and denomination. First we want to look at the point of rupture when the sect protests to the point of breaking with the denomination or church. Second, we will trace the evolutionary pattern that most sects follow which eventually leads them to denominational status.

THE FORMATION OF SECTS

We stated earlier that the fundamental theme of the religious sect is protest—protest which leads to schism and a breaking away from the parent religious group, be it church or denomination. Such action, however, is not the only method of resolving conflict within a religious group. One method historically employed by church-type religious groups—of which the Roman Catholic Church is a paramount example—is by allowing, often in fact encouraging, the formation of specialized groups within the larger body. If some persons feel they cannot worship properly in the established ritual form of ordinary local congregational groups (the reasoning goes), then allow them to form a subgroup or religious order within the larger body that emphasizes extensive contemplation and private meditation, or one that encourages active participation in social and political activities, or one that engages in spontaneous, emotional, pentecostal-type behaviors. Monastic orders within the Roman Catholic Church have served this purpose admirably. Even today the tacit permission if not encouragement of pentecostal subgroups within such standard denominations as the Catholic, Lutheran, Presbyterian, and Episcopalian Churches is an excellent example of this tactic of channeling deviant and/or specialized groups within the overarching structure of the denomination.

Probably the most familiar method of resolving dissatisfaction within a denomination is simply for individuals or families to withdraw—either to drift from organized religion altogether or to affiliate with another religious group that seems to satisfy one's wishes and concerns more fully. How many present-day denominational switches are such expressions of religious protest, we do not know. Undoubtedly many are relatively simple transfers of convenience when a family moves and cannot find its denomination represented nearby; or when upward mobility (as opposed to ideological conflict) suggests to a person that he or she should forsake, say, his or her Baptist background and affiliate with a "higher-status" Presbyterian or Episcopalian congregation; or when an interfaith marriage leads one partner to switch to the mate's religious group as a matter of form and convenience.

Another way of resolving religious conflict is for those who are dissatisfied simply to split off and form another denomination. We will soon emphasize that a prime ingredient in sect formation is the factor of social class. But if social class is not a particularly primary factor in a given controversy and the issue is more strictly political or ideological, then a denomination may simply split into two. The division of both the Baptists and the Presbyterians into northern and southern denominations during the Civil War are good examples of this process. The split within the Presbyterian Church in the 1930s over certain doctrinal issues is another example; not a sect but another denomination formed as a result. Similarly in nineteenth century Europe, Reform Judaism separated from Orthodox Judaism not as a sect but as a denomination.

The final method of resolving religious group conflict is the one we keep referring to—the process of sect formation. What happens in this process and why? Ostensibly the issue is almost invariably doctrinal or theological. Potential sect members are likely to talk about the loss of true Christianity in the parent denomination—about how doctrine has become liberalized and people are not living their Christianity the way they should. Some members finally opt out and form their own small group in order to preserve or recapture the basics and the essence of true religion and save themselves from further theological contamination and perversion. Undoubtedly most sectarians are sincere and truly believe that theological or doctrinal issues are the real issues. Yet one suspects there is more to it than that. The social scientist continually looks for latent factors lurking behind manifest behaviors, definitions of the situation, and rationalizations. We are thus particularly intrigued when we observe that sectarians are quite predominantly of lower-class social status. Aware that social status influences all manner of social behavior and attitudes, sociologists thus regard it very likely that social status also relates in some way with the sectarian break from the denomination.

Liston Pope, in his classic analysis of the interrelationship of religion and social structure, reviews several hypotheses that try to account for the phenomenon of sect formation. Most writers, he notes, pay serious attention to the status dimension, or at least by implication suggest that lower social status is somehow significantly involved in the motivation for sectarian involvement.[5] For example, the "cultural shock" hypothesis of John B. Holt suggests that migrants to cities seek out or form sects as a means of preserving rural religious lifestyles and values, and as a defense against the anonymity of the city and the urban denominational congregations.[6] Although such factors may be relevant for some persons, Holt's analysis does not account for the formation of sects in rural and small-town settings. Holt does point out, however, that persons attracted to sects, whether migrants experiencing cultural shock or not, are predominantly lower class.

Many theorists, then, see sect formation as some form of compensation for those deficiencies epitomized by inferior social status. Pope notes that sects "substitute religious status for social status."[7] The sectarian is likely to say something like, "I may not be high society, but I'm on God's first string, " or "I may not have a big house, a fancy car, and a college education, but I've got what's really important—I've got true religion." Pope observes: "They transmute poverty into a symptom of Grace."[8] Socially separated from those above them in the stratification system, they then emphasize separation from "the world" as a virtue. Although they feel excluded from fellowship with those of higher education and social and economic position, they in turn exclude from their fellowship those who dance, play cards, smoke, drink, and bet on the races. Unable to afford jewelry, they make wearing of any such adornment a sin. Pope again observes: "Excluded from secular society, they set up a religious society of their own, in which standards of membership are more rigid than those of the general culture that has ignored them."[9] Reaching heaven, which is the supreme, ultimate reward, becomes eminently more important than earthly success and the good life here and now, which is only temporal and not eternal.

THE IMPACT OF DEPRIVATION
ON SECT DEVELOPMENT

To this point we have been concentrating on a rather simplistic distinction between high and low socioeconomic status. Charles Y. Glock has added specifi-

[5] Liston Pope, *Millhands and Preachers* (New Haven: Yale University Press, 1942), pp. 133–34.

[6] John B. Holt, "Holiness Religion: Cultural Shock and Reorganization," *American Sociological Review* 5, no. 5 (1940), 740–47.

[7] Pope, *Millhands and Preachers,* p. 137.

[8] Ibid.

[9] Ibid., p. 138.

cation to this general hypothesis by introducing the concept of "deprivation" and making distinctions among five types of deprivation.[10] First, there is *economic deprivation*, which consists of limited income and access to the material necessities of life. It may be objectively defined and measured as well as subjectively experienced and perceived. That is, although a person may technically not be categorized as living at the poverty level, he or she may perceive of himself or herself as poor. Such a perception can influence his or her behavior and attitude as much as or more than the objective facts of his or her existence.

Second, *social deprivation* refers to the relative absence of such societal rewards as prestige, power, social status, and opportunity for participation in various activities and organizations. This is frequently a concomitant of economic deprivation in the sense that low economic status likely means low prestige or respect, little power or influence over others, and exclusion from much of the social and organizational life of the community. But social deprivation is not necessarily strictly correlated with economic deprivation. A person may be socially deprived yet be economically solvent, even successful. Social deprivation is one of the main emphases of the women's liberation movement. "Although I can buy all that my heart desires, I'm considered 'just a housewife' because it's my husband's income I'm spending." "I may be receiving a very livable salary, but it's less than that of a man doing comparable work." And so on. Or social deprivation may be along age lines. Consider the very young and the very old who have relatively little power and prestige even though economically they may be facing no difficulty. Further, the minority-group member, such as a Chicano or black or American Indian, may be economically successful yet a second-class citizen on other dimensions of status.

A third type of deprivation is *organismic*. This refers to the deprived condition of some in society along the dimensions of physical and mental health and biological-physical abilities. Some suffer from neuroses or psychoses; some are deaf or blind; some are paraplegics; some are mentally retarded; others suffer from one or more of an almost infinite variety of other conditions.

Another type of deprivation is what Glock calls *ethical*. This exists when persons come to feel that the dominant values and norms of the society no longer provide them with a meaningful way of organizing their lives. Ethically deprived persons have trouble finding meaning in their lives and cannot decide where to go or how to proceed to find it. Above all, these persons seek a body of ethical prescriptions on how to organize their lives and want an alternative value system to inform and guide them.

Finally there is *psychic deprivation*, which affects the person who may enjoy the material rewards of society and may subscribe to society's norms but

[10] Charles Y. Glock, "The Role of Deprivation in the Origin and Evolution of Religious Groups," in *Religion and Social Conflict*, eds. Robert Lee and Martin E. Marty (New York: Oxford University Press, 1964), pp. 24–36.

who nevertheless lacks an adequate share of psychic rewards—the person does not *feel* satisfied or really accepted in society. Such deprivation frequently accompanies social deprivation—for example, the black professional in American society who has superior specialized skill and education, who may be economically successful, but who still feels looked down upon because of his or her color, and who in many situations is made to feel inferior, second-rate. Whereas social deprivation is more or less an objective measure or dimension, psychic deprivation is a psychological matter and thus highly subjective.

To relate these types of deprivation to the sources of sectarianism, we can first of all observe with Glock that the emergence of any protest movement or group—religious or otherwise—requires some feeling of deprivation on the part of the participants.[11] They face a problem that is either not being met by the groups they are presently affiliated with or is in some way produced by a group or groups with which they are affiliated (or both). Glock suggests, however, that while some felt deprivation is a necessary condition for protest group formation, it is not a sufficient condition—there are additional requirements. The deprivation must be shared with others, and these people need to find one another; a leader must emerge to suggest a solution; and no alternative existing institutional arrangements or processes must appear to be available.[12] When such factors combine, a protest group can get underway.

But what form will it take? For example, will it be a secular group or movement, or will it be a religious organization such as a sect breaking away from a denomination? If the deprivation is either economic or social, it is likely that a religious route will be followed (1) when the nature of the deprivation is inaccurately perceived or inadequately understood—that is, when people do not realize that a prime factor in their unhappiness and frustration is their economic or social position relative to others; or (2) when, even though the nature of the deprivation is accurately perceived, people feel powerless to work directly at eliminating its causes.[13] In either case, persons may retreat into an emotionally releasing, rationalizing, otherwordly sectarian religious group and activity as a conscious or subconscious means of escaping from the harsh realities of economic or social deprivation. On the other hand, if people accurately perceive the problem and feel capable of attacking and resolving it through social change, then they are more likely to form a secular organization or attempt some other secular resolution. In other words, religious resolutions such as the formation of sects are essentially compensatory mechanisms for alleviating feelings of deprivation, while secular resolutions try to strike directly at the causes of the deprivation.

A striking example of both of these attempts can be seen in the black community in the United States. Historically much black religious behavior

[11] Ibid., p. 29
[12] Ibid.
[13] Ibid.

and involvement has tended to be of the sect variety, quite clearly responding to economic and social deprivation in a compensatory way. More recently, however, as more blacks have become cognizant of the real nature of their problems, have rejected doctrines of inherent inferiority, and have become convinced that the system could be effectively challenged, the civil rights movement has flowered. Young blacks in particular have increasingly turned to secular organizations, such as CORE, Operation Breadbasket, and the Black Panthers, or in some cases to groups like the Black Muslims, rather than to traditional black religious organizations. More on this phenomenon and on black religion in general appears in Chapter 11.

When social deprivation is not intimately associated with or reinforced by economic deprivation, another route may be followed that is neither sectarian nor secular—very simply, another religious denomination may result. Again we turn to the American black community for an example. The African Methodist Episcopal Church came into being not as a sect but as a denomination when freed blacks, many of them of essentially middle-class economic status, reacted to unequal participation privileges and unequal voice in the white-dominated Methodist Episcopal Church and broke away in 1796.

Although we have not discussed the cult as a specific type of religious organization, we should mention at this point that either ethical or psychic deprivation is less likely to result in sectarian development and more likely, for reasons that will become evident later, to cause people to form or be attracted to a religious cult. It is of course also possible that ethical or psychic deprivation may be a prelude to secular solutions and the formation of nonreligious groups.

THE EVOLUTION OF SECTS

So much for the phenomenon of sect formation. We now turn to the issue of sect evolution and an investigation of the factors involved in the nearly universal tendency of sects (if they survive at all) to change and to move away from their original "pure" state—in fact, to move toward eventual denominational status and to begin manifesting the characteristics of an organization from which they originally withdrew and which they earlier repudiated. We refer to the sect in its pure state as a religious group composed of the exclusive "elect" or select few, who practice what they see as "pure," authentic religion and who avoid secular involvement and contamination; and we begin with the empirical observation that a sect cannot remain a sect.

A major causative factor in the evolution of sect to denomination is quite nonreligious and very sociological. We refer here to the laws of increasing group size that we outlined in the previous chapter. For these laws to apply, we assume, of course, that the originally small sect grows. And even if a sect does not grow enough to call into play the laws of increasing group size, other nonreligious factors apply that we will discuss later. But assuming a sect adds to its numbers—as most do, since they usually want to spread their gospel and share their discovery of true religion—then some inevitable developments come about. More people automatically means a greater diversity of background. New members will not share precisely the same experiences of the original core group, and some will have significantly different personal objectives and goals that they expect the group to fulfill. Thus problems of unanimity and total consensus arise, even though all may sincerely believe that they subscribe to the same goals and norms as everyone else. The foundation is therefore laid for ultimate modification of the sect's central goals and values.

As a group increases in size, subgroups inevitably develop. Although this phenomenon occurs the moment any few people form a group, it intensifies in geometric proportion as the group grows. Subgroups develop their own unique combinations of goals, norms, and roles while still subscribing to the overarching ideology of the larger group and respecting its structure. Subgroups not only provide internal diversity, but represent the distinct possibility that a particular subgroup may become increasingly more deviant, gain more adherents, and ultimately dominate the larger group and assume guiding control. Obviously under such circumstances the group will change.

We just mentioned deviance. As groups increase in size, deviance increases, largely through subgroup action. But not only that. Tolerance of deviance increases, either because the deviance is unknown or unrecognized, or because the task of enforcing strict normative behavior on the membership becomes more and more difficult. Clearly the original conformity and unanimity is breaking down.

A prime need for groups as they grow larger is greater coordination. Strictly democratic decision making in all matters becomes impractical and impossible. Responsibility for coordinating the activities of many persons and roles is centralized in specialists. A side effect will likely be a declining intensity of commitment and sense of involvement among ordinary members. Also, the distance between elite and rank-and-file members will increase. The person who sees original principles changed or lost will find it increasingly difficult to communicate his or her concern to the elites in the group. Not only will change remain unchecked, but the individual who objects to change will become increasingly dissatisfied and disenchanted (while others, of course, will applaud the change).

A result may well be a legitimacy crisis, with some concluding that they must reject the authority of the leaders and coordinators. But perhaps they are voiceless or powerless. What to do? Go along silently but unhappily, or leave and form a new group—a new sect that can once again restore purity and truth to religion.

But what if a sectarian religious group manages to avoid the problems inherent in organizational growth by simply not growing, or at least by not growing to the extent where a bureaucratic structure develops and members become isolated from one another? Even with no growth or only limited growth, sources of change are present and begin to work. Almost immediately after formation a formalization of norms begins and the group loses some of its spontaneity and flexibility. Then the group must answer two questions: (1) Where does authority lie? In a book? With a leader? In a doctrinal statement? That is, who or what is the ultimate arbiter? (2) What are correct beliefs? What are we going to teach our children and the adults who knock on our door and inquire about coming in?

With each development the group is becoming more stabilized, it is formalizing its norms; structurally it is becoming just a bit more like the group from which it severed itself. There is a little less chance for innovations; it is becoming a little more difficult to substantiate that the Holy Spirit is working through you to bring new insight. It becomes increasingly more necessary to reconcile that which is newly introduced with what the group has already established as normative in answering the two questions above.

Furthermore, the group must provide for leadership succession. If the group begins with a charismatic leader, what happens if he or she dies or is incapacitated or is discredited as morally or otherwise unfit to continue as leader? Norms must therefore be established that outline the process of leader selection and succession. Perhaps it will involve a training program for potential leaders. Above all, it will require specification of the qualifications and duties of the leader. After all, if we bring in a new leader, he or she has to know what the duties are. At this point something highly significant has happened—the leader has become an officeholder. The leader's role has been routinized and formalized. And one observes the beginning of formal structure and ultimately perhaps bureaucracy itself.

Also, any expansion beyond the few initial individuals or families will require attention to financial matters. A hall for meetings must be rented or purchased; some minimal equipment and fixtures must be provided; a checking account must be opened at a local bank. And again we see the spontaneous, flexible group becoming structured and routinized. It is taking an early short but definite step down the road toward the type of organization from which it came. "That church I used to belong to paid too much attention to everyday, worldly matters like meeting budgets, fundraising, and building maintenance. It didn't pay enough attention to spiritual matters—the really important things." So says the sectarian. Yet the sect itself must soon begin to have similar concerns, though at first on a smaller scale of course.

Another factor contributing to change in the sect is the strong tendency within any group for higher-status persons to assume positions of power and be elected to office. The sect is no exception. Low-status members of a group tend to defer to those with more education, a higher-status job, and greater prestige. The result tends to be a conservative influence on the group—conservative in the sense that such higher-status leaders are likely to want to modify and tone down extremes in the sect's stance and ideology. They have more at stake in the surrounding community and do not want their names associated with too weird a group. Thus the sect begins to change, to accommodate itself, and it becomes more compatible with the surrounding culture.

A final important factor involved in turning the sect around and leading it back toward the denominational form is the upward status mobility of some of its members. Insofar as sect formation is primarily a lower-status phenomenon, what happens when some of these lower-status members improve their social and economic condition? They will either bring the group with them along the lines of modification and accommodation just discussed, or they will leave the group and affiliate with another group (more denominational in character) that is more compatible with their enhanced social status. If they stay, conceivably they could even more or less force those in the group who have not begun to change their status level and conditions to pull out and form a new sect; this could be done consciously or unconsciously. What is involved here is effectively and poignantly stated by John Wesley, himself a founder of a sect—a sect that has become the Methodist Church in its various denominational forms:

> *Wherever riches have increased, the essense of religion has decreased in the same proportion. Therefore, I do not see how it is possible, in the nature of things, for any revival of religion to continue long. For religion must necessarily produce both industry and frugality, and these cannot but produce riches. But as riches increase, so will pride, anger, and love of the world in all its branches. . . . Is there no way to prevent this—this continual decay of pure religion? We ought not to prevent people from being diligent and frugal; we must exhort all Christians to gain all they can, and to save all they can; that is in effect to grow rich. What way then can we take, that our money may not sink us into the nethermost hell?*[14]

In other words, the sect has an inherent problem—in Marxian phraseology, a seed of self-destruction or change—that leads it out of its "pure" state and into something it rebelled against at an earlier point in time. And out of a sect grows a denomination. This is precisely what happened with Wesley's Methodists; indeed, it is a pattern that has also been followed by most of the other major Christian denominations today. Such groups as the Baptists, the Lutherans, the Presbyterians, and the Seventh-Day Adventists all began at one point as sects, but each has evolved to full-fledged denominational status today. David Harrell, who focuses on this manner of development in tracing the evolution of the Church of Christ sect, mentions that the evolution of some of these sectarian groups is directly related to the changing character of the membership of the group: "The cultured element in the movement . . . simply [begins] the search for a more sophisticated type of religion."[15]

[14] Quoted in H. Richard Niebuhr, *The Social Sources of Denominationalism* (New York: Meridian Books, 1957), pp. 70–71.

[15] David E. Harrell, Jr., *Emergence of the "Church of Christ" Denomination* (Lufkin, Tex.: Gospel Guardian Company, 1967), p. 28.

THE INSTITUTIONALIZED SECT

Another important type of religious organization is what Yinger calls the *established sect* and what others call the *institutionalized sect*.[16] It has been necessary to develop this concept to cover a route that sects occasionally take as an alternate to the predominant sect-to-denomination pattern. There is of course yet a third path that many sects follow—the sect-to-oblivion route. In fact, most sects do not survive long. Internal rivalries and personality clashes, problems with leadership succession, the geographic mobility of members, urban renewal that disperses constituencies and removes facilities—all conspire to make most sects transitory. Those that survive tend to evolve into denominations. However, some become institutionalized sects. Such groups manage to retain elements of their radical protest and a strong commitment to ideology while avoiding the accommodation and modification that would turn them into a denomination. Some denominational characteristics, however, usually become incorporated into the group—the group becomes somewhat bureaucratized; its norms and procedures become formalized; some of its members gain higher social status. Yet it does not become a denomination, even though it is no longer a pure sect either. An institutionalized sect is halfway between the denomination and the sect on the church-sect continuum. What is of crucial significance, however, is that it is in a state of arrested development—the evolutionary process has been brought to a standstill.

Some examples will help clarify this type of religious organization. Religious cooperative and utopian groups such as the Amish, the Hutterites, the Dukhobors, and various Mennonite groups are excellent examples. The Quakers (Society of Friends) are a fairly well-known group that also qualifies quite well as an institutionalized sect. These groups are like the pure sect in the sense of being relatively small in numbers, engaging in protest against both the way religion has been routinized in denominations and the society itself, and emphasizing democratic involvement of members and thereby avoiding extensive bureaucratization. In fact, many such groups do not employ full-time clergy. These groups are unlike pure sects, however, in that they are somewhat more bureaucratically organized than the latter. The Quakers, for example, have organized two agencies for political influence in Washington and elsewhere and for performing various service and social action functions that are well-organized lobbying groups—the American Friends Service Committee and the Friends' Committee on National Legislation.

Members of institutionalized sects are unlike members of ordinary sects in that their socioeconomic status is often higher. Further, their religious expression in worship is less emotionally charged, and they are more concerned about education than the newly formed sect, which is primarily a fellowship of adults.

---

[16] J. Milton Yinger, *The Scientific Study of Religion* (New York: Macmillan, 1970), pp. 266–73.

How does one account for the arrested development of the institutionalized sect? The cooperative religious groups provide one significant element in suggesting an answer to this question. Groups such as the Amish have avoided unsettling influences from the surrounding society and from other religious groups by the rather dramatic tactic of withdrawing to a considerable degree from the surrounding society. As mentioned in the previous chapter, this includes physical or geographic isolation, to the degree that such is possible in a modern society, by establishing themselves exclusively in rural environments. In the process their members collectively become nearly self-sufficient, depending on the outside world for little except machinery, fuel, and building materials. Thus their members engage in only minimal contact with people outside their group. Such groups further increase their isolation by forbidding television sets and radios and by limiting the education of the children to elementary school. By specifying a very simple lifestyle and adopting distinctive clothing, they deliberately set themselves apart from others and maintain a readily discernable identity, besides avoiding the interaction with the outside world involved in keeping up with new styles. By deliberately minimizing contact with the outside, by making a virtue out of their uniqueness, and by carefully socializing their children, they contribute significantly to their protracted period of "suspended animation." Some of these groups have existed for hundreds of years with very little change, and show essentially no signs of accelerating their pace of change today.

The Quakers, on the other hand, have not physically isolated themselves. In fact, among their members are many high-status, highly educated professionals. Quakers, moreover, are politically and socially motivated and involved. Yet the Quaker sect, which originated in the mid-1600s, has not become a full-fledged denomination. The Methodist Church and the Society of Friends today are quite different kinds of organizations, although both started out as sectarian movements. Yinger contrasts these two groups in making a very important theoretical suggestion concerning why one group will proceed along the continuum to denominational status while another will stop short at the institutionalized-sect stage. He states that differential status improvement could not be a cause, since members of both groups have moved up the class ladder in fairly equal proportions. There does seem to be some difference, however, in intensity of persecution. Quakers were more vigorously opposed and persecuted than Methodists everywhere. Thus conceivably the Quakers could have developed a stronger feeling of cultural isolation and thus greater internal solidarity.

But at best Yinger suggests that such could only be a proximate cause. The really important question is, Why were the Quakers more vigorously opposed than the Methodists? Answering this question requires examining the nature of the group's original protest. Yinger's suggestion is that those sects that emphasize problems of individual anxiety, sin, and salvation tend to evolve into denominations, while sects whose concern is focused on social evils and injustices will become established or institutionalized sects.[17] Radically different kinds of protest distinguished the early Methodists from the early Quakers. The Wesley brothers and other early Methodists were concerned primarily with individual morality and worked primarily to rescue people from their sin. Quakers, however, attacked society and called for political reforms, for an end to societal injustice and discrimination, for an end to poverty. Certainly society could more easily tolerate, even encourage, the Methodists' emphasis yet feel threatened by the Quakers', a fact that goes far in explaining why one sect was persecuted vigorously and the other not nearly so much.

The point here is not so much that as a result of societal persecution and opposition a group (such as the Quakers) may be forced back on its own resources and develop higher group identification and morale. The point is that such a group finds its feeling of estrangement from society intensified—it feels less at home in society and is less likely to evolve to full-blown denominational status, one characteristic of which is a relatively cozy, supportive relationship with the governing structure of the society. The stance the Quakers adopted placed them in a role more like that of an antagonist, and less like that of even "loyal opposition," as we understand that term from British parliamentary politics.

In a sense, the physical isolation of the cooperative religious groups is matched by the political and social isolation of the Quakers. Moreover, the established cooperative sects are also in opposition to much that exists in society, which is viewed as basically evil and as a source of contamination. Many of these groups do not even vote in national or local elections. Established sects such as the Quakers, on the other hand, do not express their opposition to society by withdrawing; they become activists and try to change society. In either case, however, such groups are inhibited in moving along the path to standard denominational status.

THE CULT

The final type of religious organization to consider is the religious cult. A *cult* is similar to a sect in its rejection of the religious patterns and formulations of denominations—or of whatever the society's dominant form(s) of religion happens to be. Cult members were either not attracted to dominant religious groups in the first place or, like sectarians, became disenchanted with commonly accepted religious forms. The cult differs from the sect, however, in that the former does not call for a return to the original, pure religion, but rather emphasizes the new—a new revelation or insight provided by a supernatural power, say, or the rediscovery of an old revelation that had been lost and unknown these many years (and which is therefore new to this age). Cults

[17] Yinger, *The Scientific Study of Religion,* pp. 266–68.

thus tend to be out of the mainstream of the dominant religious system in a society. Although there will usually be some overlapping of ideology and terminology, cults deliberately contrast themselves with dominant traditional religious groups. As might be expected, cults frequently employ new terminology and symbols. Discourses of some groups, such as the Great I Am, are hardly intelligible to the uninitiated. The themes of cults tend to be mystical and esoteric. Further, a cult is more likely than any other type of religious group to be centered around a charismatic leader—that is, a person who is believed to have been given special revelation or knowledge and the ability to open the door of truth and insight to the uninitiated. Father Divine, Daddy Grace, Mary Baker Eddy, the Reverend Jim Jones, and the Reverend Moon are such types.

Cults also have a strong individualistic emphasis, stressing peace of mind and getting the individual in tune with the supernatural, while exhibiting relatively little concern with social change. Cults tend to be urban centered, in part because they have traditionally not attracted great hordes of people and therefore need a large population to draw from, but likely also in part because cults tend to attract the disenchanted, those persons looking for meaningful attachments to counterbalance their anonymity—persons who are probably more likely to be found in urban settings. Cults seldom develop much of an organizational structure, often tend to remain small and informal, and can be quite casual about membership requirements. They may not even require followers to sever their other religious affiliations.

Cults tend to be rather transitory and short-lived. Being dependent on a charismatic leader, they tend to dissolve when the leader dies, disappears, or is discredited. Occasionally, however, a cult persists, develops a structure and means of leadership succession, grows in size, and actually moves toward denominational status on the church-sect continuum. In a study of cults in Alberta, Canada, W. E. Mann found the following characteristics of members: Anglo-Saxon by ethnic background, more female than male, individuals rather than family units, avid readers with above average educational attainment, highly mobile, and although of comfortable financial means, seeming to lack full middle-class acceptance.[18] Although a few writers have placed the cult beyond the extreme end of the church-sect continuum, another way of viewing it is to see it as an alternate to the sect at one end which may move onto the continuum at some point and give evidence of evolution toward denominational or quasi-denominational status. Figure 5–1 shows what we are suggesting. The dotted line associated with the cult indicates the possibility that it may change, not die, and get on the evolutionary road toward denominational status. A classic example is Christian Science, which began as a cult (with Mary Baker Eddy as its leader), but which today exhibits most of the characteristics

---

[18] W. E. Mann, *Sect, Cult, and Church in Alberta* (Toronto: University of Toronto Press, 1955), pp. 5–8, 37–40.

FIGURE 5–1

of a standard denomination. Similarly, the Nation of Islam ("Black Muslims"), which originally met all the criteria of a cult—it began as a small group with a charismatic leader (Elijah Muhammed) who preached a new doctrine of Black supremacy and Islam (out of the mainstream of Christianity), it emphasized individual self-help rather than societal reform, and it was primarily urban—is now showing definite signs of moving toward a denominational pattern.

It must be noted that cults constitute a most viable phenomenon today. If anything, their numbers and popularity are increasing. Faith-healing cults continue to abound; cults that center around Eastern religious ideas and individual gurus have gained in popularity; interest in the occult and the formation of groups around the practice of the occult have increased; and segments of the drug culture that celebrate the use of mind-expanding drugs as a religious enterprise continue to emerge. All of these constitute groups or movements. The cult phenomenon is very much alive and well, although individual cults themselves may be extremely transitory as they flower today and wither tomorrow.

JIM JONES'S PEOPLES TEMPLE AS CULT

To illustrate some of the points we have made concerning cults we shall look somewhat specifically at the Reverend Jim Jones's Peoples Temple as a representative religious cult. Although Jim Jones started off traditionally enough as an ordained minister in a standard denomination that had only some slight sectarian tendencies, he gradually began sounding like a cult leader with a new message to bring.

First, that new message.[19] The date is November, 1969; the place is a bona fide Christian church—the Peoples Temple Christian Church in Ukiah, California. The Reverend Jim Jones is preaching.

> The King James Bible is full of contradictions and errors. . . . If there were a God in Heaven, do you think he would let me say these things about his Holy Word? If there is a God in Heaven, let him strike me dead![20]

[19] All quotations are as attributed to the Rev. Jim Jones by Jeannie Mills. Reprinted by permission of A & W Publishers, Inc., New York, from *Six Years with God: Life Inside Rev. Jim Jones's Peoples Temple* by Jeannie Mills. Copyright © 1979 by MBR/Investments, Inc.

[20] Mills, *Six Years with God*, p. 121. Reprinted by permission of A & W Publishers, Inc.

Was this a "new" message? If not new, it was unusual—to say the least—from a Christian pulpit. Note that Jones is not calling for a return to the original message or intent of Scripture as a sectarian would. He simply discredits the Bible and substitutes a new message. As Jones continues he sounds more and more like a cult leader.

> I have seen by divine revelation the total annihilation of this country and many other parts of the world. San Francisco will be flattened. The only survivors will be those people who are hidden in the cave that I have been shown in a vision. Those who go into this cave with me will be saved from the poisonous radioactive fallout that will follow the nuclear bomb attack. This cave is what led our church to migrate to this little valley from Indianapolis, Indiana. I have been shown that this cave goes deep into the earth. All the members of my church will stay in it until it is safe to come out. We have gathered in Redwood Valley for protection, and after the war is over we will be the only survivors. It will be up to our group to begin life anew on this continent.[21]

In a cult a charismatic leader[22] not only brings a new message but is frequently deified—or something very close to it. For example, Father Divine openly called himself God and his followers regarded him as such. By way of another example, in the Unification Church it is very difficult to distinguish when references to God are to God as commonly viewed in Judeo-Christian terms or to Reverend Moon himself. Often it does indeed seem to be Moon.

We note the same pattern with Jim Jones.

> Jim looked around the room again and in a loud voice called out, "Wilson." The room became silent.
>
> "Yes?" This time it was a middle-aged black woman sitting near the front.
>
> "You have been having a dull pain in your stomach even as you sit here today."
>
> "Yes."
>
> "To give you more faith I want you to know that I can see a bottle of aspirin in your bathroom medicine chest. It's sitting beside a prescription bottle that was given to you by a Dr. Edwards."
>
> Mrs. Wilson, who had been speaking softly, suddenly shouted out, "Yes, Lord!"
>
> "Who can know these things?" Jim asked with a sweet smile.
>
> Tears were flowing down her cheeks as she answered, "Only God could know."
>
> "You have a cancer in your stomach. You don't even know it is there but by the power of love I will make it pass."
>
> Mrs. Wilson went into the restroom with one of the women that Jim indicated was a nurse and a few minutes later they returned. The nurse was holding a

---

21 Mills, *Six Years with God,* p. 122. Reprinted by permission of A & W Publishers, Inc.

22 A charismatic leader (a concept introduced into sociology by Max Weber) is a person thought by his or her followers to (1) possess special qualities superior to ordinary people, sometimes to the point of seeing the leader as divine; (2) have access to special knowledge or revelation; (3) be directed to lead his or her followers down a new, perhaps revolutionary, path; and (4) be able to create a special relationship with his or her followers—what amounts to a "calling" to them to a level of trust, love, and obedience that they had not known before.

mass of smelly flesh covered with blood in a handful of tissues. Jim asked the nurse to take it around to show those who might be skeptical. He took his dark glasses off for a moment as he looked lovingly at the woman and said, "This is the cancer that left your body, and I tell you that it will never return. Praise God!" And praise she did, along with everyone else in the room. But the praise was not for God, it was all directed toward Jim Jones.[23]

Additional evidence of the centrality and power of the leader in a cult can be seen in the following reflections by Jeannie Mills.

> I was amazed at how little disagreement there was between the members of this church. Before we joined the church, Al and I couldn't even agree on whom to vote for in the presidential election. Now that we all belonged to a group, family arguments were becoming a thing of the past. There was never a question of who was right, because Jim was always right. When our large household met to discuss family problems, we didn't ask for opinions. Instead, we put the question to the children, "What would Jim do?" It took the difficulty out of life. There was a type of "manifest destiny" which said the Cause was right and would succeed. Jim was right and those who agreed with him were right. If you disagreed with Jim, you were wrong. It was as simple as that.[24]

. . .

> He began to hint broadly that he was none other than "God Almighty." In a secret meeting he told us that he knew his previous incarnations. He bragged that he had been Buddha, the Bab, Jesus Christ, and, most recently, Lenin. "Of course," he warned them, "this is highly confidential and you aren't to tell anyone else. The members might not understand, especially about that last incarnation."
>
> When he realized that his staff members were awed by this revelation, he decided that the rest of his members would probably be impressed, too. In the next Sunday service he announced that he was going to tell those who were present one of his greatest secrets. With a great deal of ceremony he announced, "I have lived on this earth before. I have come for a special mission and you who are following me are my chosen people. Most of you have been with me during some of my previous incarnations. I lived thousands of years ago as Buddha. Then I spent a short incarnation as the Bab, the person who founded the Bahai faith. I have lived on earth as Jesus the Christ, and my last incarnation was in Russia as Vladimir Lenin." He spoke with such authority and sincerity that we all believed him.
>
> It was a wonderful secret and we felt privileged that he had shared it with us. "We are so fortunate to be able to follow him" was the sentiment expressed by most of the members. I'm sure that if Jim had known what was just around the corner he wouldn't have been so anxious to make these astounding claims. He was openly bragging that he was God Almighty by the time the San Francisco temple was ready to be used as a worship center.[25]

---

[23] Mills, *Six Years with God*, pp. 123–24. Reprinted by permission of A & W Publishers, Inc.

[24] Mills, *Six Years with God*, p. 147. Reprinted by permission of A & W Publishers, Inc.

[25] Mills, *Six Years with God*, pp. 180–81. Reprinted by permission of A & W Publishers, Inc.

Sometimes the charismatic leader is viewed as having extraordinary, miracle-working power. Note Jones the miracle worker in the following scene, described by Jeannie Mills.

There were more people than usual at the Sunday service, and for some reason the church members hadn't brought enough food to feed everyone. It became apparent that the last fifty people weren't going to get any meat. Jim announced, "Even though there isn't enough food to feed this multitude, I am blessing the food that we have and multiplying it—just as Jesus did in biblical times."

Sure enough, a few moments after he made this startling announcement, Eva Pugh came out of the kitchen beaming, carrying two platters filled with fried chicken. A big cheer came from the people assembled in the room, especially from the people who were at the end of the line.

The "blessed chicken" was extraordinarily delicious, and several of the people mentioned that Jim had produced the best-tasting chicken they had ever eaten. One of the members, Chuck Beikman, a man who had come with Jim from Indianapolis, jokingly mentioned to a few people standing near him that he had seen Eva drive up a few moments earlier with buckets from the Kentucky Fried Chicken stand. He smiled as he said, "The person that blessed that chicken was Colonel Sanders."

During the evening meeting Jim mentioned the fact that Chuck had made fun of his gift. "He lied to some of the members here, telling them that the chicken had come from a local shop," Jim stormed. "But the Spirit of Justice has prevailed. Because of his lie Chuck is in the men's restroom right now, wishing that he was dead. He is vomiting and has diarrhea so bad he can't talk!"

An hour later a pale and shaken Chuck Beikman walked out of the men's room and up to the front, being supported by one of the guards. Jim asked him, "Do you have anything you'd like to say?"

Chuck looked up weakly and answered, "Jim, I apologize for what I said. Please forgive me."

As we looked at Chuck, we vowed in our hearts that we would never question any of Jim's "miracles"—at least not out loud. Years later, we learned that Jim had put a mild poison in a piece of cake and given it to Chuck.[26]

Although the charisma of the leader is important in maintaining a cult, it is also necessary that the group have important goals and aspirations. The group needs more substance than hero worship by itself. The ostensible goals of the Peoples Temple are epitomized in Jim Jones's words, as follows:

"I have the answers to the problems of society. Someday I will be the ruler of the United States. I will eliminate racism, political oppression, ecological imbalances, and the problem of the superrich and the superpoor. I will make the whole country become like our community. I call this "Apostolic Socialism."[27]

It probably needs to be said at this point, in all fairness, that much of the time the group strenuously opposed racism, was itself highly integrated ra-

[26] Mills, *Six Years with God*, pp. 151–52. Reprinted by permission of A & W Publishers, Inc.

[27] Mills, *Six Years with God*, p. 218. Reprinted by permission of A & W Publishers, Inc.

cially, and provided for the care of scores of lost, homeless, and desperate people. It hardly needs mentioning of course that some of these were among those who lost their lives in Jonestown.

In the following vignette we note the introduction of the idea of mass suicide that became the ultimate test of dedication to the "Cause" as identified by Jones in the preceding quote. The year is 1973, five years before the deaths at Jonestown.

> One afternoon the P.C.[28] counsellors received an emergency message. "Come to the church immediately for a special meeting." We dropped what we were doing and left as instructed. When we arrived it was obvious that Jim was very upset.
>
> He began, "Eight people left the church last night. They cut the telephone wires so Tom couldn't call to warn us." He was speaking in a low voice as though he were afraid the walls might hear what he was saying. "No one knows why they left, but Jim and Terry Cobb, Wayne Pietila, Micki Touchette, and four others all disappeared. Don't worry, though, I'll find them." Jim tried to sound confident, but then he shook his head in despair. "These eight people might cause our church to go down. They could say things that would discredit our group. This might be the time for all of us to make our translation together." He had mentioned the idea of a "translation" a few times before, but no one had ever taken it seriously. His idea was that all the counsellors would take poison or kill themselves at the same time, and then he promised we would all be translated to a distant planet to live with him for eternity. The few who believed this fairy tale said they'd be happy to do it anytime. Now, however, faced with death, it became obvious that there were many who didn't want to.
>
> "What about the other church members, and our children?" Linda Amos asked.
>
> "Oh, yes, that's the problem. Those who would be left behind." Jim was speaking slowly and deliberately now, and it seemed that he was trying to formulate his ideas as he spoke. "Perhaps we could devise a plan where the children would be sent to another country first." I relaxed as I realized that his plan wasn't as well thought out as I had feared. Since he hadn't worked out these important details, I was sure he couldn't insist that we all kill ourselves right now.
>
> "I want to take a vote today to find out how dedicated you all are," Jim said. "Life is a bore. Surely no one here is enamored with his existence. You've seen too much reality in all the hours of counselling at the P.C. meetings. How many of you here today would be willing to take your own lives now to keep the church from being discredited? Perhaps this way we will go down in history as revolutionaries. We could leave a note saying that we were doing this as a sign that we want peace on earth, or that we couldn't exist as an apostolic socialist group, or something like that."[29]

But one begins to see, once the commitment to the group and its leader has been made and dependency upon the group has been established, most anything becomes believable. Note the following account by Mills.

---

[28] The Peoples Council — the inner core leaders comprising some thirty to fifty people.

[29] Mills, *Six Years with God*, pp. 230–31. Reprinted by permission of A & W Publishers, Inc.

Jim told us another big secret that night. "One of the things that Carolyn had been doing was negotiating the purchase of an atomic bomb for us." He was talking almost in a whisper in case the room was bugged. "We have everything but the detonator, and we are trying to get one right now. It is important for our group to have power, and any person with an atomic bomb has power." He began to explain to us how he believed World War III would start. "I believe that someone will probably sneak up from South America and detonate an atom bomb in the United States. Then our country will assume that the bomb was sent from Russia. Our country will retaliate by sending a bomb over there, and within a short time, there will be a nuclear holocaust. Everyone will be destroyed, except the people who are living below the equator."

It was a wild theory, and most of us assumed it was another scare tactic, like the first bomb theory and his cave in Redwood Valley. The part that did impress us, though, was that we were the owners of an atomic bomb. We now felt we had enough power to make people respect and fear our group.[30]

But in the end, all Jim Jones had was potassium cyanide and the promise of an immortality that comes with dying for a cause you believe in. Yet that was enough. And a religious cult had flourished, but now is gone.

REFINEMENTS OF THE CHURCH-SECT TYPOLOGY

Although the church-sect typology that has been presented and applied in this chapter is time honored, and although we continue to see it as helpful, particularly in its descriptive capacity, the concept has not been without its critics. In fact a very substantial literature has emerged in the last twenty-five years on this topic.[31] Some of the critics suggest refinements; others suggest alternatives.

Actually, in a very real sense of the term, much of what we have presented in this chapter has been in the nature of refinements of the original church-sect typology. The concepts "denomination," "institutionalized sect," and "cult" are all refinements of the original typology proposed by Troeltsch and Weber.

---

[30] Mills, *Six Years with God,* pp. 277–78. Reprinted by permission of A & W Publishers, Inc.

[31] See for example, Benton Johnson, "A Critical Appraisal of the Church-Sect Typology," *American Sociological Review* 22, no. 1 (1957), 88–92; idem, "On Church and Sect," *American Sociological Review* 28, no. 1 (1967), 64–68; idem, "Church-Sect Revisited," *Journal for the Scientific Study of Religion* 10, no. 2 (1971), 124–37; Erich Goode, "Some Critical Observations on the Church-Sect Dimension," *Journal for the Scientific Study of Religion* 6, no. 1 (1967), 69–77; idem, "Further Reflections on the Church-Sect Dimension," *Journal for the Scientific Study of Religion* 6, no. 2 (1967), 270–75; N. J. Demerath III, "In a Sow's Ear," *Journal for the Scientific Study of Religion* 6, no. 1 (1967), 77–84; Allan W. Eister, "Toward a Radical Critique of Church-Sect Typologizing," *Journal for the Scientific Study of Religion* 6, no. 1 (1967), 85–90; J. Kenneth Benson and James Dorsett, "Church-Sect Replaced," *Journal for the Scientific Study of Religion* 10, no. 2 (1971), 138–51; James A. Beckford, "Religious Organization," *Current Sociology* XXI, no. 2 (1975), 5–170, particularly 96–102.

Another approach by way of refinement has been to elaborate the list of characteristics of sects and/or churches. For example, Liston Pope makes twenty-one distinctions between the church and the sect in his classic study of the religious life of Gastonia, North Carolina.[32]

Benton Johnson went in the opposite direction and suggested that there is really only one essential distinction between the church and the sect. That distinction is whether a religious group accepts or rejects its larger social environment. The sect rejects; the church or denomination accepts.[33] This distinction is of course highly compatible with all of our discussion in this chapter. Johnson is simply trying to distill everything into its essence. The sect opposes and challenges and rejects much of what it sees in the surrounding society and its culture; the church or denomination compromises, reinforces, and accepts most of that same society and culture.

Before Johnson's single-variable measure (1963), Yinger (1957) had proposed two criteria for differentiating churches from sects: degree of inclusiveness-exclusiveness of the group, and degree of attention paid by the group to the task of social integration as opposed to satisfaction of personal need.[34] By 1970 Yinger added Johnson's criterion and changed his earlier second criterion to emphasize degree of bureaucratization and success in integrating a variety of subunits into one structure.[35]

Roland Robertson has suggested two criteria: the basis of legitimacy as perceived by the leaders of the religious group, and the principle of membership implemented by the group.[36] The legitimacy measure contrasts views of religious leaders: (1) the view that one's group is only one among other sets of acceptable or valid religious vehicles (religious pluralism), (2) the view that one's group is the only valid religious form (unique, true religion). The membership principle contrasts "relatively demanding standards of admission and/or religious performance" (exclusivism) with low standards of acceptance (inclusivism).[37]

Another interesting modification has been contributed by Stephen Steinberg. He has analyzed the emergence of Reform Judaism from its "parent," Orthodox Judaism, not as formation of a sect but as a "church movement." That is, Reform Judaism did not object to any "perversion of true religion" embodied in Orthodox Judaism but to the continued insistence by

[32] Liston Pope, *Millhands and Preachers* (New Haven: Yale University Press, 1942), pp. 122–24.

[33] Benton Johnson, "On Church and Sect," *American Sociological Review* 28, no. 4 (1963), 539–49.

[34] J. Milton Yinger, *Religion, Society, and the Individual* (New York: Macmillan, 1957), pp. 147–48.

[35] J. Milton Yinger, *The Scientific Study of Religion* (New York: Macmillan, 1970), p. 257.

[36] Roland Robertson, *The Sociological Interpretation of Religion* (New York: Schocken Books, 1970), pp. 123ff.

[37] Robertson, *The Sociological Interpretation of Religion*, p. 124.

Orthodox Judaism on retaining the "old ways"—the Reform movement sought to "modernize" Judaism. Building on Benton Johnson's single-variable distinction between church and sect that we earlier described—in which a religious organization accepting the surrounding social environment is defined as a church and one rejecting it as a sect—Steinberg points out that the rebel group (Reform Judaism) did not follow the common route of the sect by rejecting its social environment, but accepted and accommodated to that environment.[38] Although Steinberg notes that conditions giving rise to such a "church movement" are rare, such a development is well worth noting. Furthermore, our understanding of the dynamics of such a development is enhanced by our understanding of what "normally" happens along the church-sect continuum.

[38] Stephen Steinberg, "Reform Judaism: The Origin and Evolution of a 'Church Movement,'" *Journal for the Scientific Study of Religion* 5, no. 1 (1965), 117–29.

III

RELIGION IN SOCIETY

6

Religion and Politics

Although politics is nearly as variously defined as religion, there is consensus about at least two characteristics. First of all, politics (like its corollary, government) consists fundamentally of norms—that is, ways of reaching decisions, procedures for carrying out certain tasks, expectations about rights and privileges. Second, politics is more concerned with the societal norms that stipulate how and by whom coercive power shall be used in the pursuit of societal goals.[1] The employment of coercive power by government appears necessary primarily because the available supply of rewards that people strive for, both individually and collectively, is limited. Such rewards include money (or other means of obtaining goods and services), prestige, honor, respect, power, love, affection, and the like. Although such rewards are not necessarily in scarce supply, their supply is finite. That is to say, it is a relatively rare person who feels satiated so far as his or her share of such rewards is concerned. Most people want at least a few more dollars, a few more things, than they presently possess. And universally people could use a little more love and affection and a little more respect, even if they are not specifically seeking fame or power over others.

The resulting discrepancy between supply and demand places people inevitably into a competitive position with respect to garnering their desired

[1] J. Milton Yinger, *The Scientific Study of Religion* (New York: Macmillan, 1970), p. 408.

share of available rewards. At this point we encounter politics and government as the social system or institution in a society that develops an order to regulate the process of reward seeking and to reduce the disruptive tendency inherent in the competition for rewards which could result in a war of all against all. Thus we understand the concept of politics to be the norms that designate the ultimate coercive power and the process by which the norms that regulate the exercise of power and authority get implemented. This accords well with Harold Lasswell's classic definition of politics as who gets what, when, and how—that is, the process of determining the distribution of society's rewards and balancing power relationships and claims.[2]

THE RELATIONSHIP OF RELIGION AND POLITICS

What, then, is the relationship of religion to politics? We should expect, considering the broad scope of our definition of politics, which implies a great diversity of processes, norms, and behavior, that there will be a variety of ways in which religion relates to the institution of politics.

This certainly has been the case. But we shall not go into all of the many types of relationships. We shall simply outline the range of possibilities and then discuss the most common pattern.

At one end of the continuum is the "pure theocracy." *Theocracy* literally means "rule by God." Thus religious leaders are seen as ruling all of society in God's name and ostensibly according to his wishes. Actually, the state as a distinct entity does not exist in a theocracy. The rule of Israel by God's prophets in the Old Testament period is an example of the pure theocracy. A prophet such as Samuel was seen as God's spokesman regarding not only religious matters but political and governmental matters as well. Interestingly, the people chafed under this arrangement, pleaded embarrassment in the face of surrounding societies who were under the rule of kings, and appealed for a similar "separation" of church and state.

Closely related is the *modified theocracy*. In this case, while the state is subordinate to the religious institution and its leaders, even in temporal affairs, the state nevertheless exists as a separate entity. The state is seen here as the enforcement agency of religion, an agency necessary because of the tendency of people to deviate from societal norms but yet to depend on religion for its authority. Most medieval European societies dominated by Roman Catholicism were of this type. Similarly, John Calvin's Geneva and the early Massachusetts Bay Colony are good examples. Further, the relationship of Buddhism to the government of Sri Lanka (Ceylon) from the third century B.C.

---

[2] Harold Lasswell, *Politics: Who Gets What, When, and How* (New York: Meridian Books, 1958).

until the nineteenth century A.D. was that of a modified theocracy. Only a Buddhist could become king, and his chief function was to protect and promote the faith. On the other hand, the Buddhist monks not only instructed and advised the royal court and conducted the king's coronation in the temple, but they held enormous political power in their influence and control over the masses. They could incite or prevent rebellion. No king could rule without their support.

It is worth noting at this point that the inclusion of the state within the religious system, or at a minimum some kind of control over the state by religion, is not simply a quaint, antiquarian phenomenon or legacy from preindustrial times. It is an almost universal feature of the utopian and millenarian groups and movements of the nineteenth and twentieth centuries—groups that endeavored to establish models of the perfect Kingdom of God—in addition to such a recent group as Jim Jones's People's Temple and the Jonestown experiment in Guyana.

At the other extreme is a *totalitarian* system, in which religion is either controlled by the state as a tool or enforcement arm of the state, or is outlawed altogether. A pure form of a totalitarian system is more theoretical than real, although the goal of the Bolshevik revolution in the Soviet Union in 1917 was such. What religion they could not eradicate entirely, they intended to control and manipulate.

Midway between the extremes of theocracy on the one hand and totalitarianism on the other is the concept of *total separation*. In this arrangement the arenas in which religion and politics operate are entirely distinct with no overlap. There one must assume that religion serves the soul, and the state the body—or that religion is entirely an individualized, subjective, internalized phenomenon, while politics and the state serve the group, deal with externals relative to survival, and are entirely secular. Such total separation has never been achieved, and thus remains purely a theoretical possibility.

Certainly *partial separation* is the most sociologically sound option. Inasmuch as both religion and politics are social institutions and consist of subgroups, norms, and people, they interact with one another; they sometimes overlap in their functions; they often involve the same people; they seek commitment and involvement from the same people. It is of course partial separation that describes the system with which we are most familiar in North America and Europe. But partial separation is itself a variable and tends to fluctuate toward one extreme or the other as implied by the range outlined in Figure 6-1. Figure 6-1 tries to present in summary graphic form the options we have been discussing. That is, the middle, neutral position would be "total separation." The relationship between church and state could then go in either direction toward total religious control and domination at one end ("pure theocracy"), or total state control at the other extreme ("totalitarianism"), with various intermediate points on the way.

| Pure
Theocracy | Modified
Theocracy | Partial
Separation | Total
Separation | Partial
Separation | Modified
Totalitarianism | Totalitarianism |

FIGURE 6–1 *A continuum of the possible relationships of Church and State.*

THE INFLUENCE OF RELIGION
ON POLITICS

We now continue our discussion of religion and politics by looking at specific ways in which religion affects, or tries to affect, politics. That is, we shall be asking to what extent and in what ways religion can be seen to be an influence on action and outcomes.

Religion and Voting Behavior

A widely recognized point of religious influence over politics is that of people's voting preference and behavior. The supporters of most every candidate for public office at all levels can be heard during the campaign talking about trying to get the "Catholic vote" or the "Jewish vote" or the "Baptist vote" or, most recently, the "Evangelical vote," or perhaps the support and vote of the "Moral Majority." Such interest gives very explicit recognition to the correlation that exists between religious affiliation and commitment on the one hand, and voting behavior on the other. That there should be a correlation is exactly what would be expected, of course, if religious affiliation and commitment mean anything at all. What one believes with respect to that which is good, true, and desirable, as well as what God intends for people and society, could be expected to influence the choices one makes in the political arena. That is, religion should affect people's voting patterns.

As we prepare to present evidence in this area we must mention one problem that we will have in interpreting the data. That is that although we will see large differences by religious affiliation and commitment, the differences cannnot be traced totally and simply to religion. For example, we will later see a fairly strong relationship between religion and social class. That is, certain religious groups tend to have disproportionate numbers of certain classes as members. If in a particular instance the members of a denomination tend to be predominately working class and also vote overwhelmingly for Democratic candidates, we have two correlations with political activity at work—both religious affiliation and social class. We want to be alert to such a problem of interpretation. But first some data.

Nearly everyone is aware of the historical tendency for American Catholics to vote Democratic and for Protestants to be more likely to favor the Republican party. From national survey data gathered in 1970, we find the following political party identifications by religious preference. Among Protestants, 44 percent identify with the Democratic party, while 55 percent of

Catholics and 67 percent of Jews so identified. Such differences are as one might expect, closely matched by differences in Republican party identification. Protestants (27 percent) are more likely than either Catholics (14 percent) or Jews (8 percent) to identify with the Republican party. Approximately equal proportions in each religious group identify themselves as Independents (22 percent of Protestants and 25 percent of both Catholics and Jews).[3] The data with respect to the 1968 presidential election in Table 6–1 are consistent with the 1970 party preference findings and support the casual observation made repeatedly that Protestants are more likely to vote Republican, Catholics and Jews more likely to vote Democratic.

As we have noted in earlier chapters, data on Protestant denominations also reflect characteristic differences. Table 6–2 shows these differences with respect to voting behavior (as reflected by respondents' self-report of voting behavior). Note that only the Baptists were more likely to vote for the Democratic candidate than for the Republican. In fact, Baptists were also more likely than other Protestant groups to vote for Wallace. The remaining denominations preferred Nixon over Humphrey by margins of more than two to one, with the margin for Episcopalians reaching nearly six to one (68.8 percent vs. 12.5 percent).

Even more recent public opinion poll data show similar patterns. George Gallup's survey of how people voted in the 1976 presidential election shows that while 57 percent of Catholics who voted cast their vote for Jimmy Carter, only 46 percent of Protestants did; and while 53 percent of Protestants who voted gave their vote to Gerald Ford, only 42 percent of Catholics did so. In each group 1 percent voted for other candidates.[4]

Although a detailed discussion of the relationship of social class to religion is reserved for a later chapter, we must point out here that an extremely important social-class factor accompanies these observed relationships between denominational affiliation and voting behavior—Episcopalians and Presbyterians, who were so extremely likely to choose Nixon over Humphrey in 1968, are also more likely than members of other Protestant groups to be of high socioeconomic status. Since higher-status persons tend to favor Republican over Democratic candidates, we find that status and religious affiliation reinforce one another and in combination yield dramatic differences in support for particular political parties and their candidates.

We suggested earlier that differences in political party affiliation and political behavior are not only related to religious affiliation but also to indexes of religiosity, including persons' perceptions of their own religious commitments and orientation. For example, Hadden reports dramatic differences

[3] Ronald L. Johnstone (director), National Opinion Research Center survey conducted for the Lutheran Council in the U.S.A., 1970.
[4] George H. Gallup, *The Gallup Poll: Public Opinion 1972–1977* (Wilmington, Del.: Scholarly Resources, 1978), p. 910.

TABLE 6–1 *Presidential Candidate Preference of Selected Religious Groups, 1968*

RELIGIOUS AFFILIATION	HUMPHREY (DEMOCRATIC)	NIXON (REPUBLICAN)	WALLACE (AMERICAN INDEPENDENT)	NO ANSWER	DIDN'T VOTE
Protestant (N = 975)	21.7%	36.5%	7.3%	3.4%	31.0%
Catholic (N = 355)	37.7	25.9	4.5	3.4	28.5
Jewish (N = 24)	83.3	8.3	0.0	4.2	4.2
Other (N = 42)	28.6	23.8	2.4	0.0	45.2
None (N = 66)	24.5	33.0	1.1	9.6	31.9

Source: Ronald L. Johnstone (director), National Opinion Research Center survey conducted for the Lutheran Council in the U.S.A., 1970.

TABLE 6–2 *Presidential Candidate Preference of Selected Protestant Denominations, 1968*

DENOMINATION	HUMPHREY (DEMOCRATIC)	NIXON (REPUBLICAN)	WALLACE (AMERICAN INDEPENDENT)	NO ANSWER	DIDN'T VOTE
Baptist (N = 333)	28.2%	20.1%	9.9%	2.1%	39.6%
Episcopalian (N = 32)	12.5	68.8	3.1	2.1	12.5
Lutheran (N = 120)	22.5	47.5	4.2	4.2	21.7
Methodist (N = 187)	20.9	44.4	5.3	2.1	27.3
Presbyterian (N = 67)	13.4	58.2	6.0	4.5	17.9
United Church of Christ (N = 51)	23.5	49.0	0.0	7.8	19.6
Others and No Preference (N = 185)	14.6	34.1	9.7	4.9	36.8

Source: Ronald L. Johnstone (director), National Opinion Research Center survey conducted for the Lutheran Council in the U.S.A., 1970.

TABLE 6–3 *Party Preference of Protestant Clergymen by Theological Position*

THEOLOGICAL POSITION	REPUBLICAN	INDEPENDENT	DEMOCRAT
Fundamentalist	68%	18%	13%
Conservative	62	22	15
Neo-Orthodox	39	26	35
Liberal	36	28	36

Source: Jeffrey Hadden, *The Gathering Storm in the Churches* (Garden City, NY.: Doubleday, 1969), p. 74.

among a sample of more than seven thousand Protestant clergy in terms of party affiliation related to their self-designation of theological inclination. The data in Table 6–3 show clearly that the more theologically liberal a clergy-member is, the less likely he or she is to prefer the Republican party and the more likely he or she is to prefer the Democrats or be an uncommitted independent.

Legislation of Morality

Another significant area in which religion influences the political structure is in the "legislation of morality." American state and local governments have been riddled with so-called blue laws, many of which are still on the books—and most of which reflect strong religious influence. Laws restricting Sunday business activity, laws specifying how close to schools and churches bars and taverns may operate, laws restricting the sale of intoxicating beverages, laws regarding the sale and distribution of birth-control devices—all these laws evidence strong influences by religious groups. Some are carry-overs from Puritan colonization; some are related to concentrations of Catholic immigrants; some are traceable to conservative Protestantism which has been influential throughout our history.

To be more specific in the area of the legislation of morality we shall look at several historical relationships between religion and the political process and structure in the United States.

Prohibition and Birth Control   The struggle against "demon rum" that eventually resulted in ratification of the Eighteenth Amendment (1919), which prohibited the sale of most intoxicating beverages in the United States, is a clear example of the influence of religious groups in the political arena. The Prohibition amendment was very largely the work of a well-organized church lobby, the Anti-Saloon League. The league was organized in the Calvary Baptist Church in Washington, D.C., in 1895, and although similar temperance societies cooperated with it, churches were the primary source of its membership, support, and leadership. Leo Pfeffer reports that between 1911 and 1925

111

an annual average of thirty thousand local churches, predominantly Baptist, Methodist, Presbyterian, and Congregational, were affiliated with the league.[5]

Pfeffer notes that the Anti-Saloon League did not deny that it was a political organization. When confronted with that charge, a league representative replied, "The Church is a machine and the League is a machine within a machine."[6] Pfeffer goes on to say

> Its effectiveness as a machine, as of any political machine, is measured by the fruits thereof; and the fruit of the league was the adoption of the Eighteenth Amendment within six years after the League formally launched its campaign for national prohibition. Though the League was less successful in retaining the victory it had won, its influence was respected and feared by many.[7]

The adoption of prohibition is a prime example of Protestant influences on the political system, while Catholics have an analogous influence with reference to birth-control legislation. Since Catholic doctrine maintains that any "artificial" interference with conception is inherently evil and sinful, the Catholic Church has worked long and hard to resist attempts to repeal or modify existing laws that prohibit the sale of birth-control devices or dissemination of information regarding their use. Earlier in American history Catholics were not alone in this stance—the "Comstock law," actually a set of laws passed by Congress in 1873 prohibiting mailing, transporting, or importing "obscene, lewd, or lascivious" materials, had support that also included Protestants and some groups that were at least ostensibly secular. Birth-control information and devices were interpreted as being included among the prohibitions detailed by these laws. Soon thereafter twenty-two states passed "little Comstock laws" that imposed strictures ranging from New York's restriction on physicians' freedom to prescribe lawful contraceptives (and then only "for the cure or prevention of disease"), to Massachusetts's ban on the publication of information and the distribution of material dealing with contraception, to Connecticut's absolute ban on birth control extending even to the private use of contraceptive devices.[8]

More recently we have seen attempts, largely unsuccessful as yet, by a variety of religious groups to influence legislatures and the Congress to repeal the liberalized abortion legislation that was passed and tested in the courts during the 1970s. Supporters of the "Pro-Life Amendment" to the United States Constitution are prominent protagonists in this area. Religious groups provide the major base of support.

---

[5] Leo Pfeffer, *Church, State, and Freedom* (Boston: Beacon Press, 1953), p. 200.

[6] Quoted in ibid., p. 200.

[7] Ibid.

[8] David M. Kennedy, *Birth Control in America* (New Haven: Yale University Press, 1970), p. 218.

Radical Right Politics and Religion—1950s Style   The so-called Radical Right political perspective of the 1950s that saw the reckless inquisition by Senator Joseph McCarthy and the destruction, or at best long interruption, of careers for many people included such ideas as opposition to communism and socialism in most any form, support for traditional free enterprise capitalism and its corollary limited government, commitment to traditional morality which would exclude and condemn such persons as "liberated" women, homosexuals, and civil libertarians, and frequently an expression of anti-Semitism as well. The Radical Right and its history in the United States is a fascinating topic in itself. But what is of primary interest to us in this text is the relationship and intermingling of radical right political philosophies and activities with fundamentalist Protestant religion. Particularly intriguing is the intimate association of fundamentalist Protestant theology with right-wing politics among many of the anti-Communist crusaders in the 1950s and 1960s. As Janson and Eismann state:

> Ultraconservative leaders have had considerable success, simply by preaching anticommunism, in rallying not only religious fundamentalists concerned about heresy but also political, economic, and social fundamentalists concerned about the liberal trends that are threatening their values.[9]

Some of the radical right groups tried to remain aloof from religion— Robert Welch's John Birch Society, for one. Welch did not reveal his personal religious convictions, if any, and said that he did not care what religion a person was. His ultimate appeal was not to religious beliefs but to what he viewed as fundamental American values. Other prominent right-wing political groups, however, made an intimate connection between the two. Fred C. Schwartz's Christian Anti-Communist Crusade, Billy James Hargis's Christian Crusade, and Carl McIntire's "20th Century Reformation Hour" were major groups with deep, explicit roots in Protestant fundamentalism. As Hargis has said, "I fight Communism . . . because it is part of my ordination vows, of my creed."[10] In his publication *Christian Crusade,* he states:

> Christian Crusade's fight against Communism is Christ's fight. Christ is using this Movement. The very fact that Christian Crusade has existed through fourteen years of opposition from powerful forces in high and low circles is proof that it is of God. . . . I know we are on the right track, getting the job done for Jesus.[11]

[9] Donald Janson and Bernard Eismann, *The Far Right* (New York: McGraw-Hill, 1963), p. 239.

[10] Billy James Hargis, television address, KAIL-TV, Fresno, California, October 25, 1964. Quoted in John H. Redekop, *The American Far Right* (Grand Rapids, Mich.: William B. Eerdmans, 1968), p. 17.

[11] Billy James Hargis, *Christian Crusade,* January-February 1962, p. 3. Quoted in Redekop, *The American Far Right,* p. 18.

The union of religious and political goals is clearly stated by Hargis: "We feel our mission to be God-given; to awaken our fellow citizens to the twin dangers of Communism and/or socialism and religious apostasy."[12] In fact, it becomes essentially impossible to separate religious from political and economic elements in these groups's positions. Such a merger is clearly seen in the following list of institutions for which the American Nazi party (another Radical Right group) is fighting: "(1) the White Race, which must be preserved above all; (2) the American Constitutional Republic; (3) the Christian traditions and culture of the West; (4) free enterprise and private property without the evil of criminal speculators."[13]

In discussing the connection between religion and politics that tends to exist among radical right groups, Murray Havens states that most of these groups "would substitute for religious tolerance an insistence on uniform acceptance not only of Christianity but of their particular highly dogmatic version of Christianity."[14] Their urging of Protestant fundamentalism merges smoothly with appeals for maximum cultural conformity based on small-town and rural America, an explicit antiintellectualism, and a defense of the status quo so far as economic and racial disparities are concerned.

It is interesting that while most authors who have analyzed radical right groups note the congruence and close association between right-wing political views and fundamentalist Protestant religion, seldom do they carry out much analysis of the relationship. One important exception is John Redekop, who discusses several intimate connections. One is a simplistic dualism. The fundamentalist sees only two categories, good and evil, with nothing in between. The radical right-winger sees fellow citizens as either Americans or Communists, one or the other. Tolerance is only for those who do not believe strongly in anything. Hatred of evil is therefore perfectly logical, and heresy hunting perfectly legitimate. Another characteristic of both fundamentalism and radical right philosophy is a conspiratorial view of the world. Satan conspires to detour people from the path of righteousness; communism does the same. Communism actually becomes the Devil personified—or better, politicized. As a result, all political discussion takes on a strong moral fervor. Politics thus becomes a crusade, and one's patriotism proof of a mature Christianity.

A third connection is the individualistic emphasis in fundamentalism (individual salvation), and a corresponding disapproval of social action and public welfare programs, which matches the radical right's laissez-faire economic and political ideology. Individuals are more important than society and are capable of satisfying their wants and needs in the free enterprise marketplace.

[12] Hargis, *Christian Crusade,* December 1962, p. 1. Quoted in Redekop, *The American Far Right,* p. 18.

[13] American Nazi Party, form letter mailed in response to routine inquiry signed by Lincoln Rockwell, commander, 1961, p. 2.

[14] Murray C. Havens, *The Challenges to Democracy* (Austin: University of Texas Press, 1965), pp. 82–83.

Governmental intervention here is morally wrong. Communism is therefore readily viewed as the epitome of evil.[15]

Although Murray Stedman is likely correct when he contends that "there is no apparent dictate in the inner logic of fundamentalism that would necessarily predispose its followers to political authoritarianism"[16]—that is, not all fundamentalists are or will become radical right-wingers—there is nevertheless a ready alliance between the two. When they coincide, as they frequently do, the connection is easy to understand, for the religious and the political views reinforce one another. It should be noted that this connection had been highly explicit in an earlier generation as well. In the early 1920s the spellbinding evangelist Billy Sunday convinced a lot of people that there was an extremely clever Satanic plot afoot in the world that true fundamentalist Christianity had to combat. The world conspiracy consisted of kaiserism (the First World War had just ended), bolshevism (the Communist Revolution in the Soviet Union occurred in 1917), evolutionism, higher criticism (modern biblical scholarship), and liberal theology in general—a mixture of certain theological, political, and scientific elements—all evil in their own right according to Billy Sunday and his followers.[17]

The New Religious Right—1980s Style   On the eve of the 1980s two developments came together to enhance very substantially the impact of the conservative or Fundamentalist-Evangelical segment in American religion and carry to a new level and to a new generation the linkage of right-wing politics and religion.

The first of these developments is the rapid development of what has come to be known as the "Electronic Church." This refers to the rapid expansion of preachers and groups, particularly from the fundamentalist wing of Protestantism, into a television minstry. It is of course true that religious broadcasting has existed since the beginnings of radio and television. In the early days, however, the programs were either extremely localized, or they were broadcast as part of the free public service obligation of the broadcasting media, which tended to put them at non-prime times such as the "God hour" Sunday mornings. What is different today is (1) the widespread outright ownership of radio and television stations by religious groups, (2) the full-time religious broadcasting on these stations that ensues from such ownership, and (3) as a corollary of this, the greater volume of religious broadcasting on radio and TV. In 1980, 1,400 radio stations and 60 television stations were wholly owned by religious groups. These stations produced thousands of hours of religious programming each week and generated $500 million in nontaxable revenue annually.

[15] Redekop, *The American Far Right,* chapter 10.

[16] Murray Stedman, *Religion and Politics in America* (New York: Harcourt Brace Jovanovich, Inc., 1964), p. 129.

[17] Erling Jorstad, *The Politics of Doomsday* (Nashville: Abingdon, 1970), p. 24.

While we do not wish to underestimate the significance of the electronic church (in fact, we are trying to feature not only its contemporary importance but even more its potential influence in the future), the extent of its audience and influence has been overplayed by the mass media themselves. William Martin pulls together some of the extravagant reports from recent books and popular magazines.[18] In a recent book by Ben Armstrong called *The Electric Church* (Nashville: Thomas Nelson, 1979), one reads about almost 130 million people drawn on Sundays to religious programs on TV and radio. The *Wall Street Journal* (July 11, 1980) credits a weekly audience of 128 million viewers for Oral Roberts, Pat Robertson, and Jerry Falwell. An article in *New York* magazine (October 6, 1980) not only sets membership in the electronic church at 130 million but asserts that contributions to teleministries total in the billions—a figure far in excess of the $500 million that is commonly credited to the combined fund-raising efforts of both radio and television ministries. Actually, many of the preachers for the electronic church are themselves becoming more modest in their claims. For example, whereas Rex Humbard's press materials once claimed an audience of "up to 100 million," his recent promotional literature says only 1.4 million.[19] There are still those at the other extreme, however. Martin notes, for example, the claims by the radio preacher Bert Clendennen, who has often told his hearers that his program reaches "one out of every two people on the face of this earth."[20]

But we do not need to rely on guesswork or projections based partly on public relations motivations, partly on a self-confident and optimistic outlook on one's work. The two major rating services for the broadcast media, Nielsen and Arbitron, have independently surveyed the audience for religious broadcasting that constitutes the electronic church and find a maximum audience for one TV preacher, Oral Roberts, to be 2,351,000.[21] Others, such as Robert Schuller, Rex Humbard, Jimmy Swaggart, and Jerry Falwell scale down from there. The total for the top ten programs is only 13,767,000.[22] We say "only" because there is no doubt that there is considerable overlap in the audiences of these programs. That is, one person will watch several and get counted several times. Martin suggests that there may be 7 to 10 million individual persons who watch these programs. That figure is probably on the generous side.

The upshot of this quick look at the numbers that might be involved in the electronic church is that although many of the popular claims of tens of millions of viewers and participants are significant overestimates, a substantial core and base remains.

---

[18] William Martin, "The Birth of a Media Myth," *The Atlantic* 247, no. 6 (January, 1981), 7–16.

[19] Ibid., 10.

[20] Ibid.

[21] A. C. Nielsen Company. Reported in Martin, "The Birth of a Media Myth," p. 11.

[22] Ibid.

Such statistics in themselves, while perhaps impressive, do not necessarily have much significance beyond the expanded religious outreach they represent. However, they loom much more significant, particularly in the political context, when we realize that an explicit goal of many contemporary religious broadcasters is political influence. Here we come face to face with the epitome of this phenomenon and trend, namely, the "Moral Majority" and its program for the 1980s.[23]

In June, 1980, the Reverend Jerry Falwell founded Moral Majority—an organization with at least five primary messages and emphases: (1) America is in a state of terrifying moral decline; (2) moral decay in this country will result in the fall of America and the rise of atheistic dictatorships if not stopped; (3) this nation is a chosen instrument of God for good in the world; (4) Christian citizens have a moral obligation and duty to vote; (5) as they vote they are to put into office candidates who pledge to support the religious principles of Moral Majority. It was reported that within sixteen months Falwell's group claimed to have signed up 72,000 ministers and 4 million lay members with chapters in every state, and had expectations of raising $5 million for support of political campaigns in 1980 alone.[24]

Four other groups with similar philosophies, tactics, and goals that share a fundamentalist Christian orientation are Christian Voice (Robert Grant, cofounder, Richard Zone, executive director), Christian Voters Victory Fund (Dale Silvers, chair), Religious Roundtable (Ed McAteer, founder), and the National Christian Action Coalition (Robert Billings, president).

In addition to coming out foursquare in support of the Republican candidate Ronald Reagan and the Republican platform he represented (they had a hand in building it), these groups opposed three major developments: the legalization of abortion-on-demand, the spread of pornography, and the tolerance of homosexuality. Three causes they championed were as follows: providing for prayer and Bible reading in public schools, nullifying the Equal Rights Amendment, and defeating liberal senators and members of Congress who were viewed as aiding and abetting moral decay. These groups set as one target for 1980 the defeat of six liberal senators.

Five of them did indeed go down to defeat in November, 1980: George McGovern of South Dakota, Frank Church of Idaho, John Culver of Iowa, Birch Bayh of Indiana, and Gaylord Nelson of Wisconsin. Only Alan Cranston of California retained his seat in the Senate. During the campaign, not necessarily with the endorsement of the national organization, epithets such as "baby killer" and accusations of promoting homosexuality were commonplace at the local level. Birch Bayh's comment is typical of those concerned about the New Religious Right movement. He said, "The cause of liberty is not

---

[23] While the Moral Majority is technically a political organization, not a religious group, its major leadership, membership, and support come from the New Religious Right.

[24] George J. Church, "Politics from the Pulpit," *Time,* 116 (October 13, 1980), 28.

served by organizations that brand public officials as being immoral or anti-God simply because they may hold different views. . . . These hate groups now have tasted blood. . . . Step out of line one time, and they'll chop your head off."[25]

In the spring primary campaign (1980) to unseat Senator George McGovern, the following list of opponents joined forces:

National Right to Life Committee
Life Amendment Political Action Committee
Committee for Survivial of a Free Congress
National Conservative Caucus
American Conservative Union
Fund for a Conservative Majority
Young Americans for Freedom
John Birch Society
Citizens for the Republic
National Right to Work Committee
Eagle Forum
Citizens' Committee for the Right to Keep and Bear Arms
Gun Owners of America
Tax Limitation Committee
Committee to Defeat the Union Bosses
Committee to Save the Panama Canal

James Wall says that the list looked like a "roll call of the New Right."[26]

Many have referred to the platform of these groups as "single issue politics." While "single issue" may be an overstatement, at most their platforms include but a few items. What they overlook is the broad array of political issues a member of Congress or a president is called upon to deal with. Further, critics point out that with their emphasis on abortion or homosexuality or prayer in public schools, there is total silence with respect to providing justice for all, care for the needy, protection of minorities, and the like. Various religious groups have gone so far as publicly to condemn or at least raise questions about their tactics and program. Among others, these include some Methodist and Lutheran groups, the National Council of Churches, the American Jewish Committee, and the Jesuit publication *America*. And local groups such as the Voice of Reason in Michigan, a group of people who consider themselves secular humanists, are forming explicitly to organize a counterattack against the Moral Majority and its cohorts. They too plan to use the me-

---

[25] "Religious Right Goes For Bigger Game," *U.S. News & World Report,* 89 (November 17, 1980), 42.

[26] James M. Wall, "The New Right Exploits Abortion," *Christian Century* 97 no. 25 (July 30–August 6, 1980), 747.

dia of radio and television and public forums and rallies to get their message out and to raise funds to support candidates they favor.[27]

In all fairness, however, it should be pointed out that more-liberal church people and the groups they represent, although not so well financed or perhaps with as much support, have also been known to wage single issue campaigns — anti-Vietnam War protesting, antinuclear demonstrations, participation in the 1960s Civil Rights movement are examples of these campaigns. The New Religious Right (sometimes called the new Christian Right) is certainly not the first coalition of religious groups to attempt to influence voters and the political structure of a country, the United States of America included.

In addition to such specific goals as mentioned earlier (legislation against abortion, pornography, and homosexuality, and defeating the Equal Rights Amendment and liberal members of Congress), there are other in one sense more important themes in the message of the New Christian Right. It is these themes that provide the initial "hook" that brings people in. Jeffrey Hadden and Charles Swann have summarized them as follows. First, they communicate the impression of absolute certainty about anything and everything. The elimination of ambiguity is central. Second, a positive attitude toward life is of crucial importance to success and happiness. Norman Vincent Peale's "Power of Positive Thinking" from the 1950s gets daily repetition and updating. Third, it is all right to look out for yourself. It is OK to seek success and reward, and to attain them.[28]

The message would seem to be much like the following: "And now that we've got your attention, have you been noticing what's going on around you? Have you sensed how far we've degenerated as a nation? Have you noticed how sinful we've become? And perhaps even worse, have you noticed how tolerant of sin we've become? Won't you help us do something about it?"

But what is really fascinating about the new Religious Right and in particular what conspired to make them loom significant sociologically is not simply their message. That is not really new. Preaching against sin, trying to improve the morality of people, and providing simple answers to complex issues and problems is far from new on the American religious scene. What is new is the pair of technological advances that the proponents employ: (1) television, and (2) direct mail technology that could come of age only with the storage and pinpointing capabilities of the computer. These two advances in technology give them the potential not only of reaching millions of people in a short time but also of mobilizing masses of fairly ordinary church members who hold conservative opinions and values in the religious sphere as well as in the political and social spheres.

[27] *Detroit Free Press,* March 8, 1981, p. 1A.

[28] Jeffrey K. Hadden and Charles E. Swann, *Prime Time Preachers* (Reading, Mass.: Addison-Wesley, 1981), pp. 101–2.

In terms of potential support, John Simpson notes that a full 30 percent
of Americans, although not necessarily members of or identified with the Moral Majority, hold to a set of four convictions espoused by the Moral Majority,
that is, opposition to abortion, homosexuality, the Supreme Court school
prayer decision, and a "modern" role for women outside the traditional home-
making, childrearing functions.[29] In addition, Simpson suggests that as many
as 70 percent of Americans can be classified as conservative in terms of the
socio-moral platform of the Moral Majority. That is, while not necessarily
supporting all points of the platform, they can be attracted to support a Moral Majority position on particular issues and combinations of issues (they espouse the Moral Majority position on at least two of the four issues identified
above).[30]

One thing becomes certain. The contest has only just begun. The New
Religious Right will definitely be heard from in the 1980s. And they will be
more influential than in the past, in significant part because they are not quite
as "single issue" as in the past. It is not the single issue of communism, for
example, as it was in the 1950s, that defines this new movement. Instead it is
a list of several "moral" issues, together with appeals for a return to free enterprise capitalism, a decrease in governmental regulation, and an increase in
defense spending, that distinguishes the New Religious Right.

In conclusion, Hadden and Swann note that the leaders of the New Religious Right—the "televangelists"—have come a long way from their prede-
cessors—the circuit riders, tent preachers, and revivalists. "No longer are they
satisfied with Sister Lou or Brother Jim finding the Lord and being born
again. For although salvation is still their goal, the sinner is not you and me
anymore; it's America. And saving a nation takes a lot of believers, a lot of
money, and a lot of power."[31]

CIVIL RELIGION

As we continue to look at the relationship of religion and politics we need to
consider a concept that has had wide attention among those trying to understand how religion and politics affect one another, particularly in the United
States. That is the concept of *civil religion*. In the briefest of terms the idea of
civil religion refers to the view which some people have that the foundation of
their society and the events that mark its progress through history are parts of
a larger, divine scheme of things; the political structure and the political acts
that flow out of that structure have a transcendental dimension—God is at
work in our nation, and as such we have a destiny.

[29] John H. Simpson, "Is There a Moral Majority?" Paper presented at the joint annual
meeting of the Society for the Scientific Study of Religion and the Religious Research Association,
Baltimore, Maryland, October 30, 1981.
[30] Ibid.
[31] Hadden and Swann, *Prime Time Preachers*, p. 6.

Robert Bellah introduced the term and describes civil religion as a substratum of common religious understandings that are quite pervasive in society, American society in particular.

> Although matters of personal religious belief, worship, and association are considered to be strictly private affairs, there are, at the same time, certain common elements of religious orientation that the great majority of Americans share. These have played a crucial role in the development of American institutions and still provide a religious dimension for the whole fabric of American life, including the political sphere. This public religious dimension is expressed in a set of beliefs, symbols, and rituals that I am calling the American civil religion.[32]

Bellah goes on to point out that America's civil religion is certainly not Christianity in anything like the specific sense such as would necessitate belief in Jesus Christ and the Atonement, but is rather more "unitarian," in the sense of regarding God as a sort of single supernatural being. But this God is not to be understood simply in the deistic tradition of an aloof Maker who set the world in motion and then left it to shift for itself. No, "he is actively interested and involved in history, with a special concern for America."[33] At the heart of civil religion within the United States is the idea that America is the promised land God has led people to—out of the land of bondage (Europe). Thus this nation is to be dedicated to order, law, and justice as God would have them carried out. Bellah quotes extensively from Washington and Jefferson, as well as from John Kennedy and Lyndon Johnson, pointing out the idea of America as charged with a divinely ordained mission to fulfill in bringing about God's will for humankind. Out of the trauma of the Civil War emerged new themes of sacrifice and rebirth. Lincoln's Gettysburg Address was replete with Christian symbolism without being specifically Christian (for example, "that those who here gave their lives, that the nation might live"). Lincoln's own "sacrificial" martyrdom enhanced the concept. Memorial Day ceremonies and to a lesser extent the ceremonies of the Fourth of July, Veterans Day, Thanksgiving Day, and Washington's and Lincoln's birthdays provided ritual vehicles for the civil religion.

Coleman formalizes a definition of civil religion and lists three central characteristics of American civil religion. He defines *civil religion* as "the set of beliefs, rites, and symbols which relates a man's role as citizen and his society's place in space, time, and history to the conditions of ultimate existence and meaning."[34] Three characteristics, according to Coleman, typify American civil religion. (1) The nation is the primary agent of God's meaningful activity in history. This belief gave rise to the doctrines of manifest destiny and world obligation. (2) The nation is the primary society in terms of which individual Americans discover personal and group identity. Like the historic church,

---

[32] Robert N. Bellah, "Civil Religion in America," in *Religion in America*, eds. William G. McLoughlin and Robert N. Bellah (Boston: Houghton Mifflin, 1968), pp. 5–6.

[33] Ibid., p. 9.

[34] John A. Coleman, "Civil Religion," *Sociological Analysis* 31, no. 2 (1970), 76.

through the doctrine of the melting pot, America was called to be "catholic." (3) The nation also assumes a churchly feature as the community of righteousness.[35]

In the 1950s and 1960s many writers, most with a strong theological orientation and commitment, reacted strongly against what Bellah subsequently called civil religion and what seemed to constitute much of the so-called religious revival of the 1950s. Martin Marty's criticism of what he calls the "religion of democracy" or "state Shinto" is typical. Marty states that in American state Shinto, "democracy becomes the ultimate, religion the handmaiden."[36]

Whether critical of such a religion of democracy as a perversion of Christianity or not, most who have analyzed the phenomenon would agree that civil religion in America is differentiated. That is, neither state nor church is in charge of it. Coleman sees this as a new development. He suggests that much of the furor in the 1950s over a sellout of Christianity to secularism and the substitution of a new American Shinto was implicit recognition that control over civil religion had fallen out of religious hands. His view is that such differentiation is "healthy for both the state which does not place itself in opposition to the church and the church which remains free to perform a prophetic religious function."[37]

Others have suggested quite a different perspective—the rejuvenation and encouragement of civil religion, and the active involvement of organized religion in that process. A writer such as J. Paul Williams sees this as the future task of religion, although he does not use the concept *civil religion* and his proposals predate Bellah's introduction of the concept. Actually, Williams blends, in a most interesting way, a couple of sociological ideas—the idea of religion as an integrating, functional entity in society, and the widely held view of the decline of institutional religion.

Williams calls the integrating factor *"societal" religion.* This is distinguished from *"private" religion,* which an individual shares with only a few other intimate persons, and *"denominational" religion,* which is simply the denominational phenomenon we have discussed several times before. Williams points out that although denominational religion has changed in response to social change, societal religion has remained quite uniform over the decades. Its essence is commitment to the democratic way of life. He quotes A. Powell Davies's description of the democratic faith or way of life, which asserts that people were meant to be free, that they can improve their level of life through the power of reason and discussion, and that human rights such as liberty and justice are by their nature universal. In final summation, Davies states: "God and history are on the side of freedom and justice, love and righteousness; and

[35] Ibid., p. 74.
[36] Martin E. Marty, *The New Shape of American Religion* (New York: Harper & Brothers, 1958), p. 78.
[37] Coleman, "Civil Religion," p. 76.

man will therefore, be it soon or late, achieve a world society of peace and happiness where all are free and none shall be afraid."[38] The central idea here is that the core values of America, which are almost by definition nearly universally accepted by Americans, are essentially religious values that in turn constitute the societal religion.

Williams deeply believes that since American democracy and the societal religion that undergirds it face threats of various kinds, they need buttressing. Such support, he feels, ought to come from denominational religion. "Americans must be brought to the conviction that democracy is the very Law of life."[39] To accomplish this, "democracy must become an object of religious dedication. Americans must come to look on the democratic ideal (not necessarily American practice of it) as the Will of God or, if they prefer, the Law of Nature."[40] William's proposal is simply this: "The churches and synagogues should not only promulgate their own denominational values, but in addition should support those broader values which are essential to the continuance and betterment of society as a whole. . . . In America the churches and synagogues should teach faith in democracy as one item of their creed."[41]

Implicitly Williams is suggesting that all would be better off if religion in America would lose much of its denominational character and get on with the important business at hand of creating and maintaining a true democracy— that is, if religion would return to its true social purpose of enhancing the integration of society. It hardly needs pointing out, however, that his proposal has not caught on in a particularly striking fashion. Many religious groups would reject it out and out—conservatives because of its tendencies to dilute traditional religious tenets and to blur the distinction between church and state, liberals because it appears to them too uncritical of existing political arrangements and of the manner in which democratic principles are expedited. Certainly many secularized Americans would raise serious questions about William's proposal in this day of political and intellectual dissent and criticism, when many can find no honest way to give democracy (as it obtains in the present, at least) such unqualified support.

RELIGION AND POLITICS IN THE THIRD WORLD

Although religious issues periodically surface as political issues in every society of the world, a politico-religious phenomenon virtually unknown in the United States but fairly common in the Third World (the underdeveloped na-

[38] Quoted in J. Paul Williams, *What Americans Believe and How They Worship* (New York: Harper & Row, Pub., 1969), p. 481.

[39] Ibid., p. 491.

[40] Ibid., p. 484.

[41] Ibid., p. 488.

tions of Asia, Africa, and Latin America) is the emergence of religious political parties—that is, political parties whose constituency is a particular religious group, and which pursue religious as well as political ends. Donald Smith distinguishes three kinds of Third World politico-religious parties.[42] There are first of all the *communal parties*, such as the Hindu Mahasabha or the Jana Sangh in India, which form within a national context of religious pluralism. Their self-styled function is to "protect and promote the largely secular economic and political interests of their respective communal groups."[43] Such political parties are better-organized manifestations of communal conflict and violence of the sort that might erupt between Hindus and Muslims if the latter was alledged to have killed sacred cows or if a Hindu procession was accused of disturbing Muslims in their mosques at prayer—violence of the sort paralleled in the West by the protracted Protestant-Catholic conflict in Northern Ireland. An excellent example of the Third World communal party is the Freedom party led by S. W. R. D. Bandaranaike that pledged itself to restore Buddhism to its rightful place in the national life of Sri Lanka (formerly Ceylon). The focus of its attack was Christianity, particularly the Roman Catholic Church, which was felt to be favored by governing authorities. Bandaranaike succeeded in becoming prime minister in the election of 1956, but was assassinated three years later. The subsequest administration under his wife found its power considerably weakened through expedient compromises with Marxists.

The second type of religious political party is the *sect-based party*. Smith cites the Ummah in the northern Sudan as a prime example. Although the northern portion of the Sudan is solidly Muslim, the Ummah is a minority political party that derives its constituency from the Ansar sect within that branch of Islam. In other words, unlike the interreligious conflict inherent in the communal parties, here there is intrareligious conflict of sect with parent religious group finding expression in political action and party formation.

The third type is the *ideological religious party* which, Smith notes, functions in societies in which religious minorities are politically unimportant. Such parties are not oriented to conflict with other religious groups but desire to speak to the ideological assumptions that undergird and shape the society. They may be conservative and attempt to preserve traditional patterns, such as many Latin American conservative parties, particularly of thirty and more years ago. Or they may be modernizing or reforming as they challenge aspects of the fundamental societal ideology. Examples of the latter are the Christian Democrats in Chile and the Masjumi in Indonesia.

The point to appreciate in this extremely brief look at religion and politics in the Third World is the widespread tendency of citizens in Third World societies to refuse to relegate religion solely to the private sphere of individual

---

[42] Donald E. Smith, *Religion, Politics, and Social Change in the Third World* (New York: Free Press, 1971), pp. 140–69.

[43] Ibid., p. 440.

faith and practice. The politico-religious conflict that ensues is aided by the onrush of social change and the inevitable challenges to traditional ideologies that social change involves. Such developments may upset traditional delicate compromises and stalemates among religions, which may lead to intergroup conflict, or religious groups may organize themselves politically to uphold traditional values in some cases or promote other values in other cases. The point, then, is that in many Third World societies religion and politics are less clearly separated than in, say, the United States.

A prime reason for this, as Smith points out, is that Third World societies began much more recently to question the view of government as ordained by God and of governmental leaders as gods or direct agents of God.[44] These societies have not become as secularized as most societies of the West, though this process seems to be accelerating. It is thus unlikely that religion will remain the political force that it has represented in the recent past. An important reason for this is that in many Third World countries religion has become intimately associated with nationalistic sentiments and activities. With political independence already a fact in many of these societies, a major purpose of the politico-religious parties has been all but eliminated. Further, as Smith points out, participation in the political process itself has an important secularizing effect.[45] The political party with an Islamic ideology, for example, may work within a pluralistic ideological milieu and find itself making deals that are politically expedient but that implicitly deny the absolutist, inviolable precepts of orthodox Islam. They compromise their ideology to capture minority votes. Smith notes that in the long run, "particularistic ideologies such as Islam give ground before universalistic ideologies such as socialism."[46]

[44] Ibid., pp. 1–2.
[45] Ibid., p. 4.
[46] Ibid.

7

Religion and the Economy

In line with an underlying principle made explicit throughout this book, namely, that religion is in a continuous reciprocal and interdependent relationship with society and its institutions, we now turn to one of society's most important institutions (some would say, *the* most important)—the economy.

We can initially observe that religion, although often legitimately viewed as a semiautonomous social system (societal institution) paralleling other institutions, is itself in various ways a part of the inclusive economic system of a society—it is an employer; it buys and it sells; it owns property; it contributes to the gross national product (the amount spent annually on all goods and services). A brief look at religion as an active participant in the economy constitutes the first section of this chapter. The major section following looks at religion's influence on economic relationships in a society. We shall then, in a third section, conclude with an assessment of how and to what degree religion has an impact on the economy and vice versa.

RELIGION AS AN ECONOMIC INSTITUTION

Two obvious ways in which organized religion plays an economic role in most societies is as an employer (providing the economic livelihood for religious professionals and their families) and as an owner of property and a builder of facilities. Although there are no precise figures available concerning the number of persons employed by religious organizations, we do know (from figures published by the National Council of Churches) that as of 1979 there were at least 497,301 clergy members in the United States.[1] But even this figure is not comprehensive, inasmuch as not all religious groups report statistics to the National Council of Churches—or to any one source, for that matter. Conservatively we would therefore estimate that there are at least 550,000 clergy members in the United States alone. Add to this the members of monastic and other religious orders in the Catholic Church; the tens of thousands of church secretaries, janitors, and sextons; employees of religious publishing companies; parochial-school teachers; clerical and secretarial staff for area, state, regional, and national denominations and ecumenical organizations; social workers employed by religious welfare agencies; and the like—and a total of 800,000 or more families deriving part or, for many, all of their family income from religious organizations would be a conservative estimate.

In 1957, church property and endowments in the United States were valued at $13.7 billion.[2] Although there was some decline in new construction by religious groups between 1965 and 1975, the value of expenditures for such new construction has increased each year since 1978 even when inflation is taken into account. Total new construction in 1978 was $749 million in 1972 adjusted dollars.[3]

Probably even more impressive are the figures for contributions to religious groups. In 1978 the American Association of Fund-Raising Councils estimated contributions to religious groups at $18.4 billion, or 46.5 percent of the total estimated amount of charitable contributions that year of $39.56 billion.[4] While not the biggest business in this country or the world, religion is nonetheless a significant element in the economy as an owner of great amounts of property and as an agent for the collection and distribution of billions of dollars annually.

Religious organizations also engage in a great number of activities and enterprises that are not intrinsically religious—they own and derive income from apartment and office buildings, parking lots, factories, and of course stocks and bonds held as endowments by local congregations, national denominations, and church workers' pension funds. The topic of tax-exempt status for such income can elicit highly animated discussion and may well be one that readers will want to engage in. We shall mention here only one illustration of the issue that might get the ball rolling. The widely publicized Ohio-based Cathedral of Tomorrow at one time owned and derived income from

[1] National Council of Churches of Christ in the U.S.A., Office of Planning and Program, *Yearbook of American Churches, 1979,* ed. Constant H. Jacquet, Jr. (Nashville: Abingdon, 1980), p. 226.

[2] David O. Moberg, *The Church as a Social Institution* (Englewood Cliffs, N.J.: Prentice-Hall, 1962), p. 169.

[3] National Council of Churches, *Yearbook,* p. 271.

[4] National Council of Churches, *Yearbook,* p. 242.

such a diversity of "secular" businesses as a shopping center, an apartment building, an electronics firm, a wire and plastics company—and the Real Form Girdle Company.[5] Regarding this last holding, *Women's Wear Daily* once quipped in a headline, "Rock of Ages on Firm Foundation."[6]

Such examples, while not unique, are also not ordinary. Most religious groups, particularly at the local level, hold no investments beyond the buildings and property in which they worship and perform their educational functions. But there is another level too. With such ventures as retirement villages, hospitals, and an office building in which a denominational headquarters resides, while on the surface at least seeming to be more consistent with the philosophy that grants tax exempt status to religious institutions, namely, the benefits they provide people and communities, there still may be profits from such enterprises and operators of competing businesses may claim unfair competition. And so the argument goes on. But our point is simply the one with which we began this section. That religious institutions are vitally involved in the economy of the society though their involvement may be quite supplemental to the religious purposes for which they organized.

RELIGION AS A SHAPER OF ECONOMIC ATTITUDES AND BEHAVIOR

Throughout history religious groups have faced a dilemma with regard to attempting to influence economic attitudes and behavior. On the one hand, there has been a tendency to treat poverty as a virtue and to discourage the faithful from becoming encumbered by material goods and concerns. Certainly the Bible extols poverty in these terms in such statements as "Blessed are the poor for they shall inherit the earth," or "How hard it is for a rich man to enter the kingdom of heaven." Buddhism extols the mendicant monk who travels light and remains free from economic concerns in order to engage in a life of contemplation.

Yet any religious group, particularly as its organization begins to get the least bit complex, requires funds to operate. The group then begins to get involved in economic affairs, whether it wants to or not. It finds itself grateful for substantial contributions from wealthy members. It may exact a tithe from its adherents. As at least some members rise out of poverty it does not kick them out, but perhaps even extols them for their industry and frugality. It is this tendency of religious groups to become fairly actively engaged in economic activities that is one of several stimuli to the formation of sects. We observed in Chapter 5 that sects tend to turn poverty into a virtue. This is what

[5] Alfred Balk, *The Religion Business* (Richmond, Va.: John Knox Press, 1968), p. 11.
[6] Quoted in Balk, *The Religion Business,* p. 11.

Max Weber calls a "theodicy of disprivilege" or "theodicy of escape,"[7]—that is, a rationalization and justification of one's disprivileged economic and social status as an advantage so far as salvation is concerned. True riches and enhanced status will accrue in the hereafter, when it really counts—when it is for eternity, not just sixty or seventy years of toil and trouble on this earth.

Just as children say, "That's the dumbest toy I ever saw—I didn't want that crummy old thing anyway" of the toy they grab from another child but have to return after a stern parental reprimand, so the sectarians of low socioeconomic status are likely to define what is denied them as evil, or at least as unimportant and undesirable. Wealth, fancy clothes, "highfalutin" manners and language? Who needs them! Actually Weber identifies three different forms that release from earthly disprivilege might take: the expectation of a better life in the hereafter (paradise or heaven); hope for oneself, or at least for one's progeny, in a new world to be created by God for the faithful called the Messianic Age or the millenium; hope for another life or rebirth in this world that will be better or higher than the present one (the concept of transmigration of souls in Hinduism, for example).[8]

On the other hand, there is the "theodicy of good fortune" identified by Weber. Here there is theological justification for superior economic and social status. "The fortunate is seldom satisfied with the fact of being fortunate. Beyond this, he needs to know that he has the *right* to his good fortune, . . . that he 'deserves' it."[9] Good fortune wants to be "legitimate" fortune. Religion legitimates the favored conditions of "religious men, the propertied, the victorious, and the healthy. In short, religion provides the theodicy of good fortune for those who are fortunate."[10]

Here we find ourselves drifting into the perspective in which religion is seen as influenced by forces outside itself—in this case, by economic factors, which are seen as influencing religious doctrine. There is of course much evidence supporting this point of view, and we will look at the matter more closely in the third section of this chapter. But first let us examine how and to what extent religion affects economic attitudes and behavior.

David Moberg mentions several ways in which religion to varying degrees of intensity and significance affects economic attitudes and behavior. First, insofar as such personal and business virtues as honesty, fair play, and honoring one's commitments are essential in economic life, and to the extent that religion is successful in inculcating such virtues in its members, religion has an impact on the economy. Second, religion on occasion stimulates con-

---

[7] Max Weber, *The Sociology of Religion*, trans. Ephraim Fischoff (Boston: Beacon Press, 1963), p. 113.

[8] Max Weber, "The Social Psychology of the World Religions," *From Max Weber: Essays in Sociology*, ed. and trans. H. H. Gerth and C. Wright Mills (New York: Oxford University Press, 1958), p. 275.

[9] Ibid., p. 271.

[10] Ibid.

sumption. Religious holidays implicitly encourage material consumption by followers, even if it is only special candles to light and special foods to eat. Third, in emphasizing one's work as a "calling," religion (Protestant Christianity in particular) has glorified and elevated work at one's job, however menial it may be. To the extent that people internalize this view it is likely to increase productivity. The individual worker may think along the following lines: "I'm working for God, not just for my employer or for myself. Therefore, I'd better put out a little more and do the best job possible."[11]

Vogt and O'Dea provide interesting evidence related to this point.[12] Although located in the same natural environment, the communities of Homestead and Rimrock (fictitious names) evidence quite different social systems. Rimrock, which stresses cooperative community effort and achieves great productivity as a consequence, appears to be strongly influenced by the Mormon ideology held by a majority of its citizens. Homestead, with its individualistic orientation and less successful farming endeavors, evidences the influence of competitive and divisive Protestant denominationalism that inhibits community-oriented cooperative efforts.

A fourth way in which religion may influence the economy is by explicitly endorsing certain economic systems or certain types of economic or business activities. For example, Liston Pope notes that religious leaders were influential in helping establish the cotton mill industry in Gaston County, North Carolina around the turn of the twentieth century. This was accomplished directly through supportive sermonizing and pronouncements that helped create public approval of the textile enterprise. Religion also indirectly influenced economic endeavor in Gaston County by supporting Prohibition. With the advent of Prohibition, economic capital which had been invested in distilleries was released for investment in the textile mills. Also, mill workers were slightly more likely to appear for work Monday mornings in good condition now that weekend "benders" were more unlikely. Above all, religion helped the mills (and thus influenced the economy) by exerting moral influence over the workers, encouraging them to do a good day's work and to do what the boss told them.[13]

Weber's Protestant Ethic and the Spirit of Capitalism

Probably the greatest single contribution to the discussion of the impact of religion on the economy is Max Weber's seminal study *The Protestant Ethic and the Spirit of Capitalism* (1905), which has stimulated massive amounts of

---

[11] Moberg, *The Church*, pp. 170–74.

[12] Evon Z. Vogt and Thomas F. O'Dea, "A Comparative Study of the Role of Values in Social Action in Two Southwestern Communities," *American Sociological Review* 18, no. 6 (1953), 645–54.

[13] Liston Pope, *Millhands and Preachers* (New Haven: Yale University Press, 1942), chapter 2.

research and discussion over the past half-century. Weber's thesis is that Calvinistic Protestantism as a theological belief system exerted an important influence on the emergence and growth of capitalism as a mode of economic organization. Quite explicitly Weber was trying to answer Karl Marx's assertion that society's normative system, including such phenomena as religious values and principles, in fact consists of epiphenomena produced, or at least conditioned in a primary way, by factors in the economy. Weber was essentially saying that at the very least the influential relationship between religion and the economy is a two-way street. Accordingly he set out to show how religion, as embodied in Calvinism, affected the economy, as represented by capitalism.

The Prime Elements in Calvinistic Theology

In order to see the relationship hypothesized by Weber we first need to understand a bit of Calvinistic theology. At the center of Calvinistic theology is the concept and goal of the *glory of God*—everything people do should somehow add to God's glory. Since God does not exist for people, but people for God,[14] it is not too surprising that an early Calvinist theologian has been quoted as saying that he would eagerly and joyfully be damned in hell if that would somehow glorify God.

A second central doctrine of Calvinism is that of *predestination*. This teaching speaks of the foreknowledge and above all the foreordaining by God of all people either to eternal salvation or eternal damnation. In Lutheran theology the attempt had been to use this doctrine as a source of comfort and encouragement to the believer. The emphasis was on God's foreknowledge. God knows in advance who will become a true and faithful follower and believer and who will not. Those whom he foresees as believing, he then predestines to heaven. God does not, however, explicitly predestine to hell those whom he foresees as rejecting him of their own free will; rather, they seal their own fate, so to speak, by rejecting opportunities to become a believer.

In Calvinism, however, God appears a bit more arbitrary. With less emphasis on God's foreknowledge, Calvinism sees God as assigning some to one fate, some to the other. An important implication of Calvinism's version of predestination was that a person has to proceed all alone down the path of life to meet the destiny decreed for him or her for eternity.[15] No priest, no church, no sacrament, nothing human can avail to the contrary. This is because what God has decided beforehand cannot be changed. Of course, someone who is damned should still belong to a church and observe the sacraments, because in such activities God is glorified. This is one's obligation as a human being. But it will not do the person any good so far as his or her eternal destiny is concerned. Such activities will not change God's mind. This

[14] Max Weber, *The Protestant Ethic and the Spirit of Capitalism*, trans. Talcott Parsons (New York: Scribner's, 1958), pp. 102–3.

[15] Ibid., p. 104.

is so because Christ died only for the "elect" (those predestined to salvation).[16] Obviously this view is a radical departure from Catholicism, which emphasized the church, the sacraments, and the priesthood as channels of God's gifts of hope and salvation to humankind.

A social consequence of this combination of predestination and obligation to glorify God was the encouragement of a rather extreme kind of individualism. Not only are you on your own in the sense that no other individual or group can help you change the direction of your predestined end, but you must be careful lest your relationships with people become too strong and important. You must not get carried away in involvement with and commitment to husband, wife, children, or friends. Your primary task is to glorify God.

We now add one more element to complete the basic theological ingredients, as Weber saw them, that provided the foundation for the Protestant (Calvinist) ethic—the concept of the "*calling*." This is a concept, elaborated by Luther, which emphasized using one's secular occupation, whether farmer, artisan, soldier, king, or housewife, to glorify God and to help your neighbor by doing a good job and faithfully carrying out your tasks. This concept taught people not to despise or belittle their job or role in life—it taught them instead to see their work as a "calling" by God. Calvinism picked up this concept and placed even greater emphasis on hard work; whatever your calling, you must carry out its duties to the best of your ability and with your last ounce of energy.

Implications for the Individual

We have to realize that the Calvinist was placed in a rather uneasy position with the combining of these three theological elements. He or she was to glorify God by working to the fullest in his or her calling, all the while aware that he or she had been predestined—yet not knowing whether to heaven or to hell. Hence a highly important question in the person's mind was, Is there any way I can know or at least infer that I'm one of the elect? Catholics had little problem with this question. If they were members of the church and performed at least the minimal ritual and confessional requirements, they had nothing to worry about. Lutherans also were little worried about predestination. Since predestination was viewed as based on God's offer of salvation, they had every reason to believe that they were numbered among the elect. Furthermore, they were promised the inner working of the Holy Spirit, who would develop in them a consciousness and conviction that they were specially chosen by God. True, they could "fall from grace"—but only if they lost their faith and rejected God's offered hand of deliverance. So as long as one believed and did not reject, one did not need to worry.

The Calvinist, however, did not have such assurance. He or she could not truly know or be convinced. But the Calvinist could make inferences from

---

[16] Ibid.

essentially empirical evidence—evidence of an ability consistently to perform well, of success in his or her calling, of the feeling that God seemed to be providing him or her with opportunities and was working through him or her. Would God be likely to choose to work through someone who was not one of his elect? The upshot was that the three theological elements mentioned earlier, in combination with a desire to know whether one was predestined to salvation produced a tremendous drive toward action. This resulted in what Weber calls "ascetic Protestantism"—a life of strict discipline. Hard work in one's calling is the best discipline. Work is not only the best prophylactic against a sensual, immoral life but also the best means for glorifying God. Time, then, becomes infinitely valuable. Thus one must avoid idle conversation, unproductive recreation, or more sleep than absolutely necessary, in order to have maximum time for work.

Now, if you work harder than people around you, if you put in more hours at your job, if you live frugally and ascetically, you will likely be economically more successful than those around you. This is not bad. In fact, it is good—in two ways. First, this might be inferential evidence that you are one of God's elect. Second, God is being glorified. In the meantime, however, you may become rich. Now what? Such wealth dare not be used for personal sensual pleasure—to buy wine, women, and frolic. It should not be used to buy early retirement from one's calling. What alternative is there, then? The answer is *investment*—investment of capital to produce more goods, which create more profits, which in turn represent more capital for investment, ad infinitum—which is the heart of entrepreneurial capitalism. The option of giving away the surplus in philanthropic activity was seldom recommended inasmuch as the poor might then be distracted from doing their duty in their calling to menial but important tasks.

Implications for Economics

This returns us to Weber's thesis regarding the effect of religious norms and patterns on economic relationships and institutions. Attempting "to ascertain whether and to what extent religious forces have taken part in the qualitative formation and the quantitative expansion of [the] spirit of capitalism over the world," Weber concludes that Calvinism was indeed just such a force. However, Weber is quick to warn that no one should be so foolish as to maintain that capitalism or the spirit of capitalism could therefore only have developed as a result of the Reformation or that it is a direct product of Calvinism.[17] Rather, he essentially maintains that Calvinism served an important stimulating and reinforcing function for capitalism. Calvinism did not create capitalism, nor was it even absolutely necessary for the triumph of capitalism. Rather, Calvinism encouraged capitalism and, if nothing else, hastened its development in those societies where Calvinism wielded an influence.

[17] Ibid., p. 91.

Weber was much more careful than some of his followers in hypothesizing about the relationship between Calvinistic Protestantism and capitalism, a point not always appreciated by those critics who represent him as arguing that the former "caused" the latter.

Alternatives to Weber's Hypothesis

At this point we shall briefly consider some of the alternatives to and modified versions of Weber's thesis that have been suggested. Kurt Samuelsson cites four early objections to Weber's position raised by Felix Rachfahl four years after Weber first made it public in a series of articles in 1905. Rachfahl first questions the validity of representing ethical-religious motivation as a crucial factor in economic activity. More reasonable factors, he suggests, are such things as the desire to enjoy life, solicitude for the family, and the urge to work for the common good, or for the nation and its welfare. Second, Rachfahl points to several limiting conditions imposed by Calvin on economic activity that taken together do not at all condone a free-for-all capitalism. Third, the differences between Catholicism and Calvinism with regard to economic activity should not be exaggerated. Catholic monastic orders such as the Benedictines, Franciscans, and Jesuits were not too different from Calvinism in this respect. Fourth, Weber's distinction between Catholic and Protestant countries and cities with regard to economic activity are not so neatly associated with one religion or the other as Weber seems to suggest. Some supposedly Protestant capitalistic cities, for example, had strong Catholic influence.[18]

R. H. Tawney also emphasizes Rachfahl's fourth point, observing that capitalism had clearly existed in medieval Italy and Flanders (both Catholic areas) and that the capitalistic spirit was "only too familiar to the saints and sages of the Middle Ages." He goes on to point out that Catholic cities were the chief commercial capitals of medieval Europe, and Catholic bankers its leading financiers.[19]

Another hypothesis is that the social situation of Calvinists rather than their theology encouraged their entrance into capitalistic ventures. Calvinists constituted a religious minority almost everywhere except Geneva, and in some countries and communities they were barred from governmental positions and professions such as medicine and law. Where else to turn but to business enterprises? Thus we observe a process similar to that affecting Jews during the Middle Ages, who undertook money-lending and money-handling positions partly by default—because Christians did not want to "dirty their hands" with such activities or break the church's laws against usury. Just as it

---

[18] Kurt Samuelsson, *Religion and Economic Action: A Critique of Max Weber*, trans. E. Geoffrey French (New York: Harper & Row, Pub., 1961), pp. 8–9.

[19] R. H. Tawney, *Religion and the Rise of Capitalism* (Gloucester, Mass.: Peter Smith, 1962), pp. 84, 316.

did not mean that Jews had some kind of genetic advantage over Gentiles so far as financial matters were concerned, so there was nothing particularly significant in Calvinist theology that was more conducive to the development of capitalism than Catholic, Lutheran, or Presbyterian theology.

Personality factors might also be suggested. Perhaps the very persons who were most energetic and independent, who were most willing to take business risks, were those most attracted by Calvinism as a theological system because of its stress on individualism and effort. That is, perhaps at least some people choose a religion because it meshes with their own value system and commitments. As such it would be incorrect to suggest that religion produced particular economic attitudes, for example.

Tawney, questioning Weber's concept of capitalism itself, does not see Calvinism fitting into the free-for-all capitalism of the eighteenth and nineteenth centuries. Rather, Tawney credits Calvinism with providing a business ethic to a "world of small traders and handicrafts."[20] The huge fortunes required and created by capitalism were not produced merely by thrift, Tawney notes, but by exploitation and by deliberately creating "opportunities."

As one scans four centuries of Calvinist theological writing, one is impressed with the dilemma mentioned earlier in this chapter—the dilemma of a fundamental distrust in wealth and a belief in its likely insidious undermining of fundamental Christian principles such as "keeping oneself unstained by the world" as opposed to the religious group's need for money in order to survive and the need to justify its members' accumulation of wealth. In this connection, some have stressed the distinction between early and later Calvinism— the theology of Calvin himself contrasted with that of later followers and interpreters. John McNeill points out that John Calvin had a profound mistrust of economic success, and he suggests that to argue that Calvin characterized the prosperity of believers as inferential proof of their election to heaven is to completely misinterpret the evidence we have of Calvin's thought, as reflected in such statements as "Wherever prosperity flows uninterruptedly its delight corrupts even the best of us. . . . The faithful are more miserable than despisers of God. . . . Prosperity like wine inebriates men. . . . Property is like rust or mildew."[21]

Indeed, only later did Calvinists rationalize economic success and interpret economic gain as a sign of virtue. It is interesting that Weber quotes extensively from Richard Baxter, a late seventeenth century Puritan-Calvinist theologian writing approximately 150 years after Calvin. Weber also quotes Benjamin Franklin, who was not only considerably removed in time from Calvin, but not a Calvinist theologian at all. Thus it was Baxter, not Calvin, who made such statements as "Be wholly taken up in diligent business of your law-

[20] Tawney, *Religion*, p. 31.
[21] John T. McNeill, *The History and Character of Calvinism* (New York: Oxford University Press, 1954), p. 222.

ful calling. . . . It is for action that God maintaineth us. . . . Keep up a high esteem of time and be every day more careful that you lose none of your time. . . . [and] if vain recreation, dressings, feastings, idle talk, unprofitable company, or sleep be any of them temptations to rob you of any of your time, accordingly heighten your watchfulness."[22]

Toward a Resolution of the Issue

While still other critiques of Weber's hypothesis could be introduced, enough have been summarized to make the point that the link between Calvinism and capitalism, if one exists at all, is far from a unitary causal one. Of course, Weber himself spoke not of cause but of strong encouragement and support—what we today tend to call *reinforcement*. Actually, most of Weber's critics grant some such supportive role for Calvinism. This is the position taken by Tawney, who says that the "capitalistic spirit," though "as old as history, found in certain aspects of Puritanism a tonic which braced its energies and fortified its already vigorous temper."[23] And Rachfahl, the first to criticize the Weberian hypothesis, points out several indirect ways in which the doctrinal positions of Protestant theologians influenced economic matters, and concludes that despite important weaknesses in Weber's interpretation of evidence, the basic contention that Calvinism had an important influence upon economic activity is valid—though not in the specific way suggested by Weber.[24] Rachfahl's observations are the following:

1. Protestantism permitted the intellect to be devoted to worldly pursuits, whereas in Catholic countries many of the best minds went into the priesthood.
2. Protestantism introduced education to the masses.
3. Protestantism reversed the tendency toward indolence and distaste for work associated with Catholic renunciation of the world.
4. Protestantism encouraged independence and personal responsibility for one's fate—something down-played in Catholicism.
5. Protestantism created a "higher type of morality" than did Catholicism.
6. Protestantism distinguished politics from religion more clearly than did Catholicism. This freed persons to engage in more diverse economic activities and, by tolerating a greater diversity of views, ultimately resulted in economic change.[25]

Although some of these points tend to make false or at least strained comparisons, in combination they constitute the essence of the observation made more recently by Hammond and Demerath. These writers suggest a way

---

[22] See Weber, *The Protestant Ethic*, pp. 262, 260, 261.
[23] Tawney, *Religion*, pp. 226–27.
[24] Quoted in Samuelsson, *Religion and Economic Action*, p. 10.
[25] Ibid.

of salvaging Weber's thesis without having to accept all that he says. They note that the advent of Protestantism—that is, the fact that it appeared at all—implies a weakening and ultimate breakdown of medieval Catholic control, resulting in greater freedom to experiment with new political and economic forms, one of which was capitalism.[26] In other words, there is a third variable out there, or a whole set of other variables, that affected *both* Calvinism and capitalism, that provided fertile soil in which both could grow.

In a very real sense, then, the success of Protestantism represented the destruction of the church type of religious organization (discussed in Chapter 5) and the introduction of religious pluralism, which is intimately associated with political, and ultimately with economic, pluralism as well. That is, people were beginning to face options and make choices—political and economic choices, and religious ones also. The positive influence of Protestantism on capitalism is of course only an indirect one, and must take second place to primary developments—the discovery and colonization of the New World, the expansion of trade, the second agrarian revolution that increased food production and thus resulted in a labor surplus available for commercial and manufacturing occupations, the Enlightenment, political revolutions, and ultimately the Industrial Revolution itself.

Guy Swanson analyzes the relationship of Protestantism and capitalism along somewhat the same lines as Rachfahl and as Hammond and Demerath by seeing the general "loosening" of the social structure as the important ingredient. But for Swanson religion is essentially the middle variable in a three-variable chain that begins with political structure and ends with social structure, of which capitalism is only one aspect. Comparing the social structures of various European states in late medieval Europe, he notes that important differences in political structure preceded and served as a base for different religious commitments (Protestantism or Catholicism). Thus societies that remained Catholic had one primary source or center of decision making. By contrast, Protestantism was more likely to appear in those societies in which there were a variety of decision-making sources. Thus political diversity encouraged Protestantism, and together they encouraged capitalism.[27]

Whether one agrees with Samuelsson that there is "no support for Weber's theories," that "almost all the evidence contradicts them,"[28] or with others who hold out for at least an indirect relationship of some kind between Calvinistic Protestantism and the growth of capitalism, one conclusion seems clear: Although religion has some impact on the economy, it is likely to be indirect and to be effective only as a supportive, reinforcing ingredient in concert with others in a complex causal chain.

[26] N. J. Demerath III and Phillip E. Hammond, *Religion in Social Context* (New York: Random House, 1969), p. 150.

[27] Guy E. Swanson, *Religion and Regime* (Ann Arbor: University of Michigan Press, 1967).

[28] Samuelsson, *Religion and Economic Action*, p. 154.

AN ASSESSMENT OF THE RELATIONSHIP BETWEEN RELIGION AND ECONOMICS

It is clear that religion is, among other things, an economic institution—in the sense that it participates in the economy and is an economic "force" as a buyer and seller of goods and services, in the sense that it is an employer, and in the sense that it influences the buying habits of believers. Even in such relatively simple, small ways as creating a market for devotional and "peace of mind" literature, and supporting industries that produce religious artifacts such as religious vestments, statues, medallions, church pews, and baptismal fonts, religion has an impact on the economy of the society.

Religion's Influence on the Economy

It is important to realize, however, that the economic influence or impact of religion is seldom radical or revolutionary. It is unlikely to send the economy in new directions. The buying-and-selling and economy-stimulating role of religion in the society is both stable and predictable. It creates few new markets, and demands few innovative products. Religion is a relatively stable employer that neither stimulates nor retards economic swings of recession, depression, or inflation. It does, however, tend to respond to economic change. During the Great Depression of the 1930s in the United States thousands of seminary graduates of all denominations went without calls to religious vocations because congregations could not afford to hire and pay them and denominations could not afford the cost of establishing new congregations that would need clergy leaders. During the period of economic expansion beginning in the late 1940s and continuing through the 1950s, when new congregations proliferated and when established congregations expanded their membership and their programs, seminaries could not launch enough graduates into the religious sea. Demand was greater than supply.

Of course, some religious leaders occasionally exert a significant influence on the economy of the society. A prime example, though not consciously directed toward economic change, consists of the attempts by religious groups to reinforce traditional moral values. Sometimes religious groups or persons attempt to ban the sale of certain "immoral" books or curtail the distribution of pornographic films. When this happens, an obvious indirect influence on the economy is made. The most dramatic and economically influential instance of this in recent times is the movement leading to enactment of the Prohibition amendment in 1919. Conservative religious forces are generally credited with pushing this amendment through the states. The economic impact upon specific segments of the economy (liquor producers, wholesalers, retailers, bootleggers, and the like) was significant, though the impact on the overall economy was not that great. Eventually minor readjustments by subunits in the economy were required, not major changes in its direction or form.

A more recent example involves the use of moral suasion by religious leaders in an attempt to influence the corporate policy of large organizations in favor of the objectives of the Civil Rights movement. Some attempts have been made by religious leaders to encourage, even force, organizations to divest themselves of stock in companies that blatantly discriminate against blacks and other minorities. Primary attention has been focused on corporations that do business with the Union of South Africa and thus implicitly support the apartheid policies of that country's government. Some leaders, for example, have tried to force the National Council of Churches and various denominations to sell the stock they hold in corporations that do business with South Africa and to withdraw savings deposits and cancel checking accounts with banks that have investments in or do business with that nation. We must observe that these attempts have not been particularly successful. And even if they were successful, the overall impact on the economy of the United States — or for that matter, of the Union of South Africa—would not be great.

A success story in this area did occur in Detroit (and in a few other cities) in the early 1960s, and involved action by black ministers designed to reduce employment discrimination in specified manufacturing and service industries. In Detroit, a group calling itself the Negro Preachers of Detroit and Vicinity followed a set procedure. First they attempted to negotiate with executives of target companies that were observed to employ only small proportions of blacks (and those few only in low-status, low-paying jobs). Failing in negotiation attempts, the next step was to contact the black ministers of the more than three hundred black churches in the Detroit area and urge them to suggest strongly to their members on a given Sunday morning to stop buying a given firm's products. Target firms included bread companies, oil companies, and milk distributors. Usually within two weeks the sales of target companies would be down by as much as 25 percent. Once the black ministers made their point, they usually secured concessions from the companies in question. It also appeared that other companies began paying attention and acted to eliminate discriminatory practices before they were faced with similar boycotts.

The Economy's Influence on Religion

Although we have been concentrating in this chapter on ways in which religion impinges on the economy, we do not mean to imply that there is no relationship between religion and the economy that proceeds in the opposite direction. In fact, many have suggested that the primary or most frequently observed relationship between religion and the economy is that of the economy influencing religion. Probably the most extreme view along these lines is the familiar perspective of Karl Marx, who saw religion—and all normative features of society, for that matter—as growing out of and reflecting economic factors and relationships. For Marx, religion was little more than a tool in the hands of the society's elites for pacifying the masses and maintaining prevailing economic patterns and the respective relationships of owners and nonowners to the means of production. First there is the economy and a stratification system that reflects the relationship of various people to the means of production within that economy; then comes religion, both reflecting these economic relationships and reinforcing them. Although we do not subscribe to the whole of Marx's point of view, some of this perspective is implicit in Chapter 5's discussion of the importance of lower socioeconomic status in sect formation. Certainly differential economic status is associated with different needs of all kinds, religious needs included. We need only recall Weber's distinction between the theodicy of escape and the theodicy of good fortune to see a relationship between economic status and religious perspective and expression.

It can hardly be accidental that most religious groups in a society implicitly, and often explicitly, support prevailing economic norms and institutional patterns. For example, one would hear few if any sermons on any given Sunday in the United States of America decrying capitalism. Social norms—in this case, economic norms—get absorbed into all institutions and most groups in a society, religious institutions and groups included. Although one could find as many precedents, examples, and specific injunctions in the New Testament for communal ownership, sharing of wealth, and giving to the needy till it truly hurts as one could find for a capitalistic economic structure and private accumulation of wealth, it is not by chance that Christian churches in nonsocialistic lands usually support a capitalistic ideology. Very simply, the dominant economic norms of a society tend to be reflected by religion in that society.

We have referred before to Liston Pope's *Millhands and Preachers.* Pope provides some fascinating documentation of the impact of economic factors on religion. For one thing, he discovered that religion prospers as the economy prospers and expands—new churches are founded, old ones add members, and all groups tend to prosper as the economic base of the community expands, attracts workers, and provides salaries and wages for those people. Pope observes that in the mill towns in Gaston County the mills provided land and built churches for the workers and often subsidized ministers' salaries. But at a price. Mill management expected and usually received religious support and reinforcement of their policies and ideology. At the very least, the mill churches and clergy kept silent on economic issues, sticking to "religious" concerns, thereby of course implicitly supporting economic policy and practice.[29]

[29] Pope, *Millhands,* ch. 8 and 9.

By way of a final summary comment we must repeat that although religion is definitely involved in, and a part of, the economy of the society in which its exists, its overall impact is relatively slight. Primarily it reinforces economic norms and patterns through participation as one among many buyers and sellers of goods and services. Although occasionally religion challenges specific aspects of economic relationships or the activities of specific economic units, its challenges tend to be of slight impact in the long run.

8

Religion and the Class System

In Chapter 5 we introduced the topic of the relationship between religion and social class (social stratification) in outlining differences between denominations and sects. In fact, we observed that one of the dominant features of sectarian religion is its close association with lower- or working-class problems and life situations, together with the responses of persons of low social status to those problems and situations.

In generalizing from investigations into the relationships between religion and social class, sociologists have made the primary observation that there are important differences in religious meaning related to social class. That is, religion tends to perform at least somewhat different functions for people in different classes. Or put another way, people tend to seek or construct different things in religion depending on their social-class position.

Such assertions that stress the importance of social class with regard to religion should not really surprise us, inasmuch as nearly every beginning student of sociology becomes aware that one of the most significant variables in social life is social class. Although not strictly determinative, one's social-class position dramatically influences one's behavior, attitudes, and aspirations—that is, both what one thinks and what one does throughout life. Depending upon peoples' social-class origins and lifetime position in the stratification system, they will find their lives affected in a multitude of ways—voting propensities, likelihood of psychosis, amount of travel, attitudes toward social issues, age of marriage, size of family, sexual behavior, even life expectancy. Small wonder, then, that important relationships between social class and religion have also been found. Differences by social-class levels can be seen in differential affiliation with various religious groups, type and degree of involvement in the activities of religious groups, perceptions of the purposes and functions of religion for people, motivation for joining and belonging to religious groups, religious knowledgeability, and the like.

DIFFERENCES IN RELIGIOUS
MEANING AND EXPRESSION
AMONG SOCIAL CLASSES

A classic distinction regarding differences in the functions of religion by social class is that made by Karl Marx. In defining religion as the "opium of the people," he was actually drawing an implicit distinction between the religion of the bourgeoisie (property-owning capitalist) and that of the proletariat (working class). For the proletariat, in Marx's view, religion is a sedative, a narcotic that dulls people's sensitivity to and understanding of the plight of their life situation; it provides an escape from the harshness of reality. But more. As Marx wrote: "Religion is the sigh of the oppressed creature, the mind of a heartless world, as it is the spirit of unspiritual conditions. . . . the removal of religion as the illusory happiness of the people is the requirement for their real happiness."[1]

By way of contrast, for the bourgeoisie and elites in society, Marx contended, religion serves both as a tool of oppression—a means of placating and keeping the proletariat in line—and as a rationalization and justification for the elite's own position of power and privilege. Inasmuch as Marx viewed the normative aspects of social life as deriving from the most fundamental fact and relationship in society—namely, the economy—religion becomes really nothing more than an expression of prevailing economic relationships and thus, in the capitalistic economy, a means of preserving and reinforcing existing class distinctions. The intertwining of capitalism and prevailing religions is so complete, and the alienation of people from their true destinies so truly reflected in religion, that Marx's associate Engels could predict that religion would disappear when the prevailing capitalistic economies disappeared.[2]

Although Max Weber objected to the unidirectional nature of the relationship that Marx portrayed between the economy and social norms and values (including religion), and although he wrote *The Protestant Ethic and the Spirit of Capitalism* in large part to refute or at least modify or offer an alternative to Marx's theory, Weber actually held much the same view of differential functions of religion for the various social classes. We have already spoken

[1] Karl Marx and Friedrich Engels, *Toward the Criticism of Hergel's Philosophy of Right* (Paris, 1843), trans. Glen Waas, quoted in Robert Freedman, *Marxist Social Thought* (New York: Harcourt Brace Jovanovich, Inc. 1968), p. 230.

[2] Friedrich Engels, *Anti-Dühring* (Moscow: Foreign Language Publishing House, 1954), pp. 438–40, quoted in Freedman, *Marxist Social Thought*, p. 228.

of Weber's distinction, between the religion of the disprivileged and that of the privileged, underlying the concepts "theodicy of despair or escape" and "theodicy of good fortune."[3] In the first case one thinks of the proletariat, for whom religion promises release and some kind of eventual "salvation" if they can only endure, and remain eternally faithful. Interestingly, according to Weber, the need for compensation and hope in the face of an adverse existence is relatively seldom colored by resentment or rebellion. In other words, some of the disprivileged appear to be satisfied that hell is reserved for wealthy sinners (recall our earlier discussion of the sect in Chapter 5). The privileged classes, however, learn and express religious justification of their good fortune and emphasize their "blessings" as evidence of the favor with which God looks upon them. Wealth and privilege for them are not a detriment to salvation, but an indication not only that all is going well for them now but that it will likely continue to do so in any future life.[4]

Liston Pope discovered similar differences by social class in his study of Gaston County, North Carolina. This county became an important textile mill center in the 1920s and 1930s and attracted thousands of unskilled and semi-skilled laborers for the mills. Quite early during this period, a division of residents between "uptown" people and mill workers was made—a distinction corresponding roughly to Marx's bourgeoisie and proletariat and to Weber's privileged and disprivileged. Religious behavior and ideology differed rather markedly among these two major segments of the population. Pope describes the religion of the mill worker as follows:

> In the theology of the mill worker, the world is a great battlefield on which the Lord and the Devil struggle for each individual soul. The "blood of Jesus" and the reading of the Bible turn the tide of victory toward the Lord. As one mill minister summarized it, "You have to carry a bucket of blood into the pulpit to satisfy these people." The principal sins, in the eyes of mill villagers, are such uptown "worldly amusements" as playing cards, dancing, gambling, drinking, and swimming with members of the opposite sex.
> . . . But the worker also looks to his church to find transvaluation of life, which may take the form of reassurance or of escape, or both. By affirmation of values denied in the economic world, the church provides comfort and ultimate assurance; in its religious services it often affords escape temporarily from the economic and social situation in which workaday life must be spent. The difficulties of life for the mill worker in this world help to explain the noteworthy emphasis on otherworldliness in his churches. Most of the hymns and sermons in village churches point toward a more placid state and have little concern with mundane economic or social relations. . . . A well-loved stanza, typical in ideas of many others, says:

[3] See Chapter 7.
[4] Max Weber, "The Social Psychology of the World Religions," in *From Max Weber*, trans. and ed. Hans Gerth and C. Wright Mills (New York: Oxford University Press, 1958), p. 276.

> While some live in splendid mansions,
> And have wealth at their command,
> I'm a stranger and a pilgrim
> Passing through this barren land.[5]

In short, religion for mill workers provides a relief or escape from the harshness of their lives. For an hour or two, once or twice a week, they can transcend the mundane, and focus on a future that promises to be far better than the present.

Pope points out, by way of contrast, that "if religion in the mill churches is largely an escape from economic conditions, religion in the uptown churches is to considerable degree a sanction of prevailing economic arrangements."[6] Pope reports that major sins for the uptown church members include sexual immorality, breaking one's word, not paying one's debts, engaging in "shady business," and failing to carry out one's civic and social obligations.[7] Although religion attempts to invade the personal life of the mill worker, religion is not to meddle in the private lives of the middle- and upper-class town residents. Pope suggests that "greater economic security breeds personal independence."[8] Such independence and individualism are also major features of the religion of the bourgeoisie according to Emile Pin. Pin states that individualism characterizes essentially every aspect of the life of the bourgeois, "who has reached, through his own efforts, a worldly 'salvation,' does not depend on religion to regulate his existence, but rather appeals to it only to assure the continuation of this salvation in the other world."[9]

Pope points out that for the privileged classes in Gaston County, religion is for the most part a specialized sphere of life. Their religious attitudes, as he observes them, are

> that a man ought to belong to a church, and should attend as often as convenient, and should bear his part of the financial burden,
> that churches are essential to the welfare of the community,
> that there is no use in getting all wrought up or emotional about religion,
> that if a person lives as decently as he can, that's all that God can expect of him,
> that a minister ought to be a good fellow in his private life, joining civic clubs, attending baseball games, and the like,
> that a minister ought to be a leader in all community enterprises, such as projects sponsored by the Chamber of Commerce.

[5] Liston Pope, *Millhands and Preachers* (New Haven: Yale University Press, 1942), pp. 88–90.

[6] Ibid., p. 92.

[7] Ibid.

[8] Ibid.

[9] Emile Pin, "Social Classes and Their Religious Approaches," in *Religion, Culture, and Society*, ed. Louis Schneider (New York: John Wiley, 1964), p. 411.

that religion ought not to meddle in politics, except where moral issues, such as prohibition, are involved,
that Holy Rollers are ignorant, and are to be pitied,
that mill churches meet the needs of mill workers very satisfactorily.[10]

Pope summarizes by saying, "The role of the uptown minister, and of his church, is not to transcend immediate cultural boundaries but to symbolize and sanction the rightness of things as they are."[11]

DIFFERENTIAL DENOMINATIONAL AFFILIATION BY SOCIAL CLASS

As would be expected, differences in the meaning and expression of religion by social class are reflected in denominational affiliation—that is, denominations differ in their social class composition. An indication of class differences is suggested in Table 8–1. There are dramatic differences by denomination in the proportion of members who have attended college for at least awhile. Jews and Episcopalians are almost three times as likely as Baptists and Lutherans to have attended college.[12]

More detailed data from the mid-1970s that include the three most commonly used empirical measures of status confirm the data in Table 8–1,

TABLE 8–1   Proportion of Denominational Membership Who Have Attended College

DENOMINATION	PERCENT COLLEGE
Jew	60%
Episcopalian	59
Presbyterian	51
Methodist	32
Catholic	29
Baptist	23
Lutheran	22
All Americans	32

Source: The SuperNORC composite samples taken between 1963 and the early 1970s by the National Opinion Research Center of the University of Chicago. Reported in Andrew M. Greeley, William C. McCready, and Kathleen McCourt, *Catholic Schools in a Declining Church* (Kansas City: Sheed and Ward, 1976), abstracted from Table 3.2, p. 44. Copyright 1976 by Andrew Greeley, William C. Mcready and Kathleen McCourt. Reprinted with permission of Andrews and McMeel, Inc. All rights reserved.

[10] Pope, *Millhands and Preachers*, pp. 93–94.

[11] Ibid., p. 95.

[12] While not by itself a perfect indicator of social class, education, particularly if it involves attendance at college, reflects class differences fairly well.

though the differences are not so dramatic. That is, the membership of some religious groups, such as Jews, Episcopalians, and Presbyterians, on the average have attained more education, have higher prestige jobs, and earn more money than others (see Table 8–2).

The factors underlying such class differences among denominations are many. In part it is a self-selection process of like seeking like—of people affiliating with a church whose current members are reasonably like themselves. There is the theological dimension also—the theological celebration of success in this world in some religious groups versus the emphasis on otherworldly salvation in others. In large part the class differences by denomination are a product of history. The highest status denominations in Tables 8–1 and 8–2, with the exception of the Jewish groups, have been well established in this country for the longest periods. Thus their members have had greater opportunities to accumulate family wealth and enhance their status. On the other hand, Lutherans and particularly Roman Catholics are composed of more recent arrivals in this country who have had less opportunity for upward mobility. The Lutherans also are predominantly rural in their constituency and hence likely to rank lower on such dimensions of status as education, cash income, and occupational prestige. Sectarians, we have earlier noted, are almost by definition more likely to be of low socioeconomic status than members of established denominations.

Probably the biggest change in the past twenty years has been the movement upward of Roman Catholics. They have moved past both Lutherans and Baptists in education, and past Lutherans, Baptists, and Methodists in family income, although thirty years ago they ranked behind them all on these dimensions. Only in occupational prestige do they still rank behind those groups. It should be noted that there is substantial variation within Roman

TABLE 8–2   Status Differences Along Three Dimensions among Selected Religious Groups

RELIGIOUS GROUP	AVERAGE EDUCATION ATTAINED (IN YEARS)	AVERAGE LEVEL OF OCCUPATIONAL PRESTIGE	AVERAGE FAMILY INCOME
Jews	13.7	50	$14,350
Episcopalians	13.6	48.4	14,100
Presbyterians	13.1	49	13,200
Congregationalists	12.7	47.3	12,045
Methodists	12	46.2	10,085
Roman Catholics	11.7	43.8	10,820
Lutherans	11.6	45.1	10,400
Baptists	11	45.8	9,245
Sectarians	10.5	45.7	8,080

Source: Wade Clark Roof, "Socioeconomic Differentials Among White Socioreligious Groups in the United States," Social Forces 58, no. 1 (September 1979); 280–89.

Catholicism on the basis of ethnicity. For example, Irish Catholics rank at the 12.7 level in education, while Spanish-speaking Catholics rank at 10.3.[13]

It is clear though that no religious group is completely class-exclusive—that is, there is a range of classes represented in every religious group. Class exclusiveness, however, is often more pronounced at the local congregational level. Thus, if a third of all Congregationalists, for example, are lower class we would not infer that a third of all the members of every local Congregational church, or even of a majority of them, are from the lower class. What it does mean is that there are some congregations with a majority of lower-class members, others with a majority of middle- and/or upper-class members. This should not be surprising inasmuch as congregations tend to attract a majority of their members from the neighborhoods in which they are located, and neighborhoods tend to be fairly class-exclusive.

This phenomenon is clearly in evidence in Pope's study of Gaston County. In 1939 Pope tallied thirty-four rural churches, only five of which had a significant minority (a minimum of 20 percent) of mill workers and none of which had a significant minority of uptown members. Similarly, of seventy-six mill churches only one had a significant minority of rural members and only eight a significant minority of uptown members. Uptown churches were less likely to be so predominantly of one class. Yet in only seventeen of thirty-five were even 20 percent of the members mill workers, and in only three were there significant minorities of rural members. In total, only 23 percent of the churches in Gaston County had significant minority membership, and only 6 percent lacked a majority group of at least 66.6 percent.[14] Clearly, then, a religious group is very likely to represent the class constituency of the geographic area in which it is located.

Demerath has pointed out that although there may be a mixture of social classes in a national denomination and even in its local congregations, the members of these classes may not be looking for or receiving the same things out of their affiliation and participation.[15] Demerath first reports Fukuyama's 1961 study demonstrating differences in religiosity among Congregationalists by social class. Fukuyama's data, reported in Table 8–3, show that the higher social classes are more likely than the lowest social class to express their religion in cultic and cognitive ways, whereas the lowest social class is more likely than the others to express religion devotionally (the differences along the creedal dimension are not significant). Demerath dichotomizes the possible relationship to one's religious group for his sample (Lutherans) into "church-like" and "sectlike" religiosity. Some of his findings are included in Table 8–4

[13] Wade Clark Roof, "Socioeconomic Differentials Among White Socio-religious Groups in the United States," *Social Forces* 58, no. 1 (September, 1979), pp. 280–89.

[14] Ibid., pp. 70–71.

[15] N. J. Demerath III, *Social Class in American Protestantism* (Chicago: Rand McNally, 1965).

TABLE 8-3 *Proportion of Congregationalists Scoring High on Selected Measures of Religiosity, by Social Class*

	SOCIOECONOMIC STATUS		
MEASURE	HIGH	MEDIUM	LOW
Cultic	53%	43%	35%
Cognitive	28	24	15
Creedal	27	28	31
Devotional	16	23	32

Source: Adapted from Yoshio Fukuyama, "The Major Dimensions of Church Membership," *Review of Religious Research* 2, no. 4 (1960), 159.

Note: Cultic = measure of church attendance and organizational participation
Cognitive = measure of knowledge of religious doctrine and congregational affairs
Creedal = measure of personal allegiance to traditional doctrine
Devotional = measure of personal prayer and expression of reliance on religion beyond the church itself

which indicates quite clearly that the lower Lutherans' social-class position, the less likely they are to exhibit a churchlike attachment to religion. As would be expected, a corresponding opposite relationship is observed with respect to sectlike commitment. The progression for high sectlike commitment from the upper through the middle, working, and lower classes is 10 percent, 15 percent, 25 percent, and 35 percent respectively.[16]

All these data indicate that social status appears to have an effect upon the meaning and expression of religion for people. This is not only evidenced by the fact that people of one status level tend to be members of particular denominations or sects, but people within a particular denomination and even within a local organization are both looking for and finding different things.

TABLE 8-4 *Churchlike Religiosity among Lutherans, by Social Class*

DEGREE OF CHURCHLIKE COMMITMENT*	SOCIOECONOMIC STATUS			
	UPPER	MIDDLE	WORKING	LOWER
High	51%	45%	32%	24%
Moderate	20	20	19	19
Low	29	35	48	57

Source: N. J. Demerath III, *Social Class in American Protestantism* (Chicago: Rand McNally, 1965), p. 87.

*Based on frequency of church attendance, participation in parish organizations, and membership in outside organizations.

[16] Ibid., p. 88.

That the meaning of religion and participation in religious activities varies among social classes is of course not unique to Western Christianity. Such differences are noted particularly in Hinduism. The division into social classes of Brahmins, Kshatriyas, Vaisyas, Shudras, and "outcasts" or "untouchables" correlates quite closely with differences in the historical meaning and expression of Hinduism as a religion. The fact that originally only the two upper classes were literate and could read and become familiar with the holy books predetermined important differences. For example, even today the upper classes tend to be monistic—they believe in one Absolute with all other gods a part of expression of the One. The common people tend to be polytheists and believe in many local gods and spirits, tend to identify the image or statue itself with the divine living reality, and believe in a heaven and hell which the higher classes do not. The upper classes believe more firmly in the doctrines of samsara (the transmigration of souls), karma (the principle of cause and effect —what you sow you reap), and dharma (the standard of determining whether you move socially upward or downward in the next life). The upper classes are more firmly committed to the belief that if you follow the rules of your caste you can move upward, from one life to another. This could be all the way to an ultimate goal of being released from the nearly endless cycle of transmigration of souls and realizing unity with the Brahman or Absolute (attain Nirvana). Noss notes that the masses have never had a clear conception of the finer points of Hinduism such as the various "ways" of salvation and release from the miseries and responsibilities of life (Way of Works, Way of Knowledge, Way of Devotion). He says that the masses go about being religious in the traditional manner of their local area. They practice and reflect animism, fetishism, shamanism, demonolatry, animal worship, and devotion to local spirits and godlings, often without the "higher" worship of the supreme deities in the Hindu pantheon.[17] Noss goes on to say that in some areas Hinduism can hardly be recognized as such; a primitive animism takes its place. This sub-Hinduism is common among the millions of "untouchables."[18]

Along a similar vein, Buddhism in its original form found little or no response among the masses. But the masses gradually became interested, as Noss observes, not in the theologian Gautama Buddha but in the man.[19] Worship of the person and the idea of salvation through various saviors became popular with the lower classes.[20] In fact, some of the untouchables, in trying to improve their degraded lot in life, adopted Buddhism, which promised some relief and release from the desperate, unredeemable character of their existence.

[17] John B. Noss, *Man's Religions* (New York: Macmillan, 1949), p. 243.
[18] Ibid., p. 244.
[19] Ibid., p. 171.
[20] Ibid., p. 188.

If we look a little more closely at the religious situation in India we discover that Hinduism and Indian culture (including its caste system) are almost one and the same. Hinduism is a comprehensive religion in the sense that there is really nothing that the Hindu does of a cultural nature—whether brushing one's teeth, preparing food, encountering people in the street, or any other act—that does not have religious significance and some kind of religious prescription wrapped around it. "Hinduism is a culture and a religion at the same time . . . religion and life are synonymous."[21]

At least this is the heritage of India's past—a caste-based society in which strict separation of classes was both cultural and religious dictum. In 1950, however, the Democratic Republican Constitution of India was adopted. This constitution, much like that of the United States, emphasizes justice, liberty, and equality—and not just in a political sense but in a social sense as well. Article 15 of the Constitution states that caste cannot be a basis for discrimination or any restrictions on access to stores, restaurants, village water sources, and the like. Further, any traditional practices based on untouchability are categorically forbidden.

However, castes continue to be identified, and such a system, though in a somewhat modified form, will continue for many years to come. This is so and will continue to be so in part because the caste system is so deeply embedded in Indian culture and society that it is a primary source of identification for people. As such it is a rallying point, a source of members of caste-restrictive political parties, a power bloc for economic and political action, an audience for caste journals and newspapers, the body of membership in particular craft unions, and the constituency of voluntary associations of various types. Such goes on quite irrespective of religious sanctions one way or the other and of a constitution that prescribes that caste be ignored and transcended.

It is worth noting too that with respect to the origin of caste the role of religion is almost assuredly one of reinforcement rather than cause. While there is not now and probably never will be total consensus on the precise cause or causes of caste in India, it is likely that several factors together provided the basis. While a common belief among the populace is that the castes "issued from the mouth, arms, thighs, and feet of Brahma," it is also widely understood that race has played a part. Sir Herbert Risley states that in eastern India "a man's status varies in inverse ratio to the width of his nose."[22] Others emphasize occupational sources of caste. That is, various occupations were status ranked differentially by the people themselves; subsequently specific occupations and occupational categories became castes. Still others point to the separateness of ancient tribes as well as the differences between invaders

[21] Trevor Ling, *Buddha, Marx, and God* (London: Macmillan, 1966), p. 211.
[22] Herbert Risely, "The Tribes and Castes of Bengal" quoted by N. Presad, *The Myth of the Caste System* (Petna: Prakashan, 1957), p. 26.

and the conquered as early sources of castes. And so on. But the point is simply that cultural and highly sociological factors have contributed to a rigid class (caste) system that, while integral within Indian religion, is not necessarily of religious origin. Further, a democratic constitution and continuous religious denunciation of caste today do not eradicate overnight or even in a generation or two what has been so integral a part of a society's political, religious, and social structure.

SOCIAL STRATIFICATION
WITHIN RELIGIOUS GROUPS

If we define social stratification as a hierarchical arrangement or ordering of people in a group according to criteria or standards determined and accepted by that group—a definition implicit in this chapter so far—then it is easy to see that such stratification is an integral part of religion. Although many religious groups preach the equality of everyone before God, this often implies only equality among the specially favored people in their own group. Religious groups are historically notorious for their clear distinction between the "ins" and the "outs," the believers and the nonbelievers, the saved and the unsaved. Moreover, stratification appears even within the group itself. Stratification is endemic in two senses. First, there is the distinction between prophet and people, or leader and followers. Those who are considered to have special insights or are credited with special revelation are accorded elevated positions relative to those who listen and follow. The person with deeper knowledge of sacred things (rituals and writings)—the teacher or priest—is ranked higher than those who are his or her pupils and followers. Second, there is the recognition that even among the followers, some follow the norms of the group more closely than others and are more holy, more knowledgeable, more dedicated than the "average" or "majority" of followers or members. Even though the majority of rank-and-file members may not personally aspire to such status, they tend to acknowledge its validity and give honor and respect to those who embody most perfectly the virtues and knowledge that the group has defined as praiseworthy. Such distinctions are readily observed in the panoply of saints in the Roman Catholic Church—persons who have gone an extra mile or two in perfecting the expression and application of the Catholic faith.

The great majority of Buddhists also recognize the elevated status of the numerous monks and "holy men" who have proceeded farther along the path in search of the ultimate goal—the elimination of desire—than has the ordinary follower of the Buddha.

Jehovah's Witnesses speak of the 144,000 higher-caste believers who will be rewarded with "heaven," while others will simply be inhabitants of "paradise." Although the sacred number of 144,000 appears to be taken more figuratively than literally today, particularly as the membership in the group has surpassed that number, the idea of a greater reward for the few who are most holy remains.

As Glenn Vernon suggests, probably the best known "celestial caste system" is that of the Roman Catholic Church, with its four levels of heaven, hell, purgatory, and limbo for persons after death—heaven for the purest believers, hell for the nonbelievers, purgatory for the believers who still need some "cleansing" before entering heaven, limbo a place to which people went before Christ's work of redemption was completed and from which he thereafter liberated them.[23]

Other groups talk of the visible church on earth—the voluntary association including not only sincere believers but also some nonbelievers and hypocrites who are professed but insincere members—as contrasted with the invisible church, which is composed only of true believers whom only God can know by looking within their heart and assessing their sincerity.

We have already mentioned the religious stratification in Hinduism that is so intimately associated with the societal stratification system. Lower-caste persons are not just lower-status socially but religiously as well. To move upward in successive lives through the process of samsara (transmigration of the soul) into higher castes in the social sense is to move upward religiously as well. One would thereby not only enjoy more and more of the amenities of life but would also come ever closer to the ultimate goal of union with or absorbtion into the timeless or eternal Brahman, thus finding release from the cycle of transmigration. In this connection Charles Eliot makes the point that it is the caste structure of Indian society that influences Hinduism, not vice versa. He states that many Hindu religious leaders have declared unequivocally that there ought to be no social distinctions among believers. But caste continually reasserts itself. Social structure and precedents, Eliot concludes, are stronger than theology.[24]

STRATIFICATION, RELIGION, AND RACE

We now turn to a somewhat extended example of how stratification and religion interrelate when a third variable, race or ethnic background, is introduced. Here again we shall see the reciprocal-interaction relationship between religion and other features of the society.

Although each of the major religions of the world has tended officially to welcome all comers into its fellowship of faith, in practice most have at some time or other discriminated against racial or ethnic groups living in the

---

[23] Glenn M. Vernon, *Sociology of Religion* (New York: McGraw-Hill, 1962), p. 380.

[24] Charles Eliot, *Hinduism and Buddhism* (London: Routledge & Kegan Paul, 1921), vol. 2, 176–78.

same society. Of course, we need to emphasize that the religious element in such discrimination is usually inextricably bound up with political and economic factors as well. This point will be amply demonstrated as we proceed.

One quick example before proceeding with our primary one. The interaction of political and religious factors is dramatically seen in India and Pakistan, where the centuries-old conflict between Hinduism and Islam culminated in the 1971 war over Bangladesh (formerly East Pakistan). When East Pakistan was still part of the larger nation, the government located in the western portion, which has a Muslim majority, systematically discriminated against Hindus within both West Pakistan and East Pakistan, which has a Hindu majority. Thus a basic ingredient of the military and political conflict was the religious antagonism between Muslims and Hindus.

Similar examples of prejudice and discrimination appear throughout the history of Western Christianity. One thinks of the Inquisition in medieval Europe, the execution of various Protestant reformers by Roman Catholic state and ecclesiastical powers, the Thirty Years' War in seventeenth-century Europe between Protestant and Roman Catholic forces, the present Prostestant-Catholic civil conflict in Northern Ireland, and, along a somewhat different line, the prejudice and discrimination in the name of religion that has been directed against blacks throughout American history. We shall focus just a bit on this last phenomenon particularly, because it so well portrays the intimate connection of the three variables mentioned above—religion, race, and social class.

By definition, slaves in any society are at the very bottom of the stratification system. This is not an issue in itself in a society that tolerates slavery and includes it in its normative system—if we assume a society has the right to determine such a structure in the face of universal human rights.[25] But the phenomenon of slavery presented a problem for the Christian religion. In fact, it became a dilemma in the sense that Christian theology had developed the principle that although slavery itself was not forbidden by God, a Christian should not hold another Christian in bondage. The dilemma arose when that principle came in contact with the conversion principle—that is, the mandate to "make disciples of all nations" and convert everyone possible.

The Early American Experience

Early in colonial American history the question arose concerning what to do about the religion of black slaves. One mandate said: Convert them to Christianity. But the other said: You should not hold a fellow Christian as a

---

[25] This is not the place to discuss whether norms that condone slavery run counter to "human nature" or violate fundamental human rights to such things as life, liberty, and the pursuit of happiness. Although we happen to agree that involuntary servitude is in direct violation of universal human rights, we need not debate the issue to understand the sociological points that this chapter is making.

slave. Therefore, what to do? Some slaveholders quite expectedly opposed the conversion of slaves. Unconverted they presented no problem, since the slaveholder would not be keeping a fellow Christian as a slave. But theologians and clergy members said it was the Christian's obligation to teach the slaves Christianity and convert them. Some Southerners resolved the issue by defining blacks as less than human. We do not convert dogs, kudus, or zebras; therefore, we do not need to convert blacks—as a lower animal form, they lack a soul to be saved.

And so the controversy went on. Ultimately a compromise was reached. Religious leaders abandoned their original position and said that the church would no longer maintain the position that conversion required emancipation. This meant that the church could save souls and the slaveholders their investment. This compromise led to substantial missionary activity among slaves, who were rapidly converted to Christianity. The mass conversions of slaves occurred in significant part of course because once the owners decided their slaves should espouse Christianity the slaves themselves, as property and with essentially no personal or civil rights, had little choice in the matter.

The process of this religious about-face is well documented for the Methodist Church and merits a somewhat extended examination as an example of social-class and economic influences on religious ideology and practice. In its beginning, American Methodism quite naturally looked to its English founder John Wesley for guidance on the issue of slavery. They did not look in vain. Among Wesley's *General Rules*, prepared in 1739, was a rule forbidding "the buying or selling of the bodies and souls of men, women, or children with an intention to enslave them."[26] And in 1772 he denounced the slave trade as "the sum of all villainies."[27] Accordingly, the Methodist Episcopal Church, organized in Baltimore in 1784, proposed and adopted the following six special rules designed to destroy slavery among its members:

1. Every slave-holding member, within twelve months, was required to execute a deed of manumission.

2. All infants who were born after these rules went into effect were to have immediate freedom.

3. Members who chose not to comply were allowed to withdraw within twelve months.

4. The sacrament of the Lord's Supper was to be denied to all such thenceforward.

5. No slaveholders were to be admitted thereafter into church membership.

6. Any members who bought, sold, or gave slaves away, except on purpose to free them, were immediately to be expelled.[28]

[26] Quoted in W. W. Sweet, *The Methodist Episcopal Church and the Civil War* (Cincinnati: Methodist Book Concern Press, 1912), p. 15.

[27] Quoted in Charles Swaney, *Episcopal Methodism and Slavery* (Boston: R. G. Badger, 1926), p. 1.

[28] Sweet, *The Methodist Episcopal Church*, p. 16.

This, then, was the official stand of the Methodist Church on the question of slavery.

Thus during these early days of Methodism in the United States there appeared to be no great problem with slavery. Apparently no members were slaveholders, and moreover, Wesley's principles were in force. Slavery, however, seems to have found its way into the Methodist Church during the Revolutionary War, probably without the knowledge of John Wesley or his American assistant Francis Asbury.[29] It seems to have entered gradually and unobtrusively. In this connection it is important to note that rather lax church administration prevailed at this time. By 1778 every English missionary preacher had returned to the mother country except Asbury, and the latter restricted himself primarily to the small state of Delaware. The job of expanding the church was thus committed to young, inexperienced, poorly educated men. Almost all of these young ministers had been born and reared in a slave culture and appeared to have no clear understanding that slavery was wrong. DeVinne states that the forty-eight preachers who had been received into the ministry during the Revolutionary War belonged almost exclusively to this class.[30] Further, the early work of these Methodist preachers was primarily in the slaveholding states. Out of a national membership of about fourteen thousand, only about two thousand resided in nonsouthern states.[31]

It is not surprising, then, that the formal resolutions of Methodist conferences and conventions during the last decade of the eighteenth century, although disapproving slavery, became ever more modified in tone.[32] Mattison reports that by 1808 "all that related to slaveholding among private members [that is, laypersons] was stricken out of the Methodist body of rules and regulations and the following put in its place: 'The General Conference authorizes each Annual Conference to form their own regulations, relative to buying and selling slaves.' "[33] It is important to note that it was the buying and selling of slaves that each conference was to regulate, not the holding of slaves. Apparently, the possession of slaves, at least by laypeople, now had the church's tacit approval. By 1840, the ownership of slave property was extended to ministers.[34]

A crisis developed in 1844 when a bishop of the Methodist Church, the Reverend James Andrew, was found to be a slaveholder. This necessitated a clear decision. Either do something with Bishop Andrew, or openly tolerate

---

[29] Daniel DeVinne, *The Methodist Episcopal Church and Slavery* (New York: F. Hart, 1857), p. 12.

[30] Ibid.

[31] Ibid.

[32] Lucius Matlack, *History of American Slavery and Methodism from 1780 to 1849* (New York: Lucius Matlack, 1849), pp. 33 ff.

[33] Hiram Mattison, *The Impending Crisis of 1860* (New York: Mason Brothers, 1859), p. 30.

[34] Ibid., p. 34.

slaveholding in the highest positions of the church. Was the Methodist Episcopal Church a slaveholding church, or was it not? The issue was essentially resolved that same year when the Methodist Episcopal Church split into what amounted to northern and southern branches—the former condemning slavery, the latter citing Scripture to support it.

What we observe quite clearly here is the influence of social and situational factors upon the institution of religion. To summarize briefly: Early American Methodist activity and growth were in the South where the issue of slavery and slave holding became an issue almost by definition. As the plantation system grew and as it became economically profitable to own slaves, Methodist laypeople, preachers, and finally bishops acceded to the practice. Bishop Asbury, residing in Baltimore, had little knowledge of or control over his fellow Methodists scattered throughout the South. Also, the Methodist ministers during this period were little educated, poorly informed, and Southerners by background, orientation, and ways of thinking.

And so, quite apart from official theological statements or the moral convictions and commitments of church leaders, social factors exerted their influence on the religious group. Economic pressures, organizational features, and characteristics both of the members and lower-level leadership combined to override theological and moral mandates. Because religion exists in society and in the subcommunities and regions of that society, it finds itself influenced by the norms and structure of that society and its subunits.

American Presbyterians followed a similar route. Murray states that most colonial Presbyterians viewed slavery as permitted by God and tended to accept the customs of the areas in which they settled.[35] As slaveholding became more economically significant, the battlelines between North and South were more clearly drawn. This was true of religious groups no less than other groups and institutions in the society. Actually, although some southern Presbyterians vigorously opposed slavery, it was not only the issue of theological liberalism but also the controversy over slavery that resulted in the "schism of 1837" between "old-school" and "new-school" Presbyterians.[36] This schism was sealed by the coming of the Civil War, as the northern and southern Presbyterians went their separate ways.

With the outbreak of the Civil War in 1861, all the major Protestant denominations either officially split into northern and southern branches or allowed local political policy to dictate the church's position. For example, C. F. W. Walther, leader of what is now known as The Luthern Church—Missouri Synod, saw the slavery issue as a matter for government, not churches, to decide. In doing so he relied on a strict interpretation of the principle of separation of church and state: Church members are to respect and abide by

[35] Andrew E. Murray, *Presbyterians and the Negro—A History* (Philadelphia: Presbyterian Historical Society, 1966), p. 12.

[36] Ibid., pp. 103 ff.

the laws established by the political process in the governmental units of which they are citizens.

Into the Present

Slight variations of this principle appear to have guided much religious thinking on the slavery issue and thus set the stage for the relative noninvolvement of religious groups in civil rights struggles following the Civil War. Most religious groups at both the national and local levels remained on balance silent on the issue of black civil rights for nearly ten decades. It was a stand of aloofness which relegated first the issue of slavery, then equal rights for blacks, to the political and social realm and asserted that it was "not the business of the church" to interfere in such social and political (that is, nonreligious) matters.[37] It is in fact this very silence which prompts our excursion into the question of the relationship of white Christianity in the United States to black Americans. White churches have tended to reinforce the class and caste gap between whites and blacks, sometimes by lending active support to claims of blacks' inherent inferiority and to justifications for their second-class citizenship, most often by remaining silent and thereby giving tacit approval to racial segregation, discrimination, and prejudice. Furthermore, racial or ethnic differences which became closely associated with class differences were reflected in religious differences. In other words, white churches were for whites, black churches for blacks. Kyle Haselden asserts that "long before the little signs—'White Only' and 'Colored'—appeared in the public utilities they had appeared in the Church."[38]

In the 1950s and 1960s, however, nearly every major religious group issued official statements and passed resolutions at their national conventions favoring equality for blacks and calling for an end to discrimination and segregation, although not always issuing clear calls for integration as such. Also during this period white faces in clerical collars became highly visible in sit-ins, marches, and demonstrations, as numerous white clergy and some laypeople as well provided leadership and helped fill the ranks of participants in the civil rights struggle. They sincerely wanted to tell the nation and the world that the white Christian churches were concerned and committed, and they wanted by example and exhortation to bring their fellow white church members along. Yet their voices and presence do not seem to have been representative or typical of the churches from which they came.

A strong antiblack animus remained within the white Christian denominations. In a nationwide survey as recently as 1967, nearly half (44 percent) of the white respondents registered basic disapproval of the black civil rights

---

[37] Ralph Moellering, *Christian Conscience and Negro Emancipation* (Philadelphia: Fortress Press, 1965), p. 76.

[38] Kyle Haselden, *The Racial Problem in Christian Perspective* (New York: Harper & Row, Pub., 1959), p. 29.

movement in this country.[39] Of significant interest, this proportion compares with from only 4 to 8 percent of clergy (some slight differences by denomination) who disapprove of the movement.[40]

Actually, it is generally believed that the 44 percent of laypeople who expressed disapproval of the Civil Rights movement represented a decline from earlier periods. Paul Sheatsley of the National Opinion Research Center believes that various polls conducted since the 1940s indicate a steady, unambiguous increase in positive sentiment toward civil rights issues.[41] While an improvement over attitudes expressed in earlier polls, a Brink and Harris poll in 1966 found that 52 percent of white Americans would be upset if blacks moved into their neighborhood, and 76 percent of whites who live in neighborhoods into which blacks would like to move would be upset at such a development.[42] Recent data from Gallup polls (1978) suggest continuing improvement in such attitudes. For example, in response to the question; "If blacks came to live next door, would you move?" only 4 percent said they definitely would move (with an additional 9 percent saying that they might move). A full 84 percent said they would not move (the remaining 3 percent expressed no opinion).[43] A follow-up question that posed a more threatening situation elicited more willingness to move. Fifty-one percent of white respondents said they either would definitely or might move if blacks came to live in great numbers in their neighborhood. Yet 45 percent said they would not move.[44]

While it is certainly possible that some of those who said the coming of blacks to their neighborhood would not bother them or motivate them to move are simply saying what they feel is acceptable, but would in fact be bothered to the point of seeking to move, the data provide continuing support for the trend that Sheatsley observed. The improvement may simply not be as dramatic as the figures above might suggest.

Religion, Social Class, and Racial
Attitudes

Quite obviously religion in the United States has not reversed, even to the degree it has tried, its long history of maintaining major class distinctions between whites and blacks. There are, however, important differences in this regard among major religious groups. Jews, for example, express far less suspi-

[39] Jeffrey K. Hadden, *The Gathering Storm in the Churches* (Garden City, N.Y.: Doubleday, 1969), p. 127.

[40] Ibid., p. 104.

[41] Paul B. Sheatsley, "White Attitudes Toward the Negro," *Daedalus* 95, no. 1 (1966), 217–38, quoted in Hadden, *The Gathering Storm,* p. 130.

[42] Reported in Hadden, *The Gathering Storm,* p. 130.

[43] George H. Gallup, *The Gallup Poll: Public Opinion 1979* (Willmington, Del.: Scholarly Resources, 1979), p. 214.

[44] Ibid., p. 215.

cion of and animosity toward blacks than do Protestants and Catholics, with Catholics slightly less likely than Protestants to express such suspicion and hostility. For example, Jeffrey Hadden found in the mid-1960s that only 43 percent of Jewish laypersons would be upset if their rabbi participated in civil rights activities; but 68 percent of Catholic laypersons and 77 percent of Protestant laypersons would be upset if their priest or minister joined in civil rights activities such as marches or sit-ins. Similarly, 59 percent, 30 percent, and 27 percent respectively of Jewish, Catholic, and Protestant laypersons agreed that Martin Luther King was an outstanding example of making Christianity relevant and meaningful.[45]

The social class of respondents also appears to be extremely relevant here. It appears that traditionally the lower the social class of people, the more likely they have been to express suspicion and resentment toward blacks. Using level of educational achievement as the independent measure of social class, we observe some dramatic contrasts in Hadden's sample, as shown in Table 8-5. On all of the questions there is a clear association between amount of education and attitudes in the areas of race and the involvement of clergy in civil rights activities.

One must note, of course, that not all religious persons of low educational attainment or low social status are opposed to black progress or express measurable prejudice against blacks. In fact, David Harrell has noted that some southern whites of working- or lower-class social status and some religious sects whose members are primarily of working-class status have related well to blacks at the same class level, express little or no racial prejudice, and engage in integrated religious activities.[46]

It has frequently been suggested that part of the reason for prejudice against blacks, particularly by whites of at least moderately low socioeconomic status, is the latter's fear of economic threat and of a potential undermining of their only "claim to fame," so to speak—namely, having higher status than at least one other category of people (the blacks around them). Christian antagonism toward Jews has some of this same flavor—not strictly a class phenomenon, but an uneasiness and resentment in the face of Jewish economic, educational, and political success and influence which is frequently seen as disproportionate to their numbers in the population.

Recent data suggest, however, that former differences in white racial attitudes that were related to educational level of respondents have been reduced, perhaps to the point of disappearance. From the 1978 Gallup polls mentioned earlier we note that the difference between the college educated and those with only a grade school education who definitely or might move if blacks came to live next door was only two percentage points (13 percent of

---

[45] Hadden, *The Gathering Storm*, pp. 136–37.

[46] David E. Harrell, Jr., *White Sects and Black Men in the Recent South* (Nashville: Vanderbilt University Press, 1971).

TABLE 8–5 *Proportion Expressing Selected Attitudes on Civil Rights Issues, by Level of Educational Attainment*

	EDUCATION			
ATTITUDE	SOME HIGH SCHOOL	HIGH SCHOOL GRADUATE	SOME COLLEGE	COLLEGE GRADUATE
"Clergy should stick to religion and not concern themselves with social, economic, and political questions."	63%	47%	38%	23%
"I would be upset if my (minister/priest/rabbi) were to participate in a picket line or demonstration."	77	72	69	49
"I basically disapprove of the Negro civil rights movement in America."	53	43	33	23
"Martin Luther King, Jr., is an outstanding example of making Christianity relevant and meaningful for our day."	27	27	32	40

Source: Adapted from Jeffrey K. Hadden, *The Gathering Storm in the Churches* (Garden City, N.Y.: Doubleday, 1969). p. 145.

the college educated, 14 percent of those with a high school diploma, and 15 percent of those with only a grade school education).[47] On the more threatening question about whether the respondents would either definitely or possibly move if blacks came in great numbers to live in their neighborhood, the contrast between the college and the grade school educated people is seven percentage points, but in *the opposite direction* (50 percent of college educated, 43 percent of grade school educated).[48]

While such data do not prove that a reversal has taken place, at the very least we must look carefully at what has been a traditional relationship between education and attitudes in the particular area in question. We need additional data and more intensive, focused research. It just could be that many lower status whites have by now come to terms with improved educational, job, and housing opportunities for blacks. On the other hand, as opportunities continue to improve for blacks, middle-class whites might feel psychological threats to their status and security that until recently have been rare.

[47] Gallup, *The Gallup Poll*, p. 214.
[48] Ibid., p. 215.

9

Women and Religion

In an age of great turmoil over the roles and rights of women, when Helen Reddy can sing, "I am woman; I can do anything,"[1] yet many children read, "Boys fix things, girls need things fixed. Boys invent things. Girls use what boys invent,"[2] it is small wonder that religious organizations worldwide have themselves become microcosms of the women's role and rights debate. An examination of the sociological relationship of women and religion from both a historical and a contemporary perspective will be the focus of this chapter.

By way of a beginning, we need to explore in at least an introductory way the context within which women have had and continue to have their relationship to religion, and within which they express themselves religiously. This is of course the society and the subgroup context within which both women and the religious institutions themselves live out their lives.

---

[1] *"I Am Woman"* Words by Helen Reddy. Music by Ray Burton. © 1971 Irving Music & Buggerlugs Music Co. (BMI). All rights Reserved. International Copyright Secured.

[2] Whitney Darrow, Jr., *I'm Glad I'm a Boy! I'm Glad I'm a Girl!* (New York: Simon and Schuster, 1970), cited in D. Stanley Eitzen, *In Conflict and Order* (Boston: Allyn & Bacon, 1978), p. 127.

THE RELATIONSHIP OF
WOMEN TO RELIGION IN
HISTORICAL PERSPECTIVE

The Societal Context

As we try to reconstruct life in early hunting and food gathering societies, at least one characteristic appears to be universal. That is that the contribution of women to the food supply and hence their importance to the community was equal to and perhaps greater than that of men. As such, the power and status of women were not appreciably reduced when compared with men. Further, her participation in and responsibility for what we would today call "religious" activities were frequently on a fairly equal plane with men.

While it is true that biological gender factors determine that at least some of women's work shall almost assuredly be different from men's work, such work was not usually seen as less important. Because of recurrent pregnancies that were in most cases necessary and desirable in hunting and gathering societies in order to replenish a population continually devastated by a high death rate, a woman's work needed to be close to camp and hut, and she herself needed to be accessible to nursing children. As such her activities centered around gathering edible plant life—roots, fruits, and berries—in the vicinity of the camp, as well as caring for the children and carrying out routine camp chores. The men hunted and traversed the more distant territory of the society's domain. While each contributed to the food supply, the women's contribution was usually the more stable and predictable portion and as such was almost by definition the most important. Thus her status was usually essentially equivalent to that of men.

As horticultural societies evolved, following the discovery of the cause-effect relationship between seed planting and harvest, women's role receded but little. The gardens that had now been created fell most often upon the women to tend (the gardens were after all on the edge of the village), while men continued to wander in search of game. Again, the stability of women's contribution to the food supply contributed to their maintenance of status. Concomitantly, matrilineal lines of descent were nearly as common as patrilineal, and sexual freedom, whether prenuptial or postnuptial, was frequently as great for women as for men. In short, there was relatively little status differentiation by sex.

With the domestication of animals and eventually the invention of the plow (that is, as agriculture began to succeed in evolutionary stages the hunting and horticulture that preceded), men's roles in the food production process began to exceed those of women. For one thing, the arduousness of breaking and tilling the ground, as well as breaking and controlling the large animals that provided the energy, required the greater physical strength possessed by men.

Eventually, as technology expanded and as industrialization transformed society, women became increasingly dependent upon men. Although they played important roles in childbearing and childrearing and in food preparation and home management, they were drawn further away from direct access to the means of production. Not only did they not own the means of production, they participated only minimally in the production process. As such, their dependency increased, and their status decreased.

Although the beginnings of industrialization in the form of cottage industries brought women back, at least for awhile, into the mainstream of the productive process, the persons involved—the men, the women, and the children alike (remember that abuses in the area of child labor began in the home cottage industry, not the factories, mines, and mills that followed after)—were all sufficiently enslaved by the cottage industry process as to do little for the status of these women. They were all members of an exploited class, dependent for bare subsistence upon the middlemen who provided the raw materials and accumulated the finished products for resale and their own profit.

It is only later, as the work of at least some women was moved out of the home—first in the textile industry, then in primary education[3]—that women began to participate in a more direct and obvious way in economic production. However, such a shift involved sufficiently few women, and jobs that were sufficiently economically exploitative, that there was still no significant improvement of women's status. However, it is in these early days of industrialization that the pioneer voices of women's liberation could be heard. The first major feminist tract, *The Vindication of the Rights of Women*, was published in 1792. The first American feminist convention, led by Lucretia Mott and Elizabeth Cady Stanton, well-known nineteenth century feminists, was held in 1848.[4]

But before we get too close to the present and too far away from our quick overview of the past, we want to parallel the relationship of women to religion and their roles in the religious patterns and institutions with the various stages of societal evolution.

THE HISTORIC PATTERNS

There is considerable archeological evidence that a great mother goddess was the supreme deity in a great many ancient societies. In fact, Merlin Stone states quite categorically: "At the dawn of religion, God was a woman."[5] Although evidence is insufficient to be certain that such was indeed true *everywhere*, a great deal of supporting evidence does exist.

[3] Jo Freeman, *The Politics of Women's Liberation* (New York: D. McKay, 1975), p. 14.
[4] Ibid., p. 13.
[5] Merlin Stone, *The Paradise Papers* (London: Quartel Books, 1976), p. 17.

The anthropologist Edwin James documents the prominent position of female deities throughout the ancient world from the Indian subcontinent and Mesopotamia, through all of the Near East and Greece and Rome, to Western Europe and the islands of the Mediterranean.[6] There were female creator gods in China, Australia, Africa, Babylon, and Egypt.

In fact, Egypt is one of the better-known ancient societies in which female deities not only appeared early but remained prominent. Already by 3000 B.C. the goddess Nut—probably derived from the more ancient Nekhebt, a goddess in early Upper Egypt—was described as having existed before anything else appeared in the world and as actually having created all else that has come into being. In fact, she first placed the familiar sun god, Ra, in the heavens.[7] At the point of recorded history, however, Ra (Re) appears to have become first among a pantheon of gods.[8] Ra represented the sun in all its fullness, combined all the forces of nature, and held absolute control over the Nile valley. Yet he appears to have been preceded by a powerful and creative mother-goddess, as we have mentioned.

It was Nut's daughter, Isis, who became the most popular and important goddess in Egyptian history—a highly beneficent deity who personified all that was vital in motherhood—a goddess who remained important for a long period of time.[9]

It is also worth noting that in early Egypt the queen was intended to have greater power than the king, and in marriage the wife was to have authority over the husband, with husbands agreeing to be obedient to their wives.[10]

What appears to have been the most important deity to the various Eskimo tribes was Sedna, a female deity. Tales relate how she sent her children across the seas to become ancestors for other cultures, what we know as European cultures in particular. When her father tried to sacrifice her to appease an evil spirit by throwing her into the sea, even cutting off her fingers as she grabbed at the side of the boat, her fingers became the seal and walrus and other sea animals crucial to the Eskimos' survival. As Sedna sinks to the bottom of the sea she becomes "Mother of the Sea Animals." One can readily infer her supreme importance from such depictions when one realizes the centrality of the seal and walrus to the Eskimo food, clothing, and tool supply. When taboos are perceived to have been violated and she withholds the

---

[6] Edwin O. James, *The Cult of the Mother-Goddess* (New York: Barnes & Noble, 1959).

[7] Stone, *Paradise Papers*, p. 52.

[8] Jacquetta Hawkes and Leonard Woolley, *Prehistory and the Beginnings of Civilization* (New York: Harper & Row, Pub., 1963), p. 724; E. O. James, *The Ancient Gods* (New York: Putnam's, 1960), p. 71.

[9] James, *The Ancient Gods*, p. 85.

[10] Reported by Diodorus and quoted in Stone, *Paradise Papers*, p. 53.

sea animals, shamans must get very busy performing appropriate rituals to appease her.[11]

Even in the region of Palestine, where Old Testament Judaism ultimately triumphed and not only excluded female deities (without even having a vocabulary word for "goddess") but severely restricted women's participation in religious activities, mother and other goddesses abounded in prehistoric times. Prominent among them were Anat, the "Lady of the Mountain" and consort and sister of Aleyan-Baal; Asherah, the arch rival of Anat who with the god El bore 70 gods and goddesses; and Astarte, a Philistine goddess of procreation and fecundity.[12]

That the female should be so prominently featured and credited with primary religious responsibilities in the earliest societies should not really surprise us if we remember observations made at the beginning of this chapter. For one thing, the female bears the most obvious productive responsibility. It is she who actually bears the children. Thus, from mother of children to "mother of the tribe," "mother of humankind," and so on would be fairly logical and easy extensions. Further, some reinforcement for the importance and centrality of "mother" would be observed in those societies which were uncertain concerning the source of conception in the first place, not really perceiving the male role and the serial relationship among coitus, conception, and birth. Men were most often perceived to be very much on the fringes of this process of reproduction and birth.

As hunters and gatherers discovered horticulture and as they began to rely increasingly on cultivation and gardening for their food supply, female goddesses continued to be prominent in the religious thought systems of these people. This is likely related in a significant way to the fact that women were in most societies the principal gardeners. However, the male gods do begin to assume greater prominence in horticultural societies. Many of the female goddesses become merely consorts and assistants or specialist supervisors over particular functions. The primary gods gradually become male—Ra in Egypt, Elyan and Bel in Syria, Yahweh in Israel, Zeus in Greece, and so on.

We have entered a time period when the religious roles of men begin to wax, those of women to wane. That is, while there still were positive roles for female deities and for ordinary women as members of the religious community as well, the role and view of women and religion became ambivalent. An excellent summary of the ambivalence, the change, and the ultimate subjugation of women religiously can be seen in India. In early Indian religion at the time of the Vedas (roughly 1000 B.C.) there were not only numerous female

---

[11] Adolph Jensen, *Myth and Cult among Primitive People* (Chicago: University of Chicago Press, 1963), pp. 141–44.

[12] James, *Cult of the Mother-Goddess*, pp. 69–77; Hawkes and Woolley, *Prehistory and the Beginnings of Civilization*, p. 736.

goddesses, but women generally enjoyed comparative freedom of movement and participation. However, by 500 B.C. and the flowering of classical Hinduism, women as a category had clearly been relegated to second-class status. There was even a common belief that no woman of any caste could as a woman gain salvation through the attainment of Nirvana. In a later life she would first have to be born a man.

For a time in the early years of Buddhism, women's status saw a beginning of modest restoration. Buddha himself (born 563 B.C.) preached the Four Noble Truths and the Eightfold Path to all who would listen, including women. Falk reports that women received a great deal of respect in the home, were allowed to manage property, give it away, and probably inherit it as well.[13] They were not forced into marriage—certainly not into child marriages as was later so common in Hindu practice. Nor did either societal or religious dictum force women to become recluses if widowed. "Most important, they were able to leave the world, study the sacred teachings of Buddhism, [and] become preachers and teachers in their own right. . . ."[14] The reference here is of course to female monastic orders. These were established fairly early, and monasticism became an alternative to marriage for some Indian women. But there was a fascinating ambivalence, and Buddhism changed within three to four centuries to closely mirror Hinduism. On the one hand, the Buddhist teaching on karma—with the goal of spiritual perfection which would eliminate the differences among living beings—maintained that continued spiritual development should result in a gradual sloughing off of sexual differences and limitations. To such goals monks and nuns alike would strive. They had virtually identical spiritual paths and charges, and dressed alike as well.

But another sexual model dominated in the society—the Hindu conception of dharma—an image of everything "in its place" and following its "nature," role, and order. Failure to coincide with one's dharma invites disaster for all concerned. The woman's dharma is to be a childbearing wife and mother. Thus, for a woman to follow a monastic role was to violate her dharma. Consistent with such a view was the most positive portrayal within Buddhism of laywomen—whose deeds and virtues could be recounted and extolled because they were following their dharma. And so, Buddhism, Hinduism, and the society itself all agreed that women's proper role was domestic.

Carmody suggests that the change is associated with the view of women as dangerous temptations—one side of the ambivalent view of women which we shall discuss later. Women in the monastic orders, even though in separate ones, were viewed by some as threats to male celibacy.[15] Buddhist literature at

[13] Nancy Falk, "An Image of Woman in Old Buddhist Literature: The Daughters of Mara," in *Women and Religion* (revised edition), eds. Judith Plaskow and Joan Arnold (Missoula, Mont.: Scholars Press, 1974), p. 105.

[14] Ibid., p. 105.

[15] Denise Carmody, *Women and World Religions* (Nashville: Abingdon, 1979), pp. 49–50.

the time warns against the ravenous sexual appetites of women and the obstacle to the perfection of male monks that they represent.[16] Thus, what Carmody calls a "deeply misogynistic strain"[17] infects both Hinduism and Buddhism. "Unless a woman is neutralized by marriage to a controlling man, Hindu imagination conjures up for her such images as the snake, death, the underworld, hell's entrance, the prostitute, and the adulteress."[18]

The record of Confucianism and Taoism in China is much like that of Hinduism and Buddhism in India. There is evidence of early respect for women generally, together with female goddesses and opportunities for women to participate in religious activities. But by the time of Confucius himself (500 B.C.) women were relegated to a distant second behind men.

In Japan it appears that women were provided a little more formal religious involvement and for somewhat longer than in the other ancient Asian societies. There is considerable evidence to suggest that early Japan was actually a matriarchy, with female shamans playing a prominent role in religious activities.[19] However, with the importation of the Confucian ethic the depreciation of women began, and women eventually lost their civil rights. It is interesting to note, though, that a curious ambivalence so far as the ideal of womanhood remained. On the one hand there was the ideal of the court lady who epitomized elegance and romance and presided over a mannered, erotic, leisured, and artistic court life.[20] On the other hand, some women were urged to overcome their female frailty and match males' fortitude and bravery.[21] They were trained already as children to repress their emotions and be able to use the dagger they were given at the onset of puberty.[22]

Once all of the major religions had reached their maturity[23] they all strongly resembled one another both in their depiction and treatment of women and in the degree and type of religious involvement granted their female adherents. Women were defined as inferior to men and dependent on them; the religious tasks open to them were peripheral or at best serving in nature.

Even to this day Orthodox Jewish men can be heard to repeat a morning prayer which says, "Blessed art thou, O Lord our God, King of the Universe who has not made me a woman." Jewish women have traditionally been discouraged from studying the holy Torah or even learning Hebrew. Women have not counted in the minyan (the quorum of ten males required for public

[16] Ibid., p. 50.
[17] Ibid., p. 51.
[18] Ibid., p. 51.
[19] Ibid., p. 84.
[20] Ibid., p. 82–83.
[21] Ibid., p. 84
[22] Ibid., p. 84.
[23] By "maturity" we mean only a further point along an evolutionary plane and intend no value judgment whatsoever.

religious services), cannot read Torah publicly or lead public services, and must frequently sit in special locations in the synagogue separated from men.[24]

Within Christianity, building as it did on a Jewish base, we find a long history of second class citizenship for women. St. Paul sets the stage and tone for nineteen centuries that follow as he says

> A woman must be a learner, listening quietly and with due submission. I do not permit a woman to be a teacher, nor must woman domineer over man; she should be quiet. For Adam was created first, and Eve afterwards; and it was not Adam who was deceived; it was the woman who, yielding to deception, fell into sin.[25]

Closely associated with the Pauline view of women as inferior to men are other themes that were enunciated early in the Christian tradition and reinforced throughout much of its history.

1. Celibacy, continence, and virginity are the better ways for persons of both sexes.
2. Sexual drives, if sexual restraint is not possible, must be released only within marriage and then for the procreation of children.
3. Women tempt and seduce; they are below man, yet they drag him down by their sexual attractiveness and wiles.
4. Women, as inferior to men, are to stay in the background of religious activities. (Note again Paul's assertions in I Tim. 2:11.)
5. Women who want to be religiously active can join specific religious orders established for that purpose. As celibates they can come closer to God, thereby benefiting both themselves and the men around them by withdrawing from interactions that could lead to infractions of God's moral code.
6. Leadership and decision making are reserved for men.
7. Preaching and interpretation of the Scriptures are reserved for men.

In fairness to Christianity it needs to be noted that Jesus himself treated women and men more evenhandedly than many of his followers did. His recorded miracles include women as well as men as recipients—the daughter of Jairus and Peter's mother-in-law benefited no less than the man born blind or the man possessed by demons, for example. Women were singled out for their expressions of strong faith as frequently as men (for example, the woman with a hemorrhage, the Samaritan woman, and the beggar woman). Although Jesus did not practice affirmative action in the selection of his twelve disciples, he did number several women among his close friends. He violated the Sabbath to help women (for example, Luke 13:10–13), and he rejected one taboo after another in speaking to the Samaritan woman at the well (John 4:7–30)—taboos against associating with impure persons (in this case doubly so—both

[24] Gail B. Shulman, "View from the Back of the Synagogue: Women in Judaism," in *Sexist Religion and Women in the Church*, ed. Alice L. Hageman (New York: Association Press, 1974), pp. 147–49.

[25] I Timothy 2:11–14. *New English Bible* (New York: Oxford University Press, 1976).

as a woman and a Samaritan) and then using her as a religious messenger to her townspeople. Carmody summarizes by saying

> Jesus treats men and women simply as individuals who need his help, or as co-workers, or friends. He offers women no separate but equal way of works; he compiles no segregating list of feminine virtues. In the face of considerable opposition, and with the consequence of provoking scandal, Jesus associates with the outcasts and marginal people of his day: the poor, sinners, tax collectors, lepers—and women.[26]

That there is this model in the New Testament as a contrast to the Pauline reinforcement for the established societal model of second-class citizenship for women is probably a primary reason that many women continue to work for reform within the Christian denominations—one of the options or routes being followed by women today (to be discussed later in this chapter). In fairness to Paul, however, there are many scholars who would attribute the New Testament books that tend to subjugate women and urge their second-class nature to writers other than Paul. Many scholars would suggest that only Romans, 1 and 2 Corinthians, Galations, and Philemon are genuinely authored by Paul. It should be noted that these books are least likely of the non-historical books of the New Testament to support inferior status for women.

By way of a brief summary of the roles of women in traditionally religious societies we turn again to Carmody. She notes first a subordinate role, as a woman gained status only through her relationship to a man—"by being the daughter of this father, the wife of this husband, the mother of that son."[27] Second, there is the dependent role. Carmody notes that Buddhist nuns were expected to serve even the newest and youngest monk; Christian wives were instructed to be silent in the churches and obedient to their husbands, or their "heads," just as Christ is the head of the Church; Muslim women were veiled through purdah from the eyes of all but their own husband.[28] Third, there was assumed intellectual inferiority. For example, Jewish women were denied opportunity to study the Torah; Chinese women did not study the Confucian classics; Hindu women did not study the Vedas.[29]

THE CHALLENGES TO
TRADITIONAL PATTERNS

As we look at the contemporary religious scene so far as the responses and participation of women are concerned we see a broad array of options that are available—challenges, if you will—all of which have proponents, all of which are in process and practice, all of which have precedents as well.

[26] Carmody, *Women and World Religions*, p. 115.

[27] Ibid., p. 16.

[28] Ibid., pp. 16–17.

[29] Ibid., p. 17.

In an attempt to provide some organization to what might at first glance seem a bewildering and unrelated set of options, we would suggest that there are three primary categories of response on the part of women to the question of their relationship to religion. Each category of response has in turn at least two subcategories.

The first we shall call the tradition-affirming response. Here we encounter two major subtypes: (1) The subordinate female religious role along the lines of the New Testament admonition for women to "keep silent" in the church and refrain from having any religious authority over men; and (2) the specialized religious role for women as best typified in the female monastic orders within Roman Catholicism.

Second, there is the tradition-reforming response, in which there is continuing strong commitment to the religious institution, but at the same time, however, there is a call for significant change (reformation) with respect to the traditional role and functions of women. Here two particular movements or emphases stand out. One is the movement to open ordination to the ministry to women. The second is a position that is newer and somewhat more inclusive than the ordination issue. That is the "radical obedience" position articulated by the women's rights leader and theologian Rosemary Radford Ruether by which she appeals for rethinking and reforming the traditional roles and perceptions of women but without either destroying the church or pulling women out of the institution.

Third, there is the revolutionary response that calls for such change in the substance of religion as traditionally expressed and organized as to be truly revolutionary. Here we include two subthemes. First, the call to "exodus" from traditional religious institutions as expressed by the Roman Catholic writer and theologian Mary Daly. Second, the proclamation of female superiority and the rejection of male dominance and direction of religious patterns through the resurrection of ancient practices and beliefs of witchcraft.

Tradition-Affirming Responses

With respect to support for traditional patterns of religious involvement for women we have to observe that they are certainly the most highly supported of all the options. That is to say, female religious orders continue to gain novices, and ladies' guilds and societies in both denominations and sects continue to flourish. This is not to say that membership in religious orders is not down from past numbers (actually membership has declined at a fairly dramatic rate), or that ladies' guilds and women's missionary societies are flourishing at their peak post–World War II levels. But it nonetheless remains true that because of the inertia of tradition if nothing else, great numbers of women continue to express themselves and find some level of satisfaction in avenues of religious expression that have been sanctioned by longstanding tradition.

We earlier mentioned the option for women of monastic orders, particularly with reference to Buddhism. The viability of this option within Christianity for a great many centuries is of course well known. The provision of a structure through which women could perform distinctly "feminine" tasks, such as nurturing and healing the sick, caring for the poor and needy, or teaching the young in schools, was well suited to use women's skills and energy in constructive ways and yet did not challenge one whit the established religious patriarchy. One might even suggest, at the risk of sounding facetious, that these women, celibate as they were required to be, were therefore not only closer to God but constituted that many fewer temptations to the men in society.

We referred earlier to the high regard for virginity and celibacy that existed in the early centuries of the Christian Church. This resulted already in the second century A.D. in the consecration of young women to remain unmarried and live either with the parental family or occasionally alone to fulfill a life of contemplation and devotion. Some widows were consecrated as deaconesses to live lives of service. Gradually communities of these celibate women developed and what we would properly think of today as a monastic order or convent emerged. This occurred at least as early as the fourth century A.D. Both male and female monastic orders began to multiply and we encounter such founders and advocates as Saint Antony, Saint Pachomius, and Saint Basil in the fourth century, and Saint Augustine, Saint Benedict, and Saint Caesarius in the fifth century. Their female counterparts and contemporaries were the sisters of Saint Pachomius and Saint Benedict, Bathilde at Chelles, Rodegund at Poitiers, Joan at Bourges, and Bridget in Sweden. They opened houses of learning, work, and devotion that were based on various elaborations of the three universal vows of chastity, poverty, and obedience.[30]

New orders continued to be established throughout the world. Taking vows of a nun became in the Roman Catholic Church and much later in a few Protestant denominations a goal for young women that was highly valued by both the women themselves and their fellow church members. In 1964 there were over one million nuns in the Roman Catholic Church alone.[31] Thus, for millions of women down through the centuries the celibate, impoverished, obedient life of the nun has been a highly legitimate religious route for women to follow. Although the number of women entering such orders continues to dwindle, the life of the nun endures as a legitimate religious road for women to walk. It is of course, without question, about as traditional a choice as there is—chaste, virginal women doing "women's work" of teaching, healing, serving the needy, and baking bread.

[30] Suzanne Cita-Malard, *Religious Orders of Women*, trans. George J. Robinson (New York: Hawthorn, 1964), p. 15.

[31] Cita-Malard, *Religious Orders*, p. 10; Marcella Bernstein, *The Nuns* (Philadelphia: Lippincott, 1976), p. 14.

The other traditional religious role for women is one with which the reader is probably very familiar. This is the role which for all but a very few has placed women in the background of religious activities—in most Christian denominations, for example, without vote in congregational matters, excluded from the pulpit and from behind the communion rail, and in charge only of chicken dinners and the pre-Christmas bazaar. This traditional role within Christianity, as well as some flavor of a contemporary woman's reaction to that traditional role vis-à-vis the traditional male role, is ably described in the following excerpt from Sharon Emswiler's essay "How the New Woman Feels in the Old Worship Service." She describes her participation in a typical worship service in a Protestant church.

I enter the sanctuary and am directed to my seat by an usher, always male, except on "Ladies' Day," that one day in the year when women are given the opportunity to "play usher." As I sit and meditate I listen to the organ prelude. If the church is a small one, I notice that the organist is a woman. However, if the church is a large, prestigious one, with an expensive organ, the position of organist is most often filled by a man.

The minister (or ministers)—male, of course—then appears to begin the service, accompanied by a lay person (male) acting as the liturgist of the morning. The call to worship is given, setting the worship service in motion. One such call to worship that sticks in my mind from a service I attended contains the line, "To be is to be a brother." Hearing those words, I instantly carry them to their logical conclusion: "I am not, and never will be, a brother. Therefore, I am not. I do not exist." The service is off to a great start!

The congregation now rises for the first hymn and I find myself singing a song such as "Men and Children Everywhere" (I wonder in which group I am to include myself), "Rise Up, O Men of God," or "Faith of Our Fathers." If it is near Christmas, the selections might be "God Rest Ye, Merry Gentlemen" or "Good Christian Men, Rejoice;" while the Easter season offers such choices as "Sing with All the Sons of Glory" or "Good Christian Men Rejoice and Sing." Other possible hymns in the service might include "Once to Every Man and Nation," "Now Praise We Great and Famous Men," "Brother Man, Fold to Thy Heart," "As Men of Old Their First Fruits Bought," or "Turn Back, O Man."

If the service is of a more contemporary style, I go in the hope that the hymns will speak to me in a way that the traditional ones do not. But here, too, I discover that while the folk tunes have a great appeal to me, I am asked to sing songs with titles like "Be a New Man," "Sons of God," "Come, My Brothers," "Brothers, Get Yourselves Together," and "Brother, How's Your Love."

As I sing I try to imagine that these songs are speaking to me, but I am not accustomed to thinking of myself as a "man" or a "brother;" and the identification is difficult, and most often impossible. The only way I can find to identify with these masculine words is to attempt either to deny or set aside my femininity. But I do not want to deny that part of my personhood; I want rather to affirm it. I want my femaleness recognized and affirmed by the Church also. As the worship progresses through the prayers, creeds, and sermon, the same language form keeps recurring—always the masculine when referring to people; always the masculine when referring to God. While I sing and during prayer I change the word "men" to "people;" "mankind" to "humankind;" "sons" to "children;" "Father" to "Parent," but I feel as though I am outshouted by the rest of the congregation. My words are swallowed up by theirs.

Listening to the minister preach his sermon for the morning, I am aware that he is not really attempting to address me or my sisters in the congregation. His illustrations all revolve around men and speak overwhelmingly to the masculine experience in our society. Suddenly, I feel as though I am eavesdropping on a conversation labeled "For Men Only." Or worse yet, I feel that the suspicion I had after the call to worship is true. I do not exist! I look down at my hands and arms and feet. I can see them; they are very real to me. But I feel that somehow I must be invisible to this preacher who has designed this service and now stands in front of me, speaking of "the brethren" and telling his congregation to be "new men."

Following the sermon, the worshippers are invited to participate in the celebration of the Lord's Supper. As the large group of male ushers marches down the aisle to receive the communion elements and distribute them to the congregation, I am suddenly struck with the irony of the situation. The chicken suppers, the ham suppers, the turkey suppers in the church are all prepared and served by the women. But not the Lord's Supper! Yes, it is pepared by the women, but the privilege of serving the Lord's Supper in worship is reserved for the men. This particular morning I find it very difficult to swallow the bread and drink the wine, knowing that within the Body of Christ, the Church, the sisters of Christ are not given the same respect and privileges as are his bothers.[32]

Such a "men only" or "men first" pattern is, as mentioned earlier in this chapter, not unique to Christianity. It has been characteristic, in some cases to an even more extreme degree, in all the major world religions. Nor is it dead. Far from it. For one thing, a great many women continue to assume such female subordinate religious roles and postures as proper and divinely ordained. Entire denominations continue to espouse such perspectives and make them tenets of doctrinal assent. In fact, a resurgent movement within many fundamentalist and conservative church bodies and congregations calling for a re-return to the "Christian family" holds out as the ideal family structure a patriarchial one in which women and children assume nurturing and obedient roles respectively behind a dominant, decision-making, sanction-disseminating husband-father. Consistent with this perspective, though not necessarily essential to it, was the "total woman" concept espoused by Marabel Morgan and made popular in the 1970s.[33] The central ideas of the total woman concept were that a woman could expect a much happier and more satisfying life if she worked hard at pleasing "her man" and remained in the traditional niche set aside for women.

Thus, what we have referred to as the traditional secondary and subordinate role for women in religious activities is certainly not extinct. In fact, one could hardly even say it is dying. While, as we will document in the concluding two sections of this chapter, there are numerous challenges and alternatives to such traditional views of women's religious roles, and a significant

---

[32] Sharon Neufer Emswiler, "How the New Woman Feels in the Old Worship Service," in *Women and Worship*, eds. Sharon Neufer Emswiler and Thomas Neufer Emswiler (New York: Harper & Row, Pub., 1974), pp. 3–5. Reprinted by permission of Harper & Row, Publishers, Inc.

[33] Marabel Morgan, *The Total Woman* (Old Tappan, N.J.: Fleming H. Revell Company, 1973).

number of women have adopted alternative definitions and modes, such challenges have actually at the same time stimulated a resurgence of support for traditional female religious roles. A quick browsing through any religious bookstore that specializes in conservative, fundamentalistic or "born again" Christian literature will immediately reinforce this observation.[34]

Reformation Responses for the Female Religious Role

Here we shall look particularly at two ways in which women wish to continue within the traditional religious organization but at the same time are dedicated to reform those organizations and their traditional patterns. Parallel to a grand tradition in British politics these would be women of the "loyal opposition." That is, they want to remain members in good standing of a standard religious group, yet are equally committed to changing certain aspects, tenets, or practices of that group, in their terms, "updating" them.

Any woman who seeks to change a local congregation's constitution that prohibits women from voting on congregational matters, serving as an elder or deacon, or assisting with the formal worship service in any visible way is part of this reformational response. Any woman who lobbies within her denomination for change in that religious group's stand on abortion or birth control is part of this response. But in the interests of brevity, we shall focus briefly on but two emphases—first, the movement toward the ordination of women as bona fide "clergymen," and second, the perspective espoused by the women's rights leader and theologian Rosemary Radford Ruether and identified in her own terms as "radical obedience."[35]

The ordination of women issue, though not brand new, is certainly of relatively recent origin so far as the span of history is concerned. In America the first woman ordained into the ministry was Congregationalist Antoinette Brown in 1856.[36] Olympia Brown followed in 1863. But such nineteenth century ordinations were rare. In fact, it has not been until this century, and very recently at that, that any significant number of religious groups have allowed the ordination of women. For example, it was not until 1956 that the United Presbyterian Church in the U.S.A. began to ordain women. The Church of the Brethren ordained its first woman in 1960. The Lutheran Church in America

---

[34] Perhaps as a postscript I should say that while I personally espouse equal rights and privileges for women in religious organizations and activities, I do not want the foregoing to be viewed as ideological or pejorative. Nor am I advocating any infringement on the right of women as individuals or churches themselves to take and provide the "traditional" religious options for women. Freedom of choice should be truly that—freedom to select among options, one of which continues to be a traditional pattern that remains alive and well.

[35] Rosemary Ruether and Eleanor McLaughlin, "Women's Leadership in the Jewish and Christian Traditions: Continuity and Change," in *Women of Spirit*, eds. Rosemary Ruether and Eleanor McLaughlin (New York: Simon & Schuster, 1979), p. 19.

[36] Margaret B. Crook, *Women and Religion* (Boston: Beacon Press, 1964), p. 235.

approved of the ordination of women in 1970. The first Jewish woman in the United States to become rabbi was formally accepted as such in 1972. And it was not until 1974 that the first women were ordained in the Episcopal Church in this country.

The provocation for raising the question of the ordination of women has been largely a social one. It is clear that when women participating in the antislavery movement in the 1830s to 1860s discovered that while their leadership and oratory were often eagerly sought out, they were not allowed to use a pulpit or church platform as a place from which to speak, their consciousness as well as their level of indignation was raised. Women such as the Grimke sisters (Angelina and Sarah), Margaret Prior, Lucy Stone, and Lydia Child led the way. When Lucretia Mott and Elizabeth Cady Stanton were exluded on the basis of sex from the World Anti-Slavery Convention in London in 1840 they began to lay plans for a new movement devoted to the cause of women.[37]

As feminism generally, and the woman's suffrage movement in particular, gained momentum at the end of the nineteenth and beginning of the twentieth centuries, culminating in the Nineteenth Amendment in 1920, some religious groups saw the incongruity and permitted women to head churches as ordained ministers (primarily in Baptist, Methodist, and Pentecostal churches). But probably more common was the alternative of being a female religious entrepreneur who possessed charismatic leadership qualities and gathered bands of local followers in sectarian groups, particularly in urban settings. Some of these women attained national and international notice and followings. Note such women as Mary Baker Eddy, founder of Christian Science, and the evangelist Aimee Semple McPherson.

Nonetheless, the door to ordination and religious leadership remained closed to most women. As we have mentioned, it was only very recently that the barriers have been knocked down in many of the major religious groups. Continuing in opposition are such major religious groups as the Orthodox Churches, The Lutheran Church—Missouri Synod, the Roman Catholic Church, and over a hundred of the 262 official denominations in the United States that report statistics to the National Council of Churches. Of course, none of these is without both male and female voices that challenge the sex-based restrictions to ordination. Even such a stronghold of religious patriarchy as the Roman Catholic Church is beginning to discuss the topic. Books, papers, and special conferences are beginning to accumulate.

With respect to those women who have been ordained in the United States three sets of data are instructive. First, there continue to be relatively few ordained women. The 1960 United States Census lists 4,727 women as

[37] Dorothy C. Bass, "Their Prodigious Influence: Women, Religion, and Reform in Antebellum America," in *Women of Spirit*, eds. Rosemary Ruether and Eleanor McLaughlin (New York: Simon & Schuster, 1979), p. 296.

"clergymen." This was 2.3 percent of all clergy. This proportion compares with 3.7 percent of all lawyers and judges, and 7 percent of physicians and surgeons. By 1970 the proportion of clergy who were women had increased to 2.9 percent. But lawyers-judges and physicians-surgeons categories had increased even more—to 4.9 percent and 9.3 percent respectively. A 1976 survey conducted by the National Council of Churches of all Protestant denominations showed 10,320 women clergy distributed among 71 denominations. Fourteen relatively small Pentecostal groups accounted for 32.2 percent of the female clergy. An additional 30.4 percent were in three denominations organized along paramilitary lines that emphasize holiness doctrine and social services (the Salvation Army, Volunteers of America, and American Rescue Mission). Of the ten major Protestant denominations that ordain women, the two with the most are relatively small denominations but have been ordaining women for several decades. They are the United Church of Christ with 400 women clergy and the Christian Church (Disciples of Christ) with 388. Yet even these numbers represent only 4.2 percent and 5.7 percent respectively of the total number of clergy in these two churches. The remaining denominations in descending order so far as numbers of women clergy are concerned are the United Methodist Church (319), the United Presbyterian Church in the U.S.A. (295), the American Baptist Church (157), the Episcopal Church (94), the Presbyterian Church in the U.S.A (75), the Lutheran Church in America (55), local churches of the Southern Baptist Convention (20), and The American Lutheran Church (18).[38] With the exception of the United Presbyterian Church in the U.S.A. at 2.1 percent, all these religious groups have less than 2 percent women clergy. For most, the proportion is less than 1 percent (United Methodist, Episcopal, Lutheran Church in America, Southern Baptist Convention, and The American Lutheran Church).

The second set of data shows that of the ordained women at work in the denominations that permit them, the proportion in the parish ministry is quite low. In 1951 only half (51.8 percent) of the ordained women were serving as pastors of churches (including those in an assistant minister capacity). What might be suggested here is the possibility that there is a tendency to separate or isolate women clergy into specialized roles, much like the more radical clergy were, according to Hammond and Mitchell's study,[39] and to assign them to nonparish roles such as the campus ministry or to various administrative roles within denominational and ecumenical bureaucratic structures. Another partial explanation may be that the role of parish minister has for so long been a male role that women may find some difficulty in filling it without at least some redefinition of the role taking place. That women can fill the role well,

[38] Constant H. Jacquet, Jr., ed., *Yearbook of American and Canadian Churches, 1978* (Nashville: Abingdon Press, 1978), p. 260.

[39] Philip E. Hammond and Robert E. Mitchell, "Segmentation of Radicalism—The Case of the Protestant Campus Minister," *American Journal of Sociology* 71, no. 2 (September 1965).

though with perhaps some redefinition of the role required to take place, is well attested in Priscilla and William Proctor's book, *Women in the Pulpit.*[40]

It is of more than passing interest that if responses by Lutherans can be taken as at all typical of Protestants, then data strongly suggest that the attitudes of lay members of churches are strongly receptive to the idea of female ordination. Lawrence Kersten's data on Detroit Lutherans, for example—data that were gathered in 1968 before any Lutheran woman had been ordained in the United States—show that a substantial majority of laypersons in the two more-liberal Lutheran denominations (73 percent of the Lutheran Church in America and 68 percent of the American Lutheran Church) were in favor of women being allowed to become ordained ministers.[41] In each case the laypeople were more supportive of the idea than the clergy (62 percent of the L.C.A. clergy and only 30 percent of the A.L.C. clergy supported the idea of the ordination of women in 1968).

Further indications of the future increase in women ordained to the ministry come from seminary enrollment data—our third set of data. Between 1972 and 1979 the enrollment of women in Protestant seminaries in the United States increased 203.9 percent. The corresponding increase for males was only 28.8 percent. The actual number of women enrolled in the Protestant seminaries increased from 3,358 in 1972 when they accounted for 10.2 percent of seminary enrollees, to 10,208 in 1979 when they constituted 21.1 percent of enrollment.[42] Our prediction is that by the turn of the century, women clergy will be commonplace; most denominations will approve their ordination; even the Roman Catholic Church will do so, at least under special circumstances.

We referred earlier to a second reforming approach so far as the relationship of women to religion is concerned. That is the approach of "radical obedience" urged by Rosemary Radford Ruether. The term is Ms. Ruether's own. She remains within the Christian Church (Roman Catholic), speaks out explicitly against some of the more radical options espoused by some women, the feminists among them in particular, (options that we shall discuss in the final section of this chapter), yet wants reformation of existing structures, not their dissolution and death. We shall neither attempt nor pretend to present fully Rosemary Ruether's position and advice, but will offer a few summary indications of her position.

While appealing for reform rather than revolution and rejection of the core of Christianity Ms. Ruether notes how women have in the past exercised some leadership and made contributions "from within" the body of the

[40] Priscilla and William Proctor, *Women in the Pulpit* (Garden City, N.Y.: Doubleday, 1976).

[41] Lawrence L. Kersten, *The Lutheran Ethic* (Detroit: Wayne State University Press, 1970), p. 125.

[42] Constant H. Jacquet, Jr., ed. *Yearbook of American and Canadian Churches, 1980* (Nashville: Abingdon Press, 1980), p. 258.

church.[43] Religious orders of nuns and sisters who are set apart for special religious work constitute an example known by everyone. But also, martyrdom has not been sex exclusive, and women have been recognized as contributing prophetic gifts in this process. Further, at times when reform movements such as millenialism have gained popularity, women could step into leadership positions because the very nature of the movement called into question some of the traditional expectations and patterns of family, religious organization, and society. She also mentions the important difference between religious organizations that have stressed lay leadership in contrast to formally trained and sanctioned clerical leadership as in the Roman Catholic Church. She notes that those "who have the gifts, rather than those authorized by the traditional institutions, are acclaimed as leaders. In this situation women too can emerge as leaders."[44] Further, she notes that the pentecostal groups and traditions have provided more opportunities for women because the "gifts of the Spirit" could come to anyone, male or female. As such the person and the message needed to be heeded without particularly noting the sex of the person who was seen as a vehicle for the Holy Spirit.

Her conclusion at this point is that women should appropriate such patterns and precedents from history to vindicate their moving forward within religious institutions in the present in order "to reshape and enlarge the vision and life of the church today."[45]

Integral to this "reshaping" must be reevaluation of both traditional and contemporary Mariology (the theology surrounding the Virgin Mary within Roman Catholicism).[46] Here she speaks of the need to excise the concept of passive femininity in which women are made to be "specialists in self-abnegating, auxiliary modes of existence,"[47] while men remain dominant and superordinate. Nor is it enough for men to adopt a "feminine side," particularly when such a feminine side is viewed as in the "nature" of women, but only auxiliary and supplemental to men.[48]

While Ruether is here enunciating in almost a classic manner the contemporary feminist demand for a true balance and transposition of so-called male and female qualities, rights, and expectations, she continues her assertions and appeals for action within the context of *reform*, "radical" for some though it may be.

---

[43] Rosemary Radford Ruether, "Women's Leadership in the Jewish and Christian Traditions: Continuity and Change," in *Women of Spirit*, eds. Rosemary Radford Ruether and Eleanor McLaughlin (New York: Simon & Schuster, 1979), pp. 19–28.

[44] Ibid., p. 21.

[45] Ibid., p. 28.

[46] Rosemary Radford Ruether, *New Woman/New Earth* (New York: Seabury Press, 1975), pp. 56–59.

[47] Ibid., p. 57.

[48] Ibid., p. 57.

Revolutionary Proposals

Among various proposals for resolving the issue of traditional inferior roles and status for women in the major world religions, Christianity in particular, we shall focus on what seem to be the two major options at the moment: (1) the religious exodus proposal, and (2) the resort to witchcraft.

The principal spokesperson for the religious exodus proposal is Mary Daly, who first caught public attention in 1968 with the publication of her book *The Church and the Second Sex.* In the book she was highly critical of the sexist perceptions, views, and practices of Christianity, Roman Catholicism in particular. But she called for reform, not revolution in the sense of destroying the old to inaugurate a new order. Fairly quickly she has moved to the point not of revolution in the strictest sense of the term, perhaps, but of *exodus* from the institution—turning one's back on the old and marching out to establish something new. She articulated this position already in 1971 in her now famous Harvard Memorial Church Sermon in which she spoke of the Women's movement as an "exodus community." She speaks of women building a new community as they are bonded in sisterhood. This sisterhood includes a number of qualities that lead eventually to the exodus. It is revolutionary as it destroys the credibility of sex stereotyping. It is revolutionary as it creates new definitions of God and invalidates patriarchal religion. It is antichurch in the sense that the institution called church remains sexist and wedded to patriarchal religious concepts. It is church itself as it becomes a community "with a mission to challenge the distortions in sexually unbalanced society, to be a counter force to the prevailing sense of reality by building up a new sense of reality."[49] It is, finally, an exodus community that goes away from the land of its fathers. In that sermon Daly then called to women to follow what had probably already been a spiritual break by giving physical expression to their exodus community by leaving, that is, literally walking out of the church building.

In her book *Beyond God the Father*, Mary Daly calls for the death of God as he has been known within the Judeo-Christian tradition—that is, as male. This concept should be replaced with one of God more like that proposed by theologian Paul Tillich—ultimate meaning and reality, a process more than a "person."

She then makes even more clear what she means in her "postchristian" introduction to a second printing of her first book *The Church and the Second Sex.* In a fascinating review of her own book of seven years earlier she describes how far she has moved from those embryonic beginnings, how she had referred to her sisters in the movement as "they," not "we," and above all had viewed the movement as one of *reform*, not the exodus-revolution she has now

[49] Mary Daly, "The Women's Movement: An Exodus Community," *Religious Education* 67 (September/October 1972), p. 332.

come to espouse. In a more recent book *Gyn/Ecology*[50] she refers to her first book as written by a "reformist foresister" (herself) whose work she had to refute. Her current position appears to be quite clearly summarized when she says that women "whose consciousness has been raised are spiritual exiles whose sense of transcendence is seeking alternative expressions to those available in institutional religion."[51] Or again, "When you can say 'No' to the institution you can begin to say a clearer and more effective 'Yes' to real movement, the movement of your sisters—past, present, and future."[52]

Another revolutionary expression so far as the relationship of women to religion is concerned is articulated by Naomi Goldenberg. Like Mary Daly, Ms. Goldenberg traces the rapid evolution of her own perceptions. She identifies her problems with traditional religion beginning when she tried to visualize women as rabbis, priests, and ministers but suddenly wondered how they as women would or could represent a male god.[53] She saw this as an impossible incongruity. She now sees in witchcraft a solution to the ancient problem of the subordination of women religiously and otherwise.

In witchcraft traditional historic religion is essentially turned upside down. Female is defined as superior; although goddesses have male consorts, and although those male beings are called gods, the goddess is more highly valued and ranks higher in prestige and power.[54] What makes witchcraft very different from most religions, particularly in the West, is not only the superiority of women it upholds, but the radical break it makes with the view of religion always implying an "other"—a god or other supernatural force or power that is "out there," so to speak. Witchcraft places divinity within—not a new idea at all of course (one thinks of pantheism, deism, Reform Judaism, to only begin a long list). Its radical, revolutionary nature is in the substitution of inner divinity for any and all traditional religious systems and expressions.

Some of the flavor of this inner divine power residing within the female and superior to that in the male, as well as a feel for some of the rage and defiance against traditional religion that women in the Witchcraft movement feel, is found in Goldenberg's description and analysis of an evening service of the first national conference on women's spirituality held in Boston on April 23, 1976, attended by several hundred women. Goldenberg's description is as follows:

[50] Mary Daly, *Gyn/Ecology: The Metaethics of Radical Feminism* (Boston: Beacon Press, 1978), p. xi.

[51] Mary Daly, "Theology after the Demise of God the Father," in *Sexist Religion and Women in the Church*, ed. Alice L. Hagemen (New York: Association Press, 1974), pp. 126–27.

[52] Mary Daly, *The Church and the Second Sex*, (New York: Harper & Row, Pub., 1968, 1975), p. 39.

[53] Naomi Goldenberg, *Changing of the Gods: Feminism and the End of Traditional Religions* (Boston: Beacon Press, 1979), p. 3. Copyright © 1979 by Naomi R. Goldenberg.

[54] Ibid., p. 103.

The keynote speeches and opening rituals were held in a church in the heart of Boston. After listening attentively to two addresses on the theme of "Woman-power: Energy Re-Sourcement," the audience became very active. In tones ranging from whispers to shouts, they chanted, "The Goddess Is Alive—Magic Is Afoot." The women evoked the Goddess with dancing, stamping, clapping and yelling. They stood on pews and danced bare-breasted on the pulpit and amid the hymnbooks. Had any sedate, white-haired clergyman been present, I am sure he would have felt the Apocalypse had arrived.

This episode during the Boston conference cannot be described as joyful. Women felt angry and bitter in a church that represented the worship of a male god. It did not matter that this particular denomination had a more liberal outlook than most. In fact, the women were angry at all religions of the fathers and took this opportunity to mock and defy those religions in a church they had rented for the occasion. The anger was not pretty but it certainly was justified. Why not be enraged with the whole Judeo-Christian tradition for centuries of degradation of the bodies and images of women? Why not display your breasts in a place that has tried to teach you that they are things to be ashamed of, features that make you unlike God or His son? Proclaiming that the "Goddess Is Alive" in a traditional church setting is proclaiming that woman is alive, that being female is divine. The women in Boston were raising up their images as fleshly female beings to defy their culture's image of God as an immaterial male spirit. At this opening of the Boston conference the Goddess represented fierce pride in female physical presence and fury at the abuse that presence has taken from male religious authorities. The Goddess was never symbolized as an idol or a picture in this or any other ritual. Instead, She was seen as the force which had motivated each woman to be present at the first national gathering in Her honor.[55]

CONCLUSION

Without belaboring issues or repeating ideas that have already been presented, one additional remark by way of conclusion seems appropriate. That is an insight contributed by Denise Carmody. She notes that there has been a worldwide tendency to view women as either much better or much worse than men, implying that only men have normal, mid-range humanity. So women have been placed on pedestals of purity, loveliness, and virginity. Correspondingly they have been denounced as evil witches, seducing sirens, and treacherous whores.[56] She adds, "What they have not been, historically, is equal sharers of humanity whose social and religious offices have been determined principally by their talents."[57] In a neat nutshell this seems to be the central issue for society and the central issue for religion as well.

[55] Goldenberg, *Changing of the Gods* , pp. 92–93. Reprinted by permission of Beacon Press.
[56] Carmody, *Women and World Religions*, p. 17.
[57] Ibid.

IV

RELIGION IN AMERICA

10

Major Historical Developments

In this chapter we shall discuss seven specific themes or developments in the history of American religion, proceeding roughly chronologically. Moreover, this discussion can be viewed within the context of two more general themes that the reader will find helpful to keep in mind as we proceed—first, that the outward manifestation or pattern of religion has constantly changed during the nearly four centuries since the initial European settlement of this country; and second, that the relationships between religion and other features of the social structure have also changed.

INTOLERANT BEGINNINGS

The first theme or stage in the history of religion in America we call the period of intolerant beginnings. Although many of the early colonists were themselves religious dissenters and minorities extolled by our history books for their courage and principles in struggling for religious freedom and liberty even to the extent of making perilous voyages in search of a place where they could practice their religious convictions unhampered, many of these same seekers and champions of religious freedom were inclined to deny to others what they demanded for themselves. Those who asked that others be tolerant of their views were themselves intolerant of the divergent religious views of still others.

During the colonial period the settlers, though speaking of a new world and a new age, had reproduced an ancient pattern of officially establishing religion that was supported by law and governmental authority. The state-church pattern predominated. Nine of the thirteen original colonies recognized officially established religious systems. Persons who dissented were frequently expelled from these colonies, or at best accorded only second-class citizenship if allowed to remain.

The situation is well summarized in the following excerpt from the U.S. Supreme Court's opinion in the historic 1947 *Everson* decision:

> Catholics found themselves hounded and proscribed because of their faith; Quakers who followed their conscience went to jail; Baptists were peculiarly obnoxious to certain dominant Protestant sects; men and women of varied faiths who happened to be in a minority in a particular locality were persecuted because they steadfastly persisted in worshipping God only as their own consciences dictated. And all of these dissenters were compelled to pay tithes and taxes to support government-sponsored churches whose ministers preached inflammatory sermons designed to strengthen and consolidate the established faith by generating a burning hatred against dissenters.[1]

These examples were particularly obvious in Massachusetts Bay Colony and Virginia. As the Puritan settlers in Massachusetts established what for all intents and purposes was a state church, the colonial government was expected, as part of its service to its citizens, to support the Congregational Church and its clergy. The Congregationalist meeting house was used for both governmental and religious activities. Colonial law compelled all people to attend church services regardless of their personal beliefs and denied equal rights to the "unorthodox." Citizens were subject to trial by the colonial government for what the church called sins but the government called crimes — heresy, blasphemy, and idolatry.

Anne Hutchinson, whose history is one of the better-known examples of such victimization, was interestingly enough not a representative of a dissenting or deviant religious group in the Massachusetts Bay Colony where she resided. Although what she taught was defined as deviant, heretical doctrine, she was technically a Congregationalist, like all the other (acceptable) residents of Boston. Her heresy lay in her stress on a "covenant of grace" — a religion in which a person could have direct access to God's love and grace — in opposition to the "covenant of works" that stressed obedience to the laws of church and state. In 1638 both she and her doctrines were tried and condemned — her teaching as heresy and she as a blasphemer of God and seducer of the faithful.

Earlier, in 1636, Roger Williams and four companions, having been banished from the same colony, settled in "Rogues' Island" (that is, Rhode Is-

---

[1] *Everson* v. *Board of Education*, 333 U.S. 1.

land) and established a community there as a haven for Quakers, Baptists, and other deviant and dissenting religious groups. Even in this tolerant colony, however, approximately a century later a law was passed restricting both citizenship and eligibility for public office to Protestants.[2]

Quakers were particularly obnoxious to the colonists in Massachusetts, as reflected by laws there specifying that any of that "cursed sect of heretics" who entered the colony were to be jailed, whipped with twenty stripes, and then expelled from the colony. Four Quakers were even hanged. Some were branded or had ears cut off. In at least one case the children of Quaker parents were sold into slavery upon authorization of a Boston court.

In Virginia, Anglicanism was established as the official church, but in a somewhat different form than Congregationalism was established in Massachusetts. Whereas in Massachusetts the church tended to control the government, in Virginia the government tended to control the church. In Virginia all citizens were required to attend Anglican services and were taxed to support the Anglican church, no non-Anglican religious group could hold services, specifically no Catholic or Quaker could hold public office, and no one who did not believe in infant baptism could even become a citizen of the colony.[3] Early Virginia laws, later reduced in severity, specified that anyone convicted a third time for failure to attend religious services was to spend six months in the galleys and that a third offense of working on the Sabbath was punishable by death.

THE CONSTITUTIONAL COMPROMISE

With the Revolution and the adoption of the Constitution, the colonial pattern became subject to forces resulting in drastic change. In the First Amendment, American society took the official stance that "Congress shall make no law respecting an establishment of religion, or prohibiting the free exercise thereof." As such the early pattern of state churches and their implicit intolerance was repudiated. It is interesting to note, however, that it was not until the passage of the Fourteenth Amendment in 1868 that this limitation was applied at the state level. Theoretically, any state could have had an official state religion up to that time; but none did after 1833, when Massachusetts rescinded its state-church commitments, the last state to do so.

In significant part this change from state churches to religious toleration and pluralism occurred because no single religious group could claim anything

---

[2] Evarts B. Greene, *Religion and the State* (New York: New York University Press, 1941), p. 51.

[3] Anson Phelps Stokes and Leo Pfeffer, *Church and State in the United States* (New York: Harper & Row, Pub., 1964), p. 7.

near the majority of supporters throughout the thirteen states necessary to establish it as the officially sanctioned religion of the new nation. Not that particular groups (Congregationalists, for example, who probably had the greatest number of members of any group), would not have wanted such status; it was simply that none had sufficient numbers to gain a majority vote. Every state had a goodly number of dissenters and minority-religious-group members; there were even substantial numbers of "free thinkers" who professed no formal religious affiliation. Therefore, only one practical solution appeared feasible, and that was to cut off churches both legally and financially from government support. Hence the clause in the First Amendment specifying that "Congress shall make no law respecting an establishment of religion."

Looking at the situation from a slightly different angle, every religious group, whether dissenting or firmly established, now found itself occupying a minority status in the context of all thirteen states, and so each was quite naturally concerned with keeping government from interfering with what it wanted to do and teach religiously. What if another religious group should later gain a majority—what would happen to us? Hence the second clause dealing with religion in the First Amendment stating that Congress shall make no law "prohibiting the free exercise thereof."

With disestablishment came voluntarism and the rise of denominationalism. People could join any religious group of their choice, or they could choose to join none at all. They could even form antireligious groups. Thus religious groups now had to find ways of becoming self-supporting. Competition for members and for scarce resources developed, and religious innovation was implicitly encouraged as a consequence.

It is difficult to overstate the significance and the dramatic impact of this severance of religion from state auspices. Sanford H. Cobb, an expert on the history of religious liberty, maintains that the American pattern of religious freedom was "the most striking contribution of America to the science of Government."[4]

As dramatic and innovative as the Constitution was with respect to the social organization of both religion and government, it appears that these arrangements provoked relatively little struggle. Martin Marty notes that in only three of the thirteen original states was there much resistance to these First Amendment provisions.[5] Further, "in most other colonies the change was made as if with a sigh of relief, in a spirit of tidying up, and with only whimpers of reactions."[6]

This is not to suggest of course that the First Amendment resolved all the issues. Part of the problem is its brevity and vagueness. As Joseph Tussman states:

[4] Quoted in Martin E. Marty, *Righteous Empire* (New York: Dial Press, 1970), p. 36.
[5] Ibid., p. 37.
[6] Ibid.

The First Amendment in its attractive brevity leaves much unstated and seems to take much for granted. Even its spirit is elusive. Is it a practical expression of "a religious people?" Or is it a tolerant statement of commitment to a secular experiment? Does it indeed put us "under God"? What is "establishment" and what is an "exercise" of religion? The Amendment does not explain itself.[7]

Although it would be of great help, it is impossible to "get into the mind," so to speak, of the framers of the Constitution and discover their intentions. Were they flaunting sociological realities? Or were they acknowledging them? That is, were they trying to do something that cannot be done—namely, separate religion from politics and government in society? Or, recognizing that interaction and overlap between the two is inevitable, were they simply trying to avoid excesses from arising therefrom?

Although throughout our history people have pointed to the First Amendment as evidence of an "official endorsement" of religion and have suggested that we are therefore fundamentally a religious people, it is not all that clear that the Founding Fathers were so much encouraging religion as they were trying to place some limitations on its power and influence. Clearly they did not want a repetition of early Massachusetts Bay Colony or Virginia at the national level. We need to remember that many of the Founding Fathers and framers of the Constitution were freethinkers, deists, and sons of the Enlightenment who doubted, if not rejected, much of traditional Christian orthodoxy. Further, at the official birth of the new nation relatively few of its citizens were formal members of churches.[8] Quite clearly the early emphasis seems to be one of limitation of religious power and influence rather than support and encouragement of such influence. If this is so, it represents quite a shift from the strong religious (Christian) influence in the early days of the colonies. Yet note the action of the Supreme Court fifty years later (1844) as it interprets the First Amendment. In 1831, Stephen Girard, a wealthy Philadelphian, provided in his will for the establishment of a college for orphans—on condition that although the orphans were to be taught the "purest principles of morality," no clergy members representing any religion whatsoever were to teach at, hold office in, or even visit the proposed institution. Daniel Webster, in challenging the will, stated: "No fault can be found with Girard for wishing a marble college to bear his name forever, but it is not valuable unless it has a fragrance of Christianity about it. . . . A cruel experiment is to be made upon these orphans to ascertain whether they cannot be brought up without religion."[9]

The Supreme Court upheld Girard's will interpreting it as bearing no animosity to Christianity, but only to clergy, since nonclergy were left free to

[7] Joseph Tussman, *The Supreme Court on Church and State* (New York: Oxford University Press, 1962), p. xiii.

[8] According to the first U.S. Census 1790, only 5 percent of U.S. citizens reported being members of churches.

[9] Quoted in Tussman, *The Supreme Court*, pp. 5–6.

teach Christian principles. In fact, regarding the requirement that teachers in the school "instill into the minds of the scholars the purest principles of morality" the Court commented; "Where can the purest principles of morality be learned so clearly or so perfectly as from the New Testament?"[10] In other words, Christianity should be taught—by lay Christians instead of clergy if necessary. Quite clearly there was a Christian bias abroad in the land, and it was certainly encouraged by the Supreme Court's interpretation of the Constitution.

Two summary observations at this point: First, despite the constitutional prohibitions against the establishment of a state church, the history of our society evidences strong favor toward religion—Christianity in particular. Second, opinion regarding how and to what extent the state is to be allowed to exercise its support for religion has fluctuated. Although we lack the space to document this point in detail, some semblance of a pendulum motion has been in operation throughout our history in terms of degree of involvement in and support for religion on the part of the state and political elements.

The United States' original Protestant-Christian bias was challenged and broadened by waves of Roman Catholic and Jewish immigrants in the nineteenth and early twentieth centuries and later by agnostics and secularists. Mormons demanded the right to practice polygamy as a free exercise of their religion, but ultimately were denied it. John T. Scopes taught evolution in a Tennessee high school in contradiction to fundamentalist Christianity and although a loser in court, was granted by many a "moral" victory because of the national publicity and lampooning of the prosecution by the press. Prohibition came and went. Oregon required that every child be educated in its public schools, but the Supreme Court declared religious (parochial) schools a valid alternative (1925). And so the pendulum has swung. To a great extent the problem centers around balancing the requirement of nonestablishment of religion and its inherent neutrality stance, on the one hand, with providing opportunity for free exercise of religion on the other. When the state emphasizes neutrality, its action is interpreted by some as antagonism. When the state encourages free exercise, it is accused of establishment. For example, if the state says it cannot allow observance of Christmas in public schools lest it thereby favor Christianity, objectors claim that their freedom to act out their religious convictions wherever they may be is infringed upon. If Christmas observances are allowed, members of non-Christian religion or those with no religious affiliation or commitment cry "foul" and "establishment of religion." Quite obviously, the First Amendment provides the political system with a built-in dilemma that shall never be fully resolved. And so the problem of separating religion from other social phenomena, which we earlier branded as sociologically impossible in the first place, is now merely compounded.

[10] Quoted in ibid., p. 6.

THE FRONTIER CHALLENGE

We mentioned in the preceding section that the Constitution's disestablishment of religion demanded innovation on the part of religious groups if they were to thrive—or perhaps just to survive. This need to innovate was significantly compounded by the opening of the frontier and increased westward migration. In a sense, the frontier almost immediately presented opportunities for religious groups to "test their mettle," so to speak. Here was territory. Here were people. And no one religious group had a monopoly on either.

Frontier Conditions

A number of characteristics of the frontier and the people who ventured there are of direct relevance both to the response and to the success or failure of religious groups in the frontier environment. One obvious feature was a sparse population located in small, widely separated settlements. This situation fostered among frontier settlers loneliness and the need for emotional outlets. These factors gave rise to an essential requirement of frontier life—a spirit of independence and self-sufficiency. If frontiersmen were going to make it, they had to do it on their own. Further, in the absence of external restraints, of social-control mechanisms for monitoring people's behavior, the task of checking antisocial behavior fell to control mechanisms internal to the individual. Overarching all this was another factor—namely, the constant threat of physical danger and insecurity, whether from disease, accident, inadequate food supply, Indian raids, or fellow citizens turned brigand. A final feature of the frontier worth mentioning is the fact that the frontier effected selective migration. Those who traveled westward were not a representative cross section of the inhabitants of the eastern seaboard. Rather, the roads west tended to fill up with those who had less at stake on the east coast—specifically, those of lower socioeconomic status and with little education. Not all of the latter traveled west of course, but primarily those with an adventuresome spirit, a willingness to work, and long-range aspirations.

Responses by Organized Religion

The established social institutions on the east coast, particularly the churches, were generally ill equipped to meet the combination of challenges described in the preceding. The established eastern churches, which were of the denominational type, tended to require a trained, professional full-time clergy member to head a self-supporting congregation. They were used to meeting in a specially dedicated, permanent facility containing the standard accouterments—pews, hymnbooks, a pulpit, and perhaps a keyboard instrument. Transplanting this pattern to the frontier was infeasible, if for no other reason than a sparse population with little ready cash cannot support such a standard religious organization.

Recognizing this problem, some eastern ecclesiastical leaders and organizations turned to sponsoring revivals and camp meetings (occasional gatherings of large groups of people at a central location for several days of spiritual exhortation and instruction)—techniques that were actually better suited to such emerging sectarian groups as the Methodists and the Baptists. Nevertheless, as a result for a brief period after the Revolution there occurred what came to be known as the Second Great Awakening. (The First Great Awakening began in 1734 in New England with the evangelistic preaching of Jonathan Edwards, George Whitfield, and others, and spread through the colonies in the 1730s to 1750s). This general religious revival was epitomized in the Cane Ridge, Kentucky, camp meeting of 1801, which twenty thousand persons are estimated to have attended. Considering the sparse population of "the West" at that time, this is an impressive number that says a great deal about the eagerness of people for human contact, for an emotional outlet, and probably for many if not most, for religious participation and expression as well. The Second Great Awakening was relatively short-lived, however, and produced no durable institutional forms.

The Baptist and Methodist Solutions

So far as religion was concerned, the Methodists and the Baptists became the inheritors of the frontier, for they were better able than the established churches to meet the challenges and brave the conditions of the frontier by innovative strategies. Thus the Methodists, who had numbered approximately nine thousand in 1776, grew to become the largest religious group in the country by 1850. Baptist growth was nearly as great. No doubt, then, about their rapid success. But why? What exactly did they do? The answer is basically twofold: (1) Both groups developed innovative organizational structures for reaching widely scattered people; (2) as sects they had rejected many traditional denominational patterns and seemed capable of adapting to and growing up with the frontier. As a consequence they enjoyed a response among frontier settlers that the established denominations could not elicit.

First, regarding strategy, the Methodists employed the technique of the *circuit-riding preacher.* Initially these were men with some theological training who were commissioned as missionaries to the frontier by John Wesley in England or by Bishop Asbury, John Wesley's representative in the colonies and then in the states. Their strategy was simply to go from house to house preaching the Gospel within the family setting, delivering sermons from a tree stump or wagon bed when a larger group could be gathered, creating "Methodists" as they went. They asked little more than food and shelter from those who received them. Periodically they would return on their circuit to rally the faithful, solemnize marriages, and conduct baptisms. They traveled thousands of miles a year along circuits that took a minimum of three to four weeks, often a month or two, to complete.

The Baptists settled on a different, though equally successful, approach—the *lay preacher*, a farmer or craftsman for six days, a preacher for one. The success of this technique required only a concentration of a few families on adjoining farms or in a small village. The genius of the Baptist plan was that it required no recruitment from the outside. Anyone with a "call" from God to preach and with some oratorical and pedagogical ability could do it. The people whom such lay preachers gathered together began to think of themselves as Baptists.

And so the Baptist and Methodist sects grew. But these groups had more going for them than their strategies for overcoming the problem of sparse populations. The preachers were like their flocks—largely uneducated and independent of spirit—and knew "where the people were coming from," so to speak. They could communicate. And they encouraged emotional response and involvement in everyone. Religion for them was not a spectator sport. Revival services were frequent and they were popular, for they met people's need for emotional release. The democratic slant of these sects—which included the concepts that anyone could interpret Scripture as God directed him (no women in the clergy role yet) and that parents were responsible for the spiritual welfare of their own children between visits by the circuit rider or Sunday gatherings for worship—agreed with the individualism and self-sufficiency of the frontiersman. The typical emphasis of these sects on internal controls in the face of all manner of temptations to sin meshed well with the need for such internal controls in the absence of external ones.

Later Religious Responses

As the harshness of the frontier waned, as towns developed, and as social structures became more stabilized, further developments arose in the religious life of the frontier. For one thing, the Methodists and the Baptists consolidated their gains, for as people improved their lot and their communities became more firmly established they did not suddenly forsake the religious group that had been serving them well. In great part such continuity was maintained because the Methodist and the Baptist religious groups evolved and developed along with the frontier. Originally sects, they became full-fledged denominations. More attention was paid to theological training, colleges and seminaries were established throughout the Midwest, circuit riders became resident clergymen, part-time Sunday preachers became full-time ministers.

As more middle-class business and professional people came west, the established eastern denominations followed and built their churches in the growing towns. Some of the upwardly mobile early settlers joined these "higher-status" Episcopalian, Presbyterian, and Congregational churches, though not in sufficient numbers to erode seriously the membership gains the Baptists and Methodists had already made.

As the nineteenth century neared and passed midpoint, groups of Lutherans from Germany and the Scandinavian countries came to settle and tame the farmland of the Midwest and the north-central United States. They brought their churches with them and by virtue of different language and religion remained relatively isolated from those Protestants who had preceded them. Catholics came also in substantial numbers and established their ethnically oriented churches in both urban and rural areas. Thus the frontier was becoming religiously diverse primarily through the immigration of groups from outside the United States.

A pair of unique frontier phenomena need yet to be mentioned. One was the emergence of two new denominations that were born essentially as denominations and did not follow the sect-to-denomination evolutionary route. These were the Disciples of Christ and the Churches of Christ. Both groups downplayed denominational differences and stepped into the developing towns and cities as the frontier moved ever westward, picking up some of the people left behind as many of the Methodist and Baptist preachers moved on to follow the scattering pioneers. These groups formed what today are often called "community" churches or "nondenominational" churches that preach an "average" Protestantism and express little interest in the denominational "brand name" a member may have had before. Many of these preachers were dissident Methodists, Baptists, and Presbyterians who did not wish to be regarded as comprising yet another denomination but did so nonetheless.

The other unique frontier religious phenomenon was the Church of Jesus Christ of Latter-Day Saints (Mormons), founded by Joseph Smith in western New York State in the early 1840s. This group, regarded by some outsiders as neither Protestant nor even Christian, experienced serious opposition from an alliance of established Protestant denominations and growing Protestant sects who otherwise only competed among themselves. To escape harassment that often reached violent proportions, the Mormons moved from New York to Ohio to Missouri to Illinois and finally to Utah. But even the Mormons, which were probably best viewed as a religious cult in the beginning, evolved. Today the Mormon church is generally acknowledged to belong among the ranks of standard religious denominations, even though it is more aggressive in proselytizing than many of the latter.

THE ORDEAL OF PLURALISM

Anti-Catholicism

Although there had really never been much doubt, by the beginning of the nineteenth century the new American nation saw itself as definitely a Protestant domain. Probably this is one important reason why citizens generally accepted so graciously the radically new concept of separation of church and state enunciated in the First Amendment. Of the approximately four and one-half million citizens at the birth of the nation, estimates suggest there were only about twenty thousand Roman Catholics—a small minority indeed. Not that they were ignored. In fact, they were almost universally mistrusted. Small wonder, then, at the chagrin, uneasiness, and outright fear many citizens experienced and expressed as substantial immigration of Roman Catholics from Ireland, Germany, and Eastern Europe began in the 1830s.

The First Amendment's protection of the free exercise of religion was now to be put to its first serious test. The concept of *religious pluralism,* of freedom of religious expression and conviction and of tolerance of religious diversity to which Protestants had paid lip service, now became a bitter pill for the many spokesmen for and supporters of the view that the United States was God's Protestant kingdom on earth. Not only were substantial efforts expended in trying to amend immigration laws to keep Catholics out of this country or, failing that, to convert them to Protestantism and thereby dilute their "poison," but the society witnessed several decades of physical abuse directed against Catholics in the middle of the nineteenth century.

Martin Marty points out that the anti-Catholic agitators had deep reservoirs of suspicion from which to draw. He summarizes the historical setting as follows:

> The original colonists had felt themselves beleaguered, with French Catholics to the north and Spanish-Portuguese Catholics to the south. They had emotionally protected themselves against Catholic intrusions into the thirteen colonies. Where possible they isolated the Catholics, mostly in Maryland. Where necessary they began to accept them, as in the case of prestigious families like the Carrolls. But with few Catholics on the scene, it had been easy for colonial parsons to exaggerate stories of Catholic superstition and horror; no one was around to refute them. People could thus constantly reaffirm the prejudices their fathers had brought with them from England and elsewhere across the Atlantic.
>
> As the 20,000 or 25,000 colonial Roman Catholics grew to a body of 40,000 at the beginning of the [nineteenth] century and multiplied forty times by 1850 to 1,606,000, there were ever-increasing levels of animus and threat in the Protestant rhetoric.[11]

Reacting to this dramatic upsurge in Catholic immigration, a few outspoken propagandists—such as Samuel F. B. Morse, who painted visions of a foreign conspiracy based in the Vatican to take over America—were able to render Protestant Americans ready to believe almost anything. By mid-century the nativist Know-Nothing political party was formed with anti-Catholicism as one of its unifying themes. At this point we observe the blooming of what R. A. Billington terms the "Protestant Crusade."[12] At the heart of this "Cru-

[11] Marty, *Righteous Empire,* pp. 127–28.
[12] Ray Allen Billington, *The Protestant Crusade, 1800–1860* (Gloucester, Mass.: Peter Smith, 1963).

sade" were Protestants who felt threatened by the waves of Catholic immigration and were willing to believe most any accusation or innuendo about
Catholics. Occasionally they reacted both impetuously and violently. There
was, for example, Louisville's "Bloody Monday"—August 5, 1855—in which
more than twenty persons were killed and several hundred wounded. This was
a conflict between Protestants and Catholics—the former having been aroused
by a "no-popery" campaign carried on by the *Louisville Journal,* all within the
context of the notoriously anti-Catholic Know-Nothing political party and
philosophy. The Philadelphia riots of 1844 represented an earlier case of anti-
Catholicism that saw Catholic churches destroyed and the homes of Catholics
burned, not to mention considerable bloodshed.

It appears that Roman Catholics in this country may have unwittingly
and quite coincidentally provided some fuel for the Protestant fires that were
smoldering. Consider, for example, the Philadelphia trustee conflict of the
1820s within the Roman Catholic church, which revolved around the question
of whether church property should be controlled by trustees representing
laypeople or by the bishop of the diocese. The issue dated back to 1808, when
St. Mary's Cathedral had been erected by the congregation and control of the
property had been vested in a board of lay trustees instead of the bishop, as
was usual. The long battle, during which the priest of the congregation was
excommunicated, ended in 1830. The church was placed under an interdict
which caused members to abandon it for other churches and thus forced the
trustees, left without financial support, to submit to the bishop.

This Philadelphia controversy did American Catholicism much harm. It
attracted the hostile attention of the entire nation, inspired a great deal of
"bad press" and negative literature, and left the impression in the minds of
many Protestants that Catholicism was the sworn enemy of democratic institutions and thus a dangerous influence in the United States.[13] Ironically, the
Philadelphia episode in fact marked an attempt by Catholic laypeople to pattern their church after typically American Protestant autonomous churches
and to establish an independent Catholic church in America.[14]

Opposition by Catholics to the reading of the "Protestant" King James
Version of the Bible in New York public schools, Protestant resentment and
suspicion of the Catholic parochial schools as "un-American" and subversive,
Catholic bloc voting as evidence of considerable political strength, "native
American" resentment of "cheap" Irish Catholic labor—all are factors that
have contributed to anti-Catholicism in this country.

By the Civil War anti-Catholic sentiment had lost much of its intensity.
And the war itself certainly diverted energy and attention away from the issue.
After the war, Catholic immigration proceeded steadily and then soared in the
late 1800s with the arrival of waves of southern and eastern European Catho-

[13] Ibid., pp. 38–40.
[14] Will Herberg, *Protestant, Catholic, Jew* (Garden City, N.Y.: Doubleday, 1956), p. 140.

lics. By now, lacking evidence of any "papal plot," American Protestants established a somewhat uneasy but workable peace with their Catholic countrymen. The flames of conflict have been kindled sporadically ever since, however, over such issues as public aid to parochial schools, birth control and abortion, and official government or presidential representation to the Vatican. But as we will observe in the next chapter, the animosities have been greatly reduced.

Anti-Semitism

The issue of religious pluralism and the challenge to Protestant domination was not limited to Catholic-Protestant relations. Significant numbers of Jews also immigrated to the United States between 1880 and the First World War. Until that time there had been relatively so few Jews in this country—in 1815, for example, there were only about three thousand—that they were not regarded as a threat to established Protestantism. Although Jews had been excluded from full political participation in some of the colonies (for example, Virginia) by Trinitarian belief requirements, and although the depiction of Jews in the denominational literature of that period would today properly be termed anti-Semitic, the small number of Jews elicited little explicit reaction from their fellow citizens. Anti-Semitism in this country began in earnest with the substantial immigration of Russian Jews in the 1880s when the Ku Klux Klan made anti-Semitism one of its major stances. Many of the Jews who immigrated to the United States after 1880, although often quite secularized (and sometimes politically radical), retained their ethnic identity, settling almost exclusively in urban areas and engaging in mutual assistance in establishing business enterprises. Other ethnic groups and Protestant "native Americans" began to resent their presence, and anti-Semitism began to surface. Jews thus found it necessary to establish various defense organizations, of which the Anti-Defamation League of the B'nai B'rith is the best known.

Anti-Semitism came to be a significant feature of American life—one which though significantly diminished is still alive today. Anti-Semitism probably reached its zenith in this country in the 1920s and 1930s, when anti-Semitic newspapers and radio columnists proliferated and reached out into many American homes. Such strident anti-Semitism has been relegated to the fringes of our society today, and many of the most blatant forms of anti-Semitic discrimination in housing, education, empolyment, and voluntary-association membership have been eliminated. Yet as recently as 1960, during a two-month period, 643 incidents of anti-Jewish swastika painting on synagogue walls, vandalism against Jewish property, and beatings of Jews were recorded in the United States.[15]

[15] Charles Y. Glock and Rodney Stark, *Christian Beliefs and Anti-Semitism* (New York: Harper & Row, Pub., 1966), p. xi.

Studies by Glock and Stark and Bernard Olson have shown a connection between conservative Protestant theology and anti-Semitism, though the nature of this connection and its intensity is not clear.[16] A serious difficulty arises in trying to separate what we might call *social anti-Semitism*—hatred of Jews as social beings, as persons—from *religious anti-Semitism,* which from the conservative Christian viewpoint is the concept that Jews need salvation and that it will be denied them until they accept Jesus as Savior. Unfortunately, these two "types" of anti-Semitism, although undoubtedly intermingled in many cases, are not adequately distinguished in existing measures and indexes of anti-Semitism.

Other groups, of course, come in for their share of aspersion and harassment. We have already mentioned the Mormons, who were literally forced to flee for their lives to new territory, ultimately standing their ground in Utah Territory. Similar though not so violent harassment has been directed against Jehovah's Witnesses in many communities. It is interesting from the sociological perspective to note that both these groups traditionally engage in vigorous conversion and missionary activities. That is, they implicitly reject the pluralism concept that includes respect for every other group's autonomy and right to be and do as it chooses. Whereas adherence to the spirit of pluralism demands that one accept diversity—in fact, that one champion it—these groups actively seek to bring everyone into their ranks—an aggressive stance that undoubtedly encourages resentment. Even German Lutherans who during World War I persisted in using the German language in their worship services and conversation were harassed in some communities.

The outcome of the religious pluralism controversy in this country has, however, been the triumph of pluralism and the peaceful acceptance of religious diversity by nearly all. This of course has not stopped many religious groups from actively proselytizing and openly criticizing the theology of other religious groups. But the practice of taking the process a step further by associating what appears theologically inadequate or incorrect from one's religious perspective with "un-Americanism," inferior citizenship, subversion, and the like has been significantly reduced.

RELIGIOUS SOCIAL CONCERN

The second half of the nineteenth century marked the beginning of a highly significant controversy within American Protestantism that continues today—a fundamental argument over the proper focus of Christianity. In simplest terms, should the focus be the salvation of souls or the improvement of society? Although few if any proponents of either alternative would have asserted that Christianity should exclusively be devoted to one or the other goal, the

[16] Ibid. and Bernard Olson, *Faith and Prejudice* (New Haven: Yale University Press, 1963).

controversy tended to place most Christians, theologian and layperson alike, into one camp or the other.

This period is known for the emergence of the so-called *social gospel* and the rise of such proponents of socially concerned Christianity as Horace Bushnell, Walter Rauschenbusch, and Washington Gladden. These were people who argued that Christianity is not fulfilled and not true to its origins and history unless and until it immerses itself in alleviating the world's miseries and social pathologies—social problems that emerged with advancing industrialization, increasing urbanization, and the appearance, already then, of decay in portions of the mushrooming cities. These spokemen contended that their emphasis on social responsibility was the old, authentic emphasis of the Bible. They pointed to the prophets in the Old Testament Scriptures and to Jesus in the New Testament Gospels, who evidenced great concern for the physical and social needs and problems of people. On the other side, those who stressed the more individualistic, salvation-centered focus for Christianity tended to stress the emphasis of the New Testament Epistles of Paul on the atonement of Jesus and his rescue of people from the wrath of a just and judging God.

Although we shall look more thoroughly into this controversy in its present-day form in Chapter 13, we want at least to highlight at this point the emergence of the "new" emphasis in Christianity (or, as many contended, the resurgence of the original one) that loomed so significant during the last century. It is of interest sociologically in part because it happened to develop concomitantly with the development of sociology as a field of study and of social concern as an emphasis in the social sciences. But the development of a social-concern emphasis in American religion is of interest sociologically primarily because of the change in American religion this represented. Although it did not turn American religion completely around, for some individuals and groups it did radically change the focus and purpose of religion; at the very least, it added a new dimension.

The establishment of hospitals, orphanages, and settlement houses, and the formation of groups such as the Salvation Army occurred after the Industrial Revolution was solidly under way and many of the latter's excesses and abuses were clearly seen adversely affecting great numbers of people. It is important to note, however, that the emphasis of religious people during the period of western industrialization was primarily an individualized one. That is, the primary concern of religious leaders was with helping individuals. First of all, they wanted to save the individual's soul. But then, out of compassion for those persons living a materially disadvantaged existence, they began establishing institutions and mechanisms for the purpose of helping the body. But again, just as the concern was for the souls of individual people, so the concern was for individual bodies. The social service activities of salvation-oriented religious groups, already begun in the 1820s, continued into the early part of the twentieth century. The emphasis was essentially that of John Wesley in

the eighteenth century—namely, concern for individuals; that is, replacing individual vices with individual virtues, changing the direction of individuals
from hell to heaven, making physically healthy bodies out of ill and broken
ones.

Later, other religious leaders, such as the aforementioned Bushnell,
Rauschenbusch, and Gladden, began to direct primary attention away from
salvation and toward physical and social well-being; above all, they began to
shift the focus from individual vices to societal ones. That is, they saw the lo-
cus of social problems not in individuals but in society and in institutional
structures and patterns beyond the immediate control of individuals. To these
social reformers the goal was one of "Christianizing" the social order, of applying the teachings of Jesus to the social and economic institutions of the society, of reforming the social environment in which people lived and worked.
They expounded what came to be known as the social gospel.

Those who followed in the footsteps of the earlier, individual-oriented religious leaders became increasingly uneasy with the social gospel, which they
felt operated at the expense of individual salvation—the preeminent responsibility of Christianity, in their view. Influential evangelistic preachers who emphasized individual salvation such as Dwight L. Moody and Billy Sunday thus
began challenging the social gospel and in fact essentially carried the day so
far as rank-and-file preachers and church members were concerned. Martin
Marty reports how the flamboyant evangelist Sunday took on the most noted
advocate of the social gospel still at work in the parish ministry, Washington
Gladden:[17]

> The setting of their encounter was Columbus, Ohio, where Gladden had piled up
> a record of achievement in a socially oriented ministry over three decades. But
> when Sunday came to town to carry on one of his pro-evangelistic and apparently
> "antisocial" revivals, Gladden quietly opposed him, and after the revival, Glad-
> den was more outspoken over the meager returns he saw garnered from Sunday's
> raucous efforts. But Gladden was attacked by the vast majority of Columbus's
> ministers of all Protestant denominations. They rose to the defense of Sunday's
> approach and clearly identified with the conversionism of the revivalist.[18]

In their attempts to discredit the social gospel, the individual-oriented
evangelists began to pull back from and react against social service and welfare
activities that they had earlier engaged in, and rededicated themselves to efforts to win souls and raise levels of individual morality by means of such tactics as emphasizing the evil of "demon rum" and supporting the Prohibition
movement. The social-gospel wing of American Christianity did not disappear,
however. It continued with minority support in the major denominations and

---

[17] Most of the social-gospel advocates were seminary professors, editors, authors, and the
like who remained largely unknown to the rank-and-file church member.

[18] Marty, *Righteous Empire*, p. 183.

through the various agencies of the Federal Council of Churches (now the National Council of Churches) that had been founded in 1908 primarily by social-gospel forces.

Thus the social-gospel movement did not wither away; in fact, it has continued to exert significant influence in American religion up to the present. It enjoyed a resurgence with its involvement in the civil rights movement in the 1950s and 1960s and in the war on poverty of the 1960s and 1970s, although with what still appears to have been a minority of church member support. More on this issue in Chapter 13.

Reconciling the great diversity of opinion and practice regarding social versus individual emphases is of course not uniquely a problem of religious institutions. Religious groups have in fact always reflected the historical ambivalence in American society at large regarding rugged individualism, self-sufficiency, and individual responsibility versus social concerns, welfarism, and mutual responsibility for one's fellow human beings. This could hardly be better exemplified than right now in the 1980s as religious and political conservatives push to slow down and remove welfare and aid programs of many types, put curbs on minority rights and funding for abortions and sex education, and promote other actions championed by the so-called Moral Majority.

GROWTH OF FUNDAMENTALISM

Another important development within American religion that is important not only in its own right but particularly with regard to understanding the contemporary religious scene is that of the emergence of what we today call *fundamentalism*. Its development is in significant part a direct outgrowth of the social-gospel–individual-salvation controversy just discussed. Those leaders we have variously designated evangelists, revivalists, individual-soul savers, and traditionalists were becoming increasingly disturbed with two developments during the last quarter of the nineteenth century. The first was what they viewed as increasing secularism in the society. This is tied up with the advancement of science and the increasing confidence in the inductive scientific method of attaining truth—at the expense of deduction from a standard repository of truth such as the Bible. Of concern to them also were such developments as the dissemination of the Marxist social philosophy, the spread of the accounts of Darwin and others concerning the evolution of people and their world, and the increasing independence of society's institutions from religious influence. In short, the traditionalists or Evangelicals as they are commonly called were disturbed by the erosion of religious influence throughout the rest of the society and its institutions. Second, they felt that the Christian religion was being betrayed from within. The increasing emphasis on social service and the social gospel by individuals and groups within the broad

Christian community was a significant part of their concern. For one thing, they felt that when social service was emphasized, the traditional emphasis was of necessity neglected, or at best put in a secondary position. For another, they felt some were rejecting the traditional message of Christianity altogether and substituting the social gospel in all particulars. This was liberal ideology as opposed to their conservative religion—this was liberal Christianity that attempted to incorporate secular values into the Christian structure. What further alarmed the Evangelicals was the development of a form of biblical scholarship known as *higher criticism,* an approach to the Bible asserting that it is a collection of human documents subject to the same principles of textual criticism as any other group of documents—a perspective that originated in German theological schools and universities in the mid-1800s and was subsequently adopted at many leading seminaries in the United States.

In an effort to combat this "creeping liberalism" and restore Christianity to what they regarded as its original nature and message, many of the Evangelicals coalesced around the publication, beginning in 1910, of their orthodox manifesto in twelve volumes titled *The Fundamentals.* As Stewart Cole says, "In this action the historian finds the clear emergence of fundamentalism."[19] This publication was the capstone to a series of Bible conferences held by conservatives throughout the country between 1876 and 1900, which Gasper views as "embryonic stirrings" of the fundamentalist movement.[20] At the most significant of these conferences, held in 1895 at Niagara, New York, a declaration was formulated that anticipated the famous "five points" of fundamentalist doctrine as expounded in the twelve volumes of *The Fundamentals.* The five independent points of traditional Protestant Christianity agreed upon at the Niagara Conference were (1) the inerrancy of the Scriptures, (2) the virgin birth of Jesus Christ, (3) the deity of Jesus Christ, (4) the substitutionary atonement (Jesus taking the punishment for sin in people's place), and (5) the physical resurrection of Jesus Christ and his anticipated bodily return.[21]

The five points of fundamentalist doctrine enunciated in the first volume of *The Fundamentals* were almost identical: (1) the verbal and inerrant inspiration of the Bible, (2) the virgin birth of Jesus Christ, (3) the substitutionary atonement of Jesus Christ, (4) the bodily ressurection of Jesus Christ from the tomb, and (5) the imminent second coming of Jesus Christ. Four closely related doctrines that could more or less be inferred from these basic five were (1) the deity of Jesus Christ, (2) the sinful nature of man, (3) salvation by faith through the free grace of God, and (4) the expectation of the bodily resurrection of true believers on the Last Day.[22] Much attention was also paid to refu-

[19] Stewart G. Cole, *The History of Fundamentalism* (Hamden, Conn.: Archon Books, 1963), p. 53.

[20] Louis Gasper, *The Fundamentalist Movement* (The Hague: Mouton, 1963), p. 11.

[21] Ibid.

[22] *The Fundamentals: A Testimony to the Truth,* vols. 1–12 (Chicago: Testimony Publishing Company, n.d. [c. 1919]).

tation of errors, such as the theory of organic evolution and higher criticism of the Bible, and to ways of relating to such heretical religious groups and movements as Roman Catholics, Mormons, Jehovah's Witnesses, Christian Science, and Spiritualism.

During this period the fundamentalists were organizing schools to combat the increasingly secular nature of both public and private colleges and universities. Gasper reports that over 160 Bible schools enrolling over twenty-five thousand students were organized to promote the centrality of Bible study and prepare leaders for the movement.[23]

The year 1925 probably marks the peak of fundamentalism, at least as an organized phenomenon. This is the date of the Scopes "monkey trial," in which the fundamentalists hoped that their political spokesman and three-time candidate for the presidency William Jennings Bryan would break the back of religious modernism or at least one vertebra—namely, the teaching of evolution in a public school. Even though Scopes was found guilty, the farcical nature of the trial and the "bad press" the prosecution received turned the legal victory of the fundamentalists into a public relations defeat, and the cohesiveness of the movement began to dissipate. Already by the following year attendance at their annual meeting had fallen off. By their 1930 convention "none of the scheduled speeches contained any reference to modernism or evolution."[24] They began to fight among themselves, and a host of subgroups formed.

Furniss suggests six reasons for the declining influence of fundamentalism: (1) The death of William Jennings Bryan immediately after the Scopes trial left the fundamentalists with no national leader of significant stature and appeal. (2) Fundamentalists had paid too little attention to creating and maintaining a cohesive national organization. (3) The prohibition issue and the fight against repeal of the 1919 Prohibition Amendment diverted the energies of many fundamentalists to this specific and in a sense peripheral issue. (4) The economic crash of 1929 induced many churches to begin working to alleviate human misery and to forget some of their theological quarrels. (5) People who were becoming more sophisticated in their knowledge, scientific and otherwise, recognized that the fundamentalists' representation of science and its theories were often distorted. (6) After losing some battles, the fundamentalists tended to pull back. They became less aggressive, more withdrawn, even petulant. That is, they appeared to lose some of their concern for reforming the theologies of their neighbors and concentrated more on attaining purity for themselves.[25] Gasper suggests that yet another possible factor was the development of a somewhat general reaction against theological liberalism in theological circles that came to be known as neo-orthodoxy—a moderately

---

[23] Gasper, *The Fundamentalist Movement*, p. 12.

[24] Norman F. Furniss, *The Fundamentalist Controversy, 1918–1931* (New Haven: Yale University Press, 1954), p. 56.

[25] Ibid., pp. 178–81.

conservative theological movement led by the Swiss theologian Karl Barth.[26] Thus some of what fundamentalism had been opposing was in fact modified, whether through the efforts of fundamentalists or of others. Certainly their "enemy" became less easy to identify and to caricature.

All of this does not mean, however, that fundamentalism died out in the 1930s. Although fundamentalists were less in public view, they were very hard at work solidifying their gains and exploring possibilities for a viable national organization. They published mightily and began extensively to utilize the new communication medium of radio.

In the early 1940s two distinct formal associations of fundamentalists were organized, and to this day they preserve a dual focus within fundamentalism. The first to organize called itself the American Council of Christian Churches and set out to perpetuate the early aggressive thrust of fundamentalists in promoting the "historic Gospel." In addition, it identified itself as an exclusivist organization explicitly barring particular individual churches and denominations from its membership. The second organization, the National Association of Evangelicals, intended to "break with apostasy" but also wanted to avoid becoming a "reactionary, negative, or destructive type of organization."[27] It explicitly set out to become an inclusivist organization acting as a "leaven" or influence throughout Protestantism wherever possible, without demanding rigid conformity to a set of absolute standards. The National Association of Evangelicals, apparently the more successful of the two organizations, includes such somewhat familiar groups as the Assemblies of God, the Free Methodist Church of North America, the Free Will Baptists, and several Mennonite and Pentecostal groups.

Following World War II there emerged a host of targets for the fundamentalists, particularly for the American Council of Christian Churches led by Carl McIntire. There was the "liberal" ecumenical movement, particularly as embodied in the National Council of Churches in the U.S.A. and the World Council of Churches, defined by the American Council as compromisers and betrayers of the true Christian Gospel. There was the United Nations, viewed as an enemy of democracy and capitalistic freedom and as a tool of the forces of communism. The supreme specter of communism was seen lurking not only within the United Nations and its numerous agencies, but even within the Christian churches. Numerous charges of sellouts to and compromises with communism were hurled against such prominent Protestant clergymen as John C. Bennett, Harry Emerson Fosdick, E. Stanley Jones, Reinhold Niebuhr, and Henry VanDusen. New translations of the Bible were judged by fundamentalists as distorting the divinely inspired Hebrew and Greek texts of the Bible and as disagreeing with the all-but-inspired King James Version of 1611. (Consider, for example, the controversy that arose over the Hebrew word

[26] Gasper, *The Fundamentalist Movement*, p. 19.
[27] Ibid., p. 25.

almah in Isaiah 7:14—translated as "virgin" in the King James Version and as "young woman" or similar, more general designations in such newer translations as the Revised Standard Version.)

Although some official support for these "causes" and campaigns was forthcoming from fundamentalist associations, particularly the American Council of Christian Churches, most of the agitation was led by individual self-styled leaders of the fundamentalist movement. Not that these persons' activities did not reflect the sentiments of many fundamentalists, but it is only fair to mention that seldom did the associations themselves take specific positions on these issues, particularly those involving opposition to particular individuals.

Throughout all this the basic thrust of fundamentalism has been evangelism, which it constantly promotes through the extensive publication of books, tracts, and magazines, through continuing wide use of radio and television broadcasts, and through such efforts as the Youth for Christ movement with its evengelism rallies for young people throughout the United States.

Fundamentalism today remains alive and well on the American religious scene. In fact, we have already discussed in Chapter 6 a highly significant resurgence, which has the potential for influence greater than ever before particularly because it has the ear of leadership in the Republican Party, and access to the twin technologies of television and direct mail systems. We refer, of course, to the New Religious Right, sometimes called Evangelicals. While more politically active than earlier generations of fundamentalists, they continue faithfully to carry forward the fundamentalist banner.

THE POST-WORLD WAR II REVIVAL

Following the Second World War the United States experienced what came to be known as a religious "revival." Beginning in the late 1940s and extending into the 1950s, church membership and attendance soared, contributions to religious organizations poured in, literally thousands of new congregations were established and quickly became self-supporting, and the value of new construction by religious groups increased dramatically, year after year. Some data will document this growth. Between 1940 and 1950 membership in churches rose from 49 to 57 percent of the population, and by 1959 had reached 63.6 percent.[28] Gallup poll data show a comparable increase in church attendance—whereas only 36 percent of the sample in 1942 reported having attended a church service during the week preceding the interview, by 1957 the figure had risen to 51 percent.[29] The value of new construction of religious

[28] Benson Y. Landis, ed., *Yearbook of American Churches 1964* (New York: National Council of Churches in the U.S.A., 1964), p. 290.

[29] Ibid., p. 283.

facilities totaled $28 million in 1935, during the depth of the Depression, and had increased to $59 million by 1940. But the really big increase was still to come—in 1950 the value of new construction was $409 million, and by 1965 the figure reached $1.2 billion. The religion business was indeed a booming one.

Further, there developed what William Lee Miller has called our national "piety along the Potomac," which included Bible breakfasts, congressional prayer groups, and a president named Eisenhower who made numerous religious allusions in his speeches and was himself baptized in the White House following his inauguration.[30] Postage stamps and folding money suddenly began to include "In God We Trust" on their faces. We inserted the phrase "under God" in the Pledge of Allegiance. Popular music and movie extravaganzas followed religious themes. Books of a religious, devotional, or inspirational nature proliferated, and many even made the best-seller lists.

The opening passage of this section referred to a religious "revival." At least this is what many called it. Many churchmen who saw their churches filling up, who saw massive building programs quickly underwritten with cash and pledges, who noted their denominations annually opening new mission congregations numbering in the dozens and even hundreds can hardly be blamed for speaking in such terms. Finally their sermons and various other efforts in a lifetime of dedication to religion were bearing some tangible fruit. Religion was really "catching on" and getting through to people. Observing these phenomena sociologically, however, we should be more cautious in assessing what was going on. As A. Roy Eckardt observes, there was "a manifest upsurge of *interest* in religion."[31] Whether this reflected a true revival in the sense of increasing dedication and commitment is difficult if not impossible to determine.

What we do know is that the period following World War II found many more people within our national boundaries, as millions of servicemen and women returned home and as the baby boom of the 1940s got underway. A fantastic building boom accompanied the population growth as many new and some older families moved to the suburbs in search of a place to start a new life. Church facilities that had barely sufficed during a Depression and a world war (when there was relatively little new construction) clearly came up short in the face of population and residential expansion. New church facilities were built where the new people now were. In some cases this meant a net gain, as the old facilities in the city remained and new facilities were built near the edges of the spreading suburban frontier. In other instances it was a trade. The downtown and inner-city churches were abandoned for the new, as a majority of the people moved out, or the former were sold for a few cents on the

---

[30] William Lee Miller, "Piety Along the Potomac," *The Reporter*, August 17, 1954, p. 25.

[31] A. Roy Eckardt, *The Surge of Piety in America* (New York: Association Press, 1958), p. 17.

dollar to the sects that emerged to serve the migrants (primarily blacks) who replaced the mobile, more affluent whites who left—a prime example of human ecological succession.

We do know that the United States was trying to piece itself together again after a long, harsh Depression and an expensive, grief-filled war. No doubt countless people were seeking moorings, eternal verities upon which they could start building something new. Paul Hutchinson wrote in 1955 about the "cult of reassurance," which he described as

> a flocking to religion, especially in middle-class circles, for a renewal of confidence and optimism at a time when these are in short supply. It is a turning to the priest for encouragement to believe that, despite everything that has happened in this dismaying century, the world is good, life is good, and the human story makes sense and comes out where we want it to come out.[32]

Further, there was in the postwar years the unsettled state of mind caused by the specter of the atomic bomb and the uneasiness of what was termed the "menace" of communism. Many people were undoubtedly seeking a firm base on which to stand and a clear perspective from which to evaluate what was happening.

Yet we cannot help but return to our prior comments about the growing population, and above all the suburban migration trends. Without a doubt something quite sociological and not particularly religious was going on as people got involved in building churches and attending them once they were built. These people were in a new place; they had left their neighborhoods of many years, perhaps even of their childhood; they were temporarily without friends or voluntary-association outlets and involvements; they were looking for human contact. A ready place which developed early in the suburban development to resolve some of these needs and problems was the church. In a real sense, the idea of religion as an integrating mechanism in society has definite meaning and relevance here—religion provided social contacts, outlets, and activities for people that were quite apart from strictly religious functions or concerns.

At the height of the religious "revival" Will Herberg suggested another partial explanation for the rise of religious interest. His suggestion revolves around the third-generation hypothesis, which says that while the children of immigrants strive to deny their heritage in their struggle to "match up" to what they perceive to be true American standards and characteristics, the grandchildren (the third generation), quite secure in their Americanism, look for further identity, for a heritage and a link with the past. This, Herberg feels, is available for nearly all Americans in religion, specifically the three equally alternative religions of our contemporary society—Protestantism, Catholicism, and Judaism. Since in the latter half of the twentieth century we in

[32] Quoted in ibid., p. 28.

the United States constitute essentially a nation of third-generation or later-generation Americans, it is therefore not surprising to see a renewal of interest in religion—a heightened interest not strictly for "religious" reasons, but for social and psychological reasons as well, as people try to identify what they are besides "just an American."[33]

Certainly some reservations are in order concerning how paramount religious identity is for the majority of people. If asked, "What are you?" would not more people respond in terms of their occupation rather than their religion? It is nevertheless likely that, for some people at least, religious identity has come to serve as an important link with the past and as a source of present identity.

At this point we refer to our discussion in the appendix of this book of a problem inherent in the measurement of religiosity. Most of the discussion of religious revival has centered around rather low-powered measures, such as church attendance and membership. There has been little assessment of changes in intensity of religious feeling or meaning, or changes in what people believed in and are committed to (ideological dimension), or changes in behavior as a result of religious influences (consequential dimension). Thus even if we could agree that a religious revival occurred in the United States from approximately 1945 to 1965, we may be referring to little more than what Eckardt noted—an increased *interest* in religion. And this may be somewhat of an overstatement. For example, what does an increase in church membership mean? In part it reflects the fact that requirements for church membership have in many groups become progressively less demanding and restrictive. That is, it appears to be easier to become a church member. Further, the high degree of geographic mobility of people during this period in our history, coupled with the tardiness of most local congregations to clear their membership lists of dropouts and people who have moved away, have undoubtedly resulted in some—in certain cases perhaps considerable—duplication hidden in comprehensive church membership figures. That is, it is likely that some people were counted two or three times within a given year's totals.

There is no point here in going further in expressing our uneasiness with unqualified assertions of a postwar religious revival, for we have made our basic point.[34] That is, although there appears to have been a definite upswing in religious interest in the post-World War II period, the upswing may not have been so great or significant as some have supposed. In a sense, religion became more highly visible. It was no longer contained solely within the walls of religious organizations. It hit the jukeboxes, the movie theaters, and the drugstore

[33] Herberg, *Protestant, Catholic, Jew*, pp. 272–75.

[34] Additional questions are raised by Charles Y. Glock, "The Religious Revival in America?" in *Religion and the Face in America*, ed. Jane Zahn (Berkeley: University Extension, University of California, 1959); Seymour Martin Lipset, "Religion in America: What Religious Revival?" *Columbia University Forum* 11, no. 2 (1959); and W. H. Hudson, "Are Churches Really Booming?" *Christian Century* 72, no. 51 (1955), 1494–96.

paperback bookracks. Religion was popularized, and it impinged on everyone's consciousness—much as any fad does. Just as any fad, however, some of the glitter and popularity began to fade. Glock and Stark even suggest that, solely in response to wide publicity given church membership growth in the late 1940s, there was "generated a commercial interest in producing and promoting religious literature, songs and plays with a religious motif, and commodities having religious connotations."[35] That is, commercial interests saw a new market, and the resultant visibility of religion through commercial exploitation tended to exaggerate the level of religious interest actually felt and expressed by people.

Although we could now preceed to examine developments in American religion following the postwar religious "revival" and thus bring our discussion up to date, we shall delay such an examination until Chapter 13. In that chapter we shall go into greater detail concerning the contemporary religious scene and what developed out of the postwar religious "revival" period. We now proceed in the next chapter to discuss a unique religious pattern on the American scene, namely, black religion and the black church.

[35] Charles Y. Glock and Rodney Stark, *Religion and Society in Tension* (Chicago: Rand McNally, 1965), p. 78.

11

Black Religion in America

In Chapter 8 we introduced the subject of religion and the black American. We focused both on the historical issue once facing American Christians of whether to convert black slaves to Christianity and on the more recent issue of the relationship of white churches to the black Civil Rights movement. In the present chapter we wish to pick up at the historical point when the issue of the conversion of slaves had been resolved, and trace the development of the black church as a social institution. In doing so we shall work within three major sections: an overview of the historical development of the institution; an examination of the role of militancy versus social pacifism so far as the black church is concerned; and a discussion of contemporary religious issues and developments within the black church and the black community, together with an assessment of the continuing role of religion in the black community.

*THE HISTORICAL
DEVELOPMENT OF THE
BLACK CHURCH AS A
SOCIAL INSTITUTION*

Following the consensus in the United States around the turn of the nineteenth century that slaves should be converted to Christianity and still remain slaves, the early pattern of worship services found black slaves and whites in the same congregations—the blacks usually occupying the balcony, the whites the main floor. Such joint worship was deemed advisable because white masters could then keep an eye on their "possessions" and be reassured that their slaves were not listening to a different message—such as a call to insurrection.

The Deculturation Process

Whether slaveholders were always conscious of it or not, for blacks conversion to Christianity and joint worship served as part of the deculturation process. At the very least, religious conversion served as a useful follow-up and capstone to the deliberate efforts by slave traders and owners to deculturate the slaves, to strip them of their African culture and heritage. This was accomplished by such tactics as breaking up families and prohibiting any two slaves from the same African village or tribe to be sold to work on the same plantation. One highly significant concomitant of this tactic was that the slaves usually shared no common language and thus could only converse in the English language that they had to learn. In short, much of the original culture of these people was stripped from them in less than a generation.

Obviously slaves could not very successfully preserve and practice many shared religious patterns either. Christianity, which was substituted for the ancient religions, itself became an agent for subduing and pacifying the slaves. What slaves heard preached was submission to authority, obedience, obligation to perform one's duty, commitment to nonviolence, and promise of splendid eternal rewards in heaven for all who led proper lives and made appropriate commitments during one's earthly sojourn. "Some God has made to be masters, some to be slaves. But we'll all receive a grand reward in the hereafter"—this is what has been waggishly referred to as "pie-in-the-sky by and by."

Kenneth Stampp has summarized well the use to which religion was put with regard to controlling the behavior of slaves:

> Through religious instruction the bondsmen learned that slavery had divine sanction, that insolence was as much an offense against God as against the temporal master. They received the Biblical command that servants should obey their masters, and they heard, too, that eternal salvation would be their reward for faithful service, and that on the day of judgment God would deal impartially with the poor and the rich, the black man and the white.[1]

Stampp also mentions a book titled *Suggestions on the Religious Instruction of the Negroes in the Southern States* written by Charles C. Jones and published by the national Presbyterian Board of Publication. Stampp cites Jones as advising missionaries to ignore the "civil condition" of slaves and to pay no attention to complaints against their masters. In preaching to slaves, ministers should condemn "every vice and evil custom," urge the "discharge

---

[1] Kenneth M. Stampp, *The Peculiar Institution* (New York: Knopf, 1956), p. 158.

of every duty," and support the "peace and order of society." They should, in sum, teach the slaves to give "respect and obedience [to] all those whom God in his providence has placed in authority over them."[2]

Emerging Independence of the Black Church

The early pattern of joint worship of masters and slaves in the same church did not remain the common one, probably in large part because the white masters wanted one message for their slaves, another for themselves. Therefore, another early pattern on the larger plantations was for the owner to provide special religious leaders and preachers for the slaves. These were not always white preachers, but occasionally trusted slaves who had a "gift" for preaching. Also fairly early the Baptists and Methodists began missionary activities among the slaves, and they enjoyed considerable success—for many of the same reasons that they succeeded with white settlers on the frontier (see Chapter 10). Thus the early pattern of joint worship in the same congregations was gradually replaced by segregated worship in white and black "congregations." Strictly speaking, except in the North and in a few border cities, slaves did not form their own independent congregations, largely because of laws forbidding slave assemblies. Informally, however, on many plantations essentially autonomous slave churches developed under "trusted" slave ministers. Of course, their services and activities were carefully monitored by the master or his overseer. Nevertheless, such congregations of slaves set the stage for the eventual emergence of the black church as the major, if not the only, formal group or organization over which blacks, after Emancipation, had essential control. Thus we can begin to understand the importance and centrality that black religious organizations have assumed in the black community to this day.

Although for various reasons whites began to tolerate separate religious organizations and activities for blacks, it was not without some apprehension. Richard Wade points out that as late as 1847 "many citizens" in Charleston expressed their discomfort over permitting religious institutions for blacks, particularly as it resulted in separate congregations. They feared the independence, the absence of the control and authority of the master, the taste of freedom it provided, and the opportunity for black leaders to emerge and learn skills.[3]

In the North, after some initial integrated worship, free blacks began to pull out and form their own congregations and, soon, their own denominations. In fact, the earliest all-black denominations, the African Methodist Episcopal Zion Church and the African Methodist Episcopal Church, orga-

---

[2] Quoted in ibid., p. 160.

[3] Richard C. Wade, *Slavery in the Cities: The South, 1820–1860* (New York: Oxford University Press, 1964), p. 83.

nized in 1796 and 1816, respectively, were founded by free blacks who had experienced harassment and "balcony segregation" in white congregations.

The Functions of the Black Church

After the Civil War and Emancipation, with most legal restrictions against black assemblies lifted, there occurred a mass withdrawal of blacks from racially mixed congregations and even denominations in order to form their own churches. What had begun as an outlet or escape and a focal institution for their lives under slavery continued to serve the same functions after Emancipation. Although the following evaluation by Richard Wade concerns the functions of religion for blacks under slavery, the pattern then established continued after Emancipation.

> Slavery had stripped [blacks] of any meaningful pattern of life beyond that of the master and their bondage. The family could furnish none. No tradition could provide roots into a history without servitude. Neither today nor tomorrow offered any expectation of a life without the present stigma. Deprived of nostalgia for the past and unable to discover any real meaning in the present, the blacks sought relief and consolation in a distant time. In the church, with their own kind, amid songs of redemption and the promises of Paradise, a lifeline could be thrown into the future.[4]

The prominent black leader and sociologist W. E. B. Du Bois states that once blacks assumed complete control over their church following Emancipation, the local black church became the center of its members' social life, the primary medium of communication and information exchange, and even the organizer of entertainment and amusement. With regard to the last function he lists such activities and functions as concerts, suppers, socials, fairs, literary exercises and debates, cantatas, plays, excursions, picnics, surprise parties, and celebrations.[5]

Gunnar Myrdal describes the black church as a "community center par excellence."[6] In most black communities the church was the only institution where blacks not only enjoyed autonomy and were free from the prying eyes of whites but also had access to physical facilities in which to conduct social activities.

But to note such a function as this is only to begin to list the important roles of the religious group or institution in the life of black Americans. First there is the economic function: "A study of economic co-operation among Negroes," Du Bois has stated, "must begin with the church group."[7] Many black

[4] Ibid., pp. 162–63.

[5] W. E. B. Du Bois, *The Philadelphia Negro* (Philadelphia: University of Pennsylvania, 1899), p. 201.

[6] Gunnar Myrdal, *An American Dilemma* (New York: Harper & Brothers, 1944), p. 938.

[7] W. E. B. Du Bois, *Economic Cooperation Among Negroes* (Atlanta: Atlanta University Press, 1907), p. 54.

churches early formed mutual-aid or "beneficial" societies designed to help members survive financial crises associated with illness or death of family members. These were actually incipient insurance companies. In rural communities the emphasis seemed to be particularly on burial "insurance" to provide the members with a "decent Christian burial."

The black churches have also played a significant role in education over the years. Frequently, black ministers established a school along with a church. Just as the original purpose of slave education had been to communicate the Christian Gospel and enable slaves to read the Bible, these minister-educators sought to raise the spiritual understanding of their people. When the Julius Rosenwald Fund aided in building over five thousand schools for blacks in the South during the first third of the twentieth century, black churches played an important role in supplementing those funds—E. Franklin Frazier notes that southern blacks contributed 17 percent of the total cost of $28 million (Rosenwald Fund, 15 percent; white friends, 4 percent; taxes, 64 percent), and that they raised much of their share through church suppers and various other church-sponsored programs.[8]

There was also impetus among the black denominations following the Civil War to erect educational institutions independent of white philanthropy. This plan was primarily motivated by the desire to provide a better-educated ministry—a project Frazier feels was not eminently successful, since the black denominational schools "never attained a high level as educational institutions . . . [and] have generally nurtured a narrow religious outlook and have restricted the intellectual development of Negroes."[9] Frazier also notes that the authoritarian demeanor and antiintellectualism exhibited by many black ministers have tended to inhibit the black churches from making a strong, positive contribution to education.[10] In other words, although certainly contributing to educational advancement for blacks, the black church has not been as significant an influence in this sphere as it might have been.

Supporting the significance of the black church's role in educating blacks, however, Wade mentions that some of the pre-Emancipation opposition to independent black churches—or, for that matter, to Christianity for blacks at all—centered around the observation that some blacks were becoming literate in the process of their religious instruction. For many whites feared black literacy as much as black independence in their religious activities.[11]

A third area of influence and involvement on the part of the black religious institution has been politics. During the Reconstruction period several black ministers and bishops in the South became federal and state officials, state legislators, and U.S. congressmen; one was even elected a U.S. senator.

[8] E. Franklin Frazier, *The Negro Church in America* (New York: Schocken, 1963), p. 40.

[9] Ibid., p. 41.

[10] Ibid., p. 42.

[11] Wade, *Slavery*, pp. 173–77.

With the end of Reconstruction and the resumption of white supremacy, however, blacks were virtually eliminated from public political life, and the black church then became, as Frazier observes, "the arena of . . . political activities" for black citizens.[12] As the sole major institution over which they had complete control, the church became the major context within which ambitious individuals could aspire to leadership and achieve distinction and status. In particular, the black church turned out to be the most likely source of power, upward mobility, and economic success for black males. Black churches thus soon overflowed with aspiring ministers, apprentice ministers, and "jackleg preachers" who literally waited in the wings for a chance to preach, prove their ability, and gather a following or congregation for themselves.

In the South the church also presented the only outlet of political expression for the black rank and file, denied the franchise in local, state, and national elections. The only place they could vote and make significant choices was in their church—as they elected local officers and denominational representatives and engaged in debate over policies for their local church.

We must note also that as the franchise was granted or returned to blacks, particularly in the North, black churches became more politically involved than most of their white counterparts. Candidates for political office were frequently invited to speak in black churches during or after Sunday services, ministers urged their followers to vote for particular candidates, and partisan campaign literature was made available in church buildings—all to a greater extent than in white churches, most of which counseled keeping politics and religion separate.

Although no hard data on the frequency with which black churches were involved in politics are available from the distant past, 1963 data on black clergymen in Detroit reveal that 45.5 percent allowed political candidates access to their churches, 62.7 percent permitted distribution of campaign literature from their churches, 67.8 percent explicitly encouraged their members to work with the political parties in their neighborhoods, and 30.5 percent even told their members whom they should vote for. Further, 24.4 percent of black clergymen in Detroit had at some time actively worked for a political party at the local level.[13]

It is important to note that the more militantly committed a black cleric is to the Civil Rights movement and its goals, the more likely he or she is to engage in the political behaviors just cited. We shall focus on important differences among contemporary black clergymen later in this chapter. At this point we simply wish to document that the black church has been and continues to be a fairly active political organization. Although no comparable hard data for white churches are available, every indication is that on the average, white

---

[12] Frazier, *The Negro Church*, p. 43.

[13] Ronald L. Johnstone, "Militant and Conservative Community Leadership among Negro Clergymen" (Ph.D. dissertation, University of Michigan, 1963), pp. 126–27.

churches have traditionally not been so politically involved. There has been some change here recently, of course, as we have seen the clergy and churches linked with the Moral Majority and similar groups become very active politically.

Political officeholders and aspirants have long known that the black clergyman is an important link in their relationship with the black community. In Floyd Hunter's study of the power structure of Atlanta, he found that leaders in the dominant white community believed that if anything was to be done through leadership channels in the black community, the black clergymen needed to be contacted first.[14] In his study of the reform movement in Philadelphia politics, James Reichly designated black clergymen as prime political leaders in the black community;[15] and T. R. Solomon found that black clergymen exerted considerable leadership and influence in Detroit so far as the black vote was concerned.[16]

At a more general level than politics per se, it is important to observe that historically the black minister was not only an important leader of black citizens in rural and small-town communities, but often virtually the only one. Even in a city such as New Orleans as recently as 1960, Daniel Thompson concluded that "Negro ministers constitute the largest segment of the leadership class."[17]

Finally, we must say that permeating all of the preceding functions of the black church is the fundamental function that the black church performs for its members of representing what Frazier calls "a refuge in a hostile white world."[18] The black church has provided a structural context for interaction in which blacks could not only express their deepest feelings and longings but also attain some measure of status (in God's eyes, if in no one else's). Earlier, religion provided black slaves some catharsis as well as hope for eventual freedom even though they were now in temporal bondage. Later, in a similar way, the "emancipated" blacks, after a brief opportunity to participate somewhat freely in the wider society during Reconstruction, were soon again excluded from participation in the white person's world except as inferiors. They were disfranchised, given a skimpy and inferior education, and accorded far less than justice by a court system that operated with a double standard of justice. These "emancipated" blacks needed escape and hope as much as their en-

---

[14] Floyd Hunter, *Community Power Structure* (Chapel Hill: University of North Carolina Press, 1953), pp. 117–18.

[15] James Reichly, *The Art of Government* (Philadelphia: Greater Philadelphia Magazine, 1958), p. 21.

[16] T. R. Solomon, "Participation of Negroes in Detroit Elections" (Ph.D. dissertation, University of Michigan, 1939), p. 65.

[17] Daniel C. Thompson, *The Negro Leadership Class* (Englewood Cliffs, N.J.: Prentice-Hall, 1963), p. 34.

[18] Frazier, *The Negro Church*, p. 44.

slaved parents and grandparents before them. Where could a black find refuge amid such hostility and discrimination? The place was predominantly the church, which whites left alone.

Most of what we have been describing in the foregoing paragraphs applies most appropriately to the black church since the days of Reconstruction. During slavery, when the black church had to be the "invisible institution," many were the sounds of freedom in black religion. Although it is difficult to distinguish whether calls for freedom in black slaves' religion were for ultimate spiritual freedom in heaven, or for temporal freedom from bondage, or perhaps a subtle and even unconscious combination of both ideas, there is evidence that black religion did encourage slaves' hopes of physical freedom. The leaders of the better-known slave uprisings, for example, used ample Biblical imagery and justification for their actions. Consider, for example, the rebellion led by Nat Turner, himself a black minister. Moreover, some of the northern black churches composed of freed blacks stood squarely for slaves' freedom as they served as important links in the Underground Railroad.

But following the Civil War, when the issue was no longer slavery but the pervasive racism that securely kept blacks "in their place," whatever small amount of past protest and calls for freedom there had been receded in the face of escapist and otherworldly emphases. It is this post-Civil War pattern of black religion that nurtured the stereotype of the black church that so many whites cling to—the revivalist or sectarian emotionalism and escapism that an accommodating Uncle Tom, albeit a fiery and eloquent preacher, supervised and promoted. Here one sees the subservient, peacemaking, don't-rock-the-boat style of black minister who knew only too well that his job was to keep his place, encourage submission and fatalistic acquiescence on the part of his congregation, and preach an otherworldly gospel. If he did his job well, his choir would receive an invitation to sing in a white church or two during the year, and he could look forward to a little free coal for the church and parsonage in the winter.[19]

The black church became overwhelmingly a haven, away from the prying eyes of whites, where blacks could exercise autonomy but where there appeared to be little challenge to the status quo. In fact, the following observation by an anonymous black preacher probably conveys even more truth than humor: "Come weal or woe, my status is quo." Rare was the black minister who took up the banner of change or social revolution at the risk of losing a fairly comfortable position whose advantages included high personal status and power, and income as great if not usually greater than the majority of his fellow blacks. Black ministers were also occasionally accused of being "bought off" by elements in the white power structure as they were accorded

---

[19] See Ronald L. Johnstone, "Negro Preachers Take Sides," *Review of Religious Research* 11, no. 1 (1969), 81.

the courtesy of speaking for or representing the black community and serving as the funnel for the table crumbs of white philanthropy.

With little impetus for challenge and change coming from black ministers, who did reasonably well for themselves under a system of racism, and with the rank-and-file black church members finding solace, escape, recreation, and temporal autonomy in the black church, it is not surprising that the black church proceeded through the decades of segregation and discrimination tacitly approving, or at least certainly not openly challenging, prevailing social structures and patterns. Not that there were no voices of protest coming from the black church and its clergy. Not that black religion was totally acquiescent in the face of a dominant racism. On the contrary, there were definite protests and other forms of aggressive reaction in the name of religion. In fact, although we have been stressing the accommodating, otherworldly, withdrawal response of black religion—essentially the sect approach—in the face of white racism and exclusion from the society's mainstream, there has always been a mildly aggressive and persistent reaction stemming from within the ranks of black religion.

MILITANCY IN THE
BLACK CHURCH

The Father Divine Style

Four types of black religious aggressiveness in the face of racism can be distinguished.[20] One is typified by the Father Divine Peace Mission that flourished in the 1930s and early 1940s. Here was a religious group that provided blacks with food and occasional job opportunities during the Great Depression as many blacks migrated to northern cities in search of employment. Although the Father Divine Peace Mission presents a fascinating study in theology (Father Divine was viewed as God himself), our interest here is in the group's commitment to a social service type of action that fed and housed thousands of needy persons over a period of years. Although this approach of course did not strike significantly at the root causes of problems facing black Americans and worked only at the remedial level of treating symptoms, there was here and in similar groups a clear manifestation of aggressiveness in the name of black religion. We are forced to conclude, however, that the overall net impact of such food and lodging efforts benefited only a small minority of needy blacks.

---

[20] *Aggressiveness* is understood here and in the discussion that follows in a very general sense of direct action of some kind that is perceived as likely to improve the condition of oneself or one's group.

The Black Nationalism Style

Another example of aggressiveness in the name of religion in the black community is similar to the foregoing, but more far-reaching and enduring. That is the self-help philosophy and activities of black nationalist religious organizations, best represented (most recently, at least) by the Nation of Islam ("Black Muslims"). Here is a group dating back to the early 1930s that stresses black supremacy, advocates racial separation, and maintains rigid membership requirements (religious dietary laws and moral discipline). Major emphases are to pool economic resources, "buy black," secure an education, learn skills, work hard, cultivate self-discipline, and in general engage in cooperative self-help—all in the name of religion (in this instance a version of Islam whose validity other branches of Islam tend not to recognize). Considerable credit has been given the Black Muslims for their success in rehabilitating ex-convicts and improving the economic welfare of their adherents. While the movement has not attracted hordes of blacks into its ranks, its success with the few it has attracted is worthy of attention. Again, our point here is simply that in the name of religion some American blacks have been aggressive with respect to improving their life situation.

The Individual Aggressive Style

A third example of black aggressiveness in the name of or from the ranks of religion would be the numerous examples of individual black ministers from the more standard black denominations who either took it upon themselves to extract philanthropy from the white community or became involved as individuals in political activities that concerned blacks. An excellent example of the latter activity is seen in Detroit in the late 1930s and early 1940s during the bitter labor struggle to unionize the Ford Motor Company. Using various ingenious techniques, Henry Ford and his aides had long kept a substantial contingent of blacks out of the labor movement. Although Ford as early as 1910 established the policy that at least 10 percent of his employees would be blacks, every prospective black employee needed a letter of recommendation from a black minister attesting to his moral fiber and (at least implicitly) his antiunion commitment. Black ministers were expected to emphasize not only what a benefactor Henry Ford was to blacks, but what a disaster unionization would be for black workers. By a system of judiciously placed contributions and periodic visits, Henry Ford kept a majority of black clergymen "in line." Three "maverick" black ministers, however, became outspoken leaders of the unionization movement and acted on the conviction that unionization would benefit their fellow blacks. The Reverends Horace White, Charles Hill, and Malcolm Dade were convinced that accommodation and an otherworldly gospel should be replaced or at least supplemented by challenges to existing structures and concern with the problems and opportunities of this world. Such religious leaders in the black community appear to have been rare, yet their presence merits noting in our summary of aggressive social action emanating from black religious sources.

Organized Militancy

A fourth example of aggressiveness from the black church is more recent. As with the example just cited, the action centers in the clergy, but is more organized and represents a greater proportion of black clergymen. The emergence of black clergymen organized for social protest action directed against institutionalized racism occurred at the height of the Civil Rights movement in the early 1960s. In various urban communities, such as Baltimore, Detroit, and St. Louis, black clergymen organized what amounted to economic boycotts, called "selective-buying" campaigns, against firms that were guilty of blatant discrimination against blacks in employment and promotion and whose representatives refused to discuss the issue.

For example, the usual procedure in Detroit was for a committee of the larger clergy group that called itself The Negro Preachers of Detroit and Vicinity to request an audience with executives of the company suspected of discrimination in order to discuss their policies and to check into the proportion of blacks employed at various levels in the organization. Following this initial contact, the committee would return with specific requests. The hope was that the company would cooperate by agreeing to hire a number of qualified black workers at various levels within the organization as requested by the black preachers. The company was then given a few weeks to implement this proposal, after which time (they would be informed) an economic boycott of their product(s) would commence if compliance with the request was not forthcoming. If, after a three-to-four-week period, the company still delayed and resisted, the committee would contact every black preacher in the community and ask that they cooperate and help their black brothers and sisters in the community by reading a letter to their congregations the following Sunday morning. That letter urged their members not to buy the products of a specified company. A typical letter announcing one of their successes is reproduced in Figure 11-1.

"The Negro Preachers of Detroit and Vicinity," a core group of some twenty to twenty-five black ministers who organized the selective-buying program and who comprised the negotiating committees, studiously avoided formalizing their organization, had no "official" name, no regular place of meeting, no formal officers, no permanent committees, and no printed constitution. The name they used to sign letters was thus deliberately chosen to present an image of solidarity among all black ministers in the area.

The cases of several other companies were handled similarly to the one referred to in the Detroit letter, and the issues effectively resolved. In fact, estimates at the time indicated that sales of the boycotted companies declined

TO ALL PASTORS COOPERATING WITH THE SELECTIVE PATRONAGE PROGRAM:

November 22, 1961

Dear Pastor:

Selective Patronage is a program aimed at opening doors of employment for our people that were formerly closed. As you know, our position is a simple one. We wish merely to see Equal Job opportunities for our people. The Taystee Bread Company was not completely providing such opportunities for our people in the past, and they were our first target in the Selective Patronage Program.

While we were aware that there were Negroes in the Taystee Bread Co., we believed that they should employ more than a token number of Negroes. When we began negotiations, there was not a single Negro driving a single Taystee Bread truck on the streets of Detroit.

HERE IS WHAT THEY HAVE DONE:

 1. They have hired two Negro Driver salesman;
 2. One Negro Swingman (men who relieve the regular drivers on their day off;
 3. One Clerk-Typist;
 4. Four more persons in the Production Department, and they have agreed that in the future there will be equal job opportunities for all with possible up-grading for those who presently qualify.

We have promised the Taystee Bread Co., that we will call on them within thirty (30) days to see if they are making further progress; in particular, hiring two more driver-salesmen and two more swingmen.

On Sunday, November 26, please announce to your congregation that we have had a successful negotiation with the Taystee Bread Co., and have begun work on another Bread Company. Committees have also been organized to negotiate with the Bottleing Industries and the Oil Companies. LOOK TO YOUR PULPITS FOR FURTHER INFORMATION!

Our eyes are open! never again will we stand by and see doors closed in the faces of our people. We cannot, therefore, in good conscience, remain silent while members of our congregations support a companies prejudice with our dollars.

Remember, Sunday, November 26 -- PLEASE MAKE THIS ANNOUNCEMENT, in your own words. After all, WE did it together.

Sincerely,

The Negro Preachers of Detroit and Vicinity

FIGURE 11–1 Letter sent to black ministers in the Detroit area by the Negro Preachers of Detroit and Vicinity.

up to 30 percent within a two-to-three-week period following the beginning of the boycott. Some companies that were contacted agreed to the clergymen's demands before a boycott was called. Black clergymen who talked to the author at the time reported that still other companies revised their hiring policies favorably with regard to blacks on their own initiative, before being contacted by the clergy group.

Types of Black Religious Leaders

Not every black clergyman in the Detroit area participated in the boycott campaigns described in the preceding, of course, although a crucial element in the organizers' strategy was to create just that impression. And not everyone who participated did so to the same degree or in the same manner. In fact, Detroit's black clergy can be divided into three fairly distinct categories or types: militants, moderates, and traditionalists. The *militants*, who constituted approximately 20 percent of the black clergy, were persons deeply committed to civil rights goals who demonstrated, marched, and picketed during the Civil Rights movement of the 1960s. They comprised the central planning unit of the boycott organization. These ministers tended to be young and highly educated, came from higher-than-average social-status backgrounds, tended toward theological liberalism, served larger-than-average black congregations, assumed an independent stance in their voting behavior, and emphasized social as opposed to otherworldly concerns. It should be noted in passing that the designation "militant" as used throughout this chapter refers to aggressive action to secure constitutionally guaranteed civil rights in an integrated society, not the more separatist militancy espoused by some black leaders after 1964.

Second, there were the *moderate* black clergy. Though committed ideologically to improving the lot of blacks in American society, they were gradualists and were more conciliatory and accommodating than the militant black clergy. On the average they were likely to be older than the militants and not so highly educated (a third of the moderates had no formal education beyond high school). Moderates lent support to the Detroit boycott activities by reading the letters from the boycott committee to their congregations, but by and large they refrained from helping plan strategy. In Detroit, 27 percent of black religious leaders fit into this category.

The third category, the *traditionalists*, were passive with regard to challenging the prevailing social order and were spiritually rather than socially oriented: "My job is to preach the Gospel and do spiritual work." They tended to be older men who had very little formal education (approximately three-fifths did not go beyond high school), came from low-social-status backgrounds, and served small congregations, often as only a part-time minister. These preachers, who constituted slightly over half of all black religious leaders, actually served fewer people in their combined congregations in Detroit than did their militant counterparts; thus although they were not directly supportive of the boycott actions, neither could they prevent a clear majority of black church members from hearing about them.

An obvious conclusion we can make on the basis of these observations about the three distinctive types of religious leaders in the contemporary black church (based on our Detroit data but likely generalizable to at least the urban north if not the urban south as well) is that the traditional otherworldly pattern of black religion is being effectively challenged. Militant social-action-and civil-rights-oriented religious leaders and perspectives have emerged and have gained substantial followings among members of black churches. Clearly it would be both misleading and blatantly inaccurate to speak of *the* black church today. The range of internal diversity is great. Clearly the militant civil rights perspective has made significant progress within black religious institutions. Yet it is equally important to note that the traditional black religious emphasis on otherworldliness and accommodation persists.

The Dilemma Posed by
Black Militancy

Because of the rapid developments in the civil rights struggle and the emergence of countless "secular" local and national organizations combating racism and discrimination in various ways, the centrality and dominance of the black church have been challenged fairly seriously during the past twenty years. It has been noted that young blacks in particular are becoming increasingly disenchanted with the churches and are less and less likely to find satisfaction there. Increasingly they have turned to other types of organizations that appear to deal more directly with their life situations and with the social problems they face. We are reminded of Glock's theory, introduced in Chapter 5, concerning relative deprivation and various possible responses to it. Recall that in the cases of economic and social deprivation, according to Glock's theory, responses are more likely to be secular than religious if the causes of the deprivation are not only accurately perceived but deemed capable of relief and change. Such seems increasingly to be the case with blacks, with young blacks in particular, perceiving greater potential in secular organizations than in the traditional religious ones.

Such observations do not of course sound the death knell for the black church. For one thing, many people in a religious organization—whether black, white, or whatever—will remain there if for no other reason than simple habit—inertia. Also, for many, disaffiliating requires a more dramatic stand than they are willing to make. Further, many people over time come to regard their associations and relationships with others in an organization (such as a church)—as well as with the organization itself—as so meaningful and important that these considerations alone prevent them from being readily convinced to substitute a new organization and commitment. Thus the historic centrality and importance of the black church in the life of the black population and community alone makes it particularly unlikely that black church members will easily or quickly forsake this organization. Also, there still is a large proportion of the black population for whom the social environment has changed little despite the progress achieved by the Civil Rights movement and subsequent affirmative action programs. If the sectarian nature of much black religion has served in the past to provide release and escape for low-status blacks, it might be expected to continue to do so today.

Note, however, that such comments about continuity of function within organized religion do not necessarily apply to those young blacks who find escape in any of the three "strategies for survival" described by Lee Rainwater: (1) the expressive lifestyle of living "cool" and "working the game" on the people around you; (2) the violent strategy of more or less blindly striking back at the social structure that holds you down; or (3) the depressive strategy of withdrawal, perhaps into drugs—"I don't bother nobody; don't nobody bother me."[21] Nor do such functions seem to apply well to those blacks who in increasing numbers are escaping the ghetto, securing advanced education, and entering previously closed or severely restricted occupations.

Observing young blacks' relative lack of enthusiasm for traditional black churches prompted black writer Joseph R. Washington essentially to predict, at the height of the Civil Rights movement in the early 1960s, the eventual demise of the black church—although in 1967 he strongly urged the black church to become involved with the black revolution because it had the potential to be of significant help, since it still had contact with many blacks.[22]

We have already shown a connection between at least a minority of black clergymen and militant civil rights activities. What connection is there between black religion generally, particularly for laypeople, and involvement in civil rights activities? In other words, so far as black Americans are concerned, does religion in any way stimulate reform, or does it inhibit social change? Gary Marx has phrased this question well in his book *Protest and Prejudice,* which includes a chapter headed, "Religion: Opiate or Inspiration of Civil Rights Militancy?"[23] Generally, Marx finds traditional otherworldly religion as expressed and practiced by blacks to be inconsistent with militant protest. For example, militants constitute a significantly lower proportion of black sects and cults than they do of black members of the more liberal Protestant denominations (15 percent among sects and cults, 43 and 36 percent among black Episcopalians and Presbyterians, respectively).[24] Of course, there is an important class bias affecting these data which eliminates virtually any possibility of making a valid inference regarding a cause-and-effect relationship between sectarianism and nonmilitancy; there is an association only. But at least it is interesting to observe that one finds relatively few militants in black sectarian religious groups as compared with the more liberal and predominantly white Protestant denominations.

Other measures of religion add support to the observation that traditional black religion of the otherworldly variety is at best not conducive to mili-

[21] Lee Rainwater, "A World of Trouble: The Pruitt-Igoe Housing Project," *The Public Interest* 8 (Summer 1967), 116–26.

[22] Joseph R. Washington, Jr., *Black Religion* (Boston: Beacon Press, 1964); idem, *The Politics of God* (Boston: Beacon Press, 1967), pp. 207–27.

[23] Gary T. Marx, *Protest and Prejudice* (New York: Harper & Row, Pub., 1967), chapter 4.

[24] Ibid., p. 99.

tancy and that the two approaches are "mutually corrosive kinds of commit-ments,"[25] if not actually mutually exclusive points of view. Marx found, for example, that the lower in importance black respondents regarded religion, the more likely they would be classed as militant in terms of civil rights philoso-phy; whereas only 22 percent of those to whom religion was "extremely im-portant" fell into the militant category, 62 percent of those who felt religion was "not at all important" were so classified.[26] Similarly, of those scoring high in orthodoxy, only 20 percent were militant, while of those scoring lowest on the orthodoxy scale, 57 percent were militant.[27]

Although our point of emphasis here is that there is an inverse relation-ship between religious orthodoxy and civil rights militancy, yet it is intriguing that there are a few civil rights militants even among the religiously traditional and orthodox. In this connection we should mention that many of the tradi-tionalist ministers appear to harbor a secret respect for at least some aspects of the militant stance. In our Detroit sample these ministers selected militants over fellow traditionalists as their opinion leaders by a ratio of six to one, even though they may not have known them personally.[28] It is also probable that the message of freedom and release in traditional black sectarian religion, which many have interpreted as salvation- or heaven-oriented, has been gener-alized by at least some to signify social and political freedom and release as well. There is consensus that the Jordan River referred to in the black spiritu-als was not solely a symbolic hurdle to cross before entering the bliss of heav-en but also was the Ohio River that separated the slave from his freedom in the North.

NEW THEMES IN
BLACK RELIGION

Although militant black clergymen have issued calls for change and have had some successes in the attainment of civil rights goals among blacks, the black church as a whole appears to have had only limited influence in the civil rights area. There has been almost no challenge from the black community to the contention, expressed more than once in this chapter, that black religion has concentrated on "religious" matters and salvation concerns to the neglect of social action and reform. Thus it is of more than passing interest that one black theologian, James Cone, has published a proposal for a "black theology of liberation" in which he contends that Christianity is in essence a religion of

[25] Rodney Stark, "Class, Radicalism, and Religious Involvement," *American Sociological Review* 29, no. 5 (1964), 703, quoted in Marx, *Protest and Prejudice*, p. 105.

[26] Marx, *Protest and Prejudice*, p. 100.

[27] Ibid.

[28] Johnstone, "Community Leadership," pp. 169–70.

liberation and that the struggle of the oppressed for political, social, and economic justice is integral to Jesus Christ's message.[29] Cone condemns the black and the white Protestant churches in the same breath: "Both have marked out their places as havens of retreat, the one to cover the guilt of the oppressors, the other to daub the wounds of the oppressed."[30] Cone is calling for the reform of black theology and of the black church. The view that such reform is crucial in the face of social change is shared by Joseph Washington, who states in a review of Cone's first book that "the future of the black church is in its critical participation in the future of black power—which is, the future of black people."[31] Undoubtedly there is less room today in the black church than in the white church for dual religious tracks—the one proclaiming traditional salvation goals, the other championing social reforms.

Cone chides the black church for emulating the white church and for feeling good when praised by whites. In reality, he asserts, the black church, just because it is black, is automatically among the rejected. He suggests that the black church must accept its true role as sufferer and follow the natural course of being black.[32] One thing this requires is excising the "most corrupting influence among the Black churches"—namely, "their adoption of the 'white lie' that Christianity is primarily concerned with an otherworldly reality. . . . The idea of heaven is irrelevant for Black Theology. The Christian cannot waste time contemplating the next world,"[33] for that reward is not a legitimate motive for action. In fact, it is a denial of the Christian faith, in addition to being a gigantic "put-on" devised by whites to keep blacks in their place.

The Reverend Albert Cleage, another black theologian, also expresses this view when he describes the gift of Christianity to the black slave by the white master:

> The religion which the master gave to his slave was designed for pacification and to support the authority of white supremacy. He said, "This is a picture of God. This is a picture of Jesus. They are both white as you can plainly see. Here are Biblical characters. They are all white. But they love you in spite of your evil Blackness, and they offer you salvation in the great beyond! You have to live such a life here on earth, that after death, when you cross over Jordan, there will be a reward for you. Sometimes you think that all the suffering that you are doing down here is passing unnoticed by God, but it is not! God is watching everything, every minute of every day. And every bit of suffering you have down here is written down in God's big book, and eventually on the other side of Jor-

---

[29] James H. Cone, *Liberation* (Philadelphia: Lippincott, 1970).

[30] James H. Cone, *Black Theology and Black Power* (New York: Seabury Press, 1969), p. 115.

[31] Jospeh R. Washington, Jr., review of *Black Theology and Black Power* by James H. Cone, *Journal for the Scientific Study of Religion* 11, no. 3 (1972), 311.

[32] Cone, *Black Theology*, p. 113.

[33] Ibid., pp. 121, 125.

dan there will be a reward, milk and honey and golden streets." So Black people had only to accept the authority of the white world to inherit a glorious reward in heaven.[34]

The point emphasized again and again by Cone and Cleage is that the black church must purge itself of such otherworldly-reward perspectives and join the black power movement. Black pride and social justice must become the dominant guiding concepts both in the ideology or theology and in the activities of the black church. Integral to this process, at least for Cleage, is acceptance of the fact that the Jesus of Christianity was in reality black. Cleage defines Jesus as a revolutionary black leader seeking to lead a black nation to freedom.[35] But more than that, Cleage reflects the ideas of Marcus Garvey, who in the late 1920s organized the African Orthodox Church and developed an entire black hierarchy of black God, black Jesus, black Madonna, and black angels.[36] The Reverend Cleage is minister of the Shrine of the Black Madonna, formerly the Central Congregational Church, in Detroit.

Cone, too, speaks of God as black, but more in a figurative sense (though he would not wish to use that adjective). God must be known as he reveals himself in his blackness, by which Cone means that "either God is identified with the oppressed to the point that their experience becomes his or he is a God of racism."[37] Cone is referring, in other words, to total identification of God with black people and their plight. "Because God has made the goal of Black people his own goal, Black Theology believes that it is not only appropriate but necessary to begin the doctrine of God with an insistence on his blackness."[38]

An intriguing observation applicable to the "radical" black theology of Cone and Cleage, though suggested earlier by Washington, is the conviction that the black church not only must reorient itself, but that it is capable of doing so. In one sense, such a belief or assumption appears sound inasmuch as the black church is still by far the largest social institution in the black community and is in contact with the greatest number of people. On the other hand, whether it can turn itself around and make a radical change in direction and focus is problematic. It is undoubtedly true that significant numbers of influential black preachers have at least begun the switch. It is also true, as Cone points out, that the black church and its clergy have retained some of the theme of freedom and injustice from their slave religion heritage.[39]

[34] Albert B. Cleage, Jr., *Black Christian Nationalism* (New York: Morrow, 1972), p. xxviii.
[35] Albert B. Cleage, Jr., *Black Messiah* (New York: Sheed & Ward, 1968), p. 4.
[36] Ibid., p. 8.
[37] Cone, *Liberation,* pp. 120–21.
[38] Ibid., p. 121.
[39] Cone, *Black Theology,* chapter 4.

Another black theologian, Olin P. Moyd, goes further by suggesting that black theological themes not only speak to the situation of blacks but can make important contributions to theological discussion and development generally. He suggests with pure sociological insight that principally because American blacks have had a different experience than whites their theology will be distinctive. He and others have further suggested that it is such black theology that will move to the forefront of theological discussion in the 1980s. While Cone and others have talked about the black theology of liberation, Moyd uses the term "redemption." In that term he incorporates three ideas: (1) "liberation" in the sense of deliverance from states of human-caused oppression, (2) "liberation" in the sense of salvation from sin and punishment for that sin, and (3) "confederation" with other people in a covenant relationship with each other and with God.[40]

He also suggests with J. Deotis Roberts that black theology turns around the assertion by Karl Barth that "God speaks, and man listens." In black theology it is, "Man cries, God hears."[41] As such, black theology has a contribution to make to theological discussion. We would suggest that such is true particularly as theologians in the face of dire human events pull back from the optimism that began with the Social Gospel movement around the turn of the century and continued through the "death of God" theme in the 1960s and 1970s, in which it was implicit that God was no longer necessary as humanity began to be successful in solving its problems by itself.

[40] Olin P. Moyd, *Redemption in Black Theology* (Valley Forge, Pa.: Judson Press, 1979).

[41] Ibid. and J. Deotis Roberts, Sr., "The Black Caucus and the Failure of Christian Theology," *The Journal of Religious Thought* (summer supplement, 1969), 15.

12

Denominational Society

The necessity of devoting a full chapter to a discussion of the denominational phenomenon in American religion is reinforced by an observation by the American sociologist Andrew Greeley to the effect that the United States is nearly unique among world societies as a denominational society.[1] By "denominational society" Greeley means one characterized by neither an established church nor a protesting sect, but in which religion and the rest of the society interrelate through a considerable number of essentially equal religious organizations. These constitute a social organizational adjustment to the fact of religious pluralism, and not a halfway house between sect and church.[2] Greeley's emphasis, which is also this chapter's, is on the social organizational aspect of denominationalism. That is, we are observing here an important social phenomenon, not simply a religious one—a type of social organization that has significant impact on social structure and social interaction in American society.

THE MULTIPLICITY OF GROUPS

The denominational character of American society is of course rooted in the fact that ours is among other things a pluralistic society, particularly insofar as religion is concerned. As we pointed out in Chapters 6 and 10, the denomi-

---

[1] Andrew Greeley, *The Denominational Society* (Glenview, Ill.: Scott, Foresman, 1972), p. 1.
[2] Ibid.

national society arose, not because everyone desired it, but because at the founding of our nation no one religion was sufficiently powerful to gain predominance, and also because of the various philosophical perspectives and commitments of those who framed the Constitution. The result has been one of the most obvious features of denominationalism within American society — that is, the subdivision of religion in American society into a host of independent religious groups. A society could be designated as a denominational society with only a few different religious groups. But American society leaves no doubt as to its diverse denominational character, for it includes literally hundreds of religious groups. Note well that we are not referring here to the thousands of local congregations, but to larger groupings of individual congregations into more or less cohesive associations. That is, several, perhaps thousands, of local congregational units identify sufficiently with one another to stand under one umbrella, so to speak, to carry out some activities and functions jointly, to share perhaps a summary statement of belief, and to think of themselves as united together and distinct from other associations of congregations who raise different umbrellas and fly different theological flags. Thus we are talking about Baptists, Methodists, Episcopalians, Presbyterians, Lutherans, Roman Catholics, Mormons, Unitarians, Orthodox Jews, Jehovah's Witnesses, and other fairly familiar religious groups or denominations, as well as a plethora of lesser-known groups, such as the Pilgrim Holiness Church, the Plymouth Brethren, the Duck River Baptists, the Free Magyar Reformed Church in America, the Macedonian Orthodox Church in America, and so on.

There are over 300 such groups that maintain membership statistics and report them to the National Council of Churches. Arthur Piepkorn has classified a grand total of 735 religious groups in North America. There are of course others that either simply fail to report or are opposed on principle to divulging such information. In addition, there are literally thousands of individual local congregations that we might call entrepreneurial churches that are autonomous and begin and end with the entrepreneurial religious leader who founded them. These are particularly numerous in the sect-prone inner-city ghettos, where they remain small, though one sees such entrepreneurial groups elsewhere as well. A fairly common pattern is for an evangelist to attract a following and give up traveling the tent-meeting circuit as he or she settles down to building a local cathedral and constituency and then broadcasts to a larger radio or television audience.

THE DIVERSITY OF GROUPS

Recognizing the multiplicity of religious groups in the United States is only an introduction to the great diversity among religious organizations that is a second prominent feature of denominationalism in this country. The differences among denominations can be seen along a variety of dimensions, some of which we have alluded to earlier in this text.

The Authority Dimension

At the level of structure and organization there is the basic distinction among episcopal, presbyterian, and congregational forms that we referred to in passing in Chapter 4. These terms refer to the structure of authority within the denomination and the relationship of the local congregation to the larger denomination with which it is affiliated. In the *episcopal* form authority proceeds from the top down—from the heads of the denomination (pope, archbishop, bishop, and so on) down to local representatives. In the *presbyterian* form authority rests more in the middle range, with elected representatives, both clergy and lay, at various levels, from that of the local congregation to the nation itself, holding regulatory and disciplinary authority over the levels below them. In the *congregational* type, authority lies, as the term implies, with the local group, with the national denomination having little authority, at least of a formal nature.

The Emotional Dimension

Another typology contrasts Apollonian with Dionysian religious orientation and worship style of liturgy.[3] The *Apollonian* style assumes that since the human being is basically rational and capable of controlling his or her biological and emotional urges, the person's communication with God should reflect such rationality and be characterized by moderation and gentility. The *Dionysian* emphasis rests on the observation that people are more than strictly rational beings. They have emotions and they need to express themselves individualistically. In fact, this orientation contends that an important, if not primary, feature of religion is the emotional dimension, including ecstatic, mystical experiences of the human with the divine. In religion one must and one does transcend the mundane rationality of life.

These descriptions of the Dionysian and Apollonian styles and orientations are likely to remind one of the religious sect and the denominational type of religious organization, respectively; and appropriately so. Yet neither should be considered an exclusive association. Some groups most properly classified as denominations nevertheless exhibit Dionysian elements, either because they have only recently evolved to denominational status and retain vestiges of their old pattern or because religious leaders, particularly at the local level, are convinced of the importance of the Dionysian element in religion and encourage it. Note, for example, the recent increase in the phenomenon of "speaking in tongues" and related pentecostal elements in such highly Apollonian denominations as the Roman Catholic, Episcopal, Presbyterian, and Lutheran Churches.

[3] See Greeley, *The Denominational Society*, p. 23.

MAJOR DENOMINATIONAL
FAMILIES

In an attempt to understand differences among the major denominations in America today it is helpful to know the source and meaning of the broad popular categories Catholic, Protestant, and Jew.[4] Each of these designations is a highly inclusive category in itself—inclusive in the sense that each has numerous subdivisions within it. We shall explore some of that internal diversity in the coming pages. But here, just a few comments about the origins of these major categories.

Judaism is of course the oldest and is in fact the source out of which Christianity grew, first as Catholicism (later divided into the Roman Catholic and the Eastern Orthodox branches), and then Protestantism. Although we will add some detail later we should mention here that Judaism in America is itself very diverse. There are five major categories of Jews: Orthodox, Conservative, Reform, Hasidic, and Cultural-Ethnic. Orthodx Judaism remains firmly rooted in historic Judaism with a heavy emphasis on the Old Testament and its laws, restrictions, and rituals. Jews who can be called Reformed, as well as those we call Cultural-Ethnic, are highly responsive to developments within contemporary society, assume that religion both does and should evolve, and have discarded much or all of the historical belief and ritual system of Judaism. Conservative Jews stand very consciously between the two extremes of Orthodox and Reform. Hasidic Judaism is a more mystical form of Judaism, truly in a class by itself.

Roman Catholicism came to be the designation for the religious group that was established by Jesus Christ and his followers in the first century A.D. and was a direct descendant of historic Judaism. It was the Christian Church that spread from Jerusalem throughout the Mediterranean world and beyond, within a few generations following the death of Christ. Catholics believe that Christ's statement to the disciple Peter recorded in Matthew 16:18, "Thou art Peter, and upon this rock I will build my church" (King James Version), marked the true founding of the Roman Catholic Church. Catholic tradition says that Peter journeyed to Rome late in life, preached there, became leader (bishop), and began to carry out Christ's directive to create one universal (catholic) church on earth. Both the catholicity and the unity were challenged by Eastern Christianity almost immediately, and in the Middle Ages[5] the Western (Roman Catholic) and the Eastern (Orthodox) Christian churches

---

[4] We shall add and discuss the Eastern Orthodox tradition as well.

[5] There is no consensus among historians on either a date or an event to mark the formal division into a Roman Catholic and an Orthodox division of Christianity, though a prime candidate would be the ninth century mutual excommunication exchanged by St. Photius, patriarch of Constantinople, and St. Nicholas of Rome. Other suggestions range all the way to 1439 A.D., with a commonly accepted date being 1054 when another mutual excommunication took place. Cf. Arthur C. Piepkorn, *Profiles in Belief*, Vol. I (New York: Harper & Row, Pub., 1977), pp. 32–33.

split, and remain separated until this day. Actually, these divisions into Byzantine and Roman have existed from the beginning, were evident in the seven ecumenical councils, were enhanced by language differences (Greek in the East and Latin in the West), and found their political counterparts engaged in war (for example, when in 1204 the armies of the West during the Fourth Crusade sacked Constantinople, the center of the Eastern Church).

Protestantism is the newest of the major categories of American religion, orginating as it did in the late Middle Ages with religious reformers such as John Huss (1369–1415), Martin Luther (1483–1546), Ulrich Zwingli (1484–1531), John Calvin (1509–1564), and John Knox (1513–1572) who wanted not so much to found new churches but to reform and restore what was already there, namely, the Roman Catholic Church. Thus we have the term "reformation." And we have the term "Protestant," which refers both to the idea of protest against what some viewed as perversions and distortions of original Christianity, within the Roman Catholic Church, and, as the term came to be used in Elizabethan England, to the idea of affirming a particular set of beliefs, of "bearing witness" to a particular confession and point of view.

Jewish Denominations in America

We mentioned earlier that along religious dimensions there are five major subgroups of Jews in the United States. We shall describe each briefly.

The most firmly rooted in historical Old Testament Judaism is that of Orthodoxy. Orthodox Jews very consciously try to maintain the teachings and rituals of the *Torah* (the first five books of the Old Testament), and perceive of themselves as the only legitimate bearers of Jewish tradition.[6] This means that they view themselves as the preservers of both traditional doctrine and ritual observances. There is a high emphasis on study of the *Torah* and the *Talmud* (the rabbinical commentary on the *Torah*) in the original Hebrew. The Torah is supreme and is believed to reveal that God has chosen the Jews to be his special people who will teach justice, peace, and love to the world. There is careful observance of festival days such as Yom Kippur and Passover. And an unqualified obligation is the keeping of a kosher house and serving kosher meals by maintaining separate sets of dishes and utensils for meat and for dairy products, as well as using only those foods that have been slaughtered or prepared under approved rabbinical conditions. In observation of the Sabbath from sunset Friday to sunset Saturday the Orthodox Jew tries to put aside the secular world and enter a world of prayer and family activities that will not allow cooking, writing, buying and selling, and any number of other everyday activities that are by definition set aside on such a special day in the week.

---

[6] Charles S. Liebman, "Orthodoxy in American Jewish Life," in *The Jewish Community in America*, ed. Marshall Sklare (New York: Behrman House, 1974), p. 134.

Reform Judaism emerged in nineteenth century Europe as a very conscious attempt by some Jewish intellectuals led by Abraham Geiger (1810–1874) in Germany to bring traditional Jewish Orthodoxy more up-to-date and in tune with modern realities. The movement rejected many traditional Jewish laws and substituted ethics for laws. The declaration of principles issued by the Frankfort Society of the Friends of Reform in 1843 is a fairly concise summary of their position.

> First, we recognize the possibility of unlimited development in the Mosaic religion. Second, the collection of controversies and prescriptions commonly designated by the name Talmud possess for us no authority from either the doctrinal or the practical standpoint. Third, a Messiah who is to lead back the Israelites to the land of Palestine is neither expected nor desired by us; we know no fatherland but that to which we belong by birth or citizenship.[7]

Isaac Mayer Wise (1819–1900), who is credited with establishing Reform Judaism in the United States when he founded the Union of American Hebrew Congregations in 1873, expressed confidence that this Reform Judaism would soon become the Judaism of all American Jews. While such did not happen, Reform Judaism did attract a substantial following and accounts for a little less than a third of American Jews.[8]

Conservative Judaism quite deliberately takes the traditionalism of Orthodoxy and the liberalism of the Reform movement and blends them. It is a distinctly American innovation for Jews who had immigrated to the United States some years earlier but were becoming highly acculturated—people who had moved out of the Jewish ghetto into neighborhoods that were predominantly non-Jewish, wanted to use English as their religious as well as social language, yet did not want as complete a divorce from historic Judaism with its host of customs and beliefs as Reform Judaism represented. The Conservative movement devised a Sunday school program for children in conformity with the Protestants around them and developed confirmation ceremonies for girls as a ritual parallel to the Bar Mitzvah for boys. Thus Jewish children could maintain a solid link with their past but also point out to the other children in their neighborhood and school that although they were Jews they were not that different from them.

---

[7] Quoted from G. F. Moore, *History of Religions,* Vol. II (New York: Scribner's, 1946), p. 94.

[8] A Boston survey found 27 percent of Jews identify themselves as Reform, 44 percent Conservative, 14 percent Orthodox, 15 percent with no preference or considering themselves as nonreligious. Cf. Morris Axelrod, Floyd J. Fowler, and Arnold Gurin, *A Community for Long Range Planning—A Study of the Jewish Population of Greater Boston* (Boston: Combined Jewish Philanthropies of Greater Boston, 1967), p. 119. A survey in Providence, Rhode Island, found 21.2 percent Reform, 19.8 percent Orthodox, 54.1 percent Conservative, and 4.9 percent other self-designations. Cf. Sidney Goldstein and Calvin Goldscheider, *Jewish Americans: Three Generations in a Jewish Community* (Englewood Cliffs, N.J.: Prentice-Hall 1968), p. 177.

Marshall Sklare points out that it became particularly difficult for truly Orthodox Jews to maintain their orthodoxy when so much of their everyday life was outside the synagogue and its immediate community.[9] In other words it was much easier to be an Orthodox Jew in a Jewish ghetto in eastern Europe than in an American city where the majority of one's contacts and activities were with non-Jews.

The compromise that is Conservative Judaism quickly showed its practical wisdom as it became the largest Jewish religious organization. This growth was particularly marked in the decades after World War II.

Sectarian Judaism consists of several small groups and movements, the best known of which is Hasidic Judaism. A Hasid is a mystic. Thus Hasidic Judaism includes persons who consider themselves Orthodox but also possess an additional dimension of mysticism, emotion, and ecstasy. Their counterparts within Protestantism in at least some ways would be the charismatic pentecostals.

The Hasidic movement arose in Poland in the eighteenth century and spread rapidly to include nearly half of eastern European Jews in its ranks.[10] Hasidic Jews are usually distinguished by their outward appearance. They will likely be dressed in black, wear large black hats sometimes of fur, be bearded, and have long curled earlocks. They are highly concentrated in circumscribed urban areas—the Labavitcher movement, for example, located predominantly in the Crown Heights section of Brooklyn, the Satmar community of about twelve hundred families, most of whom are located in the Williamsburg and Borough Park sections of Brooklyn, and the Skvirer Hasidim in Rockland County, New York, that left Brooklyn to establish a separate community in which they could exercise greater internal social control.[11]

The final Jewish subgroup we would mention is not religious at all, strictly speaking. These are those people of Jewish ethnicity who feel some kinship with others of Jewish origin but have rejected the religious elements of Judaism. Hence the designation we used earlier of "cultural-ethnic Jews."

Roman Catholicism

Roman Catholicism in the United States has suffered the effects of minority status since the beginning. Even when millions of immigrants from eastern and southern Europe and Ireland swelled the ranks of the Catholic Church in the nineteenth and early twentieth centuries, Roman Catholicism continued to be viewed with suspicion and distrust by other Americans. They saw Roman Catholic subjection to the Pope in Rome as an expression of a di-

[9] Marshall Sklare, *Conservative Judaism: An American Religious Movement* (New York: Schocken Books, 1972), pp. 45–46.

[10] Martin Buber, *Hasidism and Modern Man*, ed. and trans. Maurice Friedman (New York: Harper & Row, Pub., 1958), p. 10.

[11] Marshall Sklare, *America's Jews* (New York: Random House, 1971), pp. 49–50.

vided loyalty that made Roman Catholics at best only half American. They also saw Roman Catholics sending their children to Roman Catholic schools that were established explicitly to help members "keep the faith," and they marked them as under suspicion. If one adds to the list of issues the opposition of Catholic theology to any kind of so-called unnatural birth control, the opposition to interfaith marriage and the requirement of a prenuptial agreement to educate any children in the Catholic faith if permission to marry outside the faith was granted at all, and a retention of many old world customs in the many Roman Catholic ethnic enclaves, and Protestant Americans became even more suspicious. Quite expectedly, though hardly helping to improve the situation, many Roman Catholics developed an "inferiority complex" and found it difficult to relate on an eyeball-to-eyeball basis with their Protestant neighbors. However, with the election of the Roman Catholic John F. Kennedy as president, with clear signs of ecumenical openness in the person and message of Pope John XXIII, with signals of doctrinal innovation and change in the second ecumenical council, with fewer Roman Catholics isolating themselves in Catholic schools, with many nuns adopting average street clothing for their works of mercy and education, with the Civil Rights movement gaining acceptance for many minorities and not just black Americans, and above all with the practices of Catholic laypeople with respect to such traditionally important issues of marriage and birth control rapidly approximating those of other Americans—with all these changes we find that Roman Catholics have definitely joined and been accepted in the mainstream of American life.

Yet Roman Catholic doctrine continues to be distinctive. There continues to be a high regard for Mary, the mother of Jesus, still believed to have been immaculately conceived, have lived a sinless life, have given birth to Christ yet with her virginity intact, have bodily ascended to heaven before death; and now believed to serve as an intermediary between people and God. There continues to be a belief in papal infallibility over matters of faith and doctrine and an emphasis on penance paid by the faithful by way of partial atonement for their sinful acts. Yet on central doctrines of historic Christianity, such as the triune nature of God as Father, Son, and Holy Spirit, world creation by God, the existence of angels both good and evil, the sinful nature of human beings and their need for God's salvation, and salvation as coming only through the death and resurrection of God's Son, Jesus Christ, Roman Catholics join most Protestant and Orthodox Christians.

Yet many areas of doctrine and practice show great discrepancies between the official doctrine and the practice of Catholic laypersons. For example, Andrew Greeley found in a 1974 sample of Roman Catholics that only 17 percent practiced monthly confession and only 18 percent would accept the church's position on even two of three items that constituted a "sexual orthodoxy" scale (no divorce, no "artificial" methods of birth control, and no premarital sex). In each case there was a significant decline from only eleven years earlier when 37 percent still practiced monthly confession and 42 percent followed the church's dictates on at least two of the three items in the sexual orthodoxy scale.[12]

We suggested earlier that such changed practices constitute one reason for greater acceptance of Catholics in the mainstream of American life. But probably more significant is the prediction that as a consequence of such changing practices doctrines will eventually change as well, although not overnight by any means. In fact, in the face of such changing behavior and practice there have been reactionary voices within Roman Catholic officialdom.

For example, although Pope John XXIII established a special commission in 1963 to investigate whether a change in the church's traditional prohibitions against birth control could and should be brought about, and although the commission voted 13 to 2 for change,[13] the closest advisors to the Pope (the Vatican Curia) persuaded the successor to John XXIII, Pope Paul VI, to conserve the traditional position of the church. His encyclical letter "Humanae Vitae," issued in 1968, reaffirmed traditional positions. Andrew Greeley, whose data on changed attitudes and practices of Roman Catholics we reported earlier, finds the encyclical "Humanae Vitae" almost entirely to blame for the rapid decline of traditional Roman Catholic practice with respect to birth control in particular.

Pope John Paul II, although charming, diplomatic, warm, open, and well received by most, whether Catholic or non-Catholic, whether liberal or conservative, still felt obliged in the early 1980s to reaffirm traditional Roman Catholic positions in such areas as birth control, the ordination of women to the priesthood, and priestly celibacy. Further, various groups of Catholic laypeople oppose many of the recent changes in doctrine and practice, and urge a return to the old ways. Not only do they not want even to hear talk about the possibility of priests being allowed to marry, but they want Latin brought back as the language of the liturgy. They have declared Pope John XXIII an inauthentic pope and the second Vatican council an invalid assembly.

It is of more than passing interest that thousands of Roman Catholic laypeople are involved in this movement commonly referred to as "Catholic Traditionalism." William Dinges estimates ten to fifteen thousand active participants. He reports that there are 230 locations throughout the United States where the old Latin Mass is celebrated regularly in violation of the mandated vernacular mass. Traditionalists support several parochial schools and have ninety priests to serve them.[14] Four organizations carry the banner of this Catholic traditionalism: The Catholic Traditionalist Movement in the United

[12] Andrew M. Greeley, "Council or Encyclical?" *Review of Religious Research,* 18, no. 1 (Fall, 1976), 11.

[13] Andrew Greeley, "The Making of the Pope, Part Four," *Detroit Free Press* (August 17, 1978), p. 11a.

[14] William D. Dinges, "Catholic Traditionalism in America: Sociological Aspects of a Value-Oriented Social Movement." Paper presented at the 1981 annual meeting of the Society for the Scientific Study of Religion and the Religious Research Association, October 30, 1981, Baltimore, Maryland.

States, the Orthodox Roman Catholic Movement, Traditional Catholics in America, and the Society of Saint Pius X.[15] The last named organization is the largest and most significant. As a religious order it has organizational capabilities and continuity that many simple voluntary associations lack. It even has the authority to train and ordain priests to propagate the message of Catholic traditionalism (ordaining over twenty priests a year at present).[16] It should also be noted that the Catholic Traditionalism movement is both larger and more aggressive in Europe. The foremost figure in the movement, Archbishop Marcel Lefebvre, who heads the Society of Saint Pius X, began his work in France and immigrated to the United States a few years ago. He stated in his 1974 "Credo" that the reforms of the second Vatican council "spring from heresy and end in heresy."

We mentioned earlier that there have been some reactionary signs among Roman Catholic officialdom. In this connection, the authorization in 1981 by the Vatican of a broad study and evaluation of all 501 Roman Catholic seminaries in the United States has prompted a great deal of suspicion among more liberal Catholics. They see this as a fairly heavy-handed attempt to return to more traditional educational methods that will train more traditional priests who will stick to their traditional ministries and avoid political and social action involvement. Some heads of American Roman Catholic seminaries fear serious infringement on hard-won academic freedom gained since the second Vatican council.[17]

It is clear that the Roman Catholic Church in America is not nearly so cohesive or unified as some common stereotypes would suggest. There are strong pressures from some constituencies to move in a more liberal direction; other constituencies push fervently back toward the past and a more conservative, traditionalist emphasis and practice. Roman Catholics are facing what Jews and Protestants have grappled with for a long time.

Protestantism

The denominations and sects that comprise Protestantism are sufficiently different among themselves as almost to doom any attempt to generalization. Not only do their forms of organization run the full range from episcopal through presbyterian to congregational, but their assent to various central orthodox Christian doctrines is far from unanimous. While some say the Lord's body and blood are truly present in the bread and wine of the Lord's Supper, others believe the presence is only symbolized by the bread and wine, perhaps also insisting that the wine be grape juice. While some see the Virgin Birth as

[15] Ibid.

[16] Ibid.

[17] *Detroit Free Press*, "Is the Vatican Out to Change the Education of Its Priests?" by Harry Cook, October 4, 1981.

not only unimportant but untrue, others make the doctrine one of only a handful of the most crucial beliefs of all. While some believe God created the universe in six days of twenty-four hours each in length, others accept evolutionary theories that do not presume divine creation of any kind. For further specification of the diversity, note the great diversity among Protestant denominations on several fairly standard Christian doctrines that is shown in Tables 12–1 and 12–2. Note that these data reflect what members of these denominations believe and not necessarily what the denominations might officially stand for.

Although we have emphasized the vast diversity within Protestantism and have implied it is almost absurd to try to generalize, there are historical reasons for generalizing about Protestantism, and there are even a few generalizations that are reasonably valid today.

We suggested earlier that Protestants got their name by protesting against Roman Catholicism. In such protest there were some implicit similarities—resentment against the Pope and religious control over political agencies, reaction against the imposition of indulgences, aversion against what amounted in many cases to worship of the saints, and the like. But there were important differences among the groups that gathered around the various reformers. For example, while someone like Martin Luther thought there was much in the Roman Catholic Church that should be retained, others such as Andreas Carlstadt (d. 1541) and Thomas Müntzer (d. 1525) insisted that everything that smacked of Romanism must go. So, while Luther thought organs and music and statues and paintings were important and must be integrated into worship and instruction, Carlstadt and Müntzer felt justified not only in keeping such ornamentations out of their churches but in destroying them when they could.

A more explicit tenet of all of Protestantism has been the right and the ability of individuals to be in touch with God, to learn religious truth, and to worship God as individuals without the necessity of an intermediary or intercessor such as a priest or the Virgin Mary. Integral to this belief is the conviction that the Bible as the sourcebook for Christianity should not only be open and available to all believers but can be understood by them as well. This emphasis on the Bible has led to near idolatry by some Protestants who make much of its "verbal inspiration" and power, yet all hold it in high regard.

Another generalization so far as Protestants are concerned is a restriction on the number of sacraments to two or less (Holy Baptism and the Lord's Supper), certainly far fewer than the traditional seven in Roman Catholicism (Baptism, Lord's Supper, Confirmation, Penance, Ordination, Matrimony, and Extreme Unction).

We have mentioned several times the great diversity within Protestantism. We shall now, as we conclude our discussion of Protestantism in general terms, identify the major groupings of Protestant religious denominations in the United States.

TABLE 12–1 Proportion of Denominational Members Agreeing with Various Doctrinal Statements

STATEMENT	CONGREGA-TIONALIST	METHODIST	EPISCO-PALIAN	DISCIPLES OF CHRIST	PRESBY-TERIAN	AMERICAN LUTHERAN	AMERICAN BAPTIST	MISSOURI LUTHERAN	SOUTHERN BAPTIST	SECTS	ROMAN CATHOLIC
"I know God really exists and I have no doubts about it."	41%	60%	63%	76%	75%	73%	78%	81%	99%	96%	81%
"Jesus is the Divine Son of God and I have no doubts about it."	40	54	59	74	72	74	76	93	99	97	86
"Jesus was born of a virgin." (% saying: "Completely true.")	21	34	39	62	57	66	69	92	99	96	81
"Jesus walked on water." (% saying: "Completely true.")	19	26	30	62	51	58	62	83	99	94	71
"Will Jesus actually return to the earth someday?" (% answering: "Definitely.")	13	21	24	36	43	54	57	75	94	89	47
"Miracles actually happened just as the Bible says they did."	28	37	41	62	58	69	62	89	92	92	74
"There is a life beyond death." (% saying: "Completely true.")	36	49	53	64	69	70	72	84	97	94	75
"A child is born into the world already guilty of sin." (% saying: "Completely true.")	2	7	18	6	21	49	23	86	43	47	68

Source: Rodney Stark and Charles Y. Glock, *American Piety* (Berkeley: University of California Press, 1968). pp. 28, 33, 34, 36, 37, and 40.

TABLE 12–2   *Proportion of Denominational Members Expressing Specified Attitudes toward Selected Theological and Religious Issues*

ATTITUDE	UNITED CHURCH OF CHRIST	METHODIST	EPISCO-PALIAN	PRESBY-TERIAN	MISSOURI LUTHERAN	OTHER LUTHERAN	BAPTIST	SECTS	ROMAN CATHOLIC	JEWISH
"The story in the Bible of Adam and Eve falling into sin is really only a story and did not actually take place."										
% definitely disagreeing	32%	44%	25%	39%	71%	46%	61%	67%	38%	13%
"The real purpose of religion should be to help people with their problems and needs rather than help them get to heaven."										
% definitely agreeing	39	45	31	49	24	40	27	21	37	71

Source: Ronald L. Johnstone (project director), National Opinion Research Center survey conducted for the Lutheran Council in the U.S.A., 1970.

The Anglican or Episcopal Churches.   While it has been said that Anglicanism has no "theology" in the sense of a comprehensive summary of doctrine, actually in a practical sense Anglicanism has a very *comprehensive*
theology in that it has very deliberately retained the traditional liturgical emphasis of the Roman Catholic Church while also incorporating an essentially
Calvinist or Reformed set of beliefs. Its continuity with Roman Catholicism is
reinforced by its emphasis on apostolic succession—the belief that its clergy
are descendents in an unbroken line from the apostles. Further, it is a sacramental church—meaning it believes that the two primary sacraments are central to the essence of the church. These Anglican churches might also be
called "Christmas churches" in the sense that they stress that God became human at the birth of the god-man Jesus Christ (the Incarnation).

The Episcopal or Anglican churches originated in the English Reformation which saw Parliament grant independence to the Church of England
around 1530 during the reign of Henry VIII. The Anglican (English) Church
was transplanted to the New World with the settlement of Jamestown, Virginia, in 1607. Following the Revolutionary War the American Anglicans
established their religious independence as the Protestant Episcopal Church in
the U.S.A.

The Lutheran Churches.   Lutherans might be said to have begun when
Martin Luther nailed his ninety-five theses to the church door in Wittenberg,
Germany, on October 31, 1517. However, it was not Luther's intent at that
time to start a new church; he wanted reform of the Roman Catholic Church
and had ninety-five issues or points he wanted to discuss and debate. The Lutheran movement spread rapidly through Germany and into the Scandinavian
countries. It arrived early on the American scene—Dutch Lutherans in New
York in 1623 and Swedes along the Delaware River in 1638. The immigration
of Lutherans continued steadily during the next three centuries and resulted in
the establishment of many ethnic communities and churches. The Norwegians,
the Swedes, the Danes, the Finns, and the Germans all established ethnic denominations—several denominations, in fact, within each ethnic group—and
the Lutherans became in the process the most ethnically divided religious family in America.[18]

Several mergers within American Lutheranism have taken place within
this century to reduce the number of Lutheran denominations to four major
ones, though there remain ten other small ones—one with only five congregations totaling less than four hundred members.

Lutherans constitute a "confessional" religious movement. That is, they
place great stress on detailed bodies of doctrine that have become official in-

---

[18] Other ethnically identified religious groups would be the Dutch Reformed and informal
subgroups within American Catholicism—Irish Catholics, Polish Catholics, Italian Catholics,
Hispanic Catholics, and so on.

terpretations of Scripture that are accepted because they correctly (it is asserted by Lutherans) interpret Scripture. Like the Roman Catholics and the Anglican-Episcopal traditions they are sacramental churches. That is, they view the sacraments of baptism and the Lord's Supper as "means of grace" through which God works directly. As such the sacraments are more than symbols; they mediate God's grace.

Their central confessional principle is the Latin expression Sola Gratia, Sola Fide, Sola Scriptura—by grace alone, by faith alone, by Scripture alone. Or to say it differently, but with another expression frequently used by Lutherans—justification by grace through faith. With the Roman Catholics and Episcopalians they are the most liturgical of the Christian church bodies. That is, Lutherans follow a fairly elaborate ritual and pattern in their worship services—one with strong historical roots and with great uniformity from one local congregation to another.

Reformed and Presbyterian Churches.   These are the denominations that most directly have followed the lead of John Calvin. The various Reformed bodies originated in Switzerland, Germany, and Holland; the Presbyterian bodies, in Scotland. Prominent themes within the Calvinist tradition are the sovereignty of God, the life of piety for God's people, and predestination or eternal election (cf. Chapter 7). Although they too use the two primary sacraments, they are seen more as symbolic acts that bring to remembrance God's acts in the past.

The first essentially Presbyterian Church was established in Massachusetts Bay Colony in 1629. The Reformed Church in America goes back to 1621 when the Dutch West India Company placed Reformed ministers in the New Netherlands Colony along the Hudson River.

In many ways the Presbyterian-Reformed tradition is the most centrist, "average" expression of Protestantism in America. All the traditional orthodox doctrines of Christianity are there with little of an extreme nature except perhaps the classic presentation of predestination. On the other hand, there are offshoots of this tradition that are not only highly conservative in theology but also in practice, and have strong overtones of the Radical Reformation that we will introduce next. We are thinking here of such groups as the Dutch Reformed, Christian Reformed, Orthodox Presbyterian, and the Bible Presbyterian Church, among others.

Churches of the Radical Reformation.   Major foundations and emphases of this tradition are articulated in the seven articles of the Schleitheim Confession of 1527.[19] These articles are as follows: baptism is for adults only; excommunication is an important means of keeping the group pure; the Lord's

---

[19] Arthur C. Piepkorn, *Profiles of Belief,* Vol. 2 (New York: Harper & Row, Pub., 1978), p. 363.

Supper is a memorial feast for adult members; the group must be separated from all evil such as Roman Catholic and any other worship services, as well as drinking establishments; the pastor must be a person of good reputation and integrity; church and state must be strictly separate, and individual Christians should not participate in the political process; oaths are absolutely forbidden.

In America the original Puritans and the various Mennonite groups were direct practitioners of the Radical Reformation. Two major Protestant groupings today that might be surprises in a list of practitioners of this track of Protestantism because they seem to be such "normal," standard Protestant denominations are the Congregational Christian and the Evangelical and Reformed Churches that merged to become the United Church of Christ in 1957, and the various Baptist denominations. The Baptists, in particular, however, continue with the view of the sacraments expressed in the Schleitheim Confession and stress moral behavior that would often forbid such activities as card playing and drinking.

Methodist Churches.   Methodism is certainly the youngest of the major Protestant denominations, founded in the eighteenth century by John and Charles Wesley as a movement within the Church of England and not formed into a separate body until after John Wesley's death in 1791. Its origin was in the pietistic revival movement that swept Europe, the British Isles, and America in the early 1700s. Wesley held to the authority of Scripture and the centrality of faith, but emphasized more than some Protestants the fruition of that faith in a life of love and good works. He talked much about the "life of perfection," which he believed was attainable by true Christians who felt God at work within them and had the experience of true conversion burning within them. Thus, knowing the moment of one's conversion became a trademark of Methodists. Also, the methodical attention to one's life to attain perfection became not only a trademark but the source of their name.

A *Life* magazine comment on the Methodist denomination, quoted by J. Paul Williams, although not totally complimentary, does catch the flavor of several major themes within Methodism:

> In many ways it is our most characteristic church. It is short on theology, long on good works, brilliantly organized, primarily middle-class, frequently bigoted, incurably optimistic, zealously missionary and touchingly confident of the essential goodness of the man next door.[20]

Holiness and Pentecostal Denominations.   An outgrowth of Methodism in the late 1800s was the Holiness movement which in turn provided the soil

---

[20] J. Paul Williams, *What Americans Believe and How They Worship,* 3rd ed. (New York: Harper & Row, Pub., 1969), p. 286, quoted from an editorial, *Life* (November 10, 1947), p. 38.

out of which the Pentecostal movement grew around the turn of this century. These are all Arminian groups with their theology rooted in the teachings of Jacob Arminius (1560–1609), who stressed both the universality of God's grace but also the freedom of people to choose for or against salvation—an emphasis implying a cooperative, human element in salvation that Lutherans and others viewed as undercutting the doctrine of salvation by God's grace alone.

The Holiness movement developed in classic sectarian form (cf. Chapter 7) as some among American Methodists felt that the goal and method of attaining Christian perfection was being neglected. As Arthur Piepkorn says so succinctly, "[They] sought to recapture Wesleyan perfectionism in order to make American Methodists into holy people."[21] They stressed the sanctified life, renounced unholy practices such as the use of alcohol and tobacco and membership in secret societies, and encouraged continuation of the Methodist-inspired camp-meeting approach to instruction, conversion, and spiritual reinforcement.

The Pentecostal movement, in most simple terms, was holiness religion to which had been added the special gift of glossolalia (speaking in tongues) as evidence of Pentecostal experience. Although the holiness people as well as what we might call the classical Methodists were not pleased with the development of Pentecostalism, Ignacio Vergara's statement that "Pentecostalism is Methodism carried to its ultimate consequences,"[22] is quite accurate.

Eastern Orthodoxy

The Eastern Orthodox Church has its origins with the very beginning of Christianity, and its theologians played the leading roles in the seven ecumenical councils that were held during the fourth through eighth centuries A.D. As mentioned earlier, the Christian Church split into the Western (Roman Catholic) and Eastern (Orthodox) Churches in the ninth century A.D. But, while the Roman Catholic Church remained formally unified under the Pope in Rome, the Eastern Church recognized four primary Patriarchs—the religious sovereign and counterpart to the Pope—in Constantinople, Alexandria, Antioch, and Jerusalem. In addition, semiautonomous churches evolved in Greece, Albania, Bulgaria, Cyprus, Romania, the Soviet Union, and Yugoslavia. Immigrants to the United States from these countries brought their churches with them. The largest and best known are the Greek Orthodox Archdiocese of North and South America and the Russian Orthodox Church in America. Other Eastern Orthodox churches are the Albanian, the Bulgarian, the Roma-

---

[21] Arthur C. Piepkorn, *Profiles of Belief,* Vol. 3 (New York: Harper & Row, Pub., 1979), p. 3.

[22] Ignacio Vergara, *El Protestanismo En Chile* (1961), pp. 126–27, quoted in the Introduction by Vinson Syman to Arthur C. Piepkorn, ibid., p. xvi.

nian, the Carpatho-Russian, Serbian Orthodox, Syrian Antiochian Orthodox, and the United Ukranian Orthodox churches.[23]

Although closer theologically to Roman Catholicism than is much of Protestantism, Orthodoxy differs from Roman Catholicism in several ways. It does not recognize the Pope in Rome as the supreme pontiff, but only one bishop among many; it contends that the Virgin Mary was cleansed from original sin at the Annunciation rather than at her conception; it rejects the Roman Catholic doctrine of the Assumption of Mary and the doctrine of purgatory. The Orthodox groups differ from most Protestants in accepting apostolic succession, subscribing to seven sacraments (called mysteries), engaging in a dramatic liturgy, de-emphasizing the sermon, employing icons in their worship, and believing that there is a supernatural link between the icon and the person it represents.

The Orthodox churches have by and large successfully resisted the pressures of the surrounding society to "modernize" and "Americanize" their doctrine and practice. To step inside an Orthodox sanctuary is to take a longer step back in time and observe an older and more original tradition than would be the case in most any other American religious group except Orthodox Judaism. Consistent with such traditionalism and resistence to change, a religious feminist movement has yet to begin in the Orthodox churches.

ECUMENISM

Despite the theological diversity we have just scanned, American denominations have shown considerable facility at coexisting peacefully. This is true historically of Protestants with Protestants primarily, of course. It has been suggested that, for Protestants at least, different denominations are regarded by most citizens as equally valid ways of being a religious American. In fact, the principal occasion for Protestant religious groups to become suspicious of other Protestant groups has been when the actions or beliefs of those others suggested less than wholehearted commitment to the American Republic. German Lutherans, for example, were prodded and occasionally harassed during World War I, as many of them continued to use the German language in their churches and schools and as some openly supported the German "fatherland." Jehovah's Witnesses have repeatedly felt legal and social pressure because of their stands against saluting the flag and serving in the armed forces. Amish fathers who refused to allow their children to attend school beyond the eighth grade were periodically jailed for their convictions until 1972, when the Supreme Court ruled in their favor. Choosing not to use the English language, refusing to salute the flag, and questioning the value of formal education raises

[23] F. E. Mayer, *The Religious Bodies of America* (St. Louis: Concordia Publishing House, 1956), pp. 19–21.

doubts in many citizens' minds about a group's loyalty and commitment to basic American principles. It hardly needs mentioning that both the Jehovah's Witnesses and the Amish are sectarian groups that protest not simply against what they view as religious error but against prevailing social structures as well.

Despite some exceptions, such as those referred to above, we can say that for most of the United States' history most religious groups have felt relatively secure and have been able to pursue their business unhampered by government, other religious groups, or fellow citizens. In short, the constitutional provision for free exercise of religion has been in fairly effective operation.

There is, of course, a fairly certain way for a religious group to bring down the wrath of other groups upon itself. That is active proselytizing and seeking converts from other religious groups. Actually, except for a few groups such as the Mormons and Jehovah's Witnesses and a few small conversionist sects, this has been no serious issue. Not that most groups have not been willing to make converts to their faith. But they have tended to concentrate on those who were not affiliated with any religious groups, those who voluntarily knocked on the door, and those with whom the group has been put in contact because of marriage with a group member. In fact, most major Protestant groups, concerned lest they inadvertently overstep the bounds of others and be accused of proselytizing, commonly establish comity arrangements with one another; particularly in expanding communities, denominations typically divide the territory among themselves so that each has designated areas in which to work and establish new congregations without competing with other denominations.

The context of cooperation and peaceful coexistence just described is an important background factor in the rise of *ecumenism*—not simply greater cooperation but joint efforts that might lead ultimately to the organic merger of two or more denominations. The ecumenical movement is essentially a phenomenon of the twentieth century and has involved much discussion and commentary. Yet despite the great volume of literature and discussion, relatively few actual mergers have taken place. There have been mergers among Lutheran denominations from various Scandinavian countries once the groups had become "Americanized," began conversing in English, and realized they all subscribed to the same confessional and creedal statements. Specifically, there have been three of these—formation of the United Lutheran Church in America in 1917, of the Lutheran Church in America in 1962, and of The American Lutheran Church in 1960. All told, these three mergers brought together ten Lutheran groups. In 1957 the Congregational Christian Churches merged with the Evangelical and Reformed Church to form the United Church of Christ. And in 1968 a merger was effected between the Evangelical United Brethren Church and the United Methodist Church. Stimulated by Eugene Carson Blake's dramatic suggestion in 1960 for a merger of most of the major Protestant denominations in the United States, discussions have been going on for over two decades within the Consultation on Church Union (COCU), which was formed to facilitate discussion and the possible ultimate merger itself. Twelve denominations originally entered the discussions of COCU. By 1972 four had withdrawn, the latest being the United Presbyterian Church, which, however, voted in 1973 to rescind its action of the previous year and rejoin the discussion. By 1980 there were nine denominations and one federation (the National Council of Community Churches) still involved in discussion and in supporting a small full-time staff. While no mergers have been brought about during its twenty years of existence, COCU sees itself as alive and well and continuing to facilitate the kinds of dialogue, interaction, and activity that could result in concrete ecumenical outcomes sometime down the road.

What those involved in COCU and other ecumenical discussions have been discovering is the extreme difficulty of blending religious groups that have unique histories, distinct theologies, and different social constituencies. Here, in a real sense, the theological differences reflected by the data in Table 12–1 become evident and important. Issues involving forms of church government (episcopal, presbyterian, or congregational), differing views of the ministry, the nature and function of the two most common Christian sacraments of baptism and holy communion (Lord's Supper), and a host of other issues make agreement and compromise extremely difficult to achieve.

But ecumenical discussion has not been limited to Protestantism. Increasingly after 1950, Catholics, Eastern Orthodox, and Jews were brought into the ecumenical discussions, and dialogues began taking place between all manner of combinations of denominations—various Protestant denominations individually, and occasionally jointly with Catholics, Eastern Orthodox, and Jews. Mostly the result has been greater mutual understanding, with occasional official recognition of agreement on certain issues. But to date there is no sign of significant progress toward actual organic unification of these diverse traditions. In fact, these broader ecumenical discussions appear to have reached their zenith in the late 1960s and early 1970s.

Certainly ecumenism has been an absorbing subject for religious leaders and groups. But sociologists have also been interested, for ecumenism is a sociological phenomenon, not simply a religious one. Sociological interest has focused less on what is going on than on why ecumenical interest has developed at all. What, if any, are the social sources of this phenomenon? Peter Berger has suggested that one primary reason is economic—that is, rising costs, particularly for buildings and staff, suggest joint effort and cost sharing.[24] It appears that denominations have become increasingly aware that duplication of effort is not only wasteful, but ultimately impossible to continue forever. Pooling resources, using one missionary governing board to supervise forty missionaries rather than two boards each supervising twenty missionaries,

---

[24] Peter Berger, "A Market Model for the Analysis of Ecumenicity," *Social Research* 30, no. 1 (1963), 77–93.

building one church edifice instead of two in a new subdivision—ideas such as these have begun to make economic sense to denominations. Such recognition would probably not have come so quickly had religious membership expansion continued past the early 1960s at its post-World War II pace. But as we will discuss in Chapter 13, by the 1970s membership growth in the major denominations had either ceased or in fact begun to decline. In the face of declining membership and a concomitant decline in contributions, denominations have been forced to become cost-conscious and to look for ways to economize and increase efficiency. At this point groups begin regarding the theological justification for ecumenism as more convincing than ever before.

A prime factor underlying the problem of stable or declining membership is that while church membership in this country has shown a fairly steady increase for nearly two centuries, the growth of churches was closely tied to population growth in the nation generally. It is very possible that denominations have "converted" and brought into their folds proportionately nearly all the people they can ever expect to. Few of those not yet convinced to join are likely to be convinced in the future. Thus one of the activities that before the mid-1960s absorbed much of the energy of local churches and of denominations—namely, home missionary activities (the establishment of new congregations to meet the demands of population shifts)—has declined and no longer commands the attention it once did. What, then, are church leaders at all levels within the structure as well as laypeople in the congregations to do by way of church work? What kind of religious frontier is left to explore and conquer? One option that excites the imagination of many is to try to break down ancient barriers that have kept denominations apart. A divided Christendom is defined as a "scandal." What with the recent emphasis in American society on overcoming prejudices, tolerating differences among people, and compromising old absolutes regarding what is good and what is evil, it is only natural that religious groups should begin to work at cleaning up their houses, so to speak, with respect to relating to other religious groups. Ecumenical discussion and activity has become popular as a consequence. The challenge for the churches during the remaining third of the twentieth century has become for many the ecumenical goal of a united Christendom. Yet at this point we need to point out again that enthusiasm and commitment in theory to ecumenism have not been enough to effect much notable success since 1968.

Robert Lee has suggested that increased interest and activity in ecumenism is a fairly natural outgrowth of a growing cultural unity within American society. Writing in 1960, Lee saw signs of growing cultural unity in such phenomena and developments as the pervasiveness of mass culture, the instantaneous dissemination of similar information throughout the land through the mass media, the replacement of sectionalism by the regional concept, and a long list of other signs. Lee of course wrote before the youth counterculture got underway, before the issue of American participation in the Vietnam War exerted its divisive influence, before the development of the black power ideology, before the loss of faith and trust associated with the Watergate revelations. Perhaps these latter developments help explain why there is less talk of ecumenism today than there was fifteen or twenty years ago.[25]

Another factor that undoubtedly fostered ecumenism in the two decades following the close of World War II is the long-term trend toward autonomous bureaucracies in the major denominations. As numerous sociological studies have shown, those persons in high-level positions in organizations are the most tolerant, accepting, and understanding of competing organizations. High-level labor union officials, for example, often interact more harmoniously with their counterparts in management, from whom they will ultimately be trying to extract concessions to union demands, than they do with the rank-and-file union members they represent. It has been suggested that such leaders may even have difficulty demanding certain things that they have come to believe, through their contacts with management, the employer cannot afford. Similarly, officials of church bureaucracies tend to interact with comparable officials of other denominations, whom they find to be much like themselves. They find it easy to get along with them and therefore counsel that the denominations themselves ought to be able to get along as well. These church bureaucrats tend to be more liberal than the rank-and-file clergy in the denominations in the first place—a fact that may by itself go far in explaining why there is so much discussion of ecumenism by religious leaders but why little of a concrete nature in terms of denominational merger and extensive cooperative endeavors seems to occur. The local churches are likely not so interested or convinced as their representatives in the denominational bureaucracies.

Suffice it to say in summarizing our discussion to this point that ecumenism, at least during this century, has paralleled denominationalism. That is to say, both have thrived, even though this would seem to involve an inherent contradiction: Denominationalism appears to be as viable as ever, and ecumenism is also alive and at least fairly well. Part of the answer to this seeming contradiction is that in ecumenical conversations and activities denominations have found themselves looking more closely not only at others but at themselves, their heritage, and their uniqueness. This analysis may have led them to a new and strong appreciation of themselves in their uniqueness. In fact, ours is a pluralistic society which today encourages its subgroups to celebrate and preserve their uniqueness so long as they support the fundamental values of the society. The upshot is that denominations may not be particularly ready to give up their identities. Yet they see much value in cooperation and certainly no value in cut-throat competition. Hence ecumenism remains viable also. While not going the whole ecumenical route and effecting outright organizational mergers, denominations feel free to cooperate and engage in joint tasks

[25] Robert Lee, *The Social Sources of Church Unity* (Nashville, Tenn.: Abingdon Press, 1960).

while each retains its identity. Even if such activities should turn out to be but a single stage or way station on the track leading to ultimate organizational union of several or even all denominations, the train will probably be able to stand at this station for a long time—energized, but with little forward movement down the track.

THE CONTINUED VIABILITY OF DENOMINATIONALISM

We now return more explicitly to the denominational phenomenon with which this chapter is concerned and discuss additional sociological reasons why the denominational phenomenon has remained so dominant a feature of American religion—of American society, for that matter. In the face of strong pressures, both theological and sociological, toward ecumenism, and given yet another unifying tendency (which we discussed in Chapter 6)—the phenomenon of civil religion, which at least implicitly would replace traditional religion with a religion focusing on the society itself—why is American society still divided into so many distinctive religious groups? It is not enough to point out, as we have already, that important doctrinal differences divide denominations, or that another factor keeping denominations distinct is the type of organizational tradition or liturgical emphasis, or the differences between Apollonian and Dionysian orientations. All of these are significant, and all represent a combination of theological and sociological factors and pressures. But there are two other factors, which are primarily sociological, that reinforce the denominational heritage which American society continually updates.

The Ethnic Factor

The first factor reinforcing denominationalism that we want to discuss— one strongly emphasized by Andrew Greeley—is the important ethnic function that religion in American society continues to serve. That is, one's religious affiliation represents for a great many people much more than commitment to a set of religious beliefs, symbols, and rituals. Religious affiliation may also become a means people use to define their identity—"who they are and where they stand in a large and complex society."[26] Greeley mentions that this definition and location of self may be the most important function religion performs for some people. For others it is intermixed with the belief system and ethical code that the religious group stands for.

The origin of religion as an American ethnic phenomenon rests with the fact that most of the nationality groups that immigrated into the United States brought their churches with them and transplanted them on American

---

[26] Greeley, *The Denominational Society*, p. 108.

soil. The Norwegians, Swedes, Finns, and Danes brought their Lutheran churches. Some Germans brought their Lutheran church; other Germans brought their Catholic church; still others brought their Reformed church. The Irish brought their Catholic church; the Italians and Poles did likewise. And so on. But there is more to it than that. The religious organization for these immigrants was immediately an important source of identification. In many cases it was a safe place for people to use their native tongue, and it linked them in their present insecurity in a new environment to a secure tradition or heritage. As the immigrants left the old cohesive communal relationship of the peasant village, with its primary relationships and awareness of who one was in relation to others, and entered a strange land of secondary relationships, they clung to their ethnic group in order to preserve some semblance of identity and a linkage with people who could provide empathy. Some of these people may not have been particularly "religious" before and perhaps would not have scored high on certain measures of religiosity in the new land, yet many found in the religious group an opportunity to meet those with whom they shared a heritage, people who spoke their language in both a literal and figurative sense. Andrew Greeley says that denominational membership makes available to Americans "a fellowship which is highly important in compensating for those intimate relationships of life which seem to have been lost when the peasant village was left behind."[27] Clearly, we see religion performing the "belonging" function emphasized by Max Weber and discussed in the chapter on religious origins (Chapter 2).

It should be noted that the opportunity for religion to serve an ethnic function, particularly for immigrant groups, was in part made possible by the religious pluralism that had existed in some of the American colonies and was authenticated in the Constitution. Religious diversity (pluralism) was valued and encouraged. Therefore, the immigrant could turn to his or her religious group as a source of belonging without undue fear of reprisal. Not that the established Americans were always happy with the religious-ethnic enclaves. But they could do little about them and still be true to the American religious heritage and precedent. That resentment and suspicion did erupt in harassment and violence is attested to in the discussion of the "Protestant Crusade" in Chapter 10; the point to be made here is that not only was anti-Catholicism being expressed, but also anti-Irish and anti–cheap urban labor sentiments as well.

Acknowledging the ethnic nature and function of religion in the United States raises some serious questions about the melting-pot hypothesis—the idea that the United States has accommodated and homogenized peoples from a diversity of cultures and backgrounds. It is hardly even the triple melting pot of Protestants, Catholics, and Jews that some have suggested. Actually, historically it was Dutch Reformed, German Lutheran, Scottish Presbyterian,

27 Ibid., p. 114.

and so on for the Protestant immigrant groups; and Polish Catholic, Serbian Catholic, Irish Catholic, and so on for the Catholic groups. It was even to some extent Russian Jew, German Jew, and so on—not simply Jewish for the third major religious family in America. That is, Americans were not only ethnically "hyphenated" as citizens (Irish-Americans, German-Americans, Polish-Americans, and so on), but they were ethnically hyphenated as members of religious groups as well. The ethnic factor has thus been more important in patterning American religion than has often been recognized.

One final comment in connection with our discussion of the ethnic feature of religion in America is that the numerical strength of American religion is in significant degree related to the ethnic factor. Because the religious group was able to serve as an ethnic rallying point and to provide an identity for people and a sense of belonging to something more intimate and meaningful than the diffuse, cold, and distant society, people gained a religious commitment that, though perhaps less intense for many as the importance of ethnic identity fades for them, they are still reluctant to cut themselves off from completely. Religion has served and does serve an important social function as an ethnic community, which exists quite in addition to any strictly "religious" function it may serve. In many cases people have even been able to live out their entire lives while only rarely leaving the religious-ethnic community. Scattered throughout the land are ethnic-religious communities where nearly 100 percent of the citizens are of a single national origin and a single religious persuasion, and where the public schools become almost parochial ones. But one need not be a farmer or a shopkeeper in such a community to live out one's life in an ethnic subcommunity. One may be a city dweller and a medical doctor, or an accountant, or an attorney, or an academician—and still serve only or almost exclusively members of the ethnic community into which he or she was born.

The Social-Class Factor

The second additional factor which reinforces denominationalism in American society is social class. We spent considerable time in Chapter 8 discussing the relationship between religion and social class, and will therefore do little more than mention it again here. But it is of considerable relevance to our present interest in denominationalism. Religion does reflect the class structure. Denominations are disproportionately constituted of different social classes, sects are almost universally a lower-social-status phenomenon, and social mobility frequently results in change in religious group affiliation that corresponds more appropriately in the eyes of the community with one's newly achieved social status.

The fact that religion reflects the class structure of the society is of course not unique to American society. Differences in religious orientation and practice have been observed in less complex societies that have religious systems at an earlier stage on Bellah's continuum of religious evolution.[28] A distinctive feature of the "archaic" stage of religious evolution, according to Bellah, is a clearly stratified society and fairly distinctive religious expressions according to class level. The upper-status people who control the political and military power usually claim superior religious status as well. Bellah states that noble families are proud of their divine descent and often have special priestly functions.[29] We can point, for example, to ancient Greece where there appears to have been a fairly clear distinction between the religion of the plebians and that of the patricians. The plebians related to gods associated with agriculture, localized gods, and gods related to magical animal symbols. The patricians were absorbed with the Olympian gods, such as Zeus, Apollo, Aphrodite, Athena, and Hermes, who oversaw broader areas of life, universal principles and emotions, and broader societal concerns. Another example is the Hindu religion. The major beliefs and practices associated with the Vedas and Upanishads and the concepts of Brahma and Brahman are largely unknown to the lower castes, who in fact have traditionally been deemed unworthy of being given the sacred truths. Instead, the lower castes learn the elemental Hindu ideas of samsara, karma, and dharma, and relate to a variety of local gods and spirits.

In American society we have fairly clear evidence of Weber's "theodicy of escape" and of Marx's and Freud's compensation-for-deprivation function of religion for the lower classes, on the one hand, and the "theodicy of good fortune" for the economically and socially successful members of the society on the other hand. The upshot is that various denominations and religious groups appeal disproportionately to different social classes. The fact that the United States has been and continues to be a highly stratified if somewhat mobile society has tended to reinforce and preserve denominational and religious diversity as different religious groups provide different things to different people.

---

[28] Robert Bellah outlines five states of religious evolution: the primitive, the archaic, the historical, the early modern, and the modern. Robert N. Bellah, "Religious Evolution," *American Sociological Review* 29, no. 3 (1964), 358–74, reprinted in idem, *Beyond Belief* (New York: Harper & Row, Pub., 1970), chapter 2.

[29] Bellah, *Beyond Belief*, pp. 30–31.

13

The Future of Religion

Those who might have predicted at any time in the past that by the late twentieth century religion would be a defunct institution would have to be quite surprised at what they can see most anywhere in the world today. Not only are many traditional signs of religion in abundance, but new manifestations seem to emerge almost daily. In the United States not only does one continue to observe bumper stickers proclaiming Jesus Saves, political candidates mouthing religious clichés, evangelists like Billy Graham still "packing them in," and freshly painted church spires dotting both countryside and town, but one observes amazing new religious sights and sounds that daily bombard the consciousness. One sees smooth-headed young men in flowing saffron robes roaming the streets chanting "Hare Krishna . . . ," jazz and rock liturgies in traditional churches, a proliferation of Eastern mystical cults, sober academic discussions in mainline Protestant churches on the "death of God," so-called Moral Majority preachers and laypeople influencing elections and moving members of Congress in directions of their religious persuasion on issues such as abortion, aid to parochial schools, capital punishment, and defense spending. In other words, there is a great deal of religious activity; there are numerous developments within religion. Some of these developments will give us clues as to what kind of future religion might have, particularly in the United States. Certainly they will influence people's thinking about the future of religion. Therefore as we try to look into the future of religion we shall focus on several major religious developments and sets of data that seem to have particular relevance.

LEVEL OF RELIGIOUS ACTIVITY

While it appeared that there would be a decline in church membership following the post–World War II religious revival that continued into the early 1960s (cf. the slight decline of church membership that began after the high in 1964 shown in Table 13–1), the decline, though continuing into 1979 (the latest date for which information is available), has moved at an extremely slow rate. Actually, we would have to observe that church membership in the United States has essentially been holding its own at an almost stable level. Only if the gradual decline continues at its recent rate for the next eight to ten years and moves back down to the 1950 level of church membership would the decline be noteworthy. At present no clear trend is in evidence.

Another piece of data to consider in assessing the relative level of religious interest and activity is the pattern of weekly attendance at religious services. The data in Table 13–2, though not completely parallel to the data in the previous table, are not inconsistent. The only difference is that the decline in church attendance started six years earlier than the decline in church membership. But there appears to have been a leveling off during the 1970s. And we have to say that patterns of church attendance in the United States do not suggest a significant change in levels of formal religious activity for American citizens at this time.

A third indicator that has been used by some, including this author, and has suggested a falling off of religious interest, activity, and commitment is the value of new construction of religious facilities. Assuming that money follows profession of one's convictions and commitments, such convictions and commitments are likely stronger during times of increasing contributions than when the money begins to fall off. Therefore, the downward trend, seen in Ta-

TABLE 13–1 *Church Membership in the United States as a Proportion of Population*

YEAR	%	YEAR	%
1930	47%	1970	62.4%
1940	49	1972	62.4
1950	57	1974	61.9
1960	63.6	1976	61.5
1964	64.4	1978	60.8
1968	63.2	1979	60.7

Source: Yearbook of American Churches (New York: National Council Press, 1959–1973; Constant H. Jacquet, Jr., ed., *Yearbook of American and Canadian Churches* (Nashville: Abingdon Press, for the years 1976, 1977, 1978, 1979, 1980, Table 1-C.

TABLE 13–2   Weekly Church Attendance in the United States as a Proportion of Population

YEAR	%	YEAR	%
1958	49%	1971	40%
1960	47	1972	40
1962	46	1974	40
1964	45	1976	42
1966	44	1978	41
1969	42	1979	40

Source: Gallup Poll data reported in Lauris B. Whitman, ed., *Yearbook of American Churches, 1969* (New York: National Council Press, 1969), p. 205, and in Constant H. Jacquet, Jr., ed., *Yearbook of American Churches*, 1980 (Nashville: Abindgon Press, 1980), p. 269.

ble 13–3, that began in 1968 and continued until 1975 seemed to suggest a gradual leveling off and perhaps incipient decline of religious interest and commitment. But since 1975, even adjusting for inflation, the value of new construction has increased.

A fourth source of evidence, one that was widely used to suggest a decline of religious interest and commitment in the late 1960s and early to mid-1970s, was a question asked periodically by the George Gallup polling organization concerning people's views on the question of whether they perceived religion to be gaining or losing influence in American life. As seen in Figure 13–1, from 1957 until 1970 a truly remarkable trend was in progress. The numbers of Americans who believed that religious influence was increasing was dropping not only steadily year by year but very dramatically as well—from a high of 69 percent in 1957 to a low of 14 percent in 1970; correspond-

TABLE 13–3   Value of New Construction of Religious Facilities in the United States

YEAR	VALUE (IN MILLIONS OF DOLLARS)	YEAR	VALUE (IN MILLIONS OF DOLLARS)
1950	$ 409 million	1972	$845 million
1955	736 "	1974	711 "
1960	1,016 "	1975	627 "
1965	1,207 "	1976	689 "
1968	1,038 "	1978	749
1970	1,056 "		

Sources: Constant H. Jacquet, Jr., ed., *Yearbook of American Churches, 1972* (Nashville: Abingdon Press, 1972), p. 260, idem, ed., *Yearbook of American Churches, 1973* (Nashville: Abingdon Press, 1973), p. 266, idem, ed., *Yearbook of American Churches, 1980* (Nashville: Abingdon Press, 1980), p. 271.

Note: Value from 1972 onward calculated in 1972 dollars.

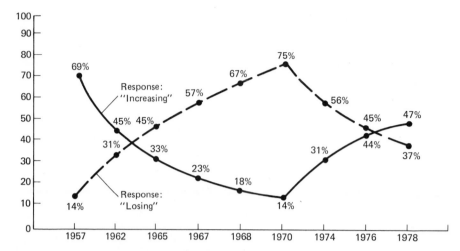

FIGURE 13–1 Proportion of adult Americans who perceive religion as increasing or losing its influence on American life. Source: George H. Gallup, The Gallup Poll (New York: Random House, 1972), 2:1482; 3:1763, 1934, 1058–59, 2193, 2240; Constant H. Jacquet, Jr., ed., Yearbook of American and Canadian Churches, 1979 (Nashville: Abingdon Press, 1979), p. 264; idem, Yearbook of American and Canadian Churches, 1980 (Nashville: Abingdon Press, 1980), p. 270.

ingly, the proportion of Americans who believed that religion was *losing* in influence was increasing dramatically—from only 14 percent in 1957 to 75 percent in 1970.

But this dramatic trend also ceased after 1970. And both the "increasing" and "losing" views have already recovered approximately two-thirds of the change from their 1957 base.

While these data are of course not indicative in any absolute sense that religion was or is actually gaining or losing influence, inasmuch as the data reflect only what people *think* is happening, it has been suggested by a number of sociologists of religion (for example, Jeffrey Hadden) that the time-honored sociological concepts of the "self-fulfilling prophecy" and the "definition of the situation" could well be in operation here. That is, people tend to behave in a manner that helps bring about what they expect and have already predicted will happen. He who predicts he will fail at a new job likely will. She who says nobody wants to be her friend will likely make few new friends. Similarly with the "definition of the situation" idea—a person's definition or understanding of reality tends to have consequences consistent with that definition or understanding.[1] Thus if enough people feel that religion is declining in influence, its influence is in fact likely to decline—if only because many of those who make such an assessment are probably showing thereby some personal

[1] Jeffrey K. Hadden, The Gathering Storm in the Churches (Garden City, N.Y.: Doubleday, 1969), pp. 25–26.

disenchantment with the institution themselves. At least it is possible that they will exert less effort on behalf of an organization that they feel is dying on the vine. As we pointed out in Chapter 1, an absolute requirement of any social group's survival is the commitment of its members and their conviction that the group is worthwhile, that it deserves expending their energies on its behalf, and that it deserves their verbal support and promotion. To the degree that members have lost such convictions, group members are likely to begin fulfilling their own negative prophecies. Half-heartedness will evidence itself in declining attendance and participation. Something of a falling-domino effect will come into operation as unenthusiastic parents who themselves are reluctant to cut their ties with formal religion nevertheless socialize their children, unconsciously perhaps, to view affiliation with institutionalized religion as a "take-it-or-leave-it" matter. The consequence is likely to be an erosion of the prime source of recruitment of new members—namely, the children of present members.

We have suggested in the previous section that what appeared to have been incipient decline in American religion beginning in the late 1960s and early 1970s at least slowed, if not stopped altogether, as the 1970s ended and the 1980s began. But at this point we must make clear that we have been using total membership and attendance figures for the nation as a whole. Therefore we should be alert to differences, possibly even substantial ones, among the various groups that in total constitute the summary figures. That is to say, some religious groups could be declining, perhaps dramatically; but others could be growing, perhaps as dramatically, or even more dramatically than others are declining. If we find it is so (and it certainly is), then we are likely to ask another question as well: What are the reasons that might account for these differences—some churches growing, some declining?

By way of a very general summary we can observe that many of what most people would consider the standard, mainline Protestant churches have been declining fairly noticeably for well over a decade. For example, some of the most dramatic declines over the period 1965 to 1979 were registered by the Presbyterians (United Presbyterian Church in the U.S.A.) with a decline in membership of 23.7 percent, the Episcopalians with a decline of 17.5 percent, and the United Church of Christ with a decline of 14.6 percent.[2] These were far from the only losers, but these were the more dramatic losers.

On the other hand, several religious groups have not only been growing, but at a substantial rate. For example, between 1965 and 1978–79 the Church of the Nazarene grew by 34.8 percent, the Seventh-Day Adventists increased by 46.9 percent, the Church of Jesus Christ of Latter-Day Saints added 65

[2] Percentages computed from data in Constant H. Jacquet, Jr., ed. *Yearbook of American Churches, 1967* (New York: National Council of Churches, 1967) pp. 198–210; Constant H. Jacquet, Jr., ed., *Yearbook of American and Canadian Churches* (Nashville: Abingdon, 1980) pp. 219–25.

percent, and the Assemblies of God grew by 126.1 percent.[3] Others are of course in between with only small fluctuations one way or the other, or alternating between small decreases some years but an increase in other years. For example, while Lutherans have declined at a modest rate for several years, 1980 saw a small increase for the two largest Lutheran groups—the Lutheran Church in America increased by 2,639 to a total of 3,046,355, and The Lutheran Church—Missouri Synod increased 1,323 to 2,719,319. These small increases were the first for the LCA since 1967; for the LC—MS, the first since 1971.

In a controversial book published in 1972 (with a second edition in 1977), *Why Conservative Churches are Growing,* Dean M. Kelley analyzed the data on growth for some, decline for others and suggested that one explanatory factor stood out in particular. That was that the growing religious organizations were the strict ones. These demand high commitment and loyalty from their members; they exert church discipline over members' beliefs and lifestyles; they put missionary zeal into practice by carrying their message to outsiders; they tend to be absolutist and clear-cut about true and correct beliefs (no relativism and little latitude).[4] In fact Kelley has since said that although overruled by his publisher he had wanted as his title, not *Why Conservative Churches Are Growing,* but *Why Strict Churches Are Strong.*[5] These strict churches demand firm allegiance, tireless devotion to proclaiming the Gospel, obedience to authority, and stoic acceptance of ridicule from the outside.

In a similar vein is the explanation for conservative growth and liberal decline proposed by George LaNoue, who notes that the conservative churches offer people a scarce commodity for which religion is the nearly unique source—namely, salvation—while the liberal churches have been trying to offer a panoply of goods and services that are also available from a host of other sources—entertainment, intellectual stimulation, and discussion and activity centering around social issues, for example. Because many secular groups can often do a better job of delivering such goods and services within their areas of specialization, liberal religious groups are likely to lose out in the competition. Small wonder, then, that conservative groups that promise delivery of a scarce commodity should grow, and liberal groups that must compete with numerous secular groups in the same business, so to speak, should be shrinking.[6]

Innately appealing as these hypotheses concerning the differential growth and decline in conservative and liberal religious groups may be, we must intro-

[3] Ibid.

[4] Dean M. Kelley, *Why Conservative Churches Are Growing* (New York: Harper & Row, Pub., 1972).

[5] Dean M. Kelley, "Commentary: Is Religion a Dependent Variable?" in *Understanding Church Growth and Decline: 1950–1978,* eds. Dean R. Hoge and David A. Roozen (New York: Pilgrim Press, 1979), p. 340.

[6] Cited in Kelley, *Why Conservative Churches Are Growing,* pp. 92–93.

duce a couple of studies that trace the changing religious affiliations of people. The reason is that a distinct disadvantage of both Kelley's and LaNoue's work is that their data represent total membership figures only, and thus cannot be used to trace the movements of individuals from one religious group to another. In fact, we cannot necessarily infer from these data any movement at all. For example, if the birth rate were higher among members of the more conservative religious groups (which is quite likely, in fact), then the growth of these groups through natural reproduction alone might account for their increasing numerical advantage over the liberal denominations. Or again, perhaps the conservative groups are gaining strength by picking up the nonaffiliated person with little or no religious background, not necessarily the dropouts from liberal denominations.

As for studies tracing changes in religious affiliations, in Stark and Glock's San Francisco Bay Area study nearly half of the Protestant respondents (46 percent) reported having changed denominational affiliation at some time in the past.[7] In seeking patterns away from and toward certain denominations, Stark and Glock conclude that the general tendency for those who change religious affiliation is to move from more conservative bodies to those that are more liberal theologically.[8]

Samuel Mueller, analyzing the same data, reached different, though not diametrically opposed, conclusions. Through the application of factor-analytic techniques he found that switches of religious affiliation occur essentially without reference to the liberal or conservative stance of the groups involved, but are made in such a way as to preserve similarity along as many dimensions as possible; that is, people tend to affiliate with a religious group similar in a sociological sense to the one they are leaving. The relevant similarities do not seem to be so much doctrinal or creedal as they are related to such factors as social status and liturgy. In other words, people seem to look for another religious group that has members like themselves and which has a form of worship similar to what they have known and practiced in the past. Some of these religiously mobile people wind up in more liberal denominations, but usually for other than theological or doctrinal reasons or motivations. And the same is true for those who move to more conservative denominations.[9]

Where does this leave us, then, with regard to the issue of the relative growth and decline of conservative and liberal churches? And at an even more general level, where do these trends fit into the observation with which this chapter began—namely, that there has been a small decline in denominational religion in the United States since peaks of activity in the 1950s and 1960s?

[7] Rodney Stark and Charles Y. Glock, *American Piety* (Berkeley: University of California Press, 1968).

[8] Ibid., p. 187.

[9] Samuel A. Mueller, "Dimensions of Interdenominational Mobility in the United States," *Journal for the Scientific Study of Religion* 10, no. 2 (1971), 76–84.

For one thing, the analyses offered by Mueller and by Stark and Glock cast some doubt on Kelley's hypothesis. Since we do not know the source of the new members in the conservative groups for which Kelley gives data—whether they are defectors from liberal denominations, converts from irreligion, or simply a result of above-average natural reproductive increase—we cannot infer that doctrinal motivations cause the discrepancy between liberal and conservative denominational growth rates as both Kelley and LaNoue at least implicitly suggest. In fact, Stark and Glock's data, as well as National Opinion Research Center data that they also examined, suggest that denominational mobility proceeds in both directions between liberal and conservative groups—moreover it proceeds, according to Mueller's analysis, in a nearly random fashion insofar as theological stances of the gaining and losing denominations are concerned.

Wade Roof and Christopher Hadaway have more recently provided very helpful information on the issue, using National Opinion Research Center General Social Survey data from 1973 through 1976 that involved a merged sample of nearly six thousand adults. One important qualification of the earlier Stark and Glock findings is that many who defect from the mainline denominations do not move to the more liberal denominations as a sort of way station to religious agnosticism and dropping out altogether, but go directly from membership in mainline denominations to nonmembership in any religious group. For example, as high a proportion as 20.4 percent of former United Presbyterians describe themselves as religious dropouts. Corresponding proportions of Lutherans, Methodists, Baptists, and Disciples of Christ were 17.8 percent, 13.4 percent, 13.8 percent, and 9.1 percent respectively. Among the Presbyterians and the Lutherans those who dropped out constituted more than those who switched to any other group.[10]

But further, at least somewhat in line with what Kelley and LaNoue have been saying, Roof and Hadaway found considerable switching out of mainline Protestant denominations into what they term the "religious fringe"—the small Protestant denominations, sect and cult groups, Mormons, and various non-Christian, non-Jewish groups. By way of example, of Presbyterians who left the United Presbyterian Church 16.8 percent went to small Protestant bodies, 9 percent to sectarian groups, and 3.6 percent to non-Christian groups; of Baptist defectors, 15.6 percent went to small Protestant denominations, 18.2 percent to sects, and 1.4 percent to non-Christian groups; of Methodist defectors, 14.7 percent went to the smaller Protestant denominations, 10.4 percent to various sects, and 1.0 percent to non-Christian groups.[11]

[10] Wade Clark Roof and Christopher Kirk Hadaway, "Denominational Switching in the Seventies: Going beyond Stark and Glock," *Journal for the Scientific Study of Religion* 18, no. 4 (1979), 372.

[11] Ibid.

In a very substantial analysis of factors that might be involved in declining memberships of mainline Protestant churches[12] various authors, looking both separately and collectively at mainline denominations, reach several similar conclusions. First, the more-highly-educated young adults who have moved in the direction of individualism, personal freedom, and tolerance of diversity appear not only to be less interested in maintaining membership in the denominations they grew up in, but are not much attracted to the even more-liberal Protestant groups either, preferring rather to defect from organized religion altogether. Dean Hoge describes a value shift among young people, particularly the more affluent and better educated among them, since the 1950s.

> The shift has been toward individualism, cosmopolitanism, and greater freedom in the areas of marriage, sexuality, sex roles, and personal morality. The total value shift has created some barriers between certain young people and the churches. Such broad contextual changes as these seem more important for explaining recent trends.[13]

If we add to this observation about defectors a second and third trend, the future of the mainline Protestant churches looks even more bleak. The two trends are the sharp decline in baptisms and the shrinking of enrollments in church schools and Sunday schools. Ruth Doyle and Sheila Kelly report that baptisms for all the major U.S. denominations that they studied (Roman Catholic, Southern Baptist Convention, United Presbyterian, United Methodist, Episcopalian, Lutheran Church in America, Lutheran Church — Missouri Synod, American Lutheran Church, and the United Church of Christ) declined from 1950–1975. They note that the declines have been especially dramatic since 1960 and, "in general, are disproportionately larger than the declines in church membership."[14] Not only do such declines result in fewer members right now, but a prime source of future members who would themselves bear children who would likely be baptized in the church are for the most part lost (some will of course come in on their own later as teens or adults).

Church school enrollment is, for most of the groups under study, a true disaster area. Of only four groups that have outstripped the growth in population under age eighteen, only one is significantly ahead of that population increase over the twenty-five-year period from 1950–1975. That group is the Roman Catholic Church. But during the last ten years of that twenty-five-year period its gains too have fallen behind population growth. The other six de-

---

[12] Dean R. Hoge and David A. Roozen, eds., *Understanding Church Growth and Decline: 1950–1978* (New York: Pilgrim Press, 1979).

[13] Dean R. Hoge, "A Test of Theories of Denominational Growth and Decline," in *Understanding Church Growth and Decline*, eds. Hoge and Roozen, ibid., p. 197.

[14] Ruth T. Doyle and Sheila M. Kelly, "Comparison of Trends in Ten Denominations 1950–75," in *Understanding Church Growth and Decline*, eds. Hoge and Roozen, ibid., p. 151.

nominations have fallen far behind population growth—actually declining from between 11.8 percent and 47 percent in church school enrollments between 1950 and 1975, while the U.S. population under age eighteen increased by 40.9 percent.[15]

The mainline Protestant churches all know that they are facing membership and participation problems. Several have conducted very substantial studies to analyze and try to reverse the pattern. But no clear answers have been forthcoming. There is an emerging consensus that from the religious perspective, growth or even holding steady so far as membership is concerned is not necessarily everything. That point is probably not more succinctly or well stated than by Robert K. Hudnut, a Presbyterian minister.

> But church growth is not the point. The point is whether the church is being true to the Gospel. And, in city after city, and town after town, it is. Indeed, because it is being faithful it is often losing members.
> Loss of growth in statistics has often meant increase in growth in the Gospel. The "dead wood" is gone. The "faithful remnant" remains.[16]

The famous neo-orthodox theologian Karl Barth raised such questions not only before the great post-World War II growth period in American religion became noticeable but certainly well before the decline in membership set in. In 1948 he said the following:

> What objection could we really make if it should please God to carry his work onward and reach his goal, not through a further numerical increase, but through a drastic numerical decrease of so-called Christendom? It seems to me the only question in this matter is: How can we free ourselves from all quantitative thinking, all statistics, all calculation of observable consequence, all efforts to achieve a Christian world order, and then shape our witness into a witness to the sovereignty of God's mercy. . .?[17]

CONTINUITY IN THE TRADITIONAL SOCIAL FUNCTIONS OF RELIGION

Here we wish to expand a little on observations made by Emile Durkheim (cf. Chapter 2)·that much of the time and in most societies religion serves as an integrating influence in society. We refer to this observation again and in fact expand on it because we believe there are several important functions for society that religion shall continue to provide in the future.

---

[15] Doyle and Kelly, ibid., p. 154.

[16] Robert K. Hudnut, *Church Growth Is Not the Point!* (New York: Harper & Row, Pub., 1975), p. ix.

[17] Karl Barth, "No Christian Marshall Plan," *The Christian Century LXV*, no. 49 (1948), 1332.

Normative Reinforcement

First, religion serves a reinforcement function in society to the degree that it teaches and emphasizes the same norms and values as the society at large. This may be at the very general level of teaching such values as human dignity and freedom, equality before the law, respect for legitimate authority, and faithfulness to one's role. Or it may be more specific, such as, "Thou shalt not kill, steal, or procreate illegitimate children." In a direct sense, religion is here being viewed as a socializing agent in the society. Although allowing that religious groups, just as all other kinds of groups, socialize their members into some norms unique unto themselves, we are here speaking of religion as one among several institutions involved in socializing citizens to the core norms of the society. Educational agencies, families, peer groups, mass media, and various voluntary associations are all involved in this process. Religion is but one such agent. But it is one that touches a majority of people with some regularity.

At a second level with respect to the reinforcement idea we observe that religion not only socializes people in the "thou shalts" and "thou shalt nots" of society in a reinforcing sense, but occasionally pushes those norms even farther. For example, society has norms against murder, but does not usually try to control what you think about your neighbor so long as you do not harm his or her person or property or infringe on his or her rights. A religious system may go farther by teaching, for example, "whosoever hateth his brother is a murderer," "Love your neighbor," and "Do good to those who despitefully use you and persecute you." If a religion is successful in inculcating norms more stringent than those the society imposes and thereby creates a "super-Christian" (or "super-Buddhist," or "super-Hindu," or whatever), to that degree one may also see a "supercitizen." That is to say, society would be even better off if people not only avoided destroying their neighbors but actually loved them and went out of their way to help them. The key here, of course, is discovering whether and to what degree religion actually produces such superior people. Undoubtedly there are some—they tend to be called "saints," and they may even be societal heroes and models for behavior. But there is no clear evidence that, on the average, religion produces a great number. Yet we must again observe: To the degree that it happens, the society would benefit and would be getting citizens with a level of commitment and dedication that they might not have in the absence of religious influence and training.

Integration into Meaningful Relationships

An exceptionally important function religion performs is that of bringing individuals into meaningful relationships with others in a group. Religious groups bring immigrants, social isolates, various minorities, and some socially maladjusted persons into a group and put them into contact with others. Not that religion reaches every such person or is successful in integrating all of those with whom it establishes contact. Nor is religion unique in performing this task or function for society—so do labor unions, fraternal lodges, newcomers' clubs, political parties, and innumerable other voluntary associations and groups of all sizes, constituencies, and purposes. However, religious groups, in large part because of their reputation for being concerned about life purposes and adjustment as well as for raising a person's sights beyond current mundane problems, attract relatively large proportions of persons in need of meaningful interpersonal contact. Society needs such groups to do this. Society needs members who can function well in their roles. People function better when they feel some personal worth and have meaningful, satisfying relationships with other people. To the extent that religious groups provide this service to some who feel isolated and who are not being relieved of their anxieties and problems elsewhere, to that extent religion is serving the society.

Catalyst and Symbol for Reaffirming
Societal Values

Another way in which religion contributes to the integration of society is by serving as a focal point or symbol—in a sense, as a catalyst—for the society to reaffirm some of its basic values. Religion everywhere does this through festivals. Think, for example, of what happens in our society in connection with the religious festival called Christmas. Although there is plenty of growling about gifts yet to buy, overdrawn checking accounts, and crass commercialism conspiring to do us all in, there is something else as well. There is a pervasive spirit in the air of good will and joviality. There are increases in gifts to charities. There is more attention given to those less fortunate than the majority. Not that what emerges is particularly enduring. Yet periodically, through such rites and festivals that reach out beyond the religious group itself, some of the fundamental values of the society are dramatized for people, and they reaffirm them at least intellectually and momentarily. Certainly not every Scrooge does an about-face, much less one that lasts beyond the festival itself; yet some do, and most citizens are at least temporarily affected.

In this connection we also think of the religious imagery and terminology, as well as the appeals to a religious authority and legitimation, that so many politicians employ—for example, "As a religious nation we reaffirm such and so and must do such and so," or "In accord with our Judeo-Christian heritage. . . ." We are reminded of the civil religion phenomenon discussed in Chapter 6.

Aid in Adjusting to Personal Crises

Another integrating function of religion that some feel is actually getting close to the fundamental purpose or essence of religion itself is the help it gives to people facing various crisis situations in their lives. To the degree that religion helps people grapple with emotional crisis, with death and bereavement, with uncertainties and disappointments of all kinds, religion is performing an important service for society. We introduced the idea of relativizing suffering and crisis in Chapter 2. Religion attempts to relativize human problems by placing them in an eternal perspective, interpreting events as God's will ("All things work for good to those who love God"), and providing "answers" for irrational events. Whether the answers and explanations are "true" is for our purposes—and for society's—beside the point. What is important is whether people feel better as a result of what religion does for them in periods of crisis and imbalance. The society needs functioning members who fill their social roles with skill and attention. Society cannot afford to have great numbers of members incapacited for extended periods of time. To the extent that religion helps with this task, society is greatly aided.

Source of Social Welfare

A final fairly major function religion performs in society is its service as a welfare institution. Religious groups were in the forefront of the nineteenth-century movement for establishing orphanages, schools for the deaf, blind, and mentally retarded, adoption and family-service agencies, hospitals, and similar welfare and service institutions. Earle E. Cairns has documented the significant impact of numerous Christian religions on drives for prison reforms, the abolition of slavery, humane treatment of the mentally ill, and improved working conditions for industrial workers in the wake of the Industrial Revolution.[18] Even today many lists of United Fund and United Way agencies include a number of organizations that either retain a religious name or were founded by a religious organization. Today most of these agencies derive the major portion of their monetary support from nonreligious sources through fees, voluntary contributions and solicitations from the general public, and governmental subsidy. But initially they were religiously motivated and funded, and represented a direct response of religious groups to human need. Although the majority of funds in social-welfare areas are today collected and distributed by the government, much of the original stimulus and efforts in these directions were religious.

THE FACTOR OF
SECULARIZATION

A concept that has been widely discussed for several decades and must be understood if we are to hope, at one level, to make sense out of contemporary developments in religion, and at a second level, to project the future of religion, is that of *secularization*. As this concept is commonly understood and

[18] Earle E. Cairns, *Saints and Society* (Chicago: Moody Press, 1960).

used it is assumed that there has been a displacement of religious interpretations of reality and religious orientations toward life by an orientation that seeks explanations for and justifications of human behavior and other phenomena in scientific and rational terms. One has undergone a secularization process if, for example, instead of asserting that marriages are made in heaven and for eternity, he or she says that marriages are made by human beings, in time, on the basis of propinquity, and in response to biological and psychological needs. The results of secularization are that, instead of more or less automatically "explaining" much that happens—death, floods, plane crashes, drought, war, peace, or whatever—as "God's will," more and more people are seeking explanations in the laws of physical science and in the social scientific "laws" of human interaction. In other words, secularization is as much a state of mind as it is a specific, measurable development.

Andrew Greeley is very much on target when he says that secularization as discussed in the United States today means essentially that religion is less important now than it was in the past.[19] If this is in fact what people mean when they refer to the secularization process at work in American society, then the decline of religion in general, and not just in its institutional manifestations, is an empirical question that clamors for sociological investigation and documentation. Much will rest on how religion is defined—whether in terms of its "essence," or as a particular traditional package of beliefs and principles (such as "our Judeo-Christian heritage"), or in terms of the vitality of its institutional forms (membership, attendance, new construction, and so on).

This problem of achieving a consensus so far as a definition of religion is concerned surfaces in many discussions of the issue of secularization wherein it happens that one person's understanding of religion does not coincide with others' understandings. Larry Shriner implies as much when he shows how *secularization* has been defined in a half-dozen ways in recent discussions.[20] Although each of these definitions has its own nuances, two basic connotations of *secularization* can be distilled from them all. First, many see secularization as a process of *replacement* of religious faith with faith in scientific principles. This concept goes back to the beginnings of modern Western science, when scientists first dared to set aside religion's view of reality, at least temporarily, in order to consider and evaluate data objectively. Thus Copernicus and Galileo were secularists in that they repudiated the belief—then a religious doctrine—that the earth is the center of the universe.

The logical extreme of secularism, in this view, is refusing to grant credence to any assertion about people, the world, or the universe that cannot be empirically verified. While some view with alarm and others with joy such a

---

[19] Andrew M. Greeley, *The Denominational Society* (Glenview, Ill.: Scott, Foresman, 1972), p. 127.

[20] Larry Shriner, "The Concept of Secularization in Empirical Research," *Journal for the Scientific Study of Religion* 6, no. 2 (1967), 207–20.

displacement of religious faith with faith in the scientific method, many on both sides see such secularization as a trend in which people evidence less and less interest in sacred and supernatural phenomena, as religious doctrines and institutions lose prestige and influence, with the possible ultimate result of a religionless society emerging.

Note, however, that no simple dichotomy exists of secular scientists hailing the replacement of religious faith with scientific faith versus religionists decrying such replacement. The popular Protestant theologian Harvey Cox, for example, welcomes secularization and sees it as a fulfillment of biblical themes and sources. He defines *secularization* in terms of "emancipation"—as the "liberation of man from religious and metaphysical tutelage, the turning of his attention away from other worlds and toward this one"[21] Cox's view may thus be regarded as a distinct variation on the "secularization-as-replacement" theme, one in which fulfillment is emphasized as a form of replacement.

The second general understanding of *secularization* is that it is a process of increasing differentiation between the religious and the secular (nonreligious) spheres of life—a process, moreover, coinciding with and perhaps in part resulting from increasing specialization within society as it grows and becomes more urbanized and industrialized.[22] Some who hold to the differentiation definition of *secularization* cite the increasing "privatization" of faith—the process of compartmentalizing the religious and the secular, of regarding religion as a mystical, personal, experiential phenomenon that one does not share with others.

Others subscribing to the differentiation view note that public manifestations of religion are becoming more scarce. One piece of evidence supporting this view would be the recent Supreme Court decisions that have tended to eliminate religious elements from public life, particularly from the public schools.

The haunting question that pervades the above discussion and a myriad of other allegations of spreading secularization is whether such signs reflect gains by "secular" forces and points of view at the expense of religion, or whether religion in its basic sense has remained essentially unaffected. Conceivably the essence of religion may be enjoying greater strength and influence today than during the heyday of the church type of religious organization in Europe or the early days of state churches in the United States. Further, "privatization" of religion need not mean that religion is not in evidence in people's actions, attitudes, and decisions. Also, many former public manifestations of religion that are no longer in evidence may have been ritualistic, pro forma actions that signified little and influenced people even less.

21 Harvey Cox, *The Secular City* (New York: Macmillan, 1965), p. 17.

22 Talcott Parsons, "Christianity and Modern Industrial Society," in *Sociological Theory, Values, and Socio-Cultural Change*, ed. Edward A. Tiryakin (New York: Free Press, 1963), pp. 33–70.

The point we are making is that before undertaking any analysis of secularization, one must specify one's operational definitions of the variables under discussion, for the conclusions one reaches about secularization are inevitably influenced by what one regards as the valuable features of religion and whether these features are perceived as threatened or disappearing, as well as by what one understands religion to be in the first place. That is, is the focus and concern on the preservation of the institution as presently constituted? Or is one concerned about what might be happening to the "essence" of religion, apart from its institutional manifestations.

But all we wish to do at this point is raise the issue of secularization, not resolve it. For one thing, we need the information and discussion that follows in this chapter to "flesh out" the issue before trying to answer the question. Secondly, establishing operational definitions of *religion* and *secularization* will be more helpful in understanding both the current status and the future of religion in the United States than will premature conclusions about secularization.

One reason that definitive conclusions about secularization are so difficult to reach is that contemporary American religion evidences numerous seeming paradoxes. While total church membership has declined somewhat from mid-1960s highs, and many mainline denominations have been experiencing membership losses, some religious groups have been advancing with firm strides if not leaps and bounds so far as membership is concerned. There is evidence of growing disenchantment with traditional religious forms among young people, yet a broad-based attempt to recapture the "real Jesus" and "authentic Christianity" constitutes the Jesus movement—a movement primarily of young people. In 1966 many Protestant theologians were busy proclaiming the "death of God," yet only seven years later over a hundred denominations and religious associations from the United States and twenty from Canada determined to "evangelize the nations" in 1973 as they banded together under the banner "Key '73"—so named after Carl F. H. Henry, editor of *Christianity Today,* and held the initial planning meetings at the Marriott Key Bridge Motor Hotel in Arlington, Virginia, under a grant from the Billy Graham Evangelistic Association. And by 1980 some religious leaders were organizing to take over political parties and processes as they joined the Moral Majority and other groups like it. Finally there is much emphasis within denominations on employing modern techniques of management, cost accounting, and computer technology, yet one observes little progress in eliminating duplication of effort by putting ecumenical ideology into practice. Such paradoxes (or seeming paradoxes) simply highlight the importance of one's decisions regarding which phenomena to consider in reaching conclusions about secularization on the one hand or "religionization" on the other. We do indeed have to be concerned about both what operational definitions and what measures of these concepts we adopt.

One of the best descriptions of secularization from the differentiation perspective is Robert Bellah's in his account of the historical evolution of religion through five stages. A dominant theme within this evolutionary process, according to Bellah, is the process of making increasingly more sophisticated distinctions and differentiations between the sacred or supernatural and the secular. This process has culminated, in the fifth stage (the modern period), in a breakdown of the dualistic distinction between the sacred and the secular, and its replacement by a multidimensional view of life and reality.[23] At this final stage, everything, including religion, is seen as revisable (though not all people see it this way, of course). Removed, or in the process of being removed, are such "either-or" dualistic descriptions of reality as *this world–other world, sacred-profane, good-evil, salvation-damnation.* Absolutism is replaced with relativity. The search of people for meaning is no longer confined within religious institutions or limited to traditional religious formulations. Such concepts as *situation ethics* and *process theology* typify the modern period. Certain traditional concepts and approaches from the past (*orthodoxy, sin,* and *moral law,* for example) are nevertheless retained by some and appear not about to disappear completely in the near future. This latter observation, of course, only reinforces Bellah's point, for a diversity of approaches and expressions and a broad range of views and interpretations are characteristic of religion in the modern period.

It is of interest that in Bryan Wilson's extended discussion of secularization[24] he suggests that denominational diversity has itself promoted secularization by providing for people a diversity of religious choice and in providing institutional expression of social differences and diversity. This can be seen as support for the view of secularization as differentiation. That is, it is not that the ideas or values of religion have necessarily become less important, but that there is increasing competition among those ideas, values, and religious systems. And there is a great deal of choice, with some traditional religious systems losing adherents and proponents that in an age gone by could have been considered guaranteed members by parentage and culture.

Consistent with this view is Wilson's suggestion that ecumenism is a manifestation, not of religious vigor, but of secularization (in a sense, weakness). Perhaps we should say, not a "manifestation of secularization," but another outcome of or response to secularization by which religious groups hope to recoup some lost influence. Or, as Wilson suggests, ecumenism can become a new focus of attention (a "new faith") when other facets of theology and faith are challenged or debunked.[25]

---

[23] Robert N. Bellah, "Religious Evolution," *American Sociological Review* 29, no. 3 (1954), 358–74.

[24] Bryan Wilson, *Religion in Secular Society* (London: C. A. Watts & Co., 1966), p. 30.

[25] Ibid., p. 126.

THE CONFLICT OVER THE
PURPOSE OF RELIGION

A fourth feature of contemporary American religion which adds a dimension to our consideration of the future of religion is the controversy over the purpose of religion. Is it for the personal benefit of its practitioners—that is, for the sake of their possible ultimate eternal salvation, in addition to their feelings of well-being, comfort, and reinforcement of life-style? Or is religion primarily a vehicle for helping those with a diversity of human needs and problems?

This debate over religion's functions and purposes, pitting social service versus self-service, is certainly not brand new. It represents a dilemma in American society at least as old as the Social Gospel movement that emerged in the last half of the nineteenth century and the counterchallenge by fundamentalism that followed. Yet the issue has been updated. Not that either perspective or emphasis ever disappeared. Both have remained viable, and in fact have in many instances coexisted within the same denomination. But the original social-gospel or social-service emphasis became institutionalized, in the sense that denominations established specialized commissions, boards, and subsidiary institutions to handle that aspect of their work. It may have been a part of the annual budget of both the local congregation and the national denomination and called "benevolences." It supported orphanages, hospitals, schools for the physically or mentally handicapped, and the like. Or it may have been supported through annual fund-raising drives as peoples' hearts were touched by an emotional appeal and they made a contribution. In any case, once a religious group's social-service and welfare concerns became primarily the responsibility of specialized personnel and agencies operating in the group's name, these same concerns were easily relegated to a peripheral dimension of most church members' lives.

However, with the emergence of the Civil Rights movement in the late 1950s and early 1960s, with the intensified American involvement in the war in Southeast Asia, and amid growing publicity and concern over such domestic social issues as poverty, capital punishment, abortion, nuclear power, and environmental pollution, individual church members and ad hoc religious groups began involving themselves in the issues. They urged their religious groups to become similarly involved and in a real sense forced an issue that had long lain dormant. Protestant, Catholic, and Jewish clergy began participating in civil rights marches, sit-ins, and demonstrations; administrators of denominational social-service programs began to urge more substantial support for existing and additional programs; Martin Luther King, Jr., challenged church people of all colors to support the struggle of black citizens for freedom and dignity. Seminaries intensified their efforts by offering new courses in social ethics and concerns and by implementing social action field-work programs. Denominations began issuing position statements supporting, at least in general terms, the rights of minority and disprivileged groups. Young seminary graduates assuming the leadership of congregations began preaching a gospel that included more than personal comfort and salvation. A "new breed" began to enter the ministry.

The outcome of all this was a crisis of direction or purpose so far as organized religion was concerned. That is, organized religion was caught in the middle of the agonizing confrontation of individual versus social concerns, personal comfort and salvation versus social welfare and help for the disprivileged.

Not that those who championed the social-concern emphasis always saw these as polar alternatives. Certainly most people who emphasized social service in the name of religion spoke of it as a concomitant of traditional individual salvation and comfort emphases, though some at least implicitly urged social service emphases at the expense of individual ones. It all became an issue when the idea left the seminaries and the resolution-forming conferences and conventions and began confronting the local congregations. Then the allegations and accusations implied by such book titles as *The Suburban Captivity of the Churches* and *The Comfortable Pew* became meaningful.[26] The message of these and similar analyses of organized religion in the 1960s was that churches not only were self-serving but probably would not change. The direct implication was that large numbers of both laypersons and clergy sought to retain the individual emphasis of the church at all costs—perhaps out of ideological commitment to the idea that salvation is the only true concern of churches, or perhaps becaue of inertia related to the comfort and security and meaningful interpersonal relationships the church provided many people.

In *The Gathering Storm in the Churches* (1969), Jeffrey Hadden provided data from various studies to support his contention that a wide gap existed between many laypersons and growing numbers of clergy on the salvation versus social service issue. Centering his discussion on support for the civil rights issue, Hadden pointed out that although a great majority of Americans interviewed in one study (86 percent) agreed that "the best mark of a person's religiousness is the degree of his concern for others," nearly half (49 percent) of the same sample felt that "clergy should stick to religion and not concern themselves with social, economic, and political questions." Further, nearly three-fourths (72 percent) admitted they would be upset if their minister, priest, or rabbi were to participate in a picket line or demonstration. Only slightly more than a third (37 percent) professed being "basically sympathetic with Northern ministers and students who have gone to the South to work for civil rights." By way of contrast, on this last issue 64 percent of the clergy interviewed expressed sympathy for such active civil rights involvement.[27]

---

[26] Gibson Winter, *The Suburban Captivity of the Churches* (Garden City, N.Y.: Doubleday, 1961); Pierre Berton, *The Comfortable Pew* (Philadelphia: Lippincott, 1965).

[27] Hadden, *The Gathering Storm*, pp. 132, 134, 136.

Such data reflect not only the conflict over the purpose of religion and the proper aims of the church, in which denominations have tended to lean strongly in one direction or the other, but also the conflict between clergy and laypeople within a given denomination, particulary those denominations that have tended to emphasize salvation. As a result of the latter conflict, Hadden feels, the traditional authority of clergy is gradually eroding and laypeople are beginning to "think for themselves" when their personal views of the purpose of religion are challenged. Such intradenominational conflicts are not new in themselves. Because the number of people involved may be greater, however, the traditional techniques religious groups have used for handling internal diversity may no longer be adequate. Agencies, "special ministries," and monastic orders with a social-service emphasis no longer seem to provide enough openings to accommodate the number of clergy and serious laypersons committed in this direction. Thus the "segmentation of radicalism" technique that Phillip Hammond and Robert Mitchell suggest has been widely used by religious groups can no longer contain the challenge to tradition as it has in the past.[28] While radicals at one time could be "kicked upstairs" into administrative positions or directed into campus ministries where contact with rank-and-file laity in standard congregations was minimal, such tactics are less effective today. It is interesting that falling back on such options assumes the group is not particularly interested in facing very directly the problems that the challengers are raising.

In general, however, the "crisis" of the salvation versus social concern issue seems to have abated somewhat. Many of the major objectives of the Civil Rights movement have been achieved, at least regarding legislation; the Vietnam War has ended; social problems and solutions that appeared simple have been recognized as complex; considerable backlash against social-welfare programs has set in; and new issues continue to surface that make a dichotomy of salvation versus social concern not so simple to maintain. Concentrating on a single, specialized issue such as women's rights, gay rights, or abortion reform need not place a protagonist at total odds with a congregation that pursues its own comfort, especially if he or she does not expect much participation or commitment from the congregation.

The whole issue of why there has been a reduction of such pressures is exceedingly complex, however, and thus the following observations are perhaps only a few of the factors that need to be considered: (1) Social-service-oriented clergy have made up the bulk of those who have left the ministry—and their numbers have been substantial in all faiths—apparently feeling that they could "do their thing" better in a secular setting. Moreover, the departure of such ministers may itself indicate that the salvation emphasis is still dominant. (2) Financial pressures have forced denominations to eliminate

---

[28] Phillip E. Hammond and Robert E. Mitchell, "Segmentation of Radicalism: The Case of the Protestant Campus Minister," *American Journal of Sociology* 71, no. 2 (1965), 133–43.

some of the administrative positions that formerly served as sources of and encouragement for dissidence. (3) The halt of growth in church membership (see Table 13–1) has tightened the job market for clergy. Not only are clergy less horizontally mobile within the denomination, but the job market outside is also less open. Such a constriction may have prompted some clergy, perhaps quite unconsciously, to accommodate themselves to the attitudes, both spoken and unspoken, of the congregations they serve. (4) In some denominations controversy has shifted to more traditional theological issues. (5) Some laypersons who objected most strongly to what they defined as at best a dilution and at worst a perversion or betrayal of the proper purpose of the church have left their denominations for more conservative ones that still emphasize salvation and personal goals. (6) A well-organized countermovement, of which the so-called Moral Majority is a prominent example (cf. Chapter 6), has arisen within the ranks of Christian denominations. Such groups explicitly aim to undo some of the earlier efforts of more liberal religious social-service efforts in the areas of welfare and abortion reform, liberalization of rights for minorities (homosexuals and women, for example), and curtailment of the military machine.

It appears that the first wave of the most recent salvation versus social action controversy is past. There is some indication that the interest in social concerns has fallen victim to the mood of the nation, as people have become more concerned with such urgent personal goals as keeping a job when others are losing theirs, maintaining financial solvency while inflation forges ahead, and staying healthy as new dangers from cancer-inducing agents are made public constantly. Further, the stridency of many of the victims of social inequities who have shouted "Black Power," "Gay Rights," and "Women's Liberation" has tended to discourage some of the more faint-hearted—they did not intend to go to "war," but only to help the helpless.

It is of more than passing interest that the "social-service" churchpeople of a liberal stripe, and the "Moral Majority" churchpeople of a conservative stripe, though far apart ideologically and theologically, proceed from a similar premise. That is that religious organizations can be used to apply political and social pressure to help bring about the social change the group desires.

As we mention again the New Christian Right it is important to note that a new twist to the salvation versus social action issue has been added only very recently. It is the new combination of conservative religion and social views of the New Christian Right, with highly explicit attempts to influence social action. That social action has included (1) high-powered urging of voters to elect some and defeat others who were running for high public office; (2) attempts to influence members of Congress and the president and advisors all around to pass Constitutional amendments and other forms of legislation that would ban abortion, permit if not require prayers in public schools, and restrict the civil rights of homosexuals; (3) a campaign to discredit the candidacy of the first female justice of the U.S. Supreme Court, Sandra Day

O'Conner, on the basis of assessment by representatives of the New Christian Right of her stands on such issues as abortion.

THE CONTINUING
TRADITIONAL THEOLOGICAL
CONTROVERSY

What we intend to discuss now is related to the discussion just completed in the sense that the question of salvation versus social service is clearly a theological issue. After all, defining the purpose of religion and of religious institutions is a central theological concern. Here, however, we wish to look at what can probably best be termed the *traditional theological question*—that is, what is true doctrine? In a real sense, then, what we observe happening in several denominations in the United States at the present time is a reenactment of the fundamentalist-modernist controversy that began around the turn of this century and culminated in 1925 with the debates between Clarence Darrow and William Jennings Bryan in the Scopes "monkey trial" (discussed in Chapter 10).

Actually the issue exists at two levels. First, some denominations that either did not face the question settled by fundamentalists to their own satisfaction fifty years ago or faced them and came down squarely on the fundamentalist side of the fence are now facing these questions anew. They find themselves arguing internally about the nature and authority of the Bible, the Virgin Birth and Resurrection of Christ, whether Jonah really lived, whether the miracles recorded in the Bible really happened as described, and so on. These are old battles, to be sure, but within some denominations they are being fought for the first time.

The second level at which doctrinal controversy is occurring is in a real sense more basic, and to some degree it affects all of American Christianity—and world Christianity, too, for that matter. This a crisis of basic faith—what Hadden calls the "crisis of belief,"[29]—by which is implied the posing of questions about the fundamental nature and basis for the Christian religion. These are *not* the ancient, enduring questions such as the proper mode of baptism (whether to immerse, pour, or sprinkle) or whether the relationship of the bread and wine to the body and blood of Christ in the Lord's Supper (Holy Communion, Eucharist) is one of transubstantiation (Catholic), representation (Reformed), or real presence (Lutheran)—these we might call superficial issues, even though protagonists for various points of view would object to such a designation. Today the issues seem more fundamental. That is, the kinds of questions frequently raised are whether God in fact exists (regardless of how you define the concept of the Trinity), whether baptism is valid and necessary

[29] Hadden, *The Gathering Storm*, pp. 15–26.

in the first place (regardless of how much water is used), whether Christ really lived and died and rose again—not whether wine or grape juice should be used in the Lord's Supper. In other words, at this second level are questions about the reality of God, as well as assumptions about the relationship of God with people, that have been essentially unchallenged until now.

Returning to the first issue or level of theological dispute, we observe that even denominations which appeared to resolve the fundamentalist-modernist issue years ago by camping on the liberal side of the fence do not evidence the internal unanimity today that one might expect. Thus although a majority of Congregationalists, Methodists, and Episcopalians cannot accept without reservation that Jesus was born of a virgin, or that miracles actually happened just as the Bible says they did, some of these people do. On the question of Jesus' Virgin Birth, for example, 21 percent of Congregationalists, 34 percent of Methodists, and 39 percent of Episcopalians accept the doctrine without reservation. Similarly, 28 percent of Congregationalists, 37 percent of Methodists, and 41 percent of Episcopalians accept the biblical account of miracles as completely true.[30] That is, although such denominations may have essentially resolved the fundamentalist-modernist controversy (if only in the sense of tolerating a diversity of views and beliefs), some of their members still hold to traditional beliefs and might even feel reasonably comfortable in another, theologically more conservative denomination.

Of even greater contemporary relevance is what is happening in religious groups which have continued to maintain an official position supporting traditional beliefs and interpretations of Scripture, and in which (according to survey data) members have consistently expressed high levels of concurrence with these doctrinal formulations, but in which an erosion of doctrinal solidarity appears to have begun. Two prime examples are the Southern Baptist Convention and The Lutheran Church—Missouri Synod. Both groups have long proclaimed their adherence to a conservative version of Christianity and continue in an official way to subscribe to traditional doctrine—essentially what we have referred to earlier as fundamentalist doctrine. However, voices throughout both groups have challenged and questioned the official traditional positions by urging a more open-ended approach to many historical definitions and understandings of Christian doctrine without necessarily denying them.

A controversy that had been going on for some time between the elected leadership of the Missouri Synod and the faculty at its major seminary (Concordia, St. Louis) heated up considerably after the church's 1973 convention in New Orleans (waggishly called the "Second Battle of New Orleans"). At that time the delegates approved as binding on all clergy and seminary professors a highly specific and conservative statement of faith, approved the censure of dissident faculty members at the St. Louis seminary, and set in mo-

---

[30] Charles Y. Glock and Rodney Stark, *Christian Beliefs and Anti-Semitism* (New York: Harper & Row, Pub., 1966), pp. 9–10.

tion procedures for purging theological deviants. The latter process proceeded to the point in early 1974 of a majority of the seminary faculty being relieved of their positions.

They promptly established a "Seminary in Exile" (Seminex), subsequently renamed Christ Seminary, that continues today as a focal point for a group of several dozen congregations that broke away from the Synod and founded the Association of Evangelical Lutheran Churches (AELC).

A powerful biblical inerrancy faction within the Southern Baptist Convention has been following a similar route to "clean up" the theological instruction at its seminaries and enforce its views of Scripture and traditional doctrinal understanding upon seminary trustees and faculty. The inerrancy proponents, under the leadership of Paige Patterson, president of the Criswell Center of Biblical Studies in Dallas, aim to cut short the drift toward "liberalism" they sense has been occurring in this large denomination. A major goal in the early 1980s is to control the election of convention presidents who appoint members to major committees within the denomination.

Quite clearly, those who oppose such deviance and diversity do not recognize the sociological realities that any large group faces, particularly as it grows larger. Any such group will inevitably have greater deviance and will find itself tolerating more deviance. In fact, we would suggest that the appearance of diversity and controversy in such groups is not nearly so amazing as the fact that these were forestalled or at least kept hidden for so long. The point is that unanimity does not exist, cannot exist, and that diversity will only increase, unless one faction accumulates sufficient power essentially to split the group formally into two groups or force out the more extreme and vocal deviates.

We now return to the second level at which the doctrinal issue or crisis of belief is operating—the questioning, or perhaps more accurately, the seeming questioning, of the basic understanding of God himself—his nature and reality and his activity in the world. As indicated before, various theologians within both Protestantism and Catholicism seem at least superficially to be characterizing fundamental religious presuppositions, such as the reality of God and how he has chosen to relate to people, as problematical. Certainly great numbers of both clergy and laypersons interpret what these theologians are saying as direct challenges to the very foundations of Christianity. Whether they are, in fact, such challenges is more difficult to determine and is certainly beyond the province of the sociologist and as such outside the scope of this volume. However, it should be noted that all such theologians—whether demythologizers such as Rudolph Bultman, or "theology of hope" proponents such as Wolfhart Pannenburg, Jurgen Moltman, and Hans Hoekendijk, or foundational theologians, or "death of God" theologians, or popularizers such as Harvey Cox and John A. T. Robinson—all seem primarily concerned with "God-language," not just with God himself. For example, when a former Church of England Bishop John A. T. Robinson says that our image of God must go, he is not denying the existence of God or proposing that somehow we banish him from the universe; rather, he is challenging our traditional conceptualization of God, a conceptualization that he regards as inadequate for today. Whether other, related theologians are similarly inclined or whether they are going farther and in fact proclaiming or even celebrating the "death" of God is a matter for theologians, not sociologists, to decide. That such suggestions have disturbed, even shocked, people in the church is, however, an understatement. That such statements and discussions have cut some people loose from "the faith" is a possibility. That such issues leave the future of Christian theology and conceptualization wide open is a certainty.

Quite clearly, then, the future of religion throughout the world promises to hold excitement, whether one is inside or outside the church, whether one is a theologian or a sociologist, for there is no doubt that new concepts, formulations, and approaches to theology are still emerging and stirring up hornets' nests of controversy and discussion. For the sociologist, following these controversies will be fascinating, and assessing possible new directions for religion will be challenging to say the least.

NEW RELIGIOUS MOVEMENTS AND CULTS

If the proverbial "person in the street" knows anything about current developments on the religious scene, he or she is likely aware of new groups that appear and behave in somewhat unusual if not bizarre ways. We may see members of the Hare Krishna movement with their shaven heads and saffron robes. We see notices and advertisements about this or that guru touring in the United States to extol the benefits of his Eastern religious philosophy. We may encounter young people in the neighborhood who talk freely about being really "turned on" to Jesus and take pride in the semiderogatory designation "Jesus freaks." We may know of someone in a traditional mainline Protestant or Catholic church who talks about his or her fantastic experiences with the Holy Spirit and how he or she has the gift of "speaking in tongues."

While one might be tempted to observe that offbeat and unconventional religious expressions are certainly nothing new, such an observation would not do justice to the proliferation of "new" religious expressions in the United States today. Although there is probably nothing in the "new"religious expressions and forms that has not appeared in another age or culture before, some of it is new to the American religious heritage.

That American society—world society, for that matter—is in a changing, fluid, uncertain state is a truism that is obvious to most and appears incredibly trite on the printed page. Yet this observation is fundamental to any discussion of new religious movements and cults. As contemporary people have begun to sense the serious, perhaps disastrous, repercussions of their past and present actions upon the future, they have become extremely discomfited. Unplanned and unlimited procreation appears to be leading to unbearable population pressures. Uncontrolled and expanding use of natural resources portends not only their disappearance but also a polluted and potentially unviable environment. Securing a college education and specialized academic training has produced a surplus of labor in a host of career fields. Blind faith in a political system and entrusting national leadership with virtually limitless power has resulted in the scandal of Watergate. The cultivation of suburban lawns and the accumulation of gas-powered engines to traverse winter snows and summer waters has resulted for many in less satisfaction and fulfillment than was confidently expected. Managed economies have on the average produced little more personal economic security than unmanaged ones. The unresponsiveness of governmental bureaucracy to personal cries of anguish, whether over undeclared wars or impoverishment and discrimination, has provoked both rebellion and cynicism, both strident assertiveness and navel-contemplating despair.

Both as a consequence and as a concomitant of these and other factors, traditional religious forms, answers, and solutions have for many become unsatisfying, even empty, and certainly quite irrelevant. Even the "civil religion" that Bellah cites as having been a unifying factor in American society almost from the founding of the nation has broken down.[31] One consequence of the dissatisfaction with traditional religious forms that many people have expressed has been that religious organizations have made attempts at restructuring and reforming themselves. Yet another consequence has been individual and small-group experimentation with new religious forms, ideologies, and structures. Most of the "new" religious activity centers around personal quests for meaning, purpose, and roots in an unsettled and quavering, if not fractured, social environment. Who am I? Where am I going? Where do I — and my whole world, for that matter—fit vis-a-vis not only the history of this planet, but the cosmos itself? These are fundamental religious questions of personal identification and relationship with forces that affect both personal and societal destinies. One result of trying to answer them has been increasing experimentation with new and reborn or rediscovered religious forms and emphases.

Neopentecostalism

We shall focus on two general types of new religious forms. The first, which appears to be as much an adult as a youth phenomenon, is the *charismatic* or *(neo-)pentecostal movement* that has emerged within both Catholic and mainline Protestant denominations. The quest for special experiences with the Holy Spirit and his special gifts in the form of glossolalia ("speaking in

---

[31] Robert N. Bellah, "Civil Religion in America," *Daedalus* 96, no. 1 (1967), 1–21.

tongues"), trances, miraculous healing, and bodily expression in dancing and spirit-possession is not at all new. A solid tradition within Protestantism that goes back to its beginnings in the fifteenth and sixteenth centuries has developed parallel to the dominant denominational Protestantism. The healing evangelists of the type of Oral Roberts and scores of other contemporary examplars are known to most everyone. The "snake cults" in Appalachia in which the special spiritual gift of handling poisonous serpents and quaffing poisonous strychnine without harm periodically hit the public press. But middle-class denominational Catholicism and Protestantism have habitually dismissed such activities as appropriate only for lower-class persons in need of some bizarre form of escape in order to adjust to their life situation, but hardly satisfying behavior for middle-class and upper-class types.

Thus what is new, and from certain perspectives surprising, is the emergence very recently of pentecostal subgroups in the traditional Christian denominations. Not that anything approaching a majority of these denominations are becoming charismatic or pentecostal, or that such a majority will appear in the future. But enough have emerged not only to elicit concern and censure from denominational authorities but to merit sociological interest. Although the numerical strength of those practicing this neopentecostalism is not overwhelming, estimates have been as high as five hundred thousand persons spread throughout the major denominations in the United States in 1972,[32] and in 1976 the Gallup poll reported an estimated three million persons involved in some way with the charismatic movement.[33]

Although the neopentecostal (now commonly called "charismatic") movement can trace its genesis back to isolated cases in the 1950s, it first gained public attention in 1960 when Dennis Bennett, an Episcopalian minister in Van Nuys, California, resigned his office in a effort to stem incipient divisiveness over pentecostal practices by himself and some members of his congregation. Apparently publicity of this episode served as a catalyst to bring to the surface other instances of charismatic activity in nonpentecostal churches. In 1961 support was added from the academic community when nineteen students and one faculty member at Yale University reported receiving the baptism of the Holy Spirit. Similar reports came out of Dartmouth and Princeton soon after. A decade later the movement had been established in all mainline Protestant denominations and among Roman Catholics and Eastern Orthodox as well.

In most cases, regardless of denominational affiliation, charismatics emphasize that they do not wish to separate from their parent churches, but simply want to aid in revitalizing their congregations, their denominations, and Christianity itself by testifying to the extraordinary work of God brought into

[32] St. Louis Post Dispatch, October 29, 1972.
[33] Reported in Constant H. Jacquet, Jr., ed. Yearbook of American and Canadian Churches, 1980 (Nashville: Abingdon Press, 1980), p. 257.

their lives through the power of the Holy Spirit. Not that such experiences are for everyone, they feel; but they are to be seen as a viable option for those who are touched.

Watson E. Miller sees a possible source of this new emphasis in traditional Christian churches in the fact that "glossolalia (the ability to speak words and phrases of a language unlearned and unknown to the speaker) may . . . be a loud protest against the cold impersonality that sometimes characterizes institutionalized worship."[34] If we add to Miller's suggestion the observation that, except for the occasional conventions of charismatics that attract hundreds and even thousands of people (such as the annual meeting of Catholic charismatics at the University of Notre Dame), charismatics tend to meet in small groups where one observes interpersonal warmth, openness, trust, and emotional support, sometimes even without "speaking in tongues," we may be explaining some of the attractiveness of the movement. Amid rapid social change, the uprooting of many traditional institutional moorings, the breaking of contact with families and friends through job mobility, and other concomitants of contemporary American life, many people are especially receptive to opportunities for open, trusting, intimate contact with others. In very simple sociological terms, they are seeking primary groups and relationships to replace those they have lost.

All such comments remain for the present essentially hypotheses, however, as little research data are yet available. It is nevertheless interesting to observe — although such observations are not well quantified or validated — that some standard demographic variables do not, on the surface at least, seem to apply to charismatics; that is, they are of both sexes, of a full age range, both urban and rural, of a wide variety of occupations and levels of educations, and of a diversity of religious backgrounds (for example, from both liturgical and nonliturgical denominations). Whether any of these or other factors are significantly related to receptivity to or participation in the charismatic movement is not yet clear. There is some indication that students who are into Catholic pentecostalism are more likely to be female than male, from a strong Catholic background and commitment, majoring in fields other than science or engineering, and neither married nor engaged.[35]

It is significant that whereas denominations at first attempted to discourage the movement by censuring congregations and particularly clergy who participated, much of that opposition has been modified. Thus the movement today, though not necessarily encouraged, is increasingly tolerated. In a sense, this growing tolerance undermines one source of growth for charismatic groups, according to Gerlach and Hine. These researchers found that among

[34] Watson E. Miller, "Glossolalia: Christianity's 'Counterculture' Amidst a Silent Majority," *Christian Century,* September 27, 1972, p. 951.

[35] Michael I. Harrison, "Sources of Recruitment to Catholic Pentecostalism," *Journal for the Scientific Study of Religion* 13, no. 1 (March, 1974), 53.

important growth factors for the groups they studied was the "psychology of persecution." Ridicule, nonacceptance, and rejection by traditional denominational churches served to stimulate growth, whereas in those instances where local denominational officials did not oppose the movement, recruitment was more difficult.[36]

From the perspective of the host institution (churches) within which the charismatic movement is occurring, such activity would normally and naturally be resisted because it is by definition beyond the control of the host organization. Charismatic activity and authority is a challenge to traditional, organizationally legitimated authority. Who knows what such open-ended authority from outside the organization (the Holy Spirit moving as and where it wills) will produce? The only apparent explanation for the relative tolerance of the movement on the part of the denominations is that most within the movement insist that they are not out to destroy the organization or even to withdraw themselves from it, but want to offer an internal, optional form of religious experience and worship; they desire simply to enrich what institutional religion already has to offer.

The Cult Movement

While the charismatic or neopentecostal movement in American religion is new by virtue of its development within standard denominational religion, pentecostalism is nonetheless an old tradition in Christianity that has attained a considerable measure of legitimacy in its own denominational forms. Another recent development in American religion, however, does not fit within standard denominational forms and is in fact an alternative, if not a challenge, to such standard forms. We are referring to what can fairly properly be called the proliferation of cults in American religion.

Cults in general are of course not at all new to American religion. They abounded in the nineteenth century, when they were represented by such religious utopian communities as the Shakers, the Oneida Perfectionists, and the Amana society, as well as by such cults as Christian Science, the Theosophical Society, and Divine Science. The first half of the twentieth century also witnessed the emergence of many cults—the Church of Truth Universal—AUM, Psychiana, and the Fellowship of Divine Truth, to name just three.

What seems new in cult development in the second half of this century are two features: (1) a change in the origin or base of the belief and practices system, and (2) a probable increase in the number of followers, though numbers are impossible to substantiate with assurance. Before we offer some tentative evidence in support of these observations, we must admit to the difficulty of making generalizations of any kind in the area of religious cults in the Unit-

---

[36] Luther P. Gerlach and Virginia H. Hine, "Five Factors Crucial to the Growth and Spread of a Modern Religious Movement," *Journal for the Scientific Study of Religion* 7, no. 1 (1968), 36.

ed States. In the first place, they exhibit a great diversity in focus and message. Thus comprehensive generalizations regarding all cults must of necessity be very broad. Secondly, consistent with our emphasis on the informal structure of cults as discussed in Chapter 5, they are likely not to have much in the way of printed material or creeds for an observer to analyze. They have fluid memberships and usually no firm membership statistics—or at least none that they are willing to publish or otherwise report publicly. Further, they are often localized and virtually unknown beyond a given locality or region.

Having acknowledged these methodological difficulties and the consequent tentativeness of our observations, we shall return to the two general features mentioned above. First, there is evidence of a strong Far Eastern religious influence in many American religious cults today, although not all contemporary cults by any means. Hinduism and Buddhism particularly serve as points of origin and orientation for many of them: Zen, Subud, Vajrayana Buddhism, Sufism, Meher Baba, I Ching, and scores of others. In most cases, these groups and their messages offer something dramatically different from most of Western religion (with the possible exception of some of the Catholic and Eastern Orthodox contemplative and eremitic monastic orders). Cults that arose during the last century and during most of this century were built strongly on either Western philosophy and Christianity or, at the farthest extreme, on Near Eastern religions such as Egyptian Rosicrucianism—but to very little extent on religions from the Far East. The exceptions to this were the New Thought and Theosophical cults that emerged seventy-five to one hundred years ago. Most modern (within the last twenty-five years) American cults share with them quite distinct strains of Hinduism and Buddhism—themes of meditation and getting right in your mind and body with the cosmic forces and fluids of the universe. It seems that Far Eastern Hindu and Buddhist influence in American cult religion is more conscious and explicit than before.

The second point we want to make about modern cults, regarding the numbers of their members, is, as already indicated, impossible to document—and we are on even less solid ground when talking about the past. Our impression is, however, that there are more people attracted to religious cults in the United States today than there were in the past. Estimates of membership numbers for some of them, made by Peter Rowley, provide a numerical context.[37]

Scientology	600,000	I Ching	125,000
Nichiren Shoshu	200,000	Yoga	125,000
Spiritual Scientists	150,000	Nation of Islam	
Transcendental		("Black Muslims")	100,000
Meditation	125,000	Bahai	100,000

[37] Peter Rowley, New Gods in America (New York: D. McKay, 1971), pp. 3–4.

Association for Research		Satanic Cults	5,000
and Enlightenment	13,000	Zen	2,000
Meher Baba	7,000	Subud	1,500
Gurdjieff	5,000	Hare Krishna	1,500
Witchcraft	5,000		

Estimates from the Gallup poll mentioned earlier suggest higher numbers later in the 1970s. Gallup reports 6 million people involved in Transcendental Meditation, 3 million in mysticism, and 2 million in Eastern religion.[38]
While there is likely much overlap in these figures (that is, many who get
counted in more than one category), and while some may have had only the
most passing and superficial of contact, the numbers are substantial and so
cannot be dismissed casually.

Another observation about contemporary cults that we might expect to
make, given the new age in which we live and the apparently greater Far Eastern influence on cults—namely, that the content of the cult message or gospel
is different today—should not be made at all. Certainly the Power, or Force,
or Spirit, or Method, or God is different from one group to another. But the
central idea inherent in cults both past and present is strikingly similar—that
is, they all emphasize a technique of "getting your mind together," of putting
mind and body in closer harmony by getting in tune with the energizing or
central power or force in the universe. It is truly striking, after listening to
members of various contemporary groups and reading their publications, to
realize that what each group defines as the problem to be overcome and what
each offers as the method for resolving that problem resemble so fundamentally every other group's definitions as to be essentially identical. The problem to
be solved is typically a highly integrated pair of issues: (1) Who am I and
where do I fit into the world? (Identity), and (2) How can I find peace and
unity of mind and body, of the spiritual and the material within me? The solution is typically a technique involving, on the one hand, meditation (perhaps
using yoga or related postures and exercises, or perhaps by repeating key
words and phrases such as one's personal mantra), and on the other hand,
small-group encouragement, support, and reinforcement. It appears to be crucial for this purpose that the cult be small and that members be capable of
close contact on a one-to-one basis or with at most a handful of others. In
this sense cults resemble, and perform functions similar to, the charismatic
groups within traditional denominations discussed in the previous section.

It is not at all surprising that such religious cults flourish today. This
author is personally surprised, not by their numbers and their followings, but
by the fact that there are not actually more people involved in them. Amid the
defilement of our natural environment, the violation of the integrity and freedom of people by all manner of exploitation, enslavement, and discrimination,

---

[38] Reported in Jacquet, *Yearbook of American Churches, 1980,* p. 257.

the hypocrisy and self-centeredness of one's fellows, the failure, as many young people see it, of science to solve our problems, and the overarching threat of planetary self-destruction, it is small wonder that many people who seek a way out find an answer in what religious cults offer.

Whether such an answer is a "cop-out" or indeed a way out we may not be certain. Is Charles A. Reich correct when he sees in the new "consciousness" typified by (though not found exclusively in) the new religious cults the great hope for America and the entire Western world?[39] Or do the ideas and strivings of these groups represent the end of the line, a last-ditch attempt by the misfits and the unloved to find peace and security? We certainly cannot say.

But we can say that the new American cults are asking religious questions and posing religious solutions, and that in many senses their members are more profoundly religious than many in standard religious organizations who have submerged the great religious questions and participate only perfunctorily and halfheartedly in ritual activities. In fact, Jacob Needleman strongly suggests that the "great value of this new 'religiosity' is that through it our young people are able to *entertain great ideas.*" In other words, part of the crisis of our civilization is that the great transcendent ideas that once dominated and defined people's lives have become choked to death by an impatient pragmatism that seldom thinks carefully before it acts.[40]

We would also suggest that the "success" of the new religious cults, in combination with the middle-aged vitality of some standard religious organizations, indicates clearly that religion, whether as an institution or as an absorbing quest for truth, is certainly not dead, nor about to die soon. People continue to ponder not only who and what they are but from whence they come and whither they are going. Is there any meaning and purpose in the world around them and, above all, is there any meaning and purpose for them as tiny, individual specks in the universe? Religion attempts to deal with such questions. As such religion has a future. In fact, it has a future to the extent that humanity has a future, because religion is an expression of the confrontation of people with their environment, both physical and social, and with each other. It is a reflection both of the precariousness of human existence and of the imperfections with which people relate to people. As such, religion in some form—or rather, in a variety of forms—not only is a part of society but will remain so.

[39] Charles Reich, *The Greening of America* (New York: Random House, 1970).

[40] Jacob Needleman, "Winds from the East: Youth and Counter-Cults," *Commonweal,* April 30, 1971, p. 189.

APPENDIX

How to Measure Religion

INTRODUCTION

The question of distinguishing the religious from the nonreligious is one that occurs in many contexts. Certainly individuals who are committed to a particular religious system are concerned about whether they meet their group's criteria for being religious: Am I a true believer? Have I committed the unpardonable sin? Are there any signs and indications that tell me whether I measure up or not?

Christian theologians talk about "marks" of Christianity, and theologians of every belief pore over sacred scriptures trying to distill the essential characteristics and behavior that sets the true believer apart from all others. "Do you believe in Jesus Christ as your only Savior?" "Do you bow toward Mecca at the specified five times daily?" "Do you belong to the Catholic Church and attend mass at least the minimum prescribed number of times a year?" "Do you abstain from pork and study Torah faithfully?"

Denominational administrators seek "indicators" of religiosity for the purpose of evaluating their programs. If, for example, certain congregations in their jurisdiction participate in a "Religious Enrichment Seminar" and consequently increase their contributions to the denomination's general fund, administrators may reason that this is a program to be urged on all the other congregations. Or if people who attended the denomination's parochial schools now attend church more often, contribute higher proportions of their income, and participate in the organizational life of the congregation more extensively than those who did not attend such schools, then such schools are most likely regarded as accomplishing their religious purpose.

Researchers in the sociology of religion also continually search for valid ways of defining the concept of "being religious"—what we will be calling religiosity from now on. Sociologists are specifically interested in identifying what constitutes religiosity for the purpose of measuring it in relation to other factors: Is the religious person different from a nonreligious person in any other respects? And if so, how? Is the religious person more humanitarian or less so? Is he or she more prejudiced or less? More economically successful or less? More likely to be politically liberal? Better "adjusted"? And so on.

One place to start in our attempt to define religiosity is the definition of religion that we arrived at in Chapter 1: Religion is a set of beliefs and practices, centered around a belief in the supernatural and an orientation toward the sacred, that are shared by members of a group. Thus we could say that anyone who is a member of a religious group, who believes certain things about the supernatural and the sacred, and who engages in certain activities associated with these beliefs is a religious person, and that everyone else is not. Would that it were so simple!

Some religious groups have approximated this approach in trying to distinguish the religious from the irreligious person. Historically, the Roman Catholic Church has maintained that any member who participated in a specified minimum number of ritual activities was a saved member of Christ's church, and that all others were not. Lutherans tended toward this approach also, identifying the true church and its members wherever the Word of God was taught and preached in purity, and wherever the sacraments were correctly administered.

Such neat definitions, however, leave several questions unanswered. Should any distinction be made, for example, between those who evidence maximum participation in the group's ritual activities and those who just "get by" with minimal participation? Or are such extremes to be considered equally religious when compared with others who do not participate in these activities at all? And what about the person who occasionally participates in the ritual but has not made a membership commitment? Is he or she therefore not religious? Or what about the person who participates occasionally, and who is a member, but actually is a disbeliever or at least doubts some of the group's central beliefs? Some people are more sincere in their religious beliefs than others; some are more enthusiastic in their ritual participation than others. Some "leave their religion at the church door," while others attempt to apply it in all life situations. Are all of these people religious? And if so, are they equally religious? And what about the person—to return to an issue left over from Chapter 1—who shares a group's belief but prefers to meditate and worship on his or her own?

Our definition of religion is less helpful than we might hope in determining people's religiosity because of a fundamental principle of sociology, namely, that most any characteristic that can be attributed to a given social phenomenon exists at some point on a *continuum*. That is, such characteristics typically are neither totally present nor totally absent, but exist to a greater or lesser degree along a range from high to low. For example, among business organizations classified as bureaucracies some organizations are more highly bureaucratized than others. Bureaucratic organizations may therefore be ranked from high to low along a continuum called "bureaucracy." Nations, to take another example, can be arranged along a continuum called "industrialization." Or people along continua called "authoritarianism," "prejudice," "self-motivation," and so on.

Similarly it is likely that people, if not organizations, may be located at various points on a continuum called "religiousness" or "religiosity." People intuitively assume this when they make statements and comparisons such as those that begin this chapter. Our problem here, however, is how to *operationalize* the concept of religiosity—how to translate such feelings into terms of observable characteristics that will permit us to make meaningful comparisons among people. Realize, of course, that we embark on this process, not in order to make invidious comparisons among people or to judge them, but solely in order to be able to determine the impact of the different ways in which people feel and express their religiosity.

Sociologists take two basic approaches to defining religiosity and applying it to their research. The first approach centers on people's affiliations with religious organizations or groups, according to which sociologists attempt to predict and observe differences in people's behavior and attitudes. Technically this approach focuses not so much on religiosity (which involves something going on inside the individual) as it does on the organization itself. This is appropriate because whenever we talk about the effect of religion on people's behavior we are assuming a religious group's influence somewhere along the line. The second approach to identifying religiosity deals with individuals and tends to disregard religious affiliations except as a possible control variable.

SOCIOLOGICAL DEFINITIONS OF RELIGIOSITY: GROUP AFFILIATION

First, we will look at the group affiliation approach. There are two principal variants here—really simply a matter of how specific the researcher wishes to become. The first is to categorize people according to major religious families, such as Protestant, Catholic, and Jewish (in Western societies), or Hindu, Muslim, Buddhist, and Christian (in Asian societies), or any number of other relevant sets of affiliations. Extensive research using such religious distinctions has been fruitful in showing different attitudes and behavior among such major groupings. For example, whereas 62 percent of the Catholics polled in one survey reported attending religious services at least once a week, only 25 percent of the Protestants polled and 12 percent of the Jews polled so reported.[1] And whereas 83 percent of Catholics and 76 percent of Protestants in the same survey reported that they regarded religion as "very important" in their lives, only 47 percent of Jews so reported.[2] In Lenski's 1959 survey in Detroit he found that while 42 percent of Jews had positive attitudes toward work, the proportions for white Protestants, black Protestants, and white Catholics were only 30 percent, 24 percent, and 23 percent respectively.[3] The same study revealed that only 11 percent of Jews, but 34 percent of white Protestants, 38 percent of black Protestants, and 66 percent of white Catholics, felt that divorce was always or usually wrong.[4] Questions about political party preference from the same survey revealed that the Republican party was preferred by 54 percent of white Protestants, 30 percent of white Catholics, 13 percent of black Protestants, and 3 percent of Jews.[5] These are only a few of the almost endless list of research findings documenting differences in attitude, behavior, and commitment among major religious groupings.

By the early 1960s, however, many sociologists began to point out that while research showing differences among such major groupings as Protestants, Catholics, and Jews may be revealing, it also tends to hide almost as much as it reveals, for these categories are still so broad that they obscure significant internal diversity. Primary objection focused on the Protestant category, which includes fundamentalists and other extremely conservative groups as well as theologically liberal groups that reject much of traditional Christian doctrine. Similar problems were seen to exist for the Catholic and Jewish categories as well—there are both liberal and conservative Catholics, and there are Reform, Conservative, and Orthodox Jews.

Moreover in surveys, even fairly large (and expensive) samples do not include enough members of, say, the various subcategories of Protestantism to make meaningful comparisons. For example, suppose you wanted to analyze social differences among various religious groups in the United States and at some point decided to make specific comparisons between Unitarians and Mennonites—two groups nearly at opposite extremes on a continuum called "Protestantism." Suppose you had been able to afford to survey a fairly large sample of one thousand persons representative of the United States population. Suppose also that your sampling techniques had worked perfectly and you had picked a truly proportionate representative sample. You would then

[1] Will Herberg, *Protestant-Catholic-Jew* (Garden City, N.Y.: Doubleday, 1956), p. 236. (Originally in "Do Americans Go to Church?" *Catholic Digest* [December, 1952], 5.)

[2] Ibid. (Originally in "How Important Religion Is to Americans," *Catholic Digest* [February, 1953], 8.

[3] Gerhard E. Lenski, *The Religious Factor* (Garden City, N.Y.: Doubleday, 1961), p. 84.

[4] Ibid., p. 150.

[5] Ibid., p. 125.

find when you went to your sample, theoretically at least, exactly eight-tenths of one Unitarian and nine-tenths of one Mennonite. You would also get only one-and-eight-tenths Seventh Day Adventists, nine Mormons, and eleven members of the United Church of Christ—hardly a sufficient number of any of these groups (not to mention a host of other small religious groups) to reach valid conclusions about any of them.

Mainline Protestant church bodies, however, such as Presbyterians, Methodists, Lutherans, Baptists, and Episcopalians, each have many more members; consequently they can provide sufficient numbers in national or area samples of a thousand or more persons to justify making comparisons among them. Thus evolved the second stage of utilizing religious affiliation as an independent variable when major subcategories of Protestants began to be studied. The research team of Charles Glock and Rodney Stark of the University of California at Berkeley, who were among the first to use this approach extensively, found significant differences among major Protestant denominations that one might have thought existed only among smaller groups which tend to hold more extreme views. For example, Glock and Stark discovered that on such a fundamental doctrinal question as the divinity of Jesus the proportion of members of major Protestant bodies who accept without reservation the traditional view—namely, that Jesus is the Son of God—and admit to having no personal doubts about it are as follows: 40 percent of Congregationalists, 54 percent of Methodists, 59 percent of Episcopalians, 72 percent of Presbyterians, 74 percent of Disciples of Christ, 74 percent of American Lutherans, 76 percent of American Baptists, 93 percent of Missouri Synod Lutherans, and 99 percent of Southern Baptists.[6] Differences among the same Protestant groups on the question of miracles is even more dramatic. The proportion of those who believe that miracles actually happened as described in the Bible are as follows: 28 percent of Congregationalists, 37 percent of Methodists, 41 percent of Episcopalians, 58 percent of Presbyterians, 62 percent of the Disciples of Christ, 62 percent of American Baptists, 69 percent of American Lutherans, 89 percent of Missouri Synod Lutherans, and 92 percent of Southern Baptists.[7] Or consider the somewhat less dramatic but still significant differences in proportion of persons who agree with the statement, "The races would probably get along just fine in this country if Communists and other radicals didn't stir up trouble": 33 percent of Congregationalists, 36 percent of Methodists and Disciples of Christ, 45 percent of both Episcopalians and American Baptists, 46 percent of Presbyterians, 50 percent of Missouri Synod Lutherans, 56 percent of American Lutherans, and 70 percent of Southern Baptists.[8] Religious affiliation among subdenominations within Protestantism apparently makes a difference.

[6] Charles Y. Glock and Rodney Stark, *Christian Beliefs and Anti-Semitism* (New York: Harper & Row, Pub., 1966), p. 7.

[7] Ibid., p. 10.

[8] Ibid., p. 168.

It is perhaps becoming obvious that we are straying from a strict definition or understanding of religiosity. What we have been doing—and will continue to do in this appendix—is indicating some of the major ways in which researchers have attempted to operationalize the concept of religiosity—that is identify a quantifiable measure that seems to measure or "get at" something of what religion is—in order to assess its effect or impact on people's behavior.

The two types of measurement we have already looked at are in reality subtypes of the affiliation measure, which focuses on the religious group to which a person belongs. In such cases how do we know whether a person is religious? We may simply consider a person religious if he or she professes to be a Protestant, a Catholic, a Jew, or a member of any other religious group, while the nonmember would be considered nonreligious, or at most less religious than the member. Although ultimately we may want to talk about the religiosity of individual people, we wind up focusing on the general or central tendencies of groups and differences among those groups—an important focus indeed, but hardly the whole package. At most, the focus on group differences measures the effect of formal religious differences among groups, primarily differences in belief and doctrine. What we lack are measures of differentiation in intensity or sincerity of belief and degree of religious interest. Such ideas are closer to the concept of individual religiosity, which presupposes a difference of degree of commitment and interest in religious ideas, religious answers or solutions, and religious participation.

SOCIOLOGICAL DEFINITIONS OF RELIGIOSITY: THE INDIVIDUAL APPROACH

We now focus on major attempts by sociologists to measure religiosity defined more narrowly as the degree and type of commitment to religious values and norms.

Although it has not always been recognized, there is great diversity within each group discussed in the preceding section, a fact illustrated by the historical development of the attempts to measure differences related to religious group affiliation. While research that contrasted the major categories of Protestants, Catholics, and Jews exposed numerous differences, such broad and inclusive categories have been recognized to be just that—inclusive of a great deal of internal diversity, as numerous studies, including those by Glock and Stark, have documented. Implicit in the data from such studies, though not always discussed, are great differences within each of the subgroups, as well. For example, although only 28 percent of Congregationalists, but 92 percent of Southern Baptists, believe in miracles, there nevertheless exists within each of these groups internal differentiation—differentiation which is even more obvious within the other Protestant groups that fall between the Congregationalists and Southern Baptists as reported earlier in this appendix. In other words, although 72 percent of Congregationalists do *not* believe in miracles, 28 percent *do* believe in them; although 42 percent of Presbyterians do not believe in miracles, 58 percent do believe in them; and so on. How do we explain such internal diversity? Why do some members of a group accept one belief, practice, or social perspective, while other members do not?

Measures of Individual Ritual
Participation

Such questions have led some researchers to ignore, at least temporarily, formal group differences and regroup—or more accurately, recategorize—people on other bases, such as types of commitment, intensity of belief, and so on. An early attempt along these lines, one which has subsequently been widely used, is based on *ritual participation*, or the frequency with which people attend the formal religious services of their religious group. Thus those who report attending weekly or nearly every week might be categorized as demonstrating a "high" degree of religiosity; those attending once or twice a month would perhaps be categorized as showing a "moderate" degree; and those attending less often would be classed "low" on this scale. Refinements of this measure into a five-point scale (with the addition of "moderately high" and "moderately low" categories), and even a seven-point scale, have been used. Other factors, such as frequency of participation in other activities sponsored by the religious group, have been included by some researchers. Commonly, when Protestants and Catholics are major components in the study, frequency of attendance at the sacrament of Communion, or the Lord's Supper, is used as a measure of religiosity. Quite obviously such measures attempt to assess variations in the intensity of commitment and the importance of religion to the individual.

But many researchers have objected that such a procedure does not really measure religiosity, that attendance statistics tell us nothing about how a given individual *feels* about attendance. A person's regular attendance may be simply a result of habit, and so it may mean relatively little to him or her personally. Or, a person's regular attendance may be due to family or other group pressures—he or she may not want to disappoint grandmother, or to give an employer cause to question his or her morality. Or perhaps a person attends regularly because he or she looks forward to the opportunity to socialize with friends after services.

Other Measures of Individual
Religiosity

Such objections have spurred attempts to measure religiosity by other means. One method has been to ask people about their prayer life—focusing again, however, as with church attendance, on frequency. The reasoning here is that if a person reports engaging frequently in personal, private prayer (where "frequently" is usually defined as at least daily), then religion is likely more meaningful and important to him or her than it is to one who prays only occasionally or one who never prays except in groups, as in formal religious services.

Other measures that try to probe just a little more into the subjective feelings and commitments of people rely on respondents' ability, in interviews and questionnaires, to categorize themselves in terms of their personal commitment to religion and to evaluate how important religion is to them personally. These measures, occasionally composites or indexes based on more than one question, vary from one study to another, but usually are based on questions such as, "How important would you say religion is in your life—very important, somewhat important, not very important, or not at all important?" Or, "All in all, how important would you say your church membership is to you?"

Evaluation of Individual Measures of
Religiosity

All the attempts to operationalize the concept of religiosity that we have mentioned in this section have in common the fact that each relies on a single measure, or on a single set of measures—for example, combining frequency of church attendance with frequency of Communion attendance, or frequency of personal prayer with extent of involvement in the total organizational life of a congregation. Such measures of religiosity have revealed significant differences among people. For example, a 1960 survey revealed that among white southern college students those who attended church were somewhat more prejudiced against blacks than those who never attended—although there were also strong indications that among the churchgoers those who attended more frequently were less prejudiced than infrequent churchgoers.[9] Or, to cite another brief example, among American middle-class men those who attend church more regularly tend to be more upwardly mobile.[10]

Differences of this sort, however, have not been so great or so consistent as some researchers had anticipated. The primary reason, according to recent research, seems to be that religiosity is not a one-dimensional phenomenon. That is, not all people are religious in the same way. A person may rank high in religiosity on one dimension or measure, but low on another or several others. Thus if certain behavior is correlated with a high score on one scale of religiosity but a low score on another, then entirely different conclusions could be reached concerning the impact of religion on that behavior, depending upon which measure of religiosity was used.

[9] R. K. Young, W. M. Benson, and W. H. Holtzman, "Changes in Attitudes toward the Negro in a Southern University," *Journal of Abnormal and Social Psychology* 60, no. 1 (1960), 131–33.

[10] Lenski, *The Religious Factor*, p. 103.

SOCIOLOGICAL MEASURES OF RELIGIOSITY: MULTIDIMENSIONAL MEASURES

Several researchers, taking a multidimensional view of religion, have either combined several specific measures into a composite of some kind or utilized several discrete measures. The rationale for such approaches is that religion is not a single, uniform entity that can be apprehended by any single measure; rather, people can "be religious" in various ways.

In works published in 1951 and 1954 Joseph Fichter distinguished four ways in which a person could be a Catholic.[11] Based on attendance at mass, participation in confession, sending children to parochial school, other involvement in church subgroups, and expressed religious interest, Fichter constructed the typology of *nuclear Catholic, modal Catholic, marginal Catholic,* and *dormant Catholic.* Nuclear Catholics go beyond minimal requirements of membership, are active in parish life, and attend Holy Communion at least weekly. Such "ideal" members in Fichter's second (1954) sample were found to comprise only 5.7 percent of all Catholics.[12] Modal Catholics comprised about 70 percent of the membership and were described by Fichter as follows:

> Since the modal parishioner holds a position midway between the nuclear and the marginal Catholic, he may be said to live up to his religion in a "middling sort of way." He generally observes the Friday abstinence and knows the difference between Advent and Lent. His name is likely to be on the roster of the Holy Name Society at some time during his life, but he hardly ever attends a meeting. He attends Sunday Mass most of the time but has difficulty "catching Mass" when holy days of obligation occur during the working week. His children fill the parochial schools, and he has a kind of aloof respect for priests and nuns.[13]

The marginal Catholic (about 20 percent of Catholics) considers himself to be a member of the Catholic church and tends to be so considered by the church itself, yet may not have attended mass during the past year, may not have received Holy Communion or participated in confession, and although he has the opportunity, does not send his children to a Catholic parochial school.[14] The dormant Catholic is one who was born into a Catholic family, baptized as a Catholic, may have been married by a priest, and perhaps asks for a priest's services as death approaches, yet is not a formal member of a Catholic congregation.[15]

[11] Joseph Fichter, *Southern Parish* (Chicago: University of Chicago Press, 1951); idem, *Social Relations in the Urban Parish* (Chicago: University of Chicago Press, 1954).

[12] Ibid., p. 24.

[13] Ibid., p. 41.

[14] Ibid., pp. 61–62.

[15] Ibid., p. 69.

It should be fairly clear from earlier comments that Fichter's typology is a simple one in the sense that his measure of religiosity essentially involves only ritual and formal participation in a religious organization. Excluded are several dimensions we have hinted at earlier and others we will be identifying as we proceed. Yet his typology made an important contribution, particularly in that it stimulated others to expand and improve on his work.

Not long after publication of Fichter's research, Charles Glock suggested that religion could be thought of as consisting of four dimensions, which he identified as the *experiential,* the *ritualistic,* the *ideological,* and the *consequential.*[16] The experiential dimension attempts to measure the degree of emotional attachment to the supernatural. The ritualistic is the by-now-familiar dimension that includes church attendance and prayer life.[17] The ideological dimension refers to the degree of commitment a person expresses in the religious beliefs of his or her group, and the consequential dimension refers to the impact of religious commitment and involvement on general behavior. Somewhat later Glock added a fifth major dimension—the *intellectual,* which measures the degree to which a person is knowledgeable about the formal beliefs of his or her religion.[18]

In 1966, Joseph Faulkner and Gordon DeJong reported their development of sets of questions for measuring each of Glock's dimensions of religiosity. We include two of these sets to give the reader an idea of how these concepts have been operationalized in research.

Ideological scale: (1) Agreement with the statement: "Do you believe that the world will come to an end according to the will of God?" (2) Agreement with the statement: "I believe in a Divine God, creator of the universe, who knows my innermost thoughts and feelings, and to whom one day I shall be accountable," rather than statements that refer to the Deity as "a power greater than myself, which some people call God and some people call Nature," or deny or doubt the existence of a supreme being altogether. (3) Agreement with the statement: "Do you believe that it is necessary for a person to repent before God will forgive his sins?" (4) Agreement with the statement: "God has and continues to act in the history of mankind." (5) Agrees that the Bible is God's word and is completely true or at least contains only some human errors while its basic moral and religious teachings are true.

[16] Charles Y. Glock, "The Religious Revival in America," in *Religion and the Face of America,* ed. Jane Zahn (Berkeley: University Extension, University of California, 1959), pp. 25–42.

[17] Stark and Glock have subsequently subdivided the ritualistic into two parts: *ritual* and *devotion.* Ritual includes such formal religious activities as attending religious services and taking Communion—what can be called public activities. Devotion includes such behavior as praying and studying sacred books and religious writings. (Rodney Stark and Charles Y. Glock, *American Piety: The Nature of Religious Commitment* [Berkeley: University of California Press, 1968].) Nudelman believes this added distinction makes sense both theoretically and empirically. (Arthur E. Nudelman, "Dimensions of Religiosity: A Factor-Analytic View of Protestants, Catholics, and Christian Scientists," *Review of Religious Research* 13, no. 1 [1971], 42–56.)

[18] Charles Y. Glock, "On the Study of Religious Commitment," *Religious Education* 62, no. 4 (1962), 98–110.

Experiential scale: (1) Strongly agrees with the question: "Would you say that one's religious commitment gives life a certain purpose which it could not otherwise have?" (2) States that at least occasionally "There are particular moments (I) feel 'close' to the Divine." (3) Agrees with the question: "Would you say that religion offers a sense of security in the face of death which is not otherwise possible?" (4) Agrees with the statement: "Religion provides the individual with an interpretation of his existence which could not be discovered by reason alone." (5) Agrees with the statement: "Faith, meaning putting full confidence in the things we hope for and being certain of things we cannot see, is essential to one's religious life."[19]

So far, the culmination of the multidimensional approach is to be found in the factor-analytic studies of church members conducted in the late 1960s by Morton King and Richard Hunt, who collated and, where necessary, elaborated the measures developed by Glock and others.[20] King and Hunt identified eleven possible ways of "being religious" and constructed multiple questions and statements to measure each. Questionnaires were then administered to several samples of church members and the results subjected to factor analysis (a research technique that brings together several variables under a common heading and shows their relationship to yet other variables) in order to find correlations among questions and measures and to make distinctions among measures. The result was to identify six primary measures of religiosity, some consisting of two or more relatively independent submeasures:

    I.   Creedal Assent (to traditional Christian doctrines)
   II.   Devotionalism (prayer life)
  III.   Congregational Involvement
      A. Church Attendance
      B. Organizational Activity
      C. Financial Support
   IV.   Religious Knowledge (knowledge of Bible, church history, and denominations)
    V.   Orientation to Religion
      A. Growth and Striving (reading the Bible and religious literature and trying to learn, understand, and apply religion)
      B. Extrinsic (religious involvement as utilitarian in social life)
  VI.   Salience
      A. Behavior (sharing and talking about religion and "witnessing")
      B. Cognition (conscious awareness of the relevance of religion for life)[21]

The advantage of this typology is not only that it combines the best insights of most of the previous attempts to measure religiosity, but also that it specifies sets of measures for each dimension. One is hard put to think of oth-

[19] Joseph E. Faulkner and Gordon F. DeJong, "Religiosity in 5-D: An Empirical Analysis," *Social Forces* 45, no. 2 (1966), 246–54.

[20] Morton B. King and Richard A. Hunt, *Measuring Religious Dimensions*, Studies in Social Science no. 1 (Dallas, Tex.: Southern Methodist University, 1972).

[21] Ibid., pp. 103–6.

er important ways in which one can be religious, at least within traditional Christianity. We must be careful of course to specify that not only was this typology developed within the context of traditional Christianity, but it applies well only there also. Quite assuredly this set does not include every possible dimension of religiosity relevant for those outside Christianity in other contexts, whether "nonreligious" Westerners or people with non-Western religious traditions.

SOCIOLOGICAL DEFINITIONS OF RELIGIOSITY: THE INTRINSIC-EXTRINSIC DISTINCTION

Another typology of religiosity, the intrinsic-extrinsic distinction, is only a dichotomy, but it has generated considerable discussion and research. The distinction between intrinsic and extrinsic religious orientations was initially made in 1950 by the psychologist Gordon Allport in *The Individual and His Religion*, although at that point they were not named as such or clearly defined. By 1960 Allport had defined these dimensions as follows:

> Extrinsic religion is a self-serving utilitarian, self-protective form of religious outlook, which provides the believer with comfort and salvation at the expense of outgroups. Intrinsic religion marks the life that has interiorized the total creed of his faith without reservation, including the commandment to love one's neighbor. A person of this sort is more intent on serving his religion than on making it serve him.[22]

In other words, "the extrinsically motivated person *uses* his religion, whereas the intrinsically motivated *lives* his religion."[23]

Working with Allport's intrinsic-extrinsic concept, Hunt and King proposed the existence of five primary components, which they described as follows:

> Universal-Parochial: Brotherhood and love of neighbor vs. ethnocentrism and exclusion of those unlike oneself.
>
> Unselfish-Selfish: Effort to transcend self-centered needs vs. self-serving, protective use for own ends.
>
> Relevance for all of life: Floods whole life with motivation and meaning vs. compartmentalized, not integrated into one's way of life.
>
> Ultimate-Instrumental: End vs. means; master motive vs. utilitarian uses.

[22] Gordon W. Allport, *Personality and Social Encounter* (Boston: Beacon Press, 1960), p. 257.

[23] Gordon W. Allport, "The Religious Context of Prejudice," *Journal for the Scientific Study of Religion* 5, no. 3 (1966), 447–57.

Associational-Communal: Involved for religious fellowship and deeper values vs. affiliation for sociability and status.[24]

Numerous other studies have sought to operationalize and refine this dichotomy. However, a major problem is that although the implicit assumption has been that a continuum is involved, the continuum is multidimensional, not unidimensional, and therefore is very difficult to utilize effectively in research. Hunt and King point out that nearly all studies that have employed this typology have documented its multidimensionality. That is, the concepts refer to several, not two, distinctive measures of religiosity. Quite possibly they are not even poles on a continuum but distinctive measures themselves.[25] They conclude that although the typology has served a useful purpose and has generated helpful research and theoretical discussion, it should be abandoned, and that attention should now be given to labels, ideas, and scales of greater specificity.[26]

SOCIOLOGICAL DEFINITIONS OF RELIGIOSITY: THE OPEN-ENDED "ULTIMATE CONCERN" APPROACH

Other researchers who have recently probed into the phenomenon of religiosity have sought to bypass institutionally related factors by defining religion in terms of theologian Paul Tillich's "ultimate concern" and then attempting to determine what people are concerned about "ultimately" and how "ultimate" and intense their concern is. This approach deliberately seeks to avoid definitions of religiosity that are closely tied to the concepts of membership and participation in traditional religious organizations and the activities that such groups encourage.

In preliminary work along these lines J. Milton Yinger has devised open-ended questions designed to steer people's thinking out of traditionally understood institutional religion and belief systems and to probe their "basic" religious feelings. For example, Yinger seeks to discover people's fundamental religious concern by posing questions like the following to his respondents:

In your most reflective moments, when you are thinking beyond the immediate issues of the day—however important—beyond headlines, beyond the temporary, what do you consider the most important issue mankind has to face? Or, to

---

[24] Richard A. Hunt and Morton King, "The Intrinsic-Extrinsic Concept: A Review and Evaluation," *Journal for the Scientific Study of Religion* 10, no. 4 (1971), 343.

[25] Ibid., pp. 351–52.

[26] Ibid., p. 354.

put the question another way, what do you see as the basic, permanent question for mankind?[27]

We might even suggest here that religiosity could be measured in terms of whether people think at all about such fundamental questions and issues and/or in terms of what questions *are* fundamental for them. Conceivably people might be more or less "religious" depending upon whether their "fundamental question" was, "How can I become economically successful in the shortest possible time?" or, "What can I do to help attain world peace and brotherhood?" or, "How can I get in tune with the ultimate divinity?"

Quite clearly Yinger is trying to get beyond understandings and definitions of religion centered around affiliation with and simple formal participation in highly institutionalized religious organizations. He is trying to get back to "basics"—to the essence of religion which may exist within institutions and may well exist outside traditional religious forms. It should be observed, however, that Yinger does not seek to define religion in strictly individualistic terms. He still pursues the group dimension. One of the questions he presents to respondents, for example, is:

> Are you a participant in or member of some group, whether large or small, for which the "basic, permanent question" and the beliefs connected with it are the focus of attention and the most important reasons for its existence? If so, please characterize the group briefly.[28]

Certainly an approach like Yinger's consciously tries to get at something different, at something that previous research into religiosity has not been able to pinpoint. Such research certainly shows great promise for pushing forward the understanding of religiosity. On the other hand, it should be pointed out that such research, while it may take us well beyond our current understanding of religion and religiosity, need not invalidate research findings that relate differences in behavior to differences in people's relationships to traditional religious organizations.

CONCLUSION

While there are many other attempts to operationalize the concept of religiosity and while it remains an ongoing challenge to sociologists of religion, our interest here is not to be encyclopedic or exhaustive of all the attempts. Our intent has rather been simply to alert the reader to two important points: (1) Defining what we mean by "religiosity" when describing people is not easy. In

---

[27] J. Milton Yinger, "A Structural Examination of Religion," *Journal for the Scientific Study of Religion* 8, no. 1 (1969), 93.

[28] Ibid., p. 93.

fact, it is quite a complicated task, especially if we want to categorize people and make comparisons in any systematic, meaningful way. (2) There are many ways social scientists have already devised to measure religiosity in at least some of its aspects. While now being familiar with a few the reader should also be alert to some of the inherent limitations and weaknesses in such measures and should gain a sharper perception of what is really being measured when a particular study purports to talk about differences in religiosity and the differential effects of various types of religiosity on the behavior and attitudes of people. The really ultimate point of it all is that people can be and are religious in different ways. It becomes important to try to discover and measure those ways and then see what effect "being religious" has upon people and what they think and do.

At this point it is important to remind the reader that there is consensus that religiosity is multidimensional. Thus a person may score high on one dimension and be termed "very religious," yet score low on one or more other measures and be identified as only "slightly religious" or even "irreligious." For example, a person may know his or her religious teachings or doctrines inside and out, yet seldom or never attend religious services, never engage in devotional activities, disbelieve what he or she knows intellectually about his or her religion, and evidence no effect of religious knowledge on his or her behavior. Obviously it is important to specify what our dimension or measuring device is when we reach conclusions about people's level or degree of religiosity. It would be convenient if one or two measures correlated highly with all the others, if one or two indicators predicted fairly accurately one's performance or commitment in terms of other indicators. Unfortunately the intercorrelations of the indicators are not high at all. For example, the fact that a person believes in and is committed to orthodox doctrine does not necessarily mean that he or she engages in an active devotional life, possesses extensive intellectual knowledge of his or her religious system, or shows any effect of faith on his or her daily life.

On a more personal note I would suggest that we must exercise extreme caution as social scientists when making judgments about the religiosity of people. Although we are reluctant to advise readers how to interact with other people, this principle would seem to apply when judging the religiosity of others in ordinary social situations. Our concern here, however, is of course primarily in confronting and evaluating research and rhetoric about religion, whether it appears from the scientific or the theological point of view. That is, we must always be careful to check the researchers' operational definitions. How is *religious* defined? Is it unidimensional or multidimensional? What specific measures are used?

In brief then, sociologically speaking, there is no single "correct" definition of religiosity. Religious commitment is multidimensional—there are several, probably many, ways to "be religious"—and the concept is therefore much too complex to be measured in only one way. The research task of the future, so far as measuring religiosity is concerned, is not finding a single measure, but isolating the various ways in which people evidence religious commitment, and deriving precise measuring instruments to distinguish them. In the meantime, readers will find examples throughout this book of quite a number of ways social scientists have operationalized the idea of "being religious." Some the readers may be more comfortable with than others; some they may find more useful for their purposes or from their perspective than others. Such differences will in themselves, at least in part, simply reflect different understandings and convictions by the readers of what "being religious" means.

Index

Aberle, David, 64
Abortion, 120
  legislation; religious influence on, 112
  opposition by New Religious Right, 117
Adolescence (*See* Conversion, age factor)
Africa; religion in, 55
African Methodist Episcopal Church, 86, 214–15
African Methodist Episcopal Zion Church, 214–15
Allport, Gordon, 52, 54, 300
Alpert, Harry, 33
American Baptist Church (Convention), 72, 178
American Baptists, 242
  beliefs of, 293
American Council of Christian Churches, 206, 207
American Jewish Committee, 118
American Lutheran Church (A.L.C.), 178, 179, 249, 265
  beliefs of, 293
American Nazi Party, 114
American Rescue Mission, 178
Amish, 78, 90, 91, 248, 249
Anglican churches (*See* Episcopal Church)
Anglicanism, 189
Animism, 27
Anthropology, 20, 26–28
Anti-Catholicism, 196–99, 254
Anti-Communism, 113
Anti-Defamation League, 199
Anti-Saloon League, 111–12
Anti-Semitism, 160, 199–200
  religious, 200
  social, 200
Apollonian religious orientation, 233
Arbitron Company, 116
Arminius, Jacob, 247
Armstrong, Ben, 116
Arnold, Joan, 168*n*
Asbury, Francis, 156, 157, 194
Assemblies of God, 206, 262
Association of Evangelical Lutheran Churches, 280
Authority:
  religious, 71, 73
  in a sect, 88
Axelrod, Morris, 236*n*

Bahai, 21, 286
Balk, Alfred, 128*n*
Bandaranaike, S. W. R. D., 124

Bangladesh, 154
Baptists, 43, 46, 71, 82, 89, 146–47, 177, 189, 243, 246, 264 (*See also* Southern Baptist Convention)
  party preference, 109
  response to frontier challenge, 194–95
  voting behavior, 109–10
Bar Mitzvah, 236
Barth, Karl, 206, 230, 266
Bass, Dorothy C., 177*n*
Baxter, Richard, 135
Bayh, Senator Birch, 117
Beckford, James A., 99*n*
Belief systems, 14
Bellah, Robert, 121, 122, 256, 273, 282
Bennett, Dennis, 283
Bennett, John C., 206
Benson, J. Kenneth, 99*n*
Benson, Purnell, 18
Benson, W. M., 296*n*
Berger, Peter, 16*n*, 250
Bernstein, Marcella, 173*n*
Berton, Pierre, 275
Bible reading; in public schools, 117
Bible translations, 206
Biblical knowledge, 43–45
Billington, R. A., 197–98
Birth control, 64
  legislation, 111–12
  religious attitudes toward, 64
Black militancy, 225–27
Black Muslims, 221, 286 (*See also* Nation of Islam)
Black nationalism, 221
Blacks:
  attitudes toward divorce, 292
  attitudes toward work, 292
Blake, Eugene Carson, 249
Borhek, James, 14, 53–54
Boycotts, 222–24
Brahma, 256
Brahman, 150
Brink and Harris Poll, 159
Bryan, William Jennings, 205, 278
Buber, Martin 237*n*
Buddha, Gautama, 24, 168
Buddhism, 10, 13, 21, 24, 65, 106–7, 128, 150, 152, 286
  and attitudes toward women, 168–69, 171
Bureaucracy in religious groups, 252
Bureaucratization of religion, 71–74

Deprivation, 225
  and blacks, 85–86
  impact on sect development, 83–86
  types, 84–85
Detroit, 139
  black churches in, 217
  black clergy in labor movement, 221
  boycott activity by black clergy, 222–24
DeVinne, Daniel, 156
Dharma, 168
Dinges, William, 239–40
Dionysian religious orientation, 233
Disciples of Christ, 196, 242, 264
  beliefs, 293
Discrimination, racial, 158
  in churches, 158
Divine Precepts cult, 55–56
Divorce; attitudes toward, 292
Doctrines (Christian), 278–79
Dorsett, James, 99n
Doyle, Ruth, 265–66
DuBois, W. E. B., 215
Durkheim Emile, 21, 22, 31–34, 90, 266

East African Revival, 55
Eastern Orthodox churches (See Orthodox [Eastern] churches)
Eastern religions, 54, 287
  influence on American cults, 286
Eckardt, A. Roy, 208, 210
Economy; and religion, 126–41
Ecumenical movement, 206
Ecumenism, 248–53, 273
Eddy, Mary Baker, 93, 177
Education; and attitudes toward civil rights, 160–61
Edwards, Jonathan, 194
Egypt, 166
Eisenhower, President Dwight, 208
Eismann, Bernard, 113
Eister, Allan W., 99n
Eitzen, D. Stanley, 163n
"Electronic Church," 115–16
Eliade, Mircea, 12
Eliot, Charles, 153
Elkind, David, 51, 54
Emswiler, Sharon N., 174–75
Emswiler, Thomas N., 175n
Endogamy, 41
Engels, Friedrich, 143
Entropy, 75
Episcopal Church, 177, 178, 233, 244
Episcopalians, 146–47, 242,–43, 265
  beliefs, 279, 293
  black, 226
  membership decline, 261
  voting behavior, 109–10
Equal Rights Amendment, 117, 119
Erickson, Donald A., 48
Ethical Culture, 13
Ethnic denominations, 244, 244n, 253–55
Evangelical and Reformed Church, 246, 249
Evangelical United Brethren Church, 249
Everson v. Board of Education, 188
Evolution; of religion, 273

Faith; religious, 30–31
Falk, Nancy, 168
Falwell, Jerry, 116, 117
Family; role in religious socialization, 51–52
Far Eastern religion (See Eastern religions)

Fascism; as a religion, 16
Father Divine, 93, 95, 220
Faulkner, Joseph, 298
Federal Council of Churches, 203
Feminist movement, 177, 181
Fichter, Joseph, 297–98
First Great Awakening, 194
Ford, Henry, 221
Ford Motor Company, 221
Fosdick, Harry Emerson, 206
Fowler, Floyd J., 236n
Frankfort Society of the Friends of Reform, 236
Franklin, Benjamin, 135
Frazer, James, 22
Frazier, E. Franklin, 216–17, 218
Free Methodist Church of North America, 206
Free Will Baptists, 206
Freeman, Jo, 165n
Freud, Sigmund, 29, 256
Fukuyama, Yoshio, 148, 149
Functional alternatives, 33
Fundamentalism, 203–7
  theology (teachings), 204–5
Fundamentalist-modernist controversy, 203–7
Fundamentalist schools, 205
Furniss, Norman F., 205

Gallup, George H., 109, 159
Gallup Poll, 159, 160, 162n, 207, 259, 260, 287
Garvey, Marcus, 229
Gasper, Louis, 204, 205, 206n
Geiger, Abraham, 236
Geneva, 106, 134
Gerlach, Luther P., 284–85
Gerth, H. H., 129, 144
Gladden, Washington, 201, 202
Glock, Charles Y., 41, 83–86, 199n, 200, 210n,
    211, 225, 242, 263, 264, 279n, 293–94,
    298, 299
Glossalalia (See Speaking in tongues)
Goals, common; characteristic of groups, 11
Goldenberg, Naomi, 182–83
Goldscheider, Calvin, 236n
Goldstein, Sidney, 236n
Goode, Erich, 99n
Goodenough, Erwin, 28
Greek Orthodox Archdiocese of North and
    South America, 247
Greeley, Andrew M., 47, 146n, 231, 233n, 238–
    39, 253, 254, 270
Greene, Evarts B., 189n
Grimke sisters, 177
Group:
  characteristics, 11–12
  definition, 61–62
  functional prerequisites, 64–66
  size, effects of, 69–70, 76, 86–87
Gurdjieff, 287
Gurin, Arnold, 236n

Hadaway, Christopher K., 264
Hadden, Jeffrey, 109, 111, 119, 120, 159n, 160,
    161, 260, 275, 278
Hageman, Alice L., 170n, 182n
Hammond, Philip E., 71, 77–78, 136–37, 178,
    276
Hare Krishna, 287
Hargis, Billy James, 113–14
Harrell, David E., Jr., 89, 160
Harrison, Michael I., 284
Harrison, Paul M., 72–73

Haselden, Kyle, 158
Havens, Murray C., 114
Hawkes, Jacquetta, 166n, 167n
Henry, Carl F. H., 272
Herberg, Will, 198n, 209–10, 292
Higher criticism, 204
Hill, Reverend Charles, 221
Hindu women, 171
Hinduism, 150, 151, 153, 154, 286
    and attitudes toward women, 168–69
Hindus, 68, 124
Hine, Virginia H., 284–85
Hoge, Dean R., 262n, 265
Holiness churches, 246–47
Holt, John B., 83
Holtzman, W. H., 296n
Homosexuality, 117, 119, 120
Hudnut, Robert K., 266
Hudson, W. H., 210n
Human nature, 6–7
Humanae Vitae (Encyclical), 239
Humanism; as a religion, 16
Humbard, Rex, 116
Hunt, Richard, 299, 300–301
Hunter, Floyd, 218
Huss, John, 235
Hutchinson, Anne, 188
Hutchinson, Paul, 209
Hutterites, 78, 90

I Ching, 286
Ideal type, 79
Identification; characteristic of group life, 12, 68
Immigration:
    Jews, 192, 199
    Lutherans, 196
    Roman Catholics, 192, 196, 197, 198–99
Importance of religion to individuals, 296
Independent political preference:
    and religious affiliation, 109–11
    and theological position, 111
India, 151–52, 153, 154
    religion in early times, 167–69
Influence of religion, 259–61
Institutionalized sects (See Sects, institutionalized)
"Iron law of oligarchy," 73
Isis (Egyptian goddess), 166
Islam, 64, 65, 125, 154 (See also Muslims)
Israel; in Old Testament period, 106

Jacquet, Constant H., Jr., 126n, 179, 200, 258n, 259n, 261n, 283, 287
Jainism, 13
James, Edwin O., 166, 167
Janson, Donald, 113
Japanese religion; and attitudes towards women, 169
Jehovah's Witnesses, 152–53, 200, 205, 248, 249
Jensen, Adolph, 167
Jesus, 201
    and attitudes towards women, 170–71
"Jesus Freaks," 54
Jewish women, 171
Jews, 39, 68, 146–47, 243, 292
    in ecumenical discussions, 250
    in the Middle Ages, 134
John Birch Society, 113
Johnson, Benton, 71, 99n, 100, 101
John Paul II, Pope, 239
Johnson, President Lyndon B., 121

Johnstone, Ronald L., 43, 45, 46, 47, 109n, 110n, 217n, 219n, 227n, 243
John XXIII, Pope, 238, 239
Jones, Charles C., 213
Jones, E. Stanley, 206
Jones, Reverend Jim, 93, 94–99, 107
Jonestown, 98, 107
Jorstad, Erling, 115n
Judaism, 24, 82, 234
    and attitudes towards women, 169–70, 171
    conservative, 234, 236, 237
    cultural-ethnic, 234, 237
    hasidic, 234, 237
    Old Testament, 167
    orthodox, 100–101, 234, 235, 237
    reform, 100–101, 234, 236
Jules-Rosette, Bennetta, 55n

Karma, 168
Kelley, Dean M., 262, 263, 264
Kelly, Sheila, 265–66
Kennedy, David B., 112n
Kennedy, President John F., 121, 238
Kersten, Lawrence K., 179
"Key '73," 272
King, Martin Luther, Jr., 274
King, Morton, 299, 300–301
Know-Nothing political party (See Political parties)
Knox, John, 235
Kotre, John, 52
Kraybill, Donald B., 48
Ku Klux Klan, 199

Labavitcher Hasidic Jews, 237
Landis, Benson Y., 207
LaNoue, George, 262, 263
Lasswell, Harold, 106
Leadership succession, 88
Learning theories:
    behavioral learning, 41
    symbolic interactionism, 40–41
Lee, Robert, 251–52
Lefebvre, Archbishop Marcel, 240
Lenski, Gerhard E., 292, 296n
Lewis, Larry M., 48
Liebman, Charles S., 235n
Lincoln, President Abraham, 121
Ling, Trevor, 151n
Lipset, Seymour M., 210n
Liturgical churches, 244, 245
Lofland, John, 55–56
Lowie, Robert, 27
Luther, Martin, 235, 241, 244
Lutheran Church in America (L.C.A.), 176–77, 178, 179, 249, 262, 265
Lutheran Church—Missouri Synod, 157, 242–43, 262, 265, 279–80, 293
    and ordination of women, 177
Lutheran churches, 233, 244–45
    definition of membership, 290
Lutherans, 43, 46, 71, 89, 118, 132, 146–47, 148, 149, 179, 200, 248, 264
    American, 242–43
    voting behavior, 110

McCarthy, Senator Joseph, 113
McCourt, Kathleen, 146n
McCready, William C., 146n
McGovern, Senator George, 117, 118
Machalek, Richard, 16n

Talmud, 235
Taoism; and attitudes towards women, 169
Tawney, R. H., 134–35, 136
Tax-exempt status for churches, 127–28
Temperance movement, 111
Theocracy:
  modified, 106–7, 108
  pure, 106, 107, 108
Theodicy:
  of disprivilege (despair, escape), 129, 140, 144, 256
  of good fortune, 129, 140, 144, 256
Theological differences among groups, 250
Theology:
  black, 227–30
  conservative, 111
  fundamentalist, 111
  liberal, 111
  neo-orthodox, 111
  traditional controversy, 278–81
Theosophy, 286
Third World, 123–25
Thomas, John L., 51
Thomas, William I., 28
Thompson, Daniel C., 218
Thouless, Robert H., 54
Tillich, Paul, 181, 301
Tiryakin, Edward A., 271n
Torah, 235
Totalitarianism, 107, 108
Totem, 31–32, 38
Traditional Catholics in America, 240
Transcendental Meditation, 286
Transfers (switching) from one denomination to another, 263, 264
Troeltsch, Ernst, 77, 99
Turner, Nat, 219
Tussman, Joseph, 190–91
Tylor, Edward, 27, 28

Underground railroad, 219
Unification Church, 65, 95
Union of American Hebrew Congregations, 236
Union of South Africa, 139
United Church of Christ, 178, 246, 261, 265
  voting behavior, 110
United Lutheran Church in America, 249
United Methodist Church, 178, 249 (See also Methodist churches)
United Nations, 206
United Presbyterian Church in the U.S.A., 176, 178, 250, 264, 265
  membership decline, 261
United States Supreme Court, 188, 191–92
Upanishads, 256
Utopian communities, 285

Vajrayana Buddhism, 286
VanDusen, Henry, 206
Vedas, 167, 171, 256
Vergara, Ignacio, 247
Vernon, Glenn, 153
Virginia, 188, 189, 191
Vogt, Evon Z., 130
Voice of Reason (Michigan), 118–19
Volunteers of America, 178
Voting behavior:
  Catholics, 108–10
  effects of religion on, 108–10
  Jews, 109–10
  Protestants, 108–10

Wade, Richard C., 214, 215
Wall, James M., 118
Wall Street Journal, 116
Wallace, Anthony F. C., 38
Walther, C. F. W., 157–58
Washington, Joseph R., Jr., 226, 228, 229
Weber, Max, 21, 22, 77, 95n, 99, 129, 130–37, 143–44, 254, 256
Welch, Robert, 113
Wesley, Charles, 246
Wesley, John, 89, 155, 194, 201–2, 246
White, Reverend Horace, 221
Whitfield, George, 194
Whitman, Lauris B., 259
Williams, J. Paul, 10, 122–23, 246
Williams, Roger, 188
Wilson, Bryan, 273
Winter, Gibson, 275
Wise, Isacc Mayer, 236
Witchcraft, 35
  number of participants, 287
  in women's movement, 182
Women:
  and religion:
    in history, 164–71
    reformation proposals, 176–80
    revolutionary proposals, 181–83
    traditional responses, 172–76
Woolley, Leonard, 166n, 167n
Work; attitudes toward, 292
World Council of Churches, 206
Worship services; attendance at, 42–44

Yinger, J. Milton, 4–5, 20n, 80, 90–92, 100, 105, 301–2
Yoga, 286
Young, R. K., 296n
Youth for Christ movement, 207

Zahn, Jane, 210n, 298n
Zen, 286–87
Zetterberg, Hans, 53
Zwingli, Ulrich, 235